Praise for *Mapping Experiences*

I've long considered *Mapping Experiences* to be the trusted guide to the craft. Jim has been one of the clearest voices in the field, with a rare ability—both in his writing and in person—to help business leaders understand and engage in the work. I've bought and loaned multiple copies of both earlier editions, and this new edition is especially timely. As AI reshapes how experiences are designed and orchestrated, Jim once again elevates how leaders and teams understand journeys, build alignment, and design with intent.

—Ronnie Battista
global lead of XD, Chubb

For years, I've pointed people to Jim's book as the definitive resource for building a serious journey mapping practice. Jim understands something most practitioners learn the hard way: the map itself is almost beside the point. What creates real alignment is the activity of mapping—and this third edition makes that lesson impossible to ignore. I can't wait to put it in the hands of my clients and students!

—Julie Francis
CX researcher and strategist
founder of BellaVia Research
Instructor of "Best Practices for Journey Mapping"

This book is a key guide to help bring your experience design to a global population. Hundreds of thousands, maybe even millions have been impacted by Jim's evangelism and practical guidance on how to empathize and redesign customer experiences.

—Mariano Suarez-Battan
cofounder of Mural and founder of Planta.co

Jim's ability to teach both the value and the practice of visualizing human experiences is priceless. This book, again, transcends tech trends and provides practical tools for ensuring your company understands the people it serves and how they interact with your products and services. Now more than ever your teams need to learn this way of working.

—Jeff Gothelf,
cofounder of Sense & Respond Learning
author of Lean UX

Long before organizations began talking about ecosystems, complexity, and interconnected systems, Jim Kalbach gave us a practical way to see them. *Mapping Experiences* remains one of the most critical works in the field, helping designers, strategists, and leaders understand how value is created across journeys, services, and organizations. It is not simply a book about mapping experiences. It is a guide to making the invisible visible.

—Greg Lakloufi,
strategic design and systems intelligence global leader

As AI drives the cost of execution toward zero, the scarce skill is no longer making the map, it's making meaning together. Kalbach saw this coming. This third edition reframes mapping not as a design artifact but as a facilitation practice, the deeply human work no model can do for us, which is exactly why it matters more now than ever.

—Douglas Ferguson,
CEO and founder of Voltage Control

Jim Kalbach has comprehensively captured the essentials of what it takes to wield wide influence in today's user experience environment. *Mapping Experiences* has become one of the books I recommend most, because every page just oozes amazing wisdom and advice.

—Jared Spool
Maker of Awesomeness, Center Centre

At its core, meaningful organizational transformation requires shifting our focus from rigid, internal silos to the lived experiences of the people we serve. This book offers a masterclass in making that shift real. Through clear, communicative illustrations, it demonstrates that the true value of journey mapping isn't just the final artifact—it's the collaborative, sociotechnical process of building it. By providing actionable frameworks that align cross-functional teams, this book helps leaders cultivate a genuinely shared strategic vision. Thoughtfully updated to reflect the sociotechnical complexities of our current landscape, this text serves as an indispensable guide for any leader committed to leveraging human insight and design strategy exactly where automated algorithms fall short.

—Elizabeth F. Churchill, PhD
department chair and professor of human computer interaction,
MBZUAI (Mohamed Bin Zayed University of Artificial Intelligence), UAE

Jim's focus on the importance of seeing big-picture views of experiences, and mapping them in a way that takes these temporal, ephemeral human stories and makes them into something concrete that teams and organizations can look at and treat like a product, is huge. Individual moments, backstage processes, and sequences no longer exist as just corporate folklore or a general idea.

Mapping Experiences has been my number one source and go-to approach across my work in both the private and public sector. The overall ethos and principles in what Jim has written about and teaches are the first place I start, and they guide me through the journey of making better experiences for people that aren't just about one-off touch-points or interfaces, but about the holistic nature of what it means to engage with any type of product or service provider over time.

That's what Jim's book and this approach teach: to treat time and relationship just like you would a product or an interface. I'm happy to have been a small part in bringing the importance of mapping experiences to the world over the years.

—Erika Flowers
systems auteur and founder at Zero Vector

Third Edition

Mapping Experiences

A Complete Guide to Activating Customer-Centered Collaboration

Jim Kalbach

O'REILLY®

Mapping Experiences

by Jim Kalbach

Published by O'Reilly Media, Inc., 141 Stony Circle, Suite 195, Santa Rosa, CA 95401.

O'Reilly books may be purchased for educational, business, or sales promotional use. Online editions are also available for most titles (*oreilly.com*). For more information, contact our corporate/institutional sales department: (800) 998-9938 or *corporate@oreilly.com*.

Acquisitions Editor: David Michelson
Developmental Editor: Angela Rufino
Production Editor: Kristen Brown
Copyeditor: Rachel Wheeler
Proofreader: Sharon Wilkey
Indexer: Potomac Indexing, LLC
Cover Designer: Susan Brown
Cover Illustrator: Karen Montgomery
Interior Designers: Ron Bilodeau and Monica Kamsvaag
Illustrator: O'Reilly Media, Inc.
Compositor: Ron Bilodeau

April 2016: First Edition

November 2020: Second Edition

July 2026: Third Edition

Revision History for the Third Edition:

2026-07-15: First release

See *http://oreilly.com/catalog/errata.csp?isbn=0642572266479* for release details.

979-8-341-67229-1

[LSI]

For my mother and father

Contents

PART 2. Creating and Activating Maps

PART 3. Mapping in Context

INTRODUCTION

It's not the map. It's the mapping.

A lot has changed since I wrote the first edition of *Mapping Experiences* in 2016. Back then, the question was: what is an experience map and how do I create one? By the time the second edition was published in 2020, I'd started getting more questions about what to do with the map when it's finished and incorporated more about the necessary follow-through.

This third edition goes one step further. It uses maps as a centripetal force for conversation and collaboration, showing that the process of mapping is just as important as the map itself.

Some practitioners argue that journey mapping is dead. They say static maps built for workshops can't keep pace with real-time data and AI-driven personalization. This critique, however, confuses the artifact with the activity.

The problem stems from treating maps as deliverables rather than catalysts for ongoing dialogue. Those decorative "wall maps" with butterflies and unicorns never had a chance to be strategic tools. They failed because no one facilitated conversations around them. They were documentation, not dialogue to challenge assumptions, foster healthy debate, drive decisions, and sustain team alignment.

Critics also tend to narrow their focus too much, typically taking aim specifically at *customer journey maps*. This is just one type of diagram. My scope for mapping experiences includes far more than maps of a current customer experience. For example:

- Service blueprints connect frontstage and backstage operations.
- Job maps show what people are trying to accomplish.
- Mental model diagrams reveal how people think.
- Day-in-the-life diagrams capture broader contexts.
- Ecosystem models show relationships among stakeholders.

Each type of map serves a unique purpose and has its own sources of information beyond just customer data. Chapter 4 reviews the full range of options in more detail.

Organizations absolutely need the real-time visibility into customer experience that journey management platforms provide. Chapter 10 is devoted entirely to this evolution. But platforms solve for data integration and visibility, not organizational alignment or fostering a broader culture of customer centricity.

Mapping experiences focuses on the very real human challenge of interpreting all the available data and facilitating team conversations. It's about helping teams move from "we see the problem" to "we're aligned on the solution."

The critics who say, "We need prescriptive, not descriptive" miss a fundamental truth: prescription without shared understanding leads to misalignment. AI can optimize journeys at scale, but it can't create the moment when a cross-functional team collectively recognizes how its silos create customer pain.

> *AI can optimize journeys at scale, but it can't create the moment when a cross-functional team collectively recognizes how its silos create customer pain.*

That shared recognition is a differentiator. When AI can handle routine interactions, your competitive advantage lies in your organization's collective ability to understand and respond to complex human needs. Mapping is part of the equation for building that capability. In my experience, mapping is one of the most frequently cited methods that demonstrates customer centricity, along with creating personas.

This book is about building collaborative sensemaking capability. All the real-time data in the world won't truly get your teams aligned on what it means and what to do about it. You need to create a shared vision of reality, and you need to act on it.

You want a valid map, to be sure; it should be represented well and visually compelling. But it is of little value if you don't activate it. The process matters as much as the artifact.

Customer Centricity Demands Better Collaboration

A key addition to this third edition is the explicit inclusion of collaborative methods. At the end of Chapters 5–14, you'll find instructions for techniques that are most compatible and most effective with mapping.

Customer centricity demands new ways of working. The customer's experience crosses departmental lines. It doesn't care about your org chart, your reporting structures, or your key performance indicators. A single customer journey might involve marketing, sales, service, operations, finance, IT, legal, and HR.

Yet while customer experience is inherently cross-functional, organizations are usually structured in silos. Journey management platforms can expose this tension by visualizing the end-to-end experience—but exposing the problem isn't the same as solving it.

To become customer-centric, organizations must strive to work differently. They need the following:

- Shared mental models across functions about what matters to customers
- Regular rhythms of collaboration that honor the cross-functional nature of customer experiences
- Facilitated conversations that surface conflicting priorities and build sustained alignment
- Trust and relationships that enable coordinated action despite siloed structures
- A common language for discussing customer needs that transcends departmental jargon

Software platforms for journey management, discussed in Chapter 10, don't provide these capabilities. The aspects of customer-centric organizations outlined here are instead cultivated through practice. Mapping, done as an ongoing collaborative exercise, is one way organizations can build customer centricity and align teams around the experience.

When marketing, operations, and IT get together to map a customer journey, they're not just documenting an experience. They're learning to see the world through the customer's eyes and discovering how their individual actions create collective outcomes. And they're building team connections that are fundamental when it comes to delivering and improving those experiences.

Modern AI-driven data platforms are powerful. But tools are only as effective as the people using them. If those people haven't learned to work collaboratively across boundaries, the most sophisticated platform in the world won't make you customer-centric.

Customer centricity demands new ways of working.

Visual artifacts contribute to strategy making, outlined in Chapter 12. A job map, a mental model diagram, or an ecosystem visualization reveals patterns and opportunities that spreadsheets and reports obscure. After all, our growth plans are ultimately driven by customer action. Mapping supports the creation of customer-centered strategies and does so in a modern, open way that invites participation and creativity.

AI and Mapping

AI is transforming how we create and analyze maps. Tools can now automatically generate draft journey maps from data, identify friction points, and surface patterns in minutes that would take humans hours to uncover. Organizations are moving from static maps to "living maps" that update continually based on real-time data.

But AI can't replace the human judgment needed to navigate ambiguous situations. It also can't replace empathy, ethical understanding, and imagination.

AI makes the human side of mapping more critical, not less. When every competitor has access to the same AI tools and real-time data, your competitive advantage lies in your organization's collective ability to understand and respond to human needs in ways AI cannot.

Consider the speed at which AI enables execution. With AI, it's now possible to go from idea to working software in hours, not weeks or months. Against this backdrop, the human side of the organization needs even more attention. Sustaining healthy, cohesive teams requires regular collaborative activities that maintain alignment and shared understanding.

But speed also changes what we can focus on. When execution time approaches zero, teams can be more strategic and visionary. They can focus more deeply on customer needs rather than getting mired in implementation details. AI-driven workflows and agents should give us more time to be more human. In this sense, mapping becomes even more strategic and critical in an AI-driven world.

As an example, consider the billing story I share at the start of Chapter 1: after research and mapping revealed that customers contesting invoices could still receive late payment warnings, a workshop produced collective outrage at this misalignment. AI couldn't create that moment, or facilitate the shared recognition of organizational failure and the commitment to change that come from humans confronting evidence together.

When execution time approaches zero, teams can be more strategic and visionary.

I view AI as a complementary tool to human decision making. While it's possible to have AI create a map with all the needed information, that misses the point: it's not the artifact (the map), it's the process (the mapping).

Further Trends

Apart from the advent of AI, several other trends have shaped this third edition:

Journey management and orchestration

Journey managers now use real-time data to coordinate diverse experiences across organizations. We're seeing the emergence of "living maps" that update continually based on behavioral data, feedback, and contextual signals. Given the high costs and technical configuration, journey management remains the purview of an elite few, while mapping is for everyone. Chapter 10 covers experience intelligence platforms and continual mapping practices.

Systems thinking in experience design

Customer experiences don't exist in isolation. They're interconnected with employee experiences, partner ecosystems, supply chains, and broader societal systems. This edition expands significantly on systems mapping approaches and frameworks for visualizing multistakeholder systems and complex interdependencies.

New models for work

The COVID-19 pandemic accelerated changes in team collaboration. Distributed teams and hybrid work are now the norm. Experience mapping has proven its value not only as a tool for building customer centricity but as a fundamental capability for organizational resilience and adaptation.

Sustainability and regenerative experiences

People increasingly evaluate experiences based on environmental and social impact, not just convenience and satisfaction. Chapter 13 introduces circular design, helping organizations visualize the environmental footprint of their services.

Each of these challenges requires organizations to step back, visualize their current state, and collectively envision better futures. Experience mapping provides the shared language and visual framework necessary for this work.

Scope of This Book

This book is about alignment diagrams: any visualization that helps align how individuals in a system engage with that system and its provider. There is no single method or approach that fits all problems or circumstances. You'll find a range of options depending on the problem you're solving.

These diagrams have been part of innovation, design, and creative disciplines for decades. You may have already used them. Reframing them as tools for sustained organizational alignment emphasizes their strategic relevance. They help flip an organization's perspective from inside-out to outside-in, building empathy and providing a model for decision making that is inclusive of the human condition.

To be clear: alignment diagrams are no silver bullet. However, the story they tell goes a long way toward achieving and maintaining alignment, particularly in larger organizations.

This book is about possibilities. My hope is that it expands your thinking about and approach to mapping in general. Don't get hung up on labels. Many distinctions are historical and based on which term was coined first. Focus on value alignment, not one specific technique. It's entirely possible to create new types of diagrams that continue to evolve the practice. I encourage you to do so.

Note that throughout the book, I use *customer* to refer to anyone an organization serves—buyers, users, consumers, partners, visitors, students, patients, citizens, and more. *Customer*, in this sense, is a generic descriptor to indicate any of the people you serve or whose experience you care about.

I also realize there is a technical difference between a *map* (where things are) and a *diagram* (how things work). However, this book does not distinguish between the two, and they are used interchangeably.

Finally, this book is not about customer experience management, service design, or user experience design. It is about diagrams and the process of alignment that spans those fields. This is also not a comprehensive book about formal techniques in graphic design, information design, or illustration. There are volumes of resources that go into much more detail on those topics.

Audience for This Book

This book is for anyone involved in planning, researching, designing, and developing experiences. It's for people who need a holistic view of the ecosystem in which their offerings are situated.

The focus is on teams working together on initiatives with a significant experiential component. While journey managers may take a more global view of coordinating experience data (covered in Chapter 10), this book is grounded in the day-to-day reality of project teams striving to align to customer needs. This includes designers, researchers, product managers, brand managers, marketing specialists, strategists, entrepreneurs, and business owners.

Regardless of your skill level in mapping, this book has something for you. The steps and processes are basic enough for beginners to start creating diagrams. The related techniques should provide new insights for experts as well.

A Note on the Diagrams

I've taken care to provide a range of diagrams that reflect different approaches to mapping experiences. My interest is in providing complete examples so you can view them in their entirety. Although I've given attention to the display and clarity of each diagram, in some cases, not all text is legible. Please see the references in the image credits and throughout the book to locate the originals online. I also encourage you to find and collect your own examples for inspiration and guidance.

Book Outline

As with previous editions, the third edition of *Mapping Experiences* is divided into three parts.

Part 1: Experience Mapping: Visualizing Value

This section establishes the conceptual foundation for mapping experiences, introducing core principles of customer-centered collaboration and alignment:

- Chapter 1, "Visualizing Value: Aligning from the Outside In," introduces the fundamental shift from inside-out to outside-in thinking, establishing value alignment as the foundation for customer-centered organizations.
- Chapter 2, "Customer-Centered Collaboration: Aligning Inside-Across," explores how mapping becomes a catalyst for ongoing dialogue and organizational transformation through regular integration of customer insights into team activities.
- Chapter 3, "Foundations of Mapping Experiences," examines the building blocks and fundamental principles of experience mapping, including key elements and design considerations.
- Chapter 4, "Map Types in Review," provides an overview of various mapping approaches and diagram types, helping practitioners select the right tool for their context.

Part 2: Creating and Activating Maps

This section provides practical guidance on executing mapping projects through a streamlined five-phase process:

- Chapter 5, "Initiate: Establishing Relevance," covers how to frame and launch mapping projects effectively, including stakeholder alignment and project scoping.
- Chapter 6, "Investigate: Grounding in Reality," details research methodologies and techniques for understanding current experiences and gathering insights.
- Chapter 7, "Illustrate: Visualizing the Experience," provides comprehensive guidance on creating compelling visual representations of experience.
- Chapter 8, "Align: Making Sense Together," explores facilitation techniques for using maps to align teams, generate insights, and support collaborative sensemaking.
- Chapter 9, "Activate: Driving Momentum and Impact," introduces frameworks and techniques for translating current state insights into future state possibilities and innovations.

Part 3: Mapping in Context

The final section examines how mapping applies to specific strategic contexts and organizational challenges:

- Chapter 10, "Journey Management: Orchestrating Experiences at Scale," addresses how organizations manage and optimize customer journeys over time at scale.
- Chapter 11, "Mapping the Employee Experience: Aligning Inside," examines the application of mapping to the employee experience and the critical connection between employee experience and customer experience.
- Chapter 12, "Activating Strategy Through Visual Alignment," details the role of visualization in strategy formation and strategic decision making.

- Chapter 13, "Mapping for the Social Good: Prosperity Beyond Profit," demonstrates how mapping principles apply beyond commercial contexts to address social challenges.
- Chapter 14, "Mapping and Jobs to Be Done," integrates jobs to be done (JTBD) theory with experience mapping to deepen understanding of customer motivations and context.

This third edition represents not just an update, but an evolution of experience mapping for our current moment. As organizations navigate unprecedented complexity and change, the need for shared understanding and aligned action has never been greater.

This book aims to equip you with the concepts, tools, and techniques to create experiences that serve human needs and build organizational resilience. The power of experience mapping lies not in perfect data and documentation, but in collaborative visioning of future possibilities.

About the Author

Jim Kalbach is a noted author, speaker, and instructor in innovation, design, customer experience, and team collaboration. He is currently chief evangelist at Mural, an online whiteboard for visual collaboration, and has also consulted with large companies around the world. Jim holds a master's degree in library and information science and a master's degree in music theory and composition, both from Rutgers University.

He has published five books over the last two decades:

- *Designing Web Navigation* (2007)
- *Mapping Experiences* (2016, 2020, and 2026)
- *The Definitive Guide to Facilitating Remote Workshops* (2018), together with Mark Tippin
- *The Jobs To Be Done Playbook* (2020)
- *Collaborative Intelligence* (2023), together with Mariano Battan

Jim is active in speaking and coaching on mapping experiences, jobs to be done, strategy, collaboration, and related topics. He offers workshops and online courses independently and through The JTBD Toolkit (*www.jtbdtoolkit.com*). Contact him on LinkedIn to learn more.

Acknowledgments for the Third Edition

The act of writing is solitary; publishing a book is collaborative. It's amazing just how many people are involved. I thank you all. Hopefully, I won't leave anyone out.

First and foremost, I'm indebted to my primary reviewers for their feedback: Julie Francis, Erika Flowers, Gerry Scullion, and Adam Connor. Thank you all for your careful reading of the book and helpful input!

The figures and images make *Mapping Experiences* uniquely accessible and engaging. A huge thanks goes out to all of the creators who agreed to have their diagrams published in the book:

- Part 1: Susan Spraragen, Carrie Chan, Paul Kahn, Chris Tallec, Nick Bowmast (*bowmast.com*), Jim Tincher (*heartofthecustomer.com*), Andy Polaine, Wolfram Nagel, Accelerom, Matt Sinclair, Brandon Schauer, Erika Flowers, Diego S. Bernardo, Jamie Thomson, Lavrans Løvlie, Ben Reason, Paige Roche, Greg Laukloufi, Trevor Connolly, Indi Young, Steve Rogalsky, Stuart Karten (*kartendesign.com*), Marc Stickdorn, Jakob Schneider, and Craig Goebel

- Part 2: Jim Tincher, Chris Risdon, Yuri Vedenin, Eric Berkman, Sofia Hussain, Hennie Farrow, Erik Hansen, Martin Ramsin, Nathan Lucy, Mark Tippin, Donna Lichaw, Jake Knapp, Jeff Gothelf, and Scott Merrill
- Part 3: Brandon Schauer, Erika Flowers, Jochem van der Veer, Chris McGrath, Rafa Vivas, Seema Jain, Pete Abilla, Nick Bowmast, Chris Risdon, Patrick Quattlebaum, Teresa Torres, Aric Wood, Sophia Hussain, Sarah Brooks, Matt Sinclair, Attila Bujdosó, Nancy Sewell, Tim May, and Elaine Matthias

Thank you also to the contributors of case studies and direct quotes used in the book: Erika Flowers for the story of service blueprinting at Inuit, Paul Kahn and Chris Tallec for their journey game, Yuri Vedenin and Jochem ven der Veer for their input on journey management, Seema Jain for her technique of mapping the customer experience and employee experience together, Matt Sinclair for the circular design mapping story, Karen Woods for her story of mapping to fight domestic violence, and Cornelius Rachieru (*ampli2de.com*) for his example of ecosystem mapping.

A special thanks goes to folks in my network for their input and encouragement as I updated the book for this third edition: Julie Francis, Nick Bowmast, Erika Flowers, Ronnie Battista, Mark Tippin, I value our conversations! Special thanks also to Greg Laukloufi, Paige Roche, and the Service Strategy & Design team at Slalom for offering diagrams to include.

Once again, a big thank you goes to Hennie Farrow for contributing the beautiful diagram in Chapters 7 and 14, as well as providing the style for the artwork throughout all editions of *Mapping Experiences*. Thanks, Hennie!

I'd also like to thank the folks at O'Reilly who made this project possible—in particular, Angela Rufino, David Michelson, Ron Bilodeau, and Kristen Brown.

Finally, I'd like to show my appreciation to everyone who gave feedback on the previous editions of *Mapping Experiences*, online or in my workshops. It's an honor to have had such a positive reception and for this third edition to be possible. Danke schön!

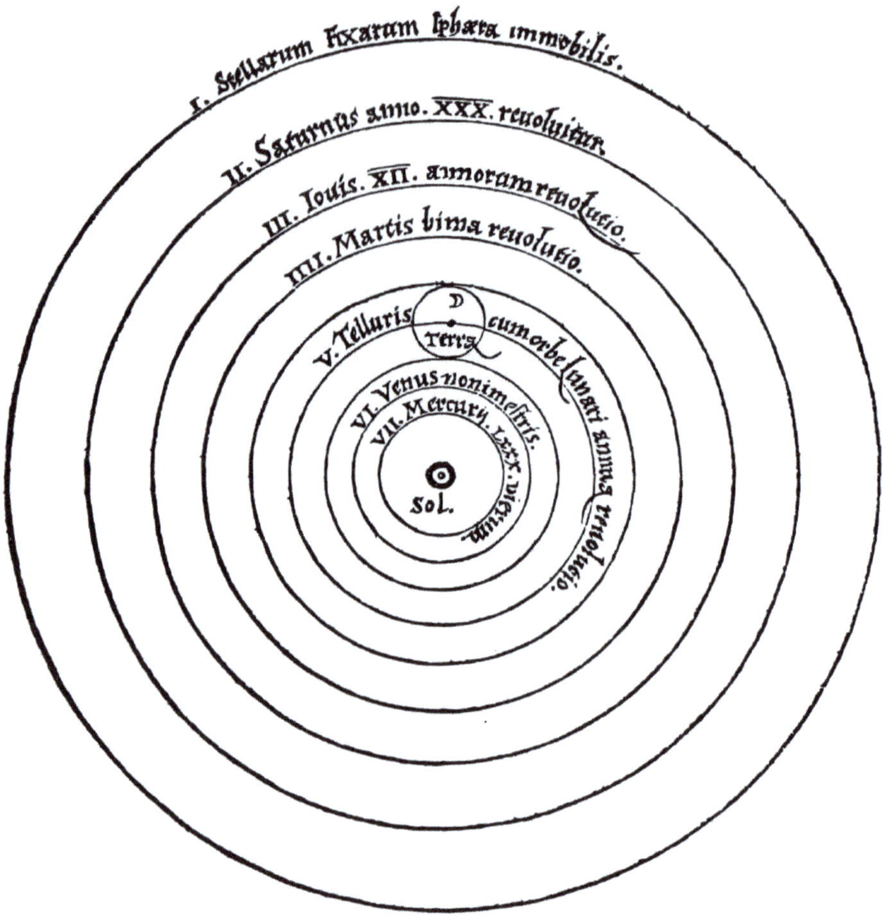

Polish astronomer Nicolaus Copernicus first proposed that the Earth revolves around the Sun, not the other way. He published his heliocentric model, shown here, shortly before his death in 1543. More than just a scientific discovery, it challenged the prevailing worldview and forced people to see the universe differently.

Similarly, companies are realizing that their customers don't revolve around them; they must revolve around their customers. Mapping experiences helps teams and organizations view their businesses in a fundamentally different way.

PART 1
Experience Mapping: Visualizing Value

I've seen it over and over: organizations get wrapped up in their own processes and lose sight of the markets they serve. Operational efficiency trumps customer satisfaction. They simply don't know what their customers go through.

But we're witnessing a shift of Copernican proportions. Customers don't revolve around the business; businesses must figure out how they fit into customers' lives. This requires a change in mindset—one that mapping can help you achieve.

Part 1 covers fundamental aspects of experience mapping:

- Chapter 1 introduces alignment diagrams. These reorient organizations from inside-out to outside-in thinking. Value alignment becomes the foundation for customer-centered organizations.
- Chapter 2 focuses on customer-centered collaboration. Mapping becomes a catalyst for ongoing dialogue, encouraging teams to continually integrate customer insights into their activities.
- Chapter 3 examines the building blocks of mapping. Although the concept of *experience* is slippery, there's a systematic way to capture it in a diagram.
- Chapter 4 reviews map types, from service blueprints, customer journey maps, and experience maps to day-in-the-life and workflow diagrams. Each has its strengths and weaknesses. Understanding these basic tools helps you decide which to use when.

You've got to start with the customer experience and work back toward the technology.

—Steve Jobs

IN THIS CHAPTER

- Aligning for value
- Experience-led growth (XLG)
- Staying human-centered in the age of AI
- Principles and benefits of mapping

CHAPTER 1

Visualizing Value: Aligning from the Outside In

"Then the Ping-Pong match begins." That's the customer quote I used to open the first edition of this book. It came from a mapping effort that visualized the invisible parts of a customer's experience in a diagram to make them tangible, allowing us to fix flaws and find new opportunities we'd otherwise miss.

In this case, the customer had received an inaccurate bill from the company I was working for and contested it—rightfully so. However, while his dispute was underway, he received a late notice for failing to pay the same incorrect bill. The ensuing communication felt like a game of Ping-Pong to him. Not a great experience.

Our mapping effort illuminated an internal misalignment: late payment notices weren't connected to bill disputes. The result was a poor experience, and not just for him; we heard similar billing complaints from other customers. And sure enough, "billing irregularities" also showed up as a top issue in Net Promoter Score (NPS) surveys—a key metric for measuring loyalty. When we presented this finding, the business stakeholders were appalled; they couldn't believe it was possible and moved quickly to address it. Mentions of billing issues decreased in later surveys as a result.

Together, we experienced the power of mapping: shifting our view from inside-out to outside-in revealed improvement opportunities the team was unaware of. Seeing the world from the customer's perspective was eye-opening.

Perhaps you've experienced a time when something suddenly clicks with your team. A pattern emerges that was hiding in plain sight. *Why do people keep calling about the same thing? Why does this step take so long?* The map shines a light in the darkness. If you've had that moment, you know why mapping matters. If not, consider these examples:

Service blueprinting at Intuit

As a principal service designer at Intuit, Erika Flowers ran mapping activities regularly. In one investigation, mapping revealed to Intuit's QuickBooks team that 20% of all customer support cases stemmed from billing and subscription confusion. This friction point cost millions in support overhead and drove customer churn. Through blueprinting activities, Intuit identified where customers got stuck, then redesigned workflows to enable self-service resolution. Journey mapping gave the company a shared view of the problem, enabling coordinated fixes across silos. The result: a significant reduction in support volume, improved retention, and millions saved annually while transforming billing from a frustration point into a seamless experience.*

Experience mapping at Airbnb

CEO Brian Chesky shared, "We created a blueprint of the Airbnb experience and used it to improve our service end-to-end."† By identifying critical friction points like booking anxiety, the team transformed insights into trust-building features: verified reviews, improved search filters, and better communication tools. The result drove measurable growth by eliminating friction, adding delight where trust formed, and creating a platform experience that feels personal rather than transactional.

Customer journey mapping at Starbucks

Starbucks used customer journey mapping to maintain its competitive edge in the coffee industry. Through cross-functional collaboration involving marketing, store operations, and product development teams, the company collected data from interviews, surveys, and digital analytics to create detailed journey maps. These maps revealed critical pain points: long wait times, inconsistent product quality, and a confusing rewards program. Armed with these insights, Starbucks developed solutions that directly addressed customer friction: Mobile Order & Pay to eliminate lines, a personalized rewards program tailored to individual preferences, improved quality control training, and digital integration in stores. The attention to the entire customer journey helped the company maintain its position as the coffee category leader.‡

I've heard dozens of stories like these over the course of the last decade. While they may not be earth-shattering breakthroughs, they reflect a commitment to continually improving the customer experience. You might not always get a game-changer with mapping, but even small changes can have a big impact.

And these examples aren't outliers: journey mapping has become standard practice for competitive organizations. According to Hanover Research, nearly half of US companies now use journey maps, and adoption continues to rise, particularly in business-to-business (B2B) sectors where the complexity of buying decisions makes understanding the people you serve critical. The investment pays off: 87% of organizations using maps report they're effective tools for decision making, 76% say the maps increase return on investment (ROI), and 79% credit them with the company becoming more customer-centric.§

This is just the tip of the iceberg. I encourage you to look for more examples and statistics online. But honestly, the greatest value you'll find from mapping experiences will come from your own stories. An internal case is more valuable than anything you can find with Google.

These stories share a common thread: visualizing experiences drives business results. In this chapter, I introduce the concept of alignment diagrams, a class of diagrams that visualize the interaction between individuals and an organization. By the end, you should understand how to model value alignment, the core commonalities underlying different diagram types, and the benefits of aligning for value.

* Reported in Erika Flowers's case study "QuickBooks Billing Experience Overhaul."

† See Chesky's post on X: *https://x.com/bchesky/status/1654137863007612930*.

‡ Carsten Krause, "Case Study: Starbucks' Success Elevating Customer Experience with Customer Journey Mapping," *CDO Times* (2023)

§ Hanover Research, *The Power of Customer Journey Mapping* (2022)

Alignment Diagrams

Customers expect some benefit when they use the products and services an organization provides. I use *customer* broadly to mean anyone an organization serves: buyers, users, patients, citizens, students, partners, and more. They want to get a job done, solve a problem, or experience an emotion. If they perceive this benefit as valuable, they'll give something in return, such as money, time, or attention.

To be successful, organizations need to capture value from their offerings. They need to earn profit, maximize reach, or improve their image. Value creation is bidirectional.

But how do we locate the source of value in such a relationship? Value creation lies at the intersection of human interaction with the provider of a service. It's where the experiences of customers in a given market intersect with the offerings of an organization (**Figure 1-1**).*

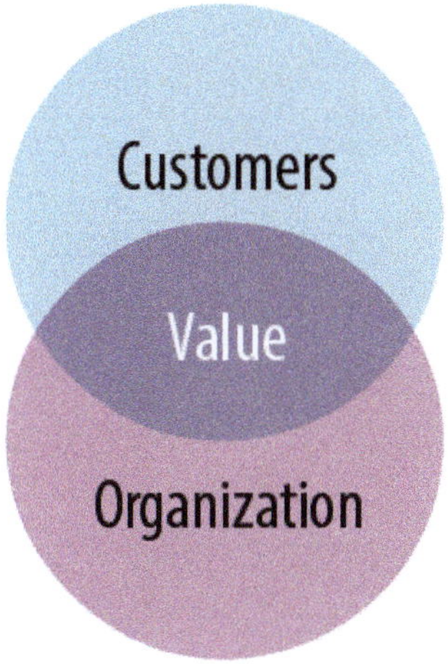

Figure 1-1. Value lies at the intersection of customers and the offerings of an organization.

Earlier in my career, prior to writing the first edition of this book, I often struggled to determine which type of diagram to use in a project: a customer journey map, mental model diagram, service blueprint, or something else. After comparing several examples, a similar set of principles became apparent: all these diagrams illustrate the value creation equation in different ways.

Viewing the commonalities of various diagrams opened up possibilities. I realized the focus shouldn't be on a specific technique, but rather on the broader concept of *alignment*.

This meant I wasn't locked into one method over another. More importantly, I could better connect the dots between human-centered design and business objectives. Focusing on alignment allowed me to speak with business leaders and stakeholders about how mapping experiences could help them reach their goals. Within a short time, I was running workshops with senior leaders and showing my diagrams to CEOs.

I use the term *alignment diagram* to refer to any map or visualization that reveals both sides of value creation in a single overview. It's a *category* of models that illustrate the interaction between people and organizations, making an otherwise invisible, abstract circumstance—a human experience—tangible and actionable.

Logically, alignment diagrams have two primary parts (**Figure 1-2**). On one side, they illustrate aspects of the individual's experience—a depiction of aggregate behavior across archetypal customers. On the other, alignment diagrams reflect an organization's offerings and processes. The points of interaction connecting the two, shown in the middle, are the means of value exchange.†

* For more on locating value visually with maps, see Jim Kalbach and Paul Kahn, "Locating Value with Alignment Diagrams," *Parsons Journal of Information Mapping* (2011), and Jim Kalbach, "Alignment Diagrams," *Boxes and Arrows* (2011).

† I owe this framing to Jess McMullin. See Jess McMullin, "Searching for the Center of Design," *Boxes and Arrows* (2003).

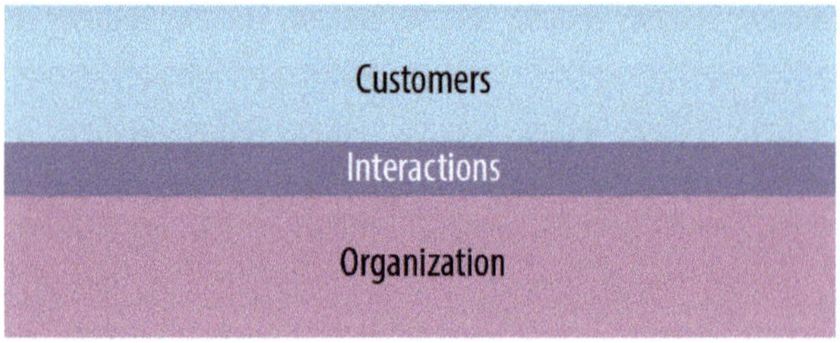

FIGURE 1-2. Alignment diagrams have two parts: a description of an experience and a description of an organization's offerings, with the interaction points between the two.

Such diagrams have become mainstream. You've probably already encountered some examples: customer journey maps, service blueprints, and experience maps, to name a few. My definition of alignment diagrams is less a proposition for a specific technique than a recognition of how existing approaches can be seen in a new, constructive way.

Take, for instance, *customer journey maps (CJMs)*. They illustrate the experiences of an individual as a customer of an organization at a high level. As the name suggests, the intent is to understand the broad arc of a "journey" over time. CJMs typically include three key phases: becoming aware of an offering, deciding to acquire it, and either staying loyal or discontinuing use.

FIGURE 1-3 shows a simple CJM of a search service for finding architects internationally. This is a modified version of a diagram I created for a project years ago, concealing the name of the product and company. The intent was to map the current state experience that customers had with the service.

The visual arrangement reflects the basic alignment diagram structure:

Individual's experience
: Phases of interaction are listed across the top, from "Become Aware" to "Renew/Upgrade." The rows show various facets of the customer experience: actions, feelings, desired outcomes, and pain points.

Organization's activities
: The bottom half illustrates key departmental activities that support the customer. An analysis of strengths, weaknesses, opportunities, and threats appears below that.

Interactions
: The primary means of interaction are listed in the middle. Moving from left to right through the chronology shows alignment between the customer's experience and the processes that intersect with it.

The team I was working with used this diagram to identify opportunities for improvement. We were able to troubleshoot half a dozen barriers to consumption that were previously unknown.

Service blueprints are another type of diagram showing the chronology of a service interaction. The intent is to provide a detailed view of a specific type of interaction, revealing the mechanisms of service provision. **FIGURE 1-4** depicts a simple example created by Susan Spraragen and Carrie Chan that illustrates a patient's interactions when going to an ophthalmologist. It reveals patient confusion about their prescription, an effect caused by two emotional states: distraction and anxiety.

Again, we see the two primary halves of the equation: the individual's frontstage experience (in pink and purple) and the backstage processes of the organization (in green and blue). The value exchange happens via interactions that cross the center line. The diagram serves as a diagnostic tool to pinpoint service inefficiencies and opportunities for improvement.

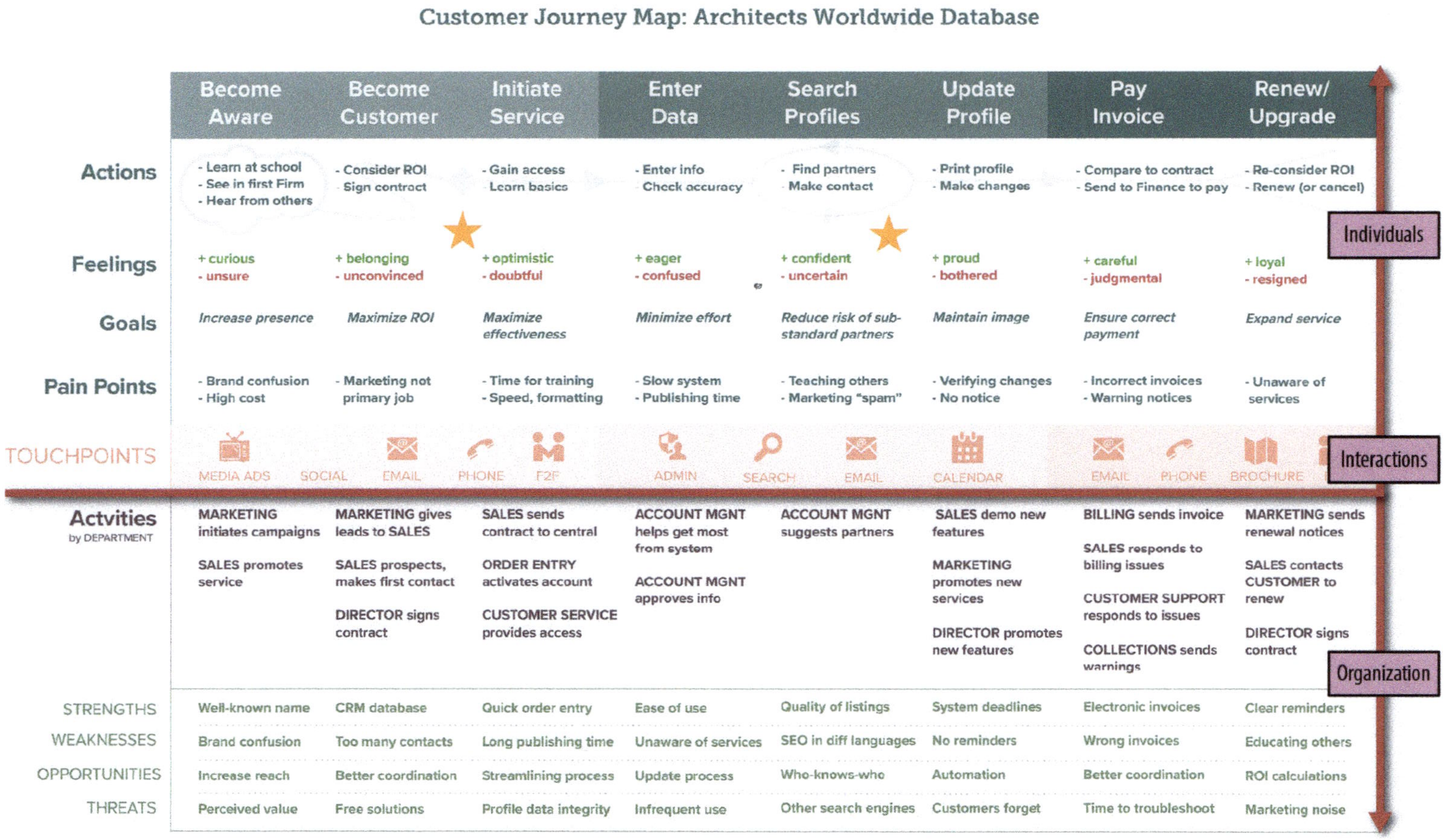

FIGURE 1-3. A simple customer journey map aligns the individual's experience with enabling activities across an organization.

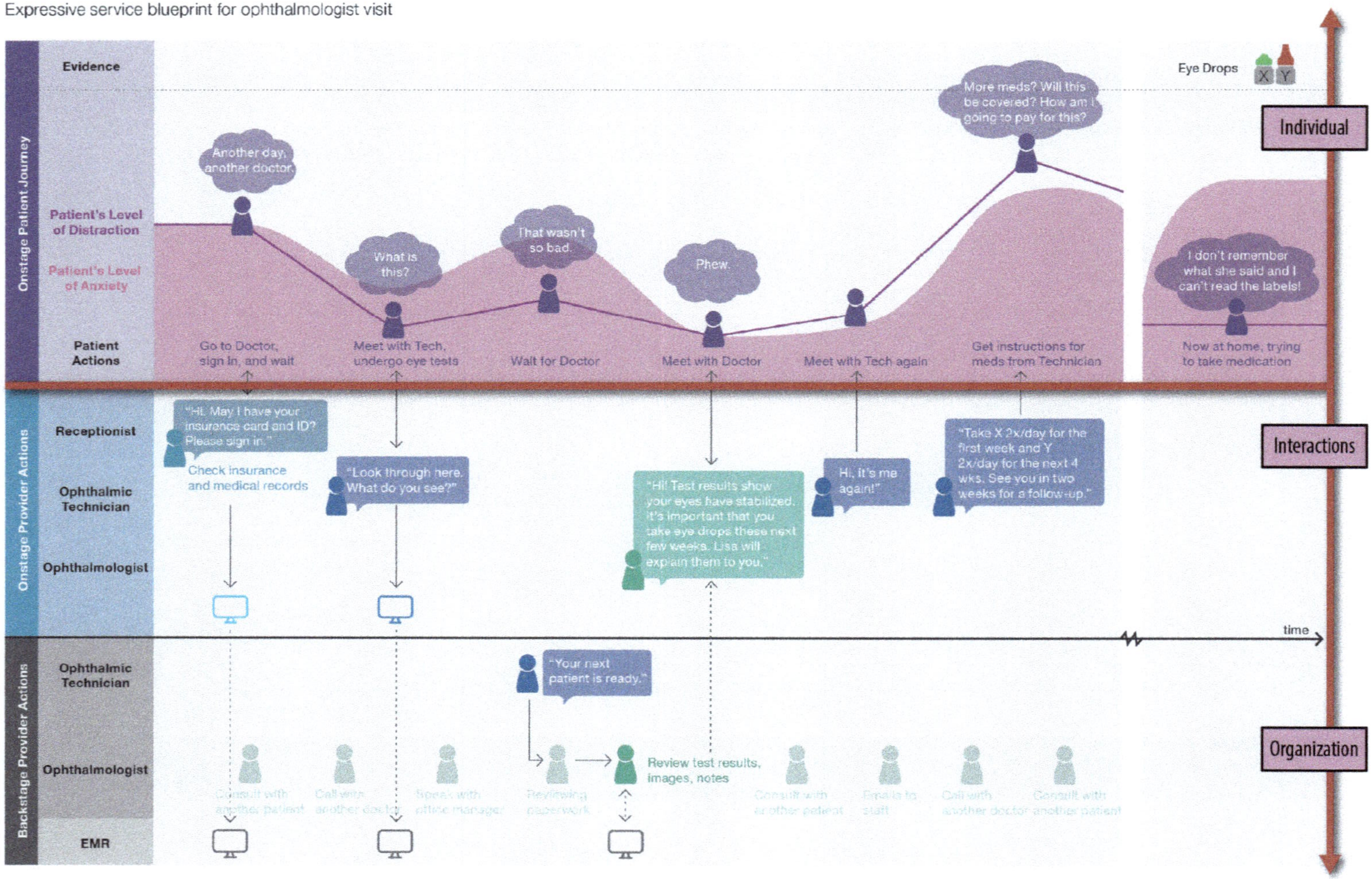

FIGURE 1-4. This example of a service blueprint, created by Susan Spraragen and Carrie Chan, depicts an encounter with an ophthalmologist.

While Chapter 4 will dive deeper into these and other specific diagram types, you can already start looking for the outside-in alignment in any map you encounter. The real power of mapping isn't about following one mapping approach over another, but rather telling the story of alignment.

How that story is told varies. For instance, a customer journey map shows a breadth of touchpoints across time, while a service blueprint details steps in a service episode to optimize delivery. Don't be overly concerned with terminology—what one person calls a customer journey map, another calls an experience map. Instead, focus on the desired outcome: outside-in alignment.

When crafted from an outside-in perspective, alignment diagrams build empathy and guide decision making. Like ethnographers, we observe the outside world and summarize it for others to understand. But unlike ethnographers, the result we produce isn't a lengthy written work but a compact visualization that serves as a springboard into action.

It's up to you to select the approach most appropriate for your situation. In the following chapters, I'll help you navigate how best to map the experiences most relevant to you.

Maps as Models and Boundary Objects

"The map is not the territory," philosopher Alfred Korzybski famously observed. Maps are models—simplified abstractions of reality that help us navigate complex situations.

Models are critical for the design of solutions and systems. Hugh Dubberly, renowned designer and business consultant, believes that models are an antidote to complexity in modern business operations. According to Dubberly:

> *A model is what you get when you put it all into one view to understand what's going on. It can be a great tool for managing the teams of people necessary to make these new products.**

Alignment diagrams are particularly effective as models because they function as what researchers call "boundary objects," or artifacts that different groups can interpret through their own professional lens while maintaining a shared understanding.†

A customer journey map, for instance, means something slightly different to marketing (touchpoint optimization), engineering (system requirements), design (interaction flows), and operations (service delivery)—yet all teams can work from the same model. I've found that a single diagram can speak to almost all groups within an organization, and they can imagine how their work is impacted by the insights from it.

This flexibility is what makes experience maps so powerful for organizational alignment. They're specific enough to be meaningful but adaptable enough to accommodate multiple perspectives.

* Hugh Dubberly, quoted in David R. Brown, "Supermodeler: Hugh Dubberly," *Gain: AIGA Journal of Design for the Network Economy* (2001).

† For more on boundary objects, see Susan Leigh Star and James R. Griesemer, "Institutional Ecology, 'Translations' & Boundary Objects," *Social Studies of Science* (1989).

Experience-Led Growth Now

Journey mapping has evolved from a specialized technique into a central activity that organizations recognize as directly tied to growth. This occurred because companies discovered that designing better experiences delivers tangible business results.

But let's be clear: this isn't new. Building on human-centered design, experience designers have focused on the full human experience for 30 years. A central argument is that understanding human behavior and experiences is business critical. As Peter Drucker, the renowned "father" of modern management, put it: "The purpose of business: to create a customer."* Everything else is a means to that end.

Maybe pushing customers through funnel stages made sense once, when the goal was to optimize conversion at each step until sales closed the deal. But customer journeys are not a straight line. We've moved from funnels to loops (**Figure 1-5**).† Customers experience the product, find value, invite others, and create expansion. The experience itself drives growth.

Yet traditional thinking persists. Product-led growth (PLG) emerged from software as a service (SaaS) in the 2010s, when companies discovered that even great products solving real problems still depended on how people experienced them. This was progress. PLG acknowledged that the path to the product mattered.

PLG also gets it wrong, though. Yes, it establishes product usage as a lever in go-to-market (GTM) motions. But it puts the product back at the center, not the experience. The product is the vehicle, not the destination. For instance, Slack "sells itself" because the experience is so much better than email that people naturally want to keep using it and invite colleagues.

Strip away the PLG buzzword, and what do you have? *Experience-led growth.*

Experience-led growth (XLG) is a strategy focused on driving profitable growth by providing distinctive customer experiences that change customer behaviors in measurable ways. Think of it as product/market fit on steroids. When you optimize the entire customer experience (not just the product, but every interaction before, during, and after), friction disappears. GTM becomes effortless because customers actually want what you're offering and recommend the service to others.

Some companies have figured this out. Amazon starts every major decision with the customer and works backward, asking not "What features can we build?" but "What customer problem are we solving?" Similarly, Intuit measures success by customer outcomes, not departmental outputs.

Steve Jobs understood this completely. For him, the experience was everything: product, packaging, retail stores, and even how the box opened. Everyone points to Apple as the example. Yet almost no one emulates what actually made the company successful. Companies copy the surface (sleek design, minimalist aesthetic) and miss the substance: organizing the entire business around creating experiences worth paying for.

Examples like these prove you can make customer experience matter more. As the data shows, this isn't soft metrics—it's hard business results around revenue and retention. Just consider these impacts:

---

* Peter Drucker, *The Practice of Management* (1954)

† See David Court et al., "The Consumer Decision Journey," *McKinsey Quarterly* (2009), and David C. Edelman, "Branding in the Digital Age," *Harvard Business Review* (2010).

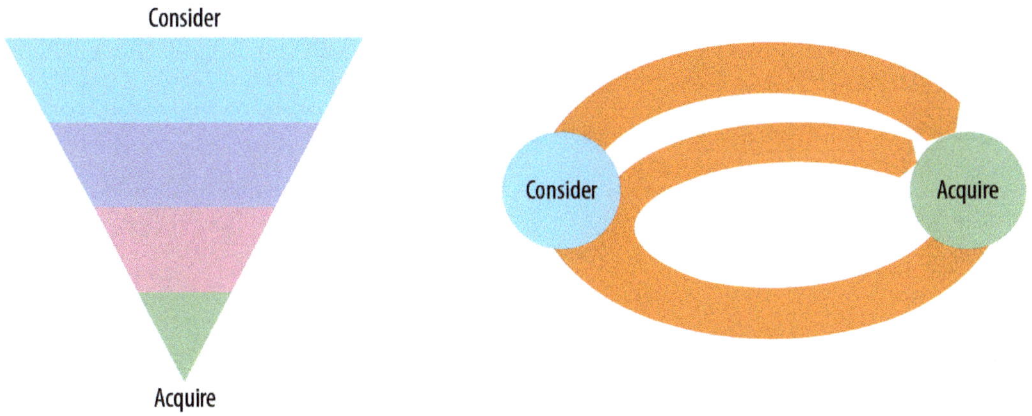

FIGURE 1-5. The funnel metaphor (left) fails to consider the "loops" of experiences customers actually have (right).

- Improving customer experience by one point can drive $1B+ in additional revenue for large companies.*
- Revenue growth of customer experience leaders is over 2x that of laggards.†
- More than half of consumers (52%) say they've stopped using a brand because of a bad experience.‡
- Customer-centric organizations achieve 51% higher retention.§

And here's the critical starting point: XLG begins with understanding the customer journey holistically, from awareness through advocacy and everything in between. It'd be hard to imagine growing via exceptional experiences without first mapping those experiences.

That's not to suggest this is an easy task. Understanding human behavior and experiences is one of the most difficult business skills. Unlike technology, with binary states of ones and zeros, human experience is messy, subjective, and emotional. People are complex, their motivations are layered, and their contexts vary. All of this matters when growth comes from creating satisfying customer experiences.

That's XLG in a nutshell. Mapping enables the necessary mindset. That's what this book is about.

Staying Human-Centered in the Age of AI

As artificial intelligence capabilities expand, it's tempting to believe that AI can automate the work of understanding customer experiences. These tools can already analyze vast amounts of customer data, identify patterns humans might miss, and even generate visual maps of customer journeys.

Sure, that's useful, and it enables the notion of broader journey management (the topic of Chapter 10). But it misses two fundamental human dimensions that make mapping effective: outside-in empathy and inside-across alignment.

* Maxie Schmidt and Sam Karpinkski, "Improving CX by 1 Point Can Drive More Than 1 Billion Dollars In Revenue," *Forrester* (2022)

† Victoria Bough et al., "Experience-Led Growth: A New Way to Create Value," *McKinsey* (2023)

‡ PwC, "PwC's 2025 Customer Experience Survey" (2025)

§ Forrester, "Forrester's 2024 US Customer Experience Index" (2024)

Outside-in: The Limits of AI Empathy

AI may provide you with more data and insights about your customers. It may even be able to create a fancy map. But it can't empathize with the people you serve.

AI can recognize patterns in sentiment data, but it cannot feel the frustration of a customer struggling with a confusing interface or the anxiety of someone making a high-stakes purchase decision. It cannot understand context the way humans can. It may identify that customers drop off at a particular step, but it won't grasp why that step feels harder to navigate on a stressed Monday morning versus a leisurely Saturday afternoon. It won't understand how cultural context shapes the meaning of interactions.

Mapping remains fundamentally human because customer experience is fundamentally human on both sides of the value equation.

Empathy requires lived experience and emotional resonance, not pattern matching. Understanding customer experiences means genuinely caring about the people behind the data, recognizing their humanity, and making ethical decisions about how to serve them. Should you optimize for engagement even if it becomes manipulative? Should you collect certain data just because you can? These are human questions that require values, judgment, and accountability.

Inside-Across: AI Can't Align Your Teams

Even if AI could perfectly understand customers, it cannot bring that understanding to life inside your organization. And it cannot align your teams to act on those insights.

The collaborative act of mapping is where the magic happens. When a cross-functional team gathers around a map making sense of customer reality, the learning sticks. The team can then align around what actions to take.

AI can't run that conversation. It doesn't know when tensions flare up between teams or how to work through the politics of naming what's not working. And it sure can't build the trust needed to get people to act.

Teams need to align with each other to deliver customer experiences. That alignment happens through human interaction, conversation, negotiation, and shared commitment.

The future of experience mapping isn't human versus AI. It's humans using AI as a powerful tool for data and pattern recognition while maintaining human elements: the empathetic understanding of customers externally and the collaborative alignment of teams internally.

Mapping remains fundamentally human because customer experience is fundamentally human on both sides of the value equation.

Principles of Alignment

Understanding the common aspects of alignment diagrams opens up possibilities—you're not limited to one approach. Here are some guidelines to keep in mind:

Show the big picture.

Alignment diagrams focus on human behavior as part of a larger ecosystem. They are not about product research. As much as possible, look at what individuals do, think, and feel in a given context.

Include multiple dimensions.

Alignment diagrams illustrate multiple facets of information simultaneously. This is what the "alignment" part of the technique is really all about.

Common aspects on the user side include actions, thoughts, feelings, states of mind, goals, and pain points. On the organization side, typical elements include processes, actions, objectives, and metrics, as well as actors or roles involved.

Show how value is exchanged.

Alignment diagrams expose touchpoints and the context of those touchpoints. The multiple layers of information come together to show an exchange of value. As a result, alignment diagrams prototype experiences. It's easy to walk through the touchpoints in slow motion, analyzing the broader circumstances around each interaction.

Visualize the experience.

Alignment diagrams make the invisible visible, adding tangibility to abstract concepts like an "experience." A 10-page report and bulleted slides summarizing the same information won't have the same impact. Visual diagrams externalize complexity, revealing patterns that remain hidden in documents. Our visual perception is fast and effective, and visualizations help overcome limitations of our working memory—they literally offload cognitive overhead.

Make it self-evident.

Alignment diagrams should need little or no explanation. People should be able to walk up to one and orient themselves relatively quickly. Keep in mind that a visual format itself does not guarantee simplicity: you'll still have to work hard to reduce information to just the most salient points.

Ensure relevancy to the organization.

Alignment diagrams must be relevant to the organization. As the mapmaker, you must investigate and understand the goals, challenges, and future plans of the organization.

Do the research.

Alignment diagrams are grounded in investigation. They require some contact with the people in the real world, through research and observation.

Benefits of Alignment Diagramming

Alignment diagrams are no panacea. They don't provide immediate answers. They are compelling visualizations that draw others into important conversations about creating value. Your ultimate goal is creating a dialogue within the organization, not creating the diagram itself.

From this perspective, mapping experiences has many benefits:

Alignment diagramming fosters empathy for customers.

It's often amazing how little organizations know about the experiences of the people they serve. Alignment diagrams shed light on real-world human conditions. In doing so, they not only instill empathy into an organization but also lead to compassionate action aimed at fulfilling individuals' needs.

Bruce Temkin, a pioneer in the customer experience movement, stressed the importance of mapping early on. In a 2010 blog post, he wrote:

> **Companies need to use tools and processes that reinforce an understanding of actual customer needs. One of the key tools in this area is something called a customer journey map.... Used appropriately, these maps can shift a company's perspective from *inside-out* to *outside-in*.***

* Bruce Temkin, "It's All About Your Customer's Journey," *Customer Experience Matters* (2010)

Looking into the organization from the outside causes a change in perspective to one more sensitive to people's thoughts and feelings.

Alignment diagramming provides a common big picture.

Diagrams serve as a shared reference, helping to build consensus. In this sense, alignment diagrams are strategic tools: they influence decision making at all levels and lead to consistency in actions.

The team at Voltage Control, a leading facilitation consultancy, has observed the effect of mapping across the hundreds of companies it advises. They write:

> **This alignment of cross-functional teams around a shared understanding of the user experience is a catalyst for change, driving the development of products and services that resonate on a deeply personal level.***

This type of alignment is crucial in designing broad information architectures and shared information environments. Alignment diagrams can provide a type of conceptual scaffolding that allows organizations to conceive of services at scale.

What's more, diagrams help preserve a common big picture as personnel changes. Team members may come and go, and diagrams help maintain continuity. In this sense, maps also play a knowledge management role.

Alignment diagrams don't provide answers directly. They facilitate conversation and stimulate reflection.

As Donella Meadows writes in *Thinking in Systems*, "The behavior of a system cannot be known just by knowing the elements of which the system is made."†

Alignment diagramming breaks down silos.

People experience a product or service holistically. Ideal solutions can easily cross an organization's department lines. Illustrations of the customer experience typically reveal divisional joints in an organization. Discussion around them sparks cross-department collaboration.

Writing for HubSpot, Diego Alamir observes:

> **One of the most powerful side effects of journey mapping is its ability to break down internal silos. When the engineering, marketing, sales, and support teams all look at the same map, they stop seeing the business from their department's perspective and start seeing it from the customer's.‡**

Don't be surprised if alignment diagrams surface inconvenient truths. That's a feature of mapping, not a bug. Silo busting is rarely simple, and pointing out flaws may meet resistance. But alignment starts by exposing inconsistencies and helping others address them for the benefit of the customer, not their own gain.

Consider also how teams at Credit Karma used mapping as a collaborative tool.§ Rather than researchers working in isolation and presenting a polished artifact later, they brought product managers, designers, and leadership into the research process from the start. The result: the teams developed shared

* Voltage Control, "Journey Mapping in Design Thinking: Best Practices & Tools" (2024)

† Donella Meadows, *Thinking in Systems* (2008)

‡ Diego Alamir, "What Is a Customer Journey Map?," *HubSpot Service Blog* (2025)

§ Reported in Tatiana Vlahovic and Pedro Rodriguez, "Using Journey Mapping as a Tool for Cross-Functional Research," *Dscout* (2022).

ownership of the journey map and used it to align their product roadmap, launch experiments, and anchor design explorations—all grounded in actual member experiences rather than assumptions.

For large enterprises, a view across functions from the individual's perspective is crucial for creating great customer experiences.

Alignment diagramming brings focus.

Many companies lack coherence in their business strategy, pulled in too many directions at once. Coherence—or incoherence, as is often the case—is the subject of *The Essential Advantage* by Paul Leinwand and Cesare Mainardi. After years of research in corporate strategy, the authors conclude:

> **To unlock the benefits of coherence, you need to take deliberate steps—to reconsider your current strategy, overcome the conventional separation between your outward-facing and inward-facing activities, and bring your organization into focus.***

Alignment diagrams represent such a deliberate step: they inherently match outward- and inward-facing endeavors. In doing so, they bring focus and coherence to organizations.

Alignment diagrams make sense of dynamic data.

Organizations today can access real-time analytics, AI-generated insights, and massive behavioral datasets. But data without context creates confusion, not clarity. Alignment diagrams provide a framework for interpreting this information, helping teams organize patterns into a coherent narrative of the human experience. Without this structure, teams risk drowning in dashboards while missing what matters. Maps transform data into shared understanding.

Just consider the fact that most journey management platforms (discussed in detail in Chapter 10) use a visual structure to display and interpret the vast amounts of data the systems can handle. Without this grounding, the people consuming that data would be lost. The structure of a map directly impacts your team's understanding of the experience, whether based on qualitative observations or quantitative metrics.

Alignment diagramming reveals opportunities.

Visualizations offer an immediacy of comprehension, providing insight into previously unnoticed value-creation opportunities.

While the diagrams themselves don't give an immediate solution, their presentation to the team often has an *aha* effect. They pinpoint areas for improvement in both operational efficiency and experience design, as well as exposing opportunities for growth.

Good diagrams are both compelling and engaging, providing an outside-in view of the organization.

Alignment diagramming goes beyond commercial settings.

In the broadest sense, an *experience* reflects the human condition, not just a customer's relationship with a service provider. While this book focuses primarily on commercial contexts, mapping techniques can be used in a range of situations, including social arenas, government, and beyond. I've seen mapping used in learning design, urban planning and improvement, and environmental protection.

Chapter 13 explores mapping for social good in greater detail.

* Paul Leinwand and Cesare Mainardi, *The Essential Advantage* (2010)

Summary

This chapter introduced alignment diagrams—visualizations that reveal both sides of value creation by showing how individuals' experiences intersect with an organization's offerings. Examples include customer journey maps, service blueprints, and experience maps. Terminology varies across the field. Don't be overly concerned with labels. Focus on the desired outcome: alignment.

XLG makes mapping critical. Companies that excel at customer experience see measurably higher revenue growth and retention. The experience drives growth, not products or GTM tactics. Journey mapping is the essential first step in any XLG strategy.

Even as AI capabilities expand, mapping remains fundamentally human work. AI cannot empathize with customers or align teams around action. The collaborative act of mapping builds shared understanding and organizational commitment that no algorithm can replicate.

Alignment diagrams offer many benefits:

- Fostering empathy for customers, shifting perspective from inside-out to outside-in
- Providing a common big picture that builds consensus
- Breaking down organizational silos
- Bringing focus and coherence to strategy
- Making sense of dynamic data
- Revealing opportunities for improvement and innovation
- Going beyond commercial settings

Alignment diagrams don't provide answers directly. They facilitate conversation and stimulate reflection. As complexity increases, such approaches are imperative tools for organizations competing on customer experience.

Further Reading

Harley Manning and Kerry Bodine, Outside In *(2012)*

This landmark book on the value of customer experience design for businesses is as relevant today as when it was written. "Customer experience is at the heart of everything you do—how you conduct your business, the way your people behave when they interact with customers and each other, the value you provide," the authors write. Mapping is a key activity to gain insight into the experience customers have with your organization.

Jim Tincher and Nicole Newton, How Hard Is It to Be Your Customer?, *2nd ed. (2022)*

This book shows how journey mapping can be used to drive customer-focused change across an organization. The authors make a broader case for mapping, not as an isolated activity but as a way to take action and effect culture changes. They bring years of experience to this volume, along with a wealth of practical advice and examples from the field. The book includes practical tools and templates you can use right away.

Simon David Clatworthy, The Experience-Centric Organization *(2019)*

This book looks at organizations holistically and discusses how to shift companies to become truly customer-centric. Despite its theoretical underpinnings, the author keeps the text approachable and quite practical. The approach is based on a maturity model with five steps toward experience-centricity. Chapter 5 deals exclusively with organizing around experience.

Lavrans Løvlie, Andy Polaine, and Ben Reason, Service Design*, 2nd ed. (2025)*

Løvlie, Polaine, and Reason provide a comprehensive, practice-focused guide to designing services that work across multiple touchpoints and channels, emphasizing research, prototyping, and measurement. This updated edition addresses AI's impact on service design and includes new frameworks for demonstrating ROI and driving organizational change. The book bridges theory and practice with case studies.

Diagram and Image Credits

Figure 1-3: Modified customer journey map by Jim Kalbach, created in Mural

Figure 1-4: Service blueprint by Susan Spraragen and Carrie Chan, used with permission

Figure 1-5: Alternative funnel model (right side in figure) adapted from David Court et al., "The Consumer Decision Journey," *McKinsey Quarterly* (2009)

Culture eats strategy for breakfast.

—Peter Drucker

IN THIS CHAPTER

- Visual models and alignment attrition
- Activating insights through collaboration
- The mapmaker as facilitator
- Three dimensions of team performance
- Behavior change: simple acts become culture

CHAPTER 2

Customer-Centered Collaboration: Aligning Inside-Across

Organizational theorist Karl Weick famously liked to retell the story of a small unit of Hungarian soldiers during World War I who became hopelessly lost in the Alps during a severe snowstorm. For days they huddled together without food, their morale collapsing as the situation grew desperate.

Then one soldier discovered a map in his pocket. With renewed confidence, they used the map to navigate their way back to safety. Once back at base camp, the lieutenant asked to see the map that had saved them. To everyone's astonishment, it was a map of the Pyrenees. The "wrong" map had guided them out of harm's way.

Weick uses this story to make a point: the soldiers were saved because the map gave them a shared reference point that broke the paralysis, aligned their efforts, and allowed them to make sense of their situation together.

To be clear: I'm not arguing for creating inaccurate experience maps. An actual map of the Alps would have been better for the group of soldiers, for sure. Your maps should absolutely reflect customer reality as faithfully as possible. But Weick's story reminds us that a map's value extends beyond its technical accuracy. That's inside-across alignment in action.

It's a two-step process (FIGURE 2-1):

1. ***Outside-in alignment:*** The organization must deeply understand the individuals it serves (buyers, users, patients, citizens, students, partners, and more), which I refer to generically as *customers*.
2. ***Inside-across alignment:*** Teams must align not only to that customer experience but also to one another.

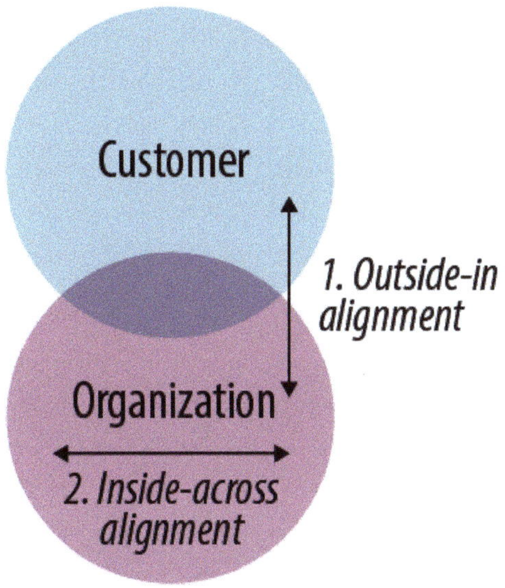

FIGURE 2-1. There are two types of alignment: alignment to the customer experience, which happens from the outside in, and internal (inside-across) alignment among the teams that create the experience.

When teams gather around an experience map—discussing it, debating it, making sense of it together—they're building the shared understanding needed to act. The map becomes the catalyst that gets everyone looking at the same thing, talking the same language, and motivated to move in the same direction.

But alignment isn't a one-time achievement. It requires maintenance. Visual representations of customer experience offer deeper, more immediate comprehension that persists over time. Regular team activities focused on customers create shared experiences that keep alignment strong, even as priorities shift and new challenges emerge.

In this light, this third edition of this book doesn't intend to defend static maps that, when printed, become wall art. It's about building the collaborative sensemaking capability that makes customer insights actually useful. It's about connecting the customer insights that are over *there* with efforts to improve the experience over *here*.

This chapter focuses on the inside-across alignment necessary to first understand and interpret experience data and then imagine solutions that will make XLG a reality. It positions mapping not as a one-off activity to produce a static artifact, but as a dynamic set of ongoing behaviors. Chapters 5 through 9 will provide specific methods and techniques for putting these collaborative principles into practice.

It's Not About the Map, It's About the Mapping

Most organizations claim to be customer-centric. Few really are. A PwC study, for instance, found that a majority of US consumers say customer experience at most companies needs improvement.* That's quite a gap.

It's not for lack of information. Companies today collect an abundance of customer data: interviews, surveys, behavioral metrics, dashboards, Net Promoter Scores (NPSs)—the list goes on. Whether qualitative or quantitative, many organizations are swimming in insights.

But there's a problem: not every company that creates experience maps knows how to put them to work. Gartner reported that while 82% of organizations have created customer journey maps, only 47% are using them effectively.†

One thing that I've realized in my work with teams around the world is that not everyone is able to imagine how insights about the individual's experience—positive, negative, or otherwise—inform what the solution should be. There's an imagination gap.

More than anything, experience maps are a key way teams gain an outside-in view of the people they serve. But the map doesn't provide all the answers outright. Instead, the real collective sensemaking emerges through dialogue and conversation.

For instance, I once consulted with a publisher to improve its relationship with its authors. I created an author experience map through direct interviews with over 20 authors and brought the resulting model back to the team. During our conversation, we noticed a trend: the publisher didn't stay in close contact with authors after they'd submitted their manuscripts.

Figure 2-2 shows this pattern overlaid on the map. The bars show our relative estimated level of involvement at each stage. With this collective observation in hand, the team then focused on ways to increase contact with authors throughout the journey. How might we make authors feel more connected? How might we create a sense of belonging?

* PwC, "Future of Customer Experience Survey" (2018)

† Cassandra Nordlund, "How to Create an Effective Customer Journey Map," *Gartner* (2019)

Figure 2-2. A simple pattern emerged through conversion that was not present in the original research insights: author involvement decreased during the production phases.

Journey management platforms (discussed in Chapter 10) may solve for data integration and visibility. They don't solve for organizational alignment. Someone still has to interpret what the metrics mean. Someone must facilitate the conversation when data reveals uncomfortable truths. Someone has to help teams move from "We see the problem" to "We're aligned on the solution."

Those are human challenges, not technical ones. And when AI can optimize journeys at scale, your competitive advantage stems from your organization's ability to make sense of experience *together* and act in concert. Visualizing the experience has a powerful ongoing aligning effect on the team.

> *Remember: the objective is not just to create a diagram, but to engage others in conversations and develop solutions together as a team.*

Design thought leader and educator Jon Kolko observes how diagrams address what he calls *alignment attrition*, or the tendency for people to get out of sync with one another. He writes:

> **A visual model becomes one of the most effective tools for minimizing alignment attrition. A visual model captures and freezes a thought in time. By building a visual model together, alignment is offloaded to and "frozen in" the diagram. Your thoughts, opinions, and views will change, but the diagram won't, and so you've added a constraining boundary to the idea—and a tool for concretely visualizing how the product vision is changing.***

Jeff Patton highlights this dynamic perfectly in his book *User Story Mapping* with the image shown in **Figure 2-3**. Three people verbally agree on a plan, each thinking they're aligned. But when they examine a shared visual model, they discover that each had completely different ideas in mind. The real breakthrough comes when they work together at the board, actively discussing and manipulating the visual elements. Only through this collaborative process do they achieve genuine shared understanding.

This is why maps become essential tools for maintaining alignment, not just achieving it. Kolko's concept of alignment attrition recognizes the natural drift that happens over time: people forget details, interpret things differently in hindsight, or shift their thinking as circumstances change. The map provides a stable reference point that teams can return to repeatedly, anchoring conversations and decisions even weeks or months later.

Part of collective sensemaking is arguing and debating. Critically, because maps focus on the people you serve rather than internal processes or departmental priorities, they offer neutral ground for productive conflict. Teams can disagree about what the map reveals without defending territorial interests. The customer's experience becomes the shared reference point that depersonalizes debate: it's not about whose department is right; it's about what's actually happening to customers.

This creates psychological safety for honest conversation. Teams are encouraged to challenge assumptions, surface uncomfortable truths, and explore alternative interpretations without triggering defensive reactions. Mapping activities foster a safe space for difficult conversations by keeping everyone focused on customer reality rather than organizational politics.

* Jon Kolko, "Dysfunctional Products Come from Dysfunctional Organizations," *Harvard Business Review* (2015)

In theory, a day might come when companies are able to completely understand and create experiences with no human intervention. In this scenario, AI systems would understand the current state, automatically diagnose the challenge to overcome, and build solutions without any teamwork.

But as soon as more than three people are involved, alignment and activation are needed. They need to not only understand the available information about an experience, but also believe in the solution and ultimately create it.

Mapping matters beyond the initial creation moment. The diagram maintains alignment even as individual perspectives shift. It becomes the stable reference point that teams can return to, measure against, and use to track how their thinking evolves.

The fundamentally human dynamics of an organization don't change in the age of AI. For the foreseeable future, inside-across team alignment will be necessary. Mapping as an activity, not just an artifact, aims at this type of alignment. But it happens only if insight is activated.

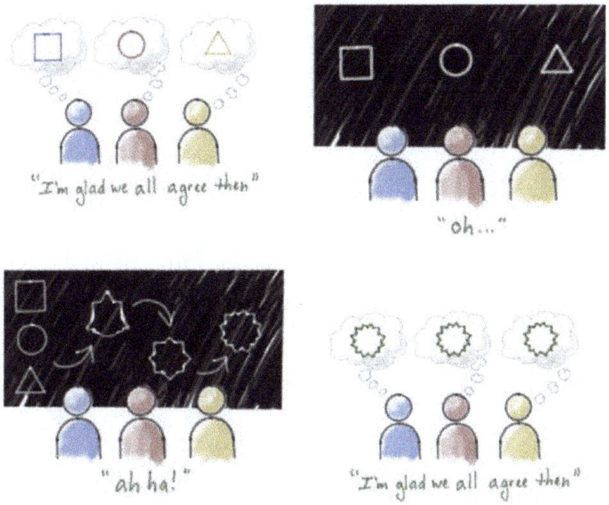

Figure 2-3. Visualizing work goes further than just verbal agreement in aligning teams.

Maps as Narrative Structures

Experience maps are narrative structures that organize a range of stories. Think of it like having a map of a city: the map shows the overall layout, the major streets, and the landmarks. But a story is a specific route through that city: the journey from the airport to your hotel, the walk from the coffee shop to the office, the detour through the park on a sunny afternoon.

If the map provides the structure, the stories bring it to life.

A journey map might show the stages a customer goes through when buying a product. But the real insight comes from the stories: A new shopper's frustration when they couldn't find pricing information. A frustrated user's relief when the chat support agent understood their problem immediately. The small business owner who almost abandoned their purchase but came back because of a well-timed email.

Each story traces a path through the map. Some follow the expected route. Others reveal surprising detours, dead ends, or shortcuts that the map didn't anticipate. These stories validate the map, challenge it, and help teams understand the emotional reality behind each stage.

When facilitating mapping sessions, encourage teams to anchor conversations in specific customer stories. Don't just say, "Customers get frustrated during onboarding." Tell the story of Alex, who spent 20 minutes trying to upload a logo in the wrong file format, gave up, and didn't come back for three days. That specificity makes the friction real and the need for change urgent.

More importantly, there's a deeper layer of storytelling at work: how the mapmaker presents customer realities to the organization. The choices you make about what to show, how to sequence it, and how to visualize it shape the narrative. Do you start with the friction points or the successes? Do you emphasize emotional highs and lows or transactional flows? Do you visualize the experience as a timeline, a cycle, or a branching path?

Maps organize, stories activate. Together, they create a shared understanding that drives action.

These are narrative choices that direct attention and frame understanding. The mapmaker becomes a translator, crafting a story about the outside world that helps internal teams see what matters most.

Stories also make maps memorable and shareable. People forget frameworks and statistics, but they remember stories. When someone from marketing tells someone from engineering about "that customer who called support three times because the button was hidden," that story carries the map's insights across organizational boundaries in ways a slide deck never could.

Maps organize, stories activate. Together, they create a shared understanding that drives action.

Customer-Centered Collaboration: Activating Insights

Organizations today talk about putting customers at the center of decisions and operations. But truly customer-centric organizations recognize that customer experience doesn't exist in isolation. This is why the most mature organizations obsess over it. They understand that creating great customer experiences requires excellent employee experiences, streamlined partner interactions, and a holistic view of all the touchpoints in their ecosystem.

Customer-centered collaboration—the regular practice of integrating customer insights into team activities and documentation to improve experiences—is what makes this possible. It has two essential parts:

1. ***Integrating experience insights:*** Teams systematically bring customer perspectives into their daily work: stand-ups, planning sessions, design reviews, and decision-making processes. Customer insights aren't locked away in research reports; they're actively present in team conversations and artifacts.
2. ***Devising solutions that improve experiences:*** Teams use these insights to create solutions explicitly designed to improve customer experiences. Every initiative, feature, or change connects back to how it will make the experience better.

The key is to avoid integrating customer insights as a one-time event or viewing them as a type of data detached from team workflows. Bring insights to life on a regular basis by leveraging diagrams of the experiences to guide the conversation.

A key way to activate insights is to design activities around them. Customer insights shouldn't be treated like data points that come and go. They should serve as a center of gravity for team collaboration, a shared reference point that pulls everyone into the same orbit.

Consider the journey mapping game created by Paul Kahn and Christophe Tallec.* The game uses a blank journey worksheet with swim lanes and a set of touchpoint cards. Teams select elements from a library—personas, goals, and touchpoints—then place the elements on

---

* See Paul Kahn and Christophe Tallec, "Customer Journey Mapping Game (Transport)," *Prezi* (2013).

the gameboard to compare and discuss different experiences. **Figure 2-4** shows the game in action.

Tallec put the game to use when a major French city wanted to reinvent urban transportation. The city's team faced a familiar challenge: getting car manufacturers, commercial firms, public transit companies, labor unions, and everyday users to see beyond their individual perspectives.

The underlying problem in these situations is always siloed thinking—each stakeholder views the challenge through their departmental lens. The game worked because it created a common language shared by everyone and dominated by no one. Participants reported increased team alignment and cross-functional collaboration after the workshops.

Activating insights with customer-centered collaboration goes beyond just journey mapping activities. Most of us spend the bulk of our workdays collaborating: meetings, workshops, emails, Slack threads, cross-functional projects. If customer understanding isn't part of those interactions, it's not really part of the work. Treat collaboration itself as a flow, with multiple touchpoints where customer insights can emerge.

There is no one standard way to activate customer insights. I encourage you to imagine and design your own activities. Here are just a few examples:

- Start meetings with a warm-up. Ask the team to rank, react to, or prioritize a real customer quote. Use AI-driven personas to make this activity more interactive.
- Use personas in breakout discussions. Assign groups to different perspectives and have them debate solutions through that lens.
- Visualize insights differently. Create posters, dashboards, or printed cards to keep customer needs visible and accessible.
- Stress-test ideas against customer needs. When making decisions, ask how they might affect each persona or segment.
- Bring customers into the room. Invite them to all-hands, retros, or team demos to share their experiences firsthand.
- Run polls or contests. Quiz the team on the current NPS, common complaints, or most surprising insights.
- Get creative. Ask teams to write a haiku or a short story based on a real customer moment. This approach may sound unusual, but it helps people connect emotionally to the experience.

Figure 2-4. Playing the journey mapping game engages everyone in the workshop.

These aren't gimmicks. They are small, intentional moves that make customer insights feel alive—something the team engages with, not just hears about. Chapters 5–14 include additional methods you can rely on to create real momentum around customer insights. See books like *Gamestorming* for even more examples.*

Beyond team rituals and collaborative activities, also look at your normal team documentation patterns. Are customer insights reflected in your documents? If not, you're missing another key opportunity:

- Product requirement documents (PRDs) should start with the customer need being addressed.
- Campaign briefs should anchor to a specific job to be done or emotional driver.
- Strategy decks should open with the voice of the customer, not just the voice of the business.

When teams see customer context embedded in every phase of work, from kickoff to rollout, they begin to internalize it. Customer centricity becomes not just a goal but a habit.

The Mapmaker as Facilitator: A Critical Role Shift

There's a fundamental shift that some teams miss: the mapmaker needs to become a facilitator. Creating a beautiful journey map or service blueprint is only the beginning. The real work happens when you bring people together to make sense of what the map reveals (**Figure 2-5**).

Too many mapping efforts follow this pattern: a small team researches and creates a map, then presents it to stakeholders in a traditional slide deck format. The map becomes a static artifact—admired, discussed briefly, then filed away. The insights remain trapped in the diagram rather than becoming fuel for collaborative action.

Experience maps aren't magic. They won't automatically clarify priorities or unlock the best ideas. The power of an experience map isn't in the artifact. It's in the conversations it enables.

But here's the crucial point: the map is the catalyst for conversations, but those conversations must be guided. When teams work together to interpret customer journeys, when they ask questions, debate patterns, and challenge assumptions, they build alignment. They gain clarity. And they're far more likely to act with confidence.

Without skilled facilitation, mapping conversations drift toward familiar internal perspectives, get stuck in defensive discussions about existing work, or jump too quickly to solutions without understanding the underlying customer reality.

Facilitation is the art of guiding group processes to help teams reach shared understanding and decisions. A facilitator doesn't provide answers or dictate direction. Instead, they create conditions for productive collaboration. This means designing activities that surface diverse perspectives, asking questions that deepen thinking, managing time and energy in the room, and ensuring that everyone's voice is heard.

Good facilitation feels invisible. The team feels a shared sense of ownership over the insights and solutions because they discovered them together. Poor facilitation either dominates the conversation (the facilitator becomes the expert) or abdicates responsibility (the meeting drifts without structure).

When mapmakers embrace facilitation, they're taking on this neutral, guiding role. They help teams make sense of the experience customers have together rather than

* Dave Gray and Sunni Brown, *Gamestorming 2.0* (2025)

telling them what it means. Facilitation is about moving things forward by doing the following:

Guiding discovery
: Teams need to work through customer insights together, not just receive them. When people participate in making sense of customer data, they develop deeper customer empathy and a stronger commitment to acting on what they learn.

Surfacing assumptions
: The most valuable moments in mapping sessions often come when team members realize that their assumptions about customer behavior don't match reality. As a facilitator, you create a safe space for these revelations.

Enabling collective problem-solving
: When teams identify friction points and opportunities through collaborative exploration, the solutions they generate have broader buy-in and a better chance of implementation.

Aligning decision making
: Ultimately, the team needs to conclude what to do next. The facilitator helps harmonize perspectives toward a collective decision.

Mapping sessions function as liminal spaces—threshold experiences where beliefs can be examined and reframed. Designer Dave Gray explores this concept in his book *Liminal Thinking*, describing how we create change by understanding and reshaping the beliefs that constrain us.

When cross-functional teams gather around a journey map, they step outside their departmental assumptions and enter ambiguous territory where new thinking becomes possible. The map creates this threshold: it's neutral ground where teams can challenge what they believe about customers without defending what they believe about themselves.

Figure 2-5. Facilitating conversations around the diagram is a critical part of mapping.

Cocreation: Bridging Internal and External Collaboration

Customer-centered collaboration doesn't stop at organizational boundaries. The most effective teams extend their collaborative practices to include customers themselves.

Think of cocreation as a bridge between inside-across alignment and outside-in alignment. Internal teams align around customer insights through mapping and shared models. But when customers join these collaborative sessions, something powerful happens: the abstract becomes concrete, assumptions come to light, and solutions emerge from direct dialogue.

Traditional customer research positions customers as data sources. Teams extract insights, then retreat to internal spaces to interpret and act on what they've learned. Cocreation flips this dynamic. Customers become collaborative partners who help identify problems, evaluate solutions, and shape direction.

This approach has roots in participatory design, a movement that emerged in Scandinavia in the 1970s. Participatory design was founded on the principle that people who will be affected by a design should have a say in the design process. The core tenet remains powerful today: the people experiencing the service or product are experts in their own experience.

When you bring customers into the design process as cocreators, you're fundamentally changing the power dynamic from "we design for them" to "we design with them." Customer experience expert Jeannie Walters defines it as follows: "Cocreation means letting your customers in on the ground floor of innovation and creating new products, services, and customer journeys in sometimes real time with them. Customers become partners and advisors, not just end users."*

Walters also notes that successful cocreation requires "discipline around prioritization, closed-loop processes, and efficient customer communications." Customers who contribute ideas need to see what happens with their input. When Starbucks credited customers for ideas like pumpkin spice lattes and loyalty program features, it reinforced that customer collaboration generates real impact.

Organizations that master cocreation find that collaborative customers become their strongest advocates. They've invested in solutions, understand the trade-offs, and feel ownership over outcomes. As Walters observes, "Customers often participate because they want to help create an experience they want, with a brand they already like."

Cocreating with Experience Maps

One of the most direct applications of cocreation in experience mapping is inviting customers to participate in building the maps themselves. Ironically, customers are often excluded from customer journey mapping sessions. But when they participate in mapping workshops, they bring an irreplaceable perspective that no amount of research can fully capture.

Cocreation in mapping can range from simple to sophisticated. You might invite a small customer cohort to a workshop session. You might ask for feedback on draft maps at key stages. Or you might work with customers to envision an "ideal state" journey that becomes the foundation for your service blueprint. With input from

* Jeannie Walters, "Co-Creation with Customers: 5 Ways to Drive Better Results," *Experience Investigators* (2019)

customers, you can create the actual experience they want before developing the supporting processes and systems required to deliver it.

This doesn't mean every mapping session needs customers present. But organizations that regularly bring customers into collaborative work develop stronger alignment both internally and with market reality.

Activities to consider when cocreating with customers include the following:

Workshop participation
: Bring customers and frontline staff together with your team to build "as-is" (current) or "to-be" (ideal) maps from scratch or to critique existing ones.

Prototype feedback
: Use map stages as tangible prototypes (e.g., paper mockups of a new app flow) during interviews to get real-time, unguarded feedback.

"Ideal state" mapping
: Focus on codesigning the future journey with customers, envisioning the perfect experience to guide innovation before building systems.

Micro-moment focus
: Identify and improve small but crucial interactions (such as a Like button) by mapping these micro-moments with user input.

Pain-point isolation
: Use maps to visualize customer frustrations (e.g., unknown taxi fares, cash payments) and collaboratively brainstorm solutions for new products, like ridesharing.

Cocreation adds most value when teams face ambiguity about customer needs, when solutions require understanding nuanced customer context, or when early concepts need validation before significant investment. Cocreation works less well when teams haven't done basic homework or when decisions are already made. Customers recognize when their input won't influence outcomes.

Team Engagement Drives Performance

Effective teams do the right work, do the work right, and do the work well. Most organizations obsess over the first two—effectiveness and efficiency—while treating engagement as secondary. That's a mistake. Engagement isn't just a feel-good factor. It's the foundation that makes the other two dimensions better.

When people care deeply about the work, they find better ways to do it and better ways to collaborate. Engaged teams bring creativity to solving problems. They are also more resilient and persist in the face of obstacles. And they tend to work more naturally across boundaries because they're united by shared purpose rather than departmental lines.

Remember: the objective is not just to create a diagram, but to engage others in conversations and develop solutions together as a team.

One of the best ways to engage people is to start with the customer's experience. This is the fundamental truth about the business that everyone is responsible for, from sales and marketing to engineering and operations and even finance and HR. I've seen it time and time again: customer insights provide common ground that transcends departmental boundaries.

When teams collaborate around real customer stories, the conversation moves from defending territorial interests to solving shared problems. Different perspectives become assets rather than obstacles. Engineers and designers find they're all trying to help the same person accomplish the same goal, just from different angles.

Experience maps serve as collaboration tools precisely because they organize information about the individual's experience in ways that multiple functions can engage with simultaneously. Each team can "see" itself in the experience. This shared understanding makes cross-functional conversations more productive because everyone starts with the same goal: delivering exceptional customer experiences.

Consider how Pixar organizes creative collaboration through its Braintrust process.* When reviewing a film in development, teams at Pixar don't gather people by hierarchy or department. They assemble cross-functional experts—directors, writers, animators, story artists—and organize the entire conversation around a single outcome: is this creating the experience we want audiences to have?

The Braintrust doesn't have the authority to mandate changes. Instead, it creates conditions for honest, productive collaboration by keeping everyone focused on the desired outcome (the audience experience) rather than internal politics or departmental agendas. This is inside-across alignment in action: different functional perspectives united by shared commitment to customer success.

One collaborative mapping session creates similar dynamics across product and go-to-market teams. When everyone examines the same customer journey together, they're no longer representing their departments; they're solving for the customer. This shift in orientation is what makes cross-functional collaboration productive rather than just procedural.

If you want to build a truly customer-focused organization, don't leave customer insights to the research team or the design function. Make them the foundation of everything from team interaction to strategy making, driving alignment, creativity, and action.

Culture Change: What You Do Is Who You Are

When IBM set out to transform its culture in the mid-2010s, the challenge was staggering.† How do you shift the mindset of nearly 400,000 employees across a sprawling global enterprise? The answer wasn't a top-down mandate or a massive training program. It was changing what people did every day.

IBM developed Enterprise Design Thinking (EDT) as a practical framework that teams could immediately apply to their work. But the real innovation wasn't the framework itself; it was how IBM scaled behavioral change across the organization. Instead of asking people to *think* differently, they were asked to *work* differently. It all started with small, repeatable practices.

For instance, teams began using *playbacks*—regular sessions where they shared work in progress with stakeholders and users, gathering feedback early and often. They also invited real customers, known as *sponsor users*, to participate directly in development and created clear statements of user value, called *hills*, to keep teams aligned on outcomes rather than outputs.

Through repetition, these practices became habits. The habits became culture. IBM directly trained over 100,000 people. But more importantly, it changed how the entire workforce collaborated around customer needs.

The transformation worked because IBM's leadership understood a fundamental truth: you don't change culture by changing what people believe; you change culture by changing what people do.

* Ed Catmull, *Creativity, Inc.* (2014)

† For a detailed account of this transformation, see Phil Gilbert, *Irresistible Change* (2025).

Frame the Customer Problem First

Teams tend to jump to solutions when given a challenge. "We need better onboarding." "Let's add a tutorial." "Build a knowledge base." But what customer problem are you actually solving?

The Double Diamond framework (**Figure 2-6**), a widespread model first developed by the British Design Council, shows why this matters. The first diamond is about understanding the problem. The second is about developing the solution.

Each diamond shape also reflects a pattern of exploration through divergent thought, followed by converging on an agreed direction. Overall, this flow has four modes of working:

Discover
: What are customers experiencing in the real world? Resist the urge to solve at this point and just seek understanding.

Define
: Which customer pain points matter most? Frame the problem before jumping to solutions.

Develop
: How might we solve the customer problem? Generate solution ideas.

Deliver
: Will this work? Decide on a direction, and test and implement it.

Most teams move too quickly through the first diamond or skip it entirely, collapsing problem and solution into a single step. While AI-driven development cycles shorten or even collapse the two diamonds, the model remains an important way of representing different modes of thinking about problems and solutions.

Mapping squarely supports the first diamond by helping teams discover and define customer problems together before developing solutions. The map becomes the shared artifact that keeps teams in problem-framing mode long enough to deeply understand what needs solving.

Use mapping to resist solution jumping. Frame the customer problem first, then solve it.

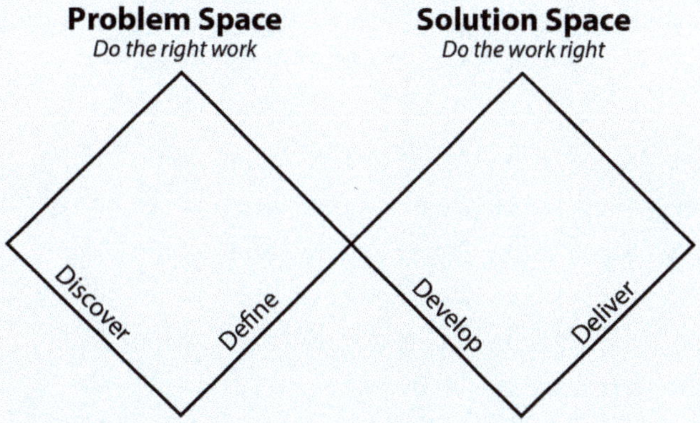

Figure 2-6. *The Double Diamond explains teamwork, from understanding the problem on the left to developing a solution on the right.*

The shift from company-centric to customer-centric thinking happens through changes in daily behavior. Simple acts, repeated, become your culture. As Ben Horowitz notes in his book of the same title, what you do is who you are.*

Jeanne Liedtka, professor at the University of Virginia Darden School of Business and a pioneering thinker in organizational design, connects the way design thinking works in organizational transformation to culture this way: "Design thinking is a social technology to affect change.... It's a holistic approach with a unique ability to create trust within teams and between teams, allowing them to have better conversations and innovate together."†

Liedtka has identified the key stages in collaborative design thinking and the effects each has on social dynamics (**Figure 2-7**). Her research maps stages in practicing design thinking (the "doing") to the experiences people have and then to the team transformations that take place (the "becoming").

This framework reveals why customer-centered collaboration creates lasting change. When teams repeatedly engage in collaborative mapping sessions, they transform into customer-driven teams. The doing shapes the becoming, as Liedtka's research shows.

If you're looking to build systematic approaches to customer-centered collaboration, frameworks such as the following offer proven methods and tools:

Stanford d.school Design Thinking

The d.school at Stanford University helped popularize design thinking with a focus on empathy, ideation, and prototyping. Its approach emphasizes understanding human needs through direct observation and iteration. The d.school's methods have become foundational for organizations seeking to embed customer understanding into innovation processes.

LUMA Institute

LUMA provides a comprehensive system of 36 methods organized around three key capabilities: Looking (observing and understanding), Understanding (analyzing and synthesizing), and Making (envisioning and prototyping). LUMA's strength lies in making simple techniques accessible across organizations.

Enterprise Design Thinking

IBM developed EDT specifically to scale human-centered practices across massive organizations. It focuses on three core principles: user outcomes, restless reinvention, and diverse, empowered teams.

Figure 2-7. Jeanne Liedtka's research shows that how teams work impacts what they become together.

* Ben Horowitz, *What You Do Is Who You Are* (2019)

† Quoted in Mural, "Maximizing the ROI of Design Thinking" (2020). See also Jeanne Liedtka et al., *Experiencing Design: The Innovator's Journey* (2021).

Design for Delight (D4D)

The guiding principles of Intuit's D4D framework are Deep Customer Empathy, Go Broad to Go Narrow (exploring many solutions before converging), and Rapid Experiments with Customers. D4D emphasizes getting customer feedback early and often through lightweight prototypes and experiments. The framework has helped Intuit maintain customer focus while scaling across multiple product lines.

Liberating Structures

While not exclusively focused on customer experience, Liberating Structures offers 33 microstructures that transform how teams interact and collaborate. Simple patterns like "1-2-4-All" and "What, So What, Now What?" can make customer-centered conversations more inclusive and productive. These structures work particularly well in mapping sessions and workshops where you need to engage diverse perspectives quickly.

Each framework has different strengths. LUMA and EDT excel at enterprise scale. D4D emphasizes rapid experimentation. The d.school provides foundational mindsets. Liberating Structures offers tactical meeting patterns. Choose based on your organization's size, culture, and maturity with customer-centered practices.

> *When teams repeatedly engage in collaborative mapping sessions, they transform into customer-driven teams.*

Capital One offers a powerful example of human-centered design operating at enterprise scale within a highly regulated industry.* Rather than organizing work around traditional functions like IT, marketing, or compliance, Capital One restructured around cross-functional product teams aligned to customer journeys and outcomes. Designers, product managers, engineers, data scientists, and risk partners were embedded together, making customer experiences a shared responsibility instead of a downstream deliverable. This structural shift hardwired collaboration around real customer needs into the organization's day-to-day decision making.

Crucially, Capital One showed that human-centered practices can coexist with—and even strengthen—governance and compliance. Customer research, journey mapping, usability testing, and data-informed insight became normal inputs to strategy and product decisions, helping teams translate complex financial and regulatory requirements into clearer, more human experiences. Design shifted from being a cosmetic layer to a strategic capability, giving the bank a durable model for customer-centered collaboration that other large, risk-averse organizations can learn from.

Cox Enterprises offers a concrete example of how human-centered design can be scaled inside a large, diversified organization using a structured system like LUMA. Through internal enablement led by the enterprise human-centered design (HCD) function, teams across the organization have been introduced to LUMA methods and tools, creating a shared language for observation, synthesis, and building. Rather than confining design thinking to a small innovation group, Cox has used LUMA as a common capability to support cross-functional work across communications, automotive, and ventures.

What makes Cox especially relevant for large companies is its complexity. As a non-design-first, multi-industry enterprise, Cox demonstrates that HCD does not require a wholesale reinvention of the organization—it requires

* Capital One, "Marking over 10 Years of Experience Design at Capital One," *Capital One Tech* (2025)

a practical, learnable system that supports collaboration around customer needs. Its adoption of LUMA reinforces the idea that scalable human-centered design is less about isolated expertise and more about equipping people across the business to observe, frame, and solve problems together.

At Cox, journey maps and visual diagrams have been used internally to understand complex experiences across its diverse businesses. In parallel with its adoption of the LUMA System, teams have applied mapping methods to synthesize insights from large-scale research and internal input, creating shared visual models that guide enterprise-wide improvement efforts and support cross-functional collaboration around customer needs.

No amount of preaching about being customer-centered will make your organization customer-centered. What matters isn't what you say. It's what you do—especially what you do together. Mapping experiences together is a primary way to achieve customer centricity that drives business results.

Summary

This chapter introduced customer-centered collaboration as the essential capability for translating customer insights into organizational action. The problem isn't lack of data; rather, it's the gap between having insights and using them to drive coordinated action.

Maps create value not through perfect accuracy but by providing shared reference points that align teams. Visual models minimize alignment attrition by freezing understanding in time. Experience maps function as narrative structures: the map provides structure, and the stories bring it to life in a sustained way.

But maps generate value only when activated through skilled facilitation. The mapmaker must become a facilitator, guiding collaborative sensemaking rather than presenting finished artifacts.

Cocreation extends collaboration beyond internal teams to include customers as partners in mapping and design processes. This bridges inside-across and outside-in alignment by bringing customer expertise directly into the collaborative process.

Team performance has three dimensions: effectiveness (right work), efficiency (work done right), and engagement (work done well). Customer insights uniquely drive engagement by providing common ground across departmental boundaries.

Customer centricity comes through behavior change, not declarations. IBM's transformation demonstrated how changing daily practices creates cultural change at scale. Simple acts, repeated consistently, become behaviors. Behaviors become culture. Organizations move from customer-aware to customer-driven through accumulated microbehaviors embedded in collaborative rituals.

The path forward: collaboration is a lever for cultural change. When you use customer insights to guide collaboration, you create not just better decisions but stronger, more customer-centered teams. What you do together is who you are.

Mapping experiences together is more than a design activity: it's a strategic practice as well. Modern strategy creation is open and inclusive, and mapping provides the forum for those dialogues to happen.

Further Reading

Priya Parker, The Art of Gathering *(2018)*

Parker challenges conventional gathering approaches by emphasizing distinctiveness and human connection over routine and tradition. Drawing on her facilitation work across diverse contexts—from corporate meetings to peace-building camps—she provides a practical framework for creating meaningful, purposeful gatherings of any size or type. This is a classic book in the field of facilitation that's highly recommended.

Sam Kaner, Facilitator's Guide to Participatory Decision-Making, *3rd ed. (2021)*

Kaner provides one of the most comprehensive guides to facilitation, with detailed frameworks for leading groups through collaborative decision-making processes. The book covers participatory methods, group dynamics, and techniques for moving teams from divergent thinking to convergent agreements.

Kursat Ozenc and Glenn Fajardo, Rituals for Virtual Meetings *(2021)*

Ozenc and Fajardo provide practical techniques for making virtual meetings more engaging and human through structured rituals that build connection and trust. The book offers concrete methods to reduce Zoom fatigue, improve group cohesion, and create meaningful interactions when teams aren't in the same physical space.

Mariano Battan and Jim Kalbach, Collaborative Intelligence *(2022)*

I wrote this book together with Mariano Battan, the cofounder and CEO of Mural. In it, we introduce collaboration design: the intentional crafting of collaborative experiences to achieve repeatable, extraordinary outcomes. The book provides practical methods for building collaboration playbooks, creating inclusive environments, and leading organizational change, whether teams work in hybrid, remote, or in-person settings.

Phil Gilbert, Irresistible Change *(2025)*

Gilbert shares the story of IBM's massive transformation across 400,000 employees in 180 countries and provides a practical playbook for earning buy-in and making change irresistible rather than enforced. The key lever in his equation: human-centered design methods scaled across the company, packaged and taught as Enterprise Design Thinking.

David Hutchens, Story Dash *(2021)*

This book provides a rapid process for finding and developing business stories that create action and engagement. Hutchens shares a tested method for identifying "narrative assets" and deploying them strategically, often in less than a day. The approach helps leaders access their natural storytelling capacity, determine which stories to tell, and build narratives that land with impact. The book emphasizes authentic leadership voice and practical application in fast-paced business environments.

Diagram and Image Credits

Figure 2-2: Customer journey map by Jim Kalbach

Figure 2-3: Diagram from Jeff Patton's book *User Story Mapping*, fair use

Figure 2-4: Image of workshop participants playing the journey mapping game by Christophe Tallec, used with permission

Figure 2-5: Diagram and photo by design research and visualization expert Nick Bowmast (*bowmast.com*), used with permission

Figure 2-7: Image showing the progression of doing to becoming, adapted from Jeanne Liedtka's research

The purpose of visualization is insight, not pictures.

—Ben Shneiderman, *Readings in Information Visualization*

IN THIS CHAPTER

- Framing the mapping effort
- Touchpoints
- Moments of truth
- Value creation

CHAPTER 3

Foundations of Mapping Experiences

The cause of the great cholera outbreak in London in 1854 was initially unclear. Prior to Louis Pasteur's germ theory, many thought the disease was in the air. John Snow, a London physician, had a different explanation. He believed cholera was in the water. After microscopic examinations were inconclusive, Snow instead analyzed the spread of cholera to prove his hunch.

To do this, he mapped cholera cases in Soho, London (FIGURE 3-1). The resulting patterns demonstrated causality: proximity to a certain water pump correlated to cholera cases with high predictability. The decline of cholera is credited to Snow's recommendation to shut down that pump.

Snow's map contained multiple layers of information—streets, houses with cholera cases, and water pumps—just enough to reveal previously undetected evidence (in this case, the cause of a disease). The approach was simple but effective, and Snow was able to generate a hypothesis based on his map: *if* the city shut down a specific pump, *then* cases of cholera would decline.

Visualizations offer an immediacy of comprehension and help us arrive at such hypotheses. Maps show interrelationships in an ecosystem.

FIGURE 3-1. John Snow's map of London during the great cholera outbreak of 1854. The red circle highlights the water pump that was the source of the disease.

It may not be immediately apparent, but Snow's example shows alignment: water (a service provided by the waterworks department), water pumps (the touchpoints to that system), and households with cholera in Soho (individuals). Snow showed that the means of treating and storing water miles away affected people in central London. This conclusion is generally credited with the start of public health practices around the world.

Today, AI might detect the statistical correlation between pump proximity and cholera cases. But Snow's map did something more. It made the causal relationship visible and undeniable, enabling immediate action. This is the power of visualization—not just finding patterns, but making them comprehensible and actionable for human decision making.

And this is why I love maps of all kinds; they provide an overview and, with some creative imagination, show new relationships leading to new insights. Armed with only a map and a few data points, John Snow was able to see what the best microscopes of the time couldn't. That's powerful.

Similarly, this is what experience mapping offers: new insight. It starts with an investigation and illustration of the human condition and then works out ways to support people's needs.

Diagrams provide a systematic overview of the experiences people have. By fostering conversations across the organization, the process of mapping helps avoid disjointed interactions and promotes coherency.

Regardless of the specific diagram type you create, you should consider the following overarching aspects of mapping experiences, covered in this chapter:

- ***Framing the effort clearly.*** Determine the point of view, scope, and focus, as well as the structure of the diagram and how you intend to use it.
- ***Identifying the various touchpoints in the system.*** This includes finding critically charged points called *moments of truth*.
- ***Focusing on creating value.*** Use the diagram to improve and innovate your offering and your business.

By the end of this chapter, you should have a greater understanding of the key decisions in mapping experiences.

Framing the Mapping Effort

The term *experience* defies precise definition. Still, we can point to some common aspects to better understand it:

Experiences are holistic.

The notion of an experience is all-encompassing, including actions, thoughts, and feelings over time.

Experiences are personal.

An experience is not an objective property of a product or service; it's the subjective perception of the individual.

Experiences are situational.

I like riding on roller coasters, but not immediately after eating a large meal. In one case, the experience is exhilarating; in the other, it's a dreadful few minutes of nausea. The roller coaster doesn't change; the situation does. Experiences differ from situation to situation.

How, then, do we approach mapping something as fluid as human experiences? Put simply, it's a matter of selection. Maps are purposefully focused. As the mapmaker, it's up to you to decide which aspects to include and which to leave out.

Cartographic maps, for instance, are selective in what they show. Consider Harry Beck's famous 1933 map of the London Underground (**Figure 3-2**). It's sparing in what it includes: tube lines, stops, exchanges, and the River Thames—nothing more. It distorts train lines into horizontal, vertical, and 45-degree angles. Stops are spaced equidistantly though distances vary greatly in reality.

That's OK. Maps are abstractions. Beck's map has remained virtually intact for over 90 years because its brilliance lies in what it *doesn't* show. Its longevity stems from its appropriateness—it fulfills a specific need extremely well.

Likewise, mapping experiences requires choice. Distortions will necessarily occur, but if your definition of the effort is on target, the overall message will be valid. And of course, the framing of your project must be relevant to the organization and address its goals.

A map that tries to be all things for all people ends up doing nothing well. Your framing decisions act as a razor: what experience are we mapping, of what actor, for whom, and for what purpose? Use these questions to figure out what to include and what to cut.

A key way to understand *experience* is to create a *model* that visually represents the experience. Models are already a common part of innovation and design. For

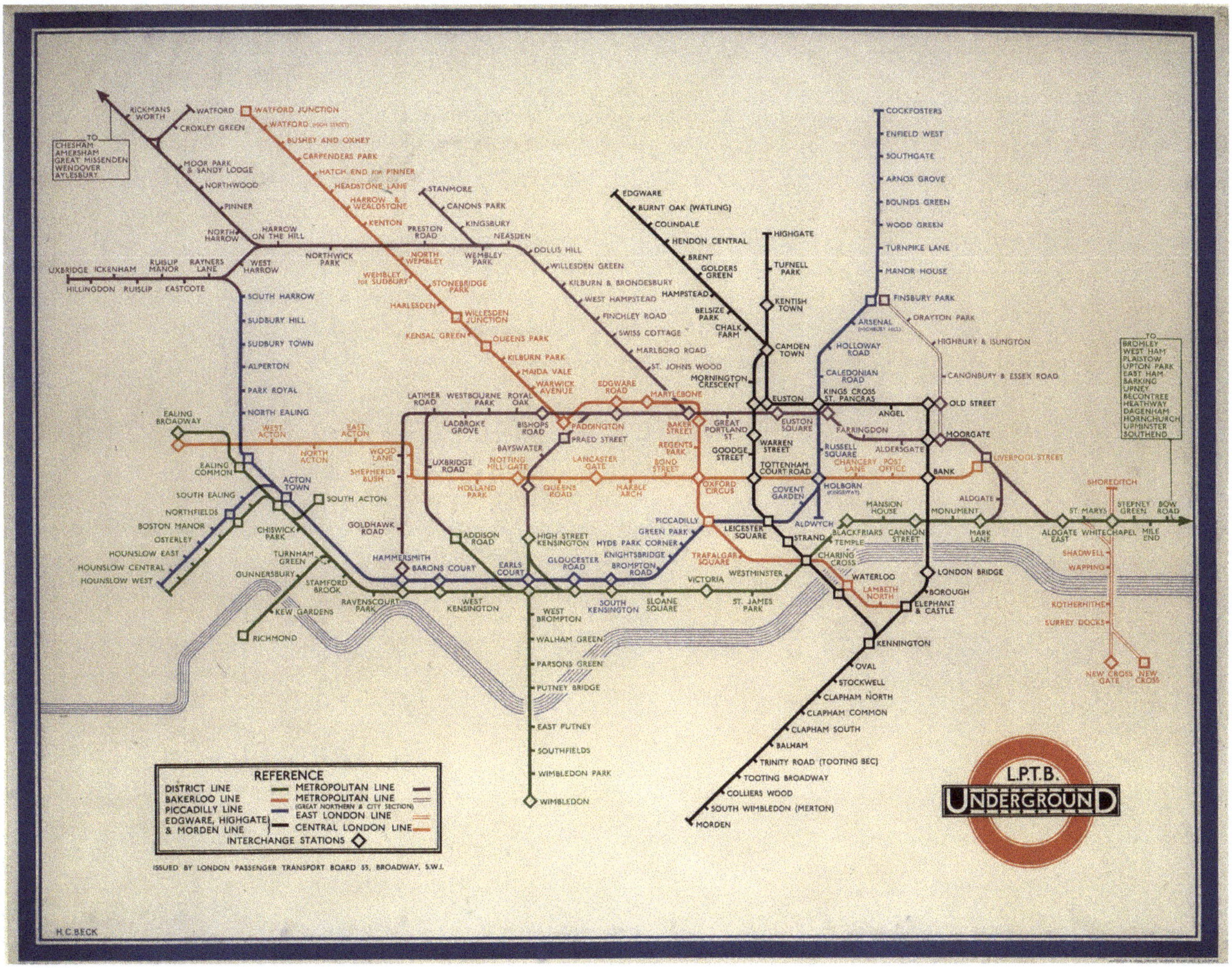

Figure 3-2. Harry Beck created his iconic map of the London Underground in 1933.

example, a persona represents people in a given market, and a business model represents how an organization can be profitable.

By illustrating all the moving parts at once, models can help organizations better understand their playing field and their markets. The model of an experience can align the perspectives of the people who have to enable that experience. This is the role of mapping experiences: a form of visual storytelling that allows teams to find solutions together.

Diagramming coordinates insights from the outside world with the teams inside an organization that create products and services to meet market needs. In other words, a model can serve as a hinge upon which we can pivot from the *problem space* into the *solution space*.

Before starting the mapping effort, there are five fundamental aspects to define, the first three of which are reflected in **Figure 3-3**:

- ***Point of view:*** Whose experience are you mapping, and which experience is included?
- ***Scope:*** When does the experience begin and end?
- ***Focus:*** What types of information will be included?
- ***Structure:*** How will the experience appear and be visualized?
- ***Use:*** What do you intend to do with it?

As the mapmaker, it's your responsibility to get agreement on each of these aspects from the key stakeholders who will ultimately be the audience of the diagram. They're discussed in detail in the following sections.

Point of View

Whose perspective are you taking in the diagram? In some cases, this may be obvious. But in other contexts—for instance, more complex B2B situations—there may be half a dozen or more actors involved in a given experience, with a variety of interdependent interactions. You'll need to first sort out which experiences to map.

Point of view is defined by two criteria: the people involved and the types of experiences they engage in.

Consider a news magazine. It might serve two distinct audiences: readers and advertisers. The interactions each has with the publisher are very different. Once you've decided on the people—let's assume readers—there are still different experiences to choose from:

Purchasing behavior

One point of view is to look at how readers purchase the publication: how they first heard of the magazine, why they bought it, whether they made a repeat purchase, and so on. Mapping an

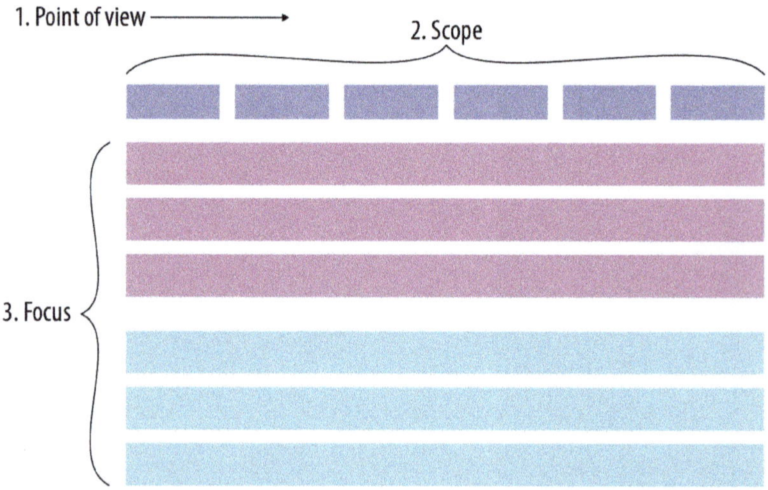

Figure 3-3. Define every mapping effort by addressing key criteria up front.

experience from this point of view makes sense if there is a need to optimize sales. A customer journey map would be a good fit.

News consumption

Another point of view might be to look at how readers consume news in general. This would situate the magazine within a broader spectrum of human information behavior. This point of view could be beneficial if the magazine is looking to expand its offering. A mental model diagram could be useful in this case.

Day in the life

You could also look at a day in the life of typical readers: How does a news magazine fit into their daily actions? Where do they come in contact with the magazine? When? What else do they do to find and read news? An experience map may be appropriate for mapping this experience.

Each of these points of view has a different unit of analysis—purchasing, consuming news, or a daily routine. And each can be beneficial, depending on the needs of the organization. Understanding the point of view of the diagram is critical in determining your approach and resulting message.

Strive to align the point of view of the map with the goals of the organization.

Typically, any given diagram reflects a single point of view. A clear perspective generally strengthens the message of a diagram. It's common to include a reference to a persona in the top corner of an experience map to clarify the point of view for the diagram's audience.

Even if you have multiple actors or experiences to consider, you'll have to define whose experiences and which specific moments to include. Often, a primary point of view is defined, and secondary perspectives are aligned to that.

There's no right or wrong answer to the question of how to determine a point of view for your mapping effort. What you decide to illustrate depends on your stakeholders' needs. Strive to align the mapping's point of view with the goals of the organization.

Scope

When does the experience begin, and when does it end? Think about scope as the left and right sides of a chronological diagram. Sometimes the scope of a mapping effort may seem self-evident, but additional concerns can extend the start and stop points you'll define.

Consider the previous example of riding a roller coaster. Does the experience begin when you get strapped into the car, or while you're waiting in line? Or does it begin before you even get to the amusement park, while you're still at home, or even before that? And when does it end—when you get out of the roller coaster car, or when you look at the photos of yourself during the ride? Or does it end when you look at those photos a month later?

It's up to you, the mapmaker, to define the scope of the experience to be illustrated. There are no universal answers; the correct scope depends on the needs of the project. I'll often find an obvious point in time to start and then go back one step to include the precursors before the beginning of an experience.

For instance, on one project, we were seeking to foster a more customer-centric mindset in employees of an organization. We initially scoped the employee experience to start around the first day of employment. However, by going back in time to the phases prior to that, including recruiting and hiring, we found even more opportunities to increase customer centricity (e.g., instilling the desired mindset during the hiring process or including our intent in the job posting).

In other cases, a broader scope isn't appropriate. Sometimes stakeholders want to zero in on a specific portion of an experience. **Figure 3-4** is a customer journey map created by Jim Tincher at Heart of the Customer (*heartofthecustomer.com*), a leading journey mapping consultancy, that focuses only on purchasing health insurance. What about submitting claims, getting reimbursed, or filing disputes? Those happen later but were intentionally scoped out to keep the map relevant for the project.

Scope is deeper than just the beginning and end of an experience, however. It also requires a trade-off in granularity. A map of an end-to-end experience reveals the big picture but leaves out detail. On the other hand, a detailed diagram may illustrate specific interactions but cover less ground.

The equally spaced Tube stops on Beck's map of the London Underground (**Figure 3-2**), for instance, allow the entire system to fit on one compact page. Actual spacing would have put the end stations far off the page. Given his scope—to show the entire system—this lack of fidelity was necessary.

Or imagine you've been contracted by the tourist bureau of a US city to improve the visitor experience, with the specific goal of increasing mobile services.

One approach could be to scope the entire visit, from planning at home to visiting the city and all the way to follow-up actions afterward. This would give you a broad picture across the entire service ecology, encompassing a range of touchpoints and stakeholders.

In another approach, you could limit the effort to experiences in the city involving mobile services. This journey might begin at the point of arrival and end at departure, but would provide greater depth on mobile touchpoints for a particular user type.

Both approaches may be valid, depending on the needs of the organization and its interests and gaps in knowledge. Are you focused on a discrete problem, or do you need a view of the entire system? The point is to be explicit about the trade-offs you're making up front and set the right expectations. Establishing the right scope will guide subsequent comprehension of the experience, as well as what strategic opportunities might emerge.

When in doubt, ask a few customers how they see the beginning and end of their experience. Their perspective often reveals scope considerations you might have missed. This doesn't require extensive, formal research; just a few short conversations with customers can clarify when the experience starts and stops.

Focus

What types of information will you include in the diagram? Think of the focus as the rows of information in a given map. That defines the content you'll include.

Again, it's up to you, the mapmaker, to choose which aspects to focus on. Strive to make it relevant to your organization's and stakeholders' needs.

There are many types of elements to consider. The ones you choose depend on how you've framed the effort (see Chapter 5) and what aspects are most salient to the organization.

I typically start with the actions, thoughts, and feelings of the individual as a default way to describe an experience. Your project may require emphasis on other foci.

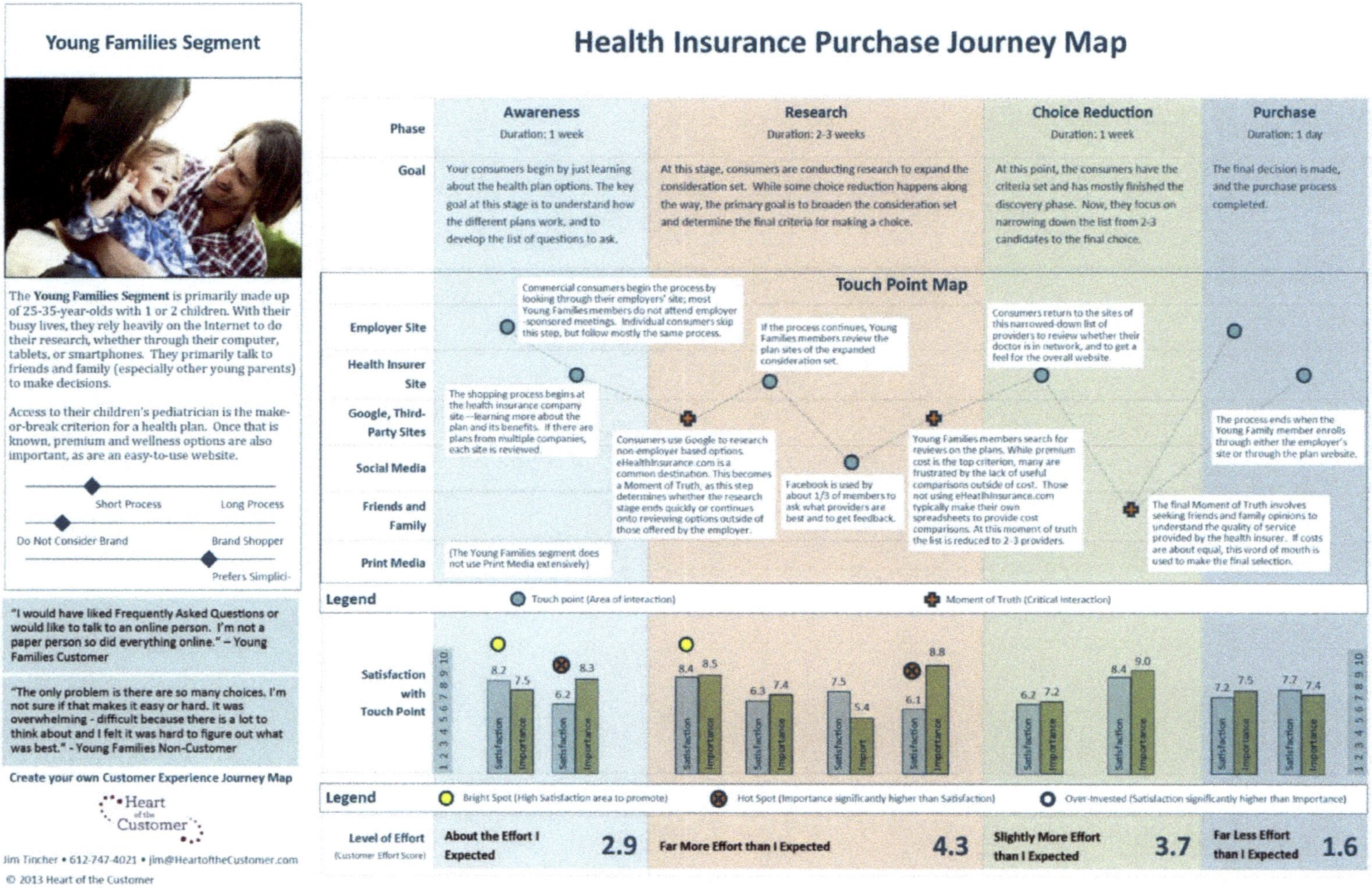

FIGURE 3-4. This journey map is scoped to just the awareness to purchase phases.

To make your map relevant to your team, you might include some of the following typical aspects:

- *Physical:* Artifacts, tools, devices
- *Behavioral:* Actions, activities, tasks
- *Cognitive:* Thoughts, views, opinions
- *Emotional:* Feelings, desires, states of mind
- *Needs:* Goals, outcomes, jobs to be done
- *Challenges:* Pain points, constraints, barriers
- *Context:* Setting, environment, location
- *Culture:* Beliefs, values, philosophy
- *Events:* Triggers, moments of truth, points of failure

Elements that describe the organization can include:

- *Touchpoints:* Mediums, devices, information
- *Offering:* Products, services, features
- *Processes:* Internal activities, workflows
- *Challenges:* Problems, issues, breakdowns
- *Operations:* Roles, departments, reporting structures
- *Metrics:* Traffic, financials, statistics
- *Evaluation:* Strengths, weaknesses, learnings
- *Effort:* Difficulties, inefficiencies, ease of interacting
- *Opportunities:* Gaps, weaknesses, redundancies
- *Goals:* Revenue, savings, reputation
- *Strategy:* Policy, design making, principles

Considering these elements is a question of balance. I recommend listing a set of target aspects that are most relevant to your mapping effort, then arranging them in a sketch of a map to see how they might fit together to meet your goals.

Keep in mind that different diagram types naturally have different foci (see **Figure 3-5**). For instance, a customer journey map may focus primarily on an experience with only a minimal description of the organization. A service blueprint, on the other hand, may highlight the service provision process across channels at the expense of a detailed description of the user experience.

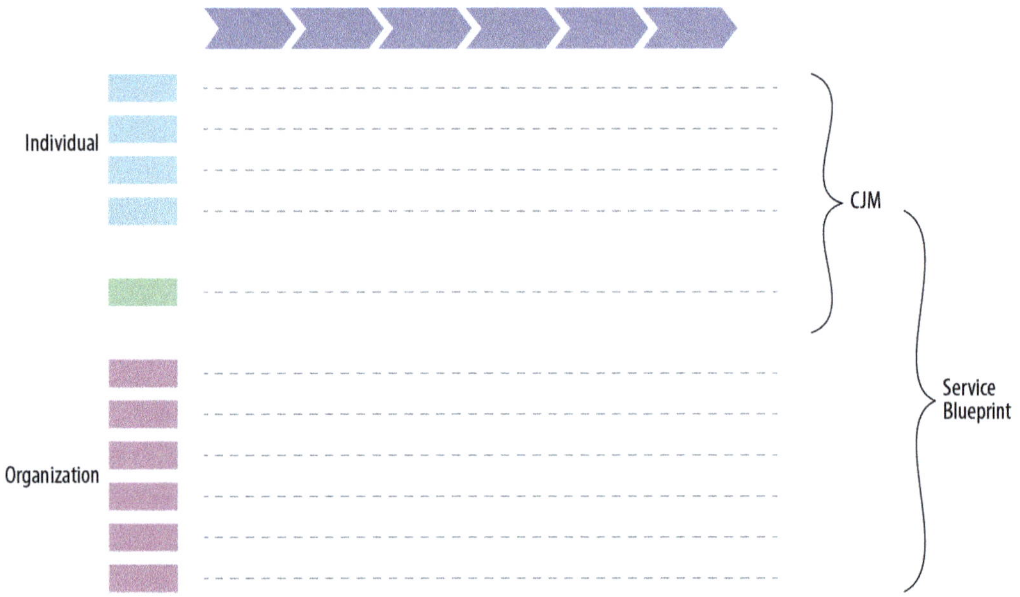

Figure 3-5. Focus differs across diagram types.

Structure

What form will the diagram take? Alignment diagrams also differ in structure. The most common scheme is chronological (FIGURE 3-6A), and many of the examples in this book have a chronological organization. However, other arrangements are possible, including hierarchical, spatial, and network structures (FIGURES 3-6B to 3-6D).

FIGURE 3-7 (on the following page) is a map of disability employment services in Australia. It's an excellent example of using a network-like structure to illustrate an experience. The focus is on touchpoints that lead to positive or negative experiences.

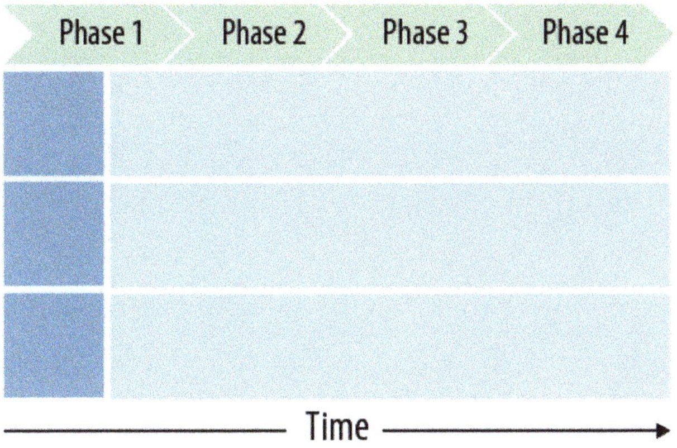

FIGURE 3-6A. CHRONOLOGICAL: Because experiences happen in real time, a chronological arrangement provides a natural sequence of human behavior. A timeline of some sort is the most prevalent way to structure alignment diagrams.

FIGURE 3-6B. HIERARCHICAL: Mapping experiences hierarchically removes the time dimension. This can have advantages when many aspects are occurring simultaneously, which is difficult to show chronologically.

FIGURE 3-6C. SPATIAL: Illustrating experiences spatially makes sense when interactions take place in a physical location—for example, in a face-to-face service encounter. Spatial diagrams can also be imposed on an experience in a metaphorical sense: spatial maps represent experiences as if they could exist in a 3D space even when they do not.

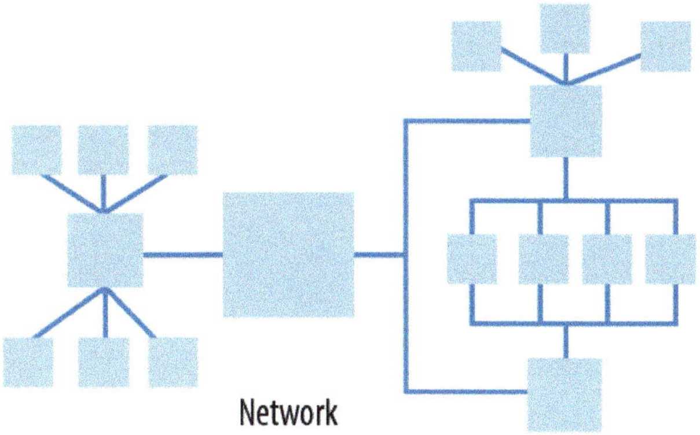

FIGURE 3-6D. NETWORK STRUCTURE: A network structure shows a web of interrelationships among aspects of an experience that are neither chronological nor hierarchical.

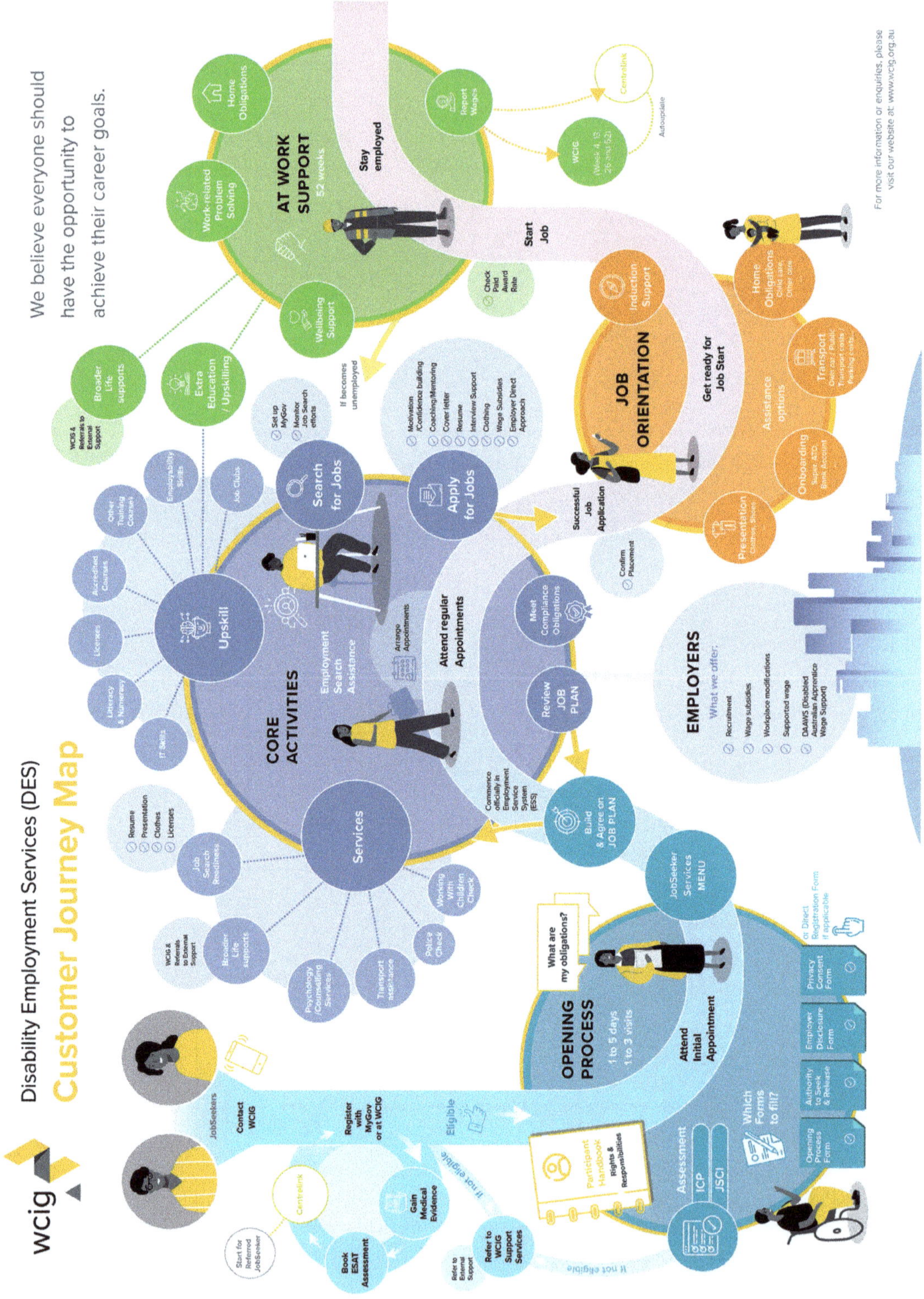

FIGURE 3-7. A network-like arrangement of actors and concepts shows positive and negative experiences for disability services from WCIG in Australia (now Opendoor).

Use

How will you activate the diagram and put it to use? This is one of the key aspects of mapping that's often an afterthought. Make it intentional and explicit from the beginning. If there's no target use for your diagram, stop and ask whether you really need it.

First, consider *who* will be consuming the information in your diagram. The London Underground map (shown previously in **Figure 3-2**) is read every day by travelers on the Tube. They use it to determine how to travel between any two points on the network. But the engineers who maintain the switching signals in the London Underground would likely find Beck's map lacking in detail—they need specifications with a much higher degree of fidelity to accomplish their work. Beck's map is not intended for that audience.

Also consider *what* you'll use your diagrams for. Frame the effort in a way that is appropriate for your team's needs. What questions does the organization have that a diagram can address? What gaps in knowledge does it fill? What problems will it help solve?

Finally, ask yourself *how* the diagram will be used. Will it be used to diagnose problems or improve the design of an existing system? Will it be used to create a strategy and plan for development? Or does your audience intend to use your alignment diagram to discover new opportunities for innovation and growth?

What Makes Good Experience Mapping?

Use these questions to assess the quality of your mapping effort:

- ***Does it reveal the exchange of value?*** Good mapping shows how value flows between individuals and the organization. You should be able to walk through the experience in slow motion, analyzing circumstances around each interaction.
- ***Is it relevant to stakeholders?*** Good mapping addresses real-world issues and organizational goals. Before creating a map, understand the challenges and future plans of the organization. The map should be constructed in such a way that stakeholders can use it to help answer their strategic questions.
- ***Is it grounded in research?*** Good mapping is based on valid investigation, not assumptions. It requires contact with real people through research and observation, not speculation in conference rooms.
- ***Does it coordinate multiple facets of information?*** Good mapping illustrates multiple dimensions simultaneously—actions, thoughts, feelings, pain points, and more. This alignment is what makes mapping useful.
- ***Does it show the bigger picture?*** Good mapping focuses on human behavior within a larger ecosystem, beyond product features or isolated workflows. It shows what people do, think, and feel in context.
- ***Is it visual and self-evident?*** Good mapping provides a composite view in a single graphical overview. The same information in a 10-page report wouldn't have the same impact. Visualizations make abstract concepts like "user experience" tangible.
- ***Does it inspire others to make sense and take action?*** Good mapping sparks conversation and drives decisions. The map should invite others in and create momentum toward action. If no one engages with it, it's not a good map.

Keep in mind that maps are not one-time artifacts. Once created, they can serve your organization over and over for sustained alignment. A well-crafted map becomes a shared reference that helps teams stay in sync as personnel changes and initiatives evolve. This longevity makes mapping an investment, not just a project expense.

As discussed in Chapter 2, a map serves as a springboard into conversations about what might be possible in the future. Put forethought into those conversations right from the start. This will not only help keep the momentum going, but also influence how you go about mapping throughout the process.

The type of mapping advocated in this book is best suited for *generative* activities. That is, teams can use maps of the current state of an experience to creatively find opportunities together. This is where customer-focused collaboration comes in. For concrete practices you can apply right away, see the "Collaborative Methods" sections at the ends of Chapters 5–14.

Mapping can also serve a *summative* function. Journey management is a rapidly growing field that coordinates live data (e.g., satisfaction scores, usage metrics) to touchpoints in customer experience for ongoing monitoring. Teams can see data about the experience people are actually having in real time at each stage in the journey. You'll find more on journey management and orchestration in Chapter 10.

Multiple Alignment

Mapping tends to focus on a single actor and a single experience. However, modern business complexity motivates us to be more inclusive in the scope of mapping efforts. *Multiple alignment* (i.e., alignment across multiple actors and/or multiple touchpoints) is possible, but techniques are still developing.

One way that I've found to map the experience of multiple actors is to create a series of related but separate diagrams for each target segment. For instance, eBay targets two distinct user groups: buyers and sellers. It's possible to illustrate separate interactions as two interlocking experiences, as reflected in **Figure 3-8**. A visual comparison between the two experiences can be made by looking at the top and bottom halves of a single column spanning the diagrams (e.g., "Take order" and "Place order" in **Figure 3-8**).

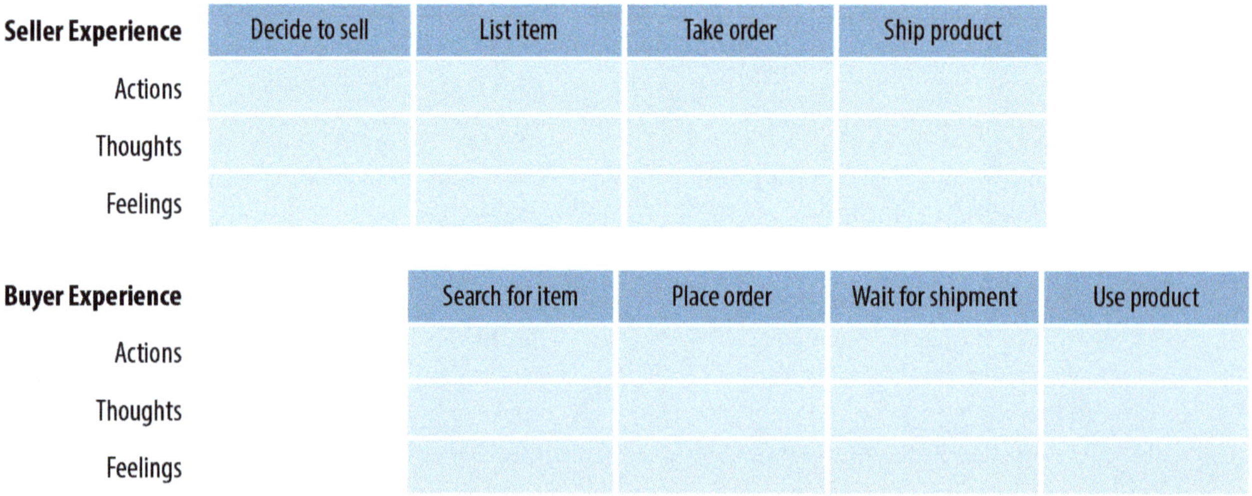

Figure 3-8. To align the experience of multiple actors, create separate but related diagrams that can be displayed together.

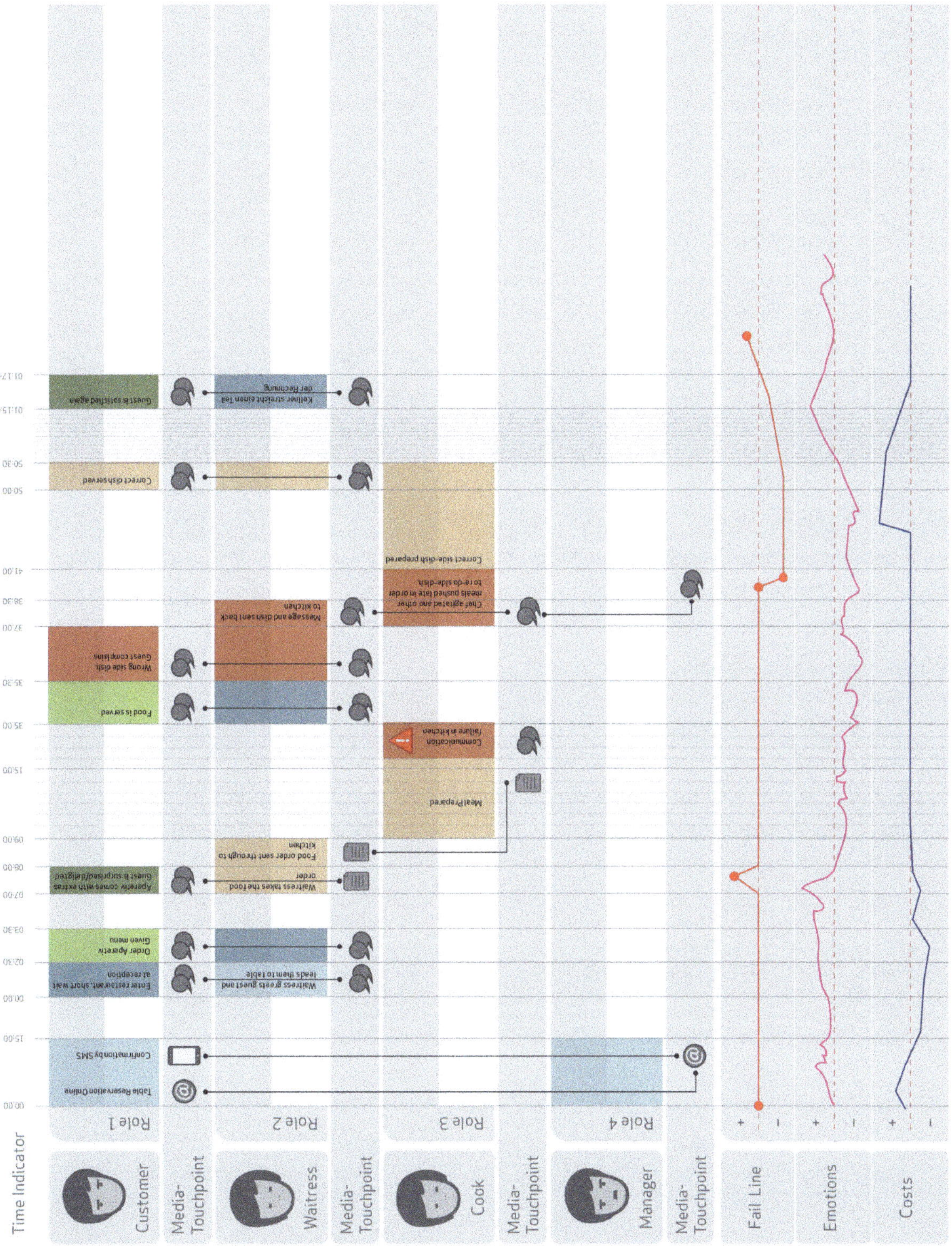

FIGURE 3-9. This expanded service blueprint by Andy Polaine includes multiple actors, each in a separate row.

It's also possible to show the interaction between three or more actors in a single diagram, placing a focus on the overall process rather than a given individual's experience. Andy Polaine, a leading service design expert, has expanded on service blueprints by mapping multiple actors simultaneously. His approach is straightforward: add a row in the diagram for each new role involved in a service ecosystem, as shown in **Figure 3-9**.*

Another issue with multiple alignment is how to show the interaction across multiple touchpoints. With many services now cloud-based and accessible on a range of devices, we must consider everything from screen types and sizes to the environmental and contextual factors surrounding use.

There are many factors to balance, and being able to comprehend them all at once is imperative. Wolfram Nagel, author of the book *Multiscreen UX Design*, suggests that designers focus on four elements: devices, users, context and content.

To view all of these elements simultaneously, Nagel recommends visualizing the interaction in a *touchpoint matrix*, as shown in **Figure 3-10**. This example shows a day in the life of a persona, with all the devices and interactions used. It's a simple but effective approach to see the movement from screen to screen and the user requirements at each transition.

Regardless of the approach, the same core principles of alignment still apply. The aim is to visually coordinate internal and external factors of the context you're operating in. The result will help align the perspectives of the teams that have to enable the intended experience.

* Andy Polaine, "Blueprint+: Developing a Tool for Service Design," SDN Conference (2009)

Identifying Touchpoints

Framing the effort, as outlined earlier in this chapter, provides a basis for illustrating the overall experience. Within that experience, you also need to consider the relationship between individuals and an organization. The concept of *touchpoints*, the means of value exchange, allows you to show the interaction between the two.

Typically, touchpoints include a range of things, such as these:

- TV ads, print ads, brochures
- Marketing emails, newsletters
- Websites, blogs, online newsletters
- Apps, software programs
- Phone calls, service hotlines, online chat
- Service counters, checkout registers
- Physical objects, buildings, roads
- Packaging, shipping materials
- Bills, invoices, payment systems

Historically, there are three primary types of touchpoints:

Static
: These touchpoints don't allow for users to interact with them. They include things such as printed materials, signage, or advertisements.

Interactive
: Websites and apps are interactive touchpoints, often with a call to action and a workflow to follow.

Human
: This type involves human-to-human interaction. Examples include a sales representative or a support agent on the phone, as well as hosted communities and forums.

Touchpoint Matrix

(daily routine | activities | environment | needs | media/service touchpoints)

Robert Sullivan

Digital pros

WHEN?	Waking up 5:30	Early in the morning 6:00	Mid-morning 7:30	Mid-day 12:30	Afternoon 15:00	Early evening 19:30	Late evening 20:30	Going to sleep 23:30
ACTIVITY WHAT?	Getting up, showering	Having breakfast, reading newspaper, sometimes on the laptop	Working, meetings, organisation	Eating, having a break, privately surfing the Internet	Working, organisation, customer meetings	Working	Sport, meeting friends, watching a film, work-related events	Going to bed, reading
LOCATION WHERE?	Bedroom (bed), bath	Dining rooom (dining table)	Office (own and employee's desk, conference room)	Office (kitchen), bar (dining table), nature (park bench)	Office (desk, employee's workplace), at the customer	Office (desk)	Restaurant (dining table), event (podium, foyer), living room (sofa)	Bedroom (bed)
ENVIRONMENT WHERE?								
NEEDS WHY? (POSITIVE / NEGATIVE)	Discipline, diligence, conscientiousness, efficiency, ambition	Order, diligence, efficiency, excellence, curiosity	Reliability, loyality, assurance, diligence, responsibility, conscientiousness, excellence, power, influency, quality, status, trailblazer	Bon vivant, recreation, well-being, phantasy, dreaminess, friendship, curiosity	Reliability, order, diligence, conscientiousness, power, influency, excellence, quality, trailblazer	Conscientiousness, diligence, excellence, quality, order, willpower, acceptance, recognition, popularity, honour, ambition	Recreation, safety, variety, enjoyment, bon vivant, well-being, stimulation, relaxation, coziness, friendship, relatedness	Curiosity, trailblazer, phantasy, enjoyment, carefreeness, relaxation, stimulation
CHANNEL WITH WHAT?								
DEVICE TOUCHPOINT WITH WHAT?								

FIGURE 3-10. A touchpoint matrix can be used to study the flow of interactions and information across devices.

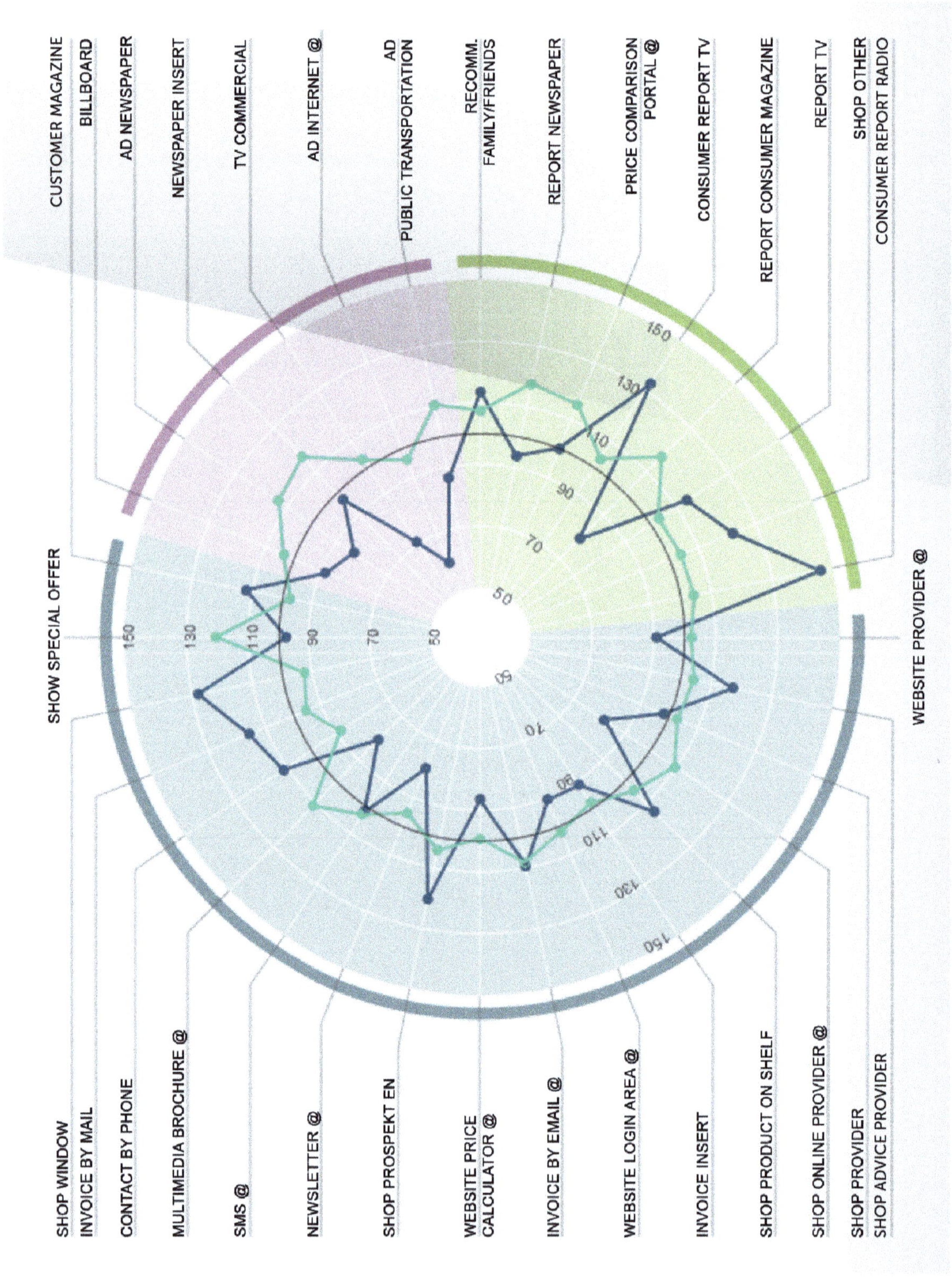

FIGURE 3-11. This 360° matrix created by the Swiss firm Accelerom illustrates a range of touchpoints.

Organizations that take an ecological view of the experiences they provide have a competitive advantage. For businesses, this impacts the bottom line. Consider the inventory of touchpoints in **Figure 3-11**. This diagram was created by the Swiss-based marketing firm Accelerom AG (*accelerom.com*), an international consultancy and research group based in Zurich, as part of its 360° touchpoint management process.* It shows the comprehensive list of touchpoints a company has with its customers.

Some people call for a broader perspective on understanding touchpoints. Design leader and author Chris Risdon, for one, defines a touchpoint as the *context* around an interaction. In his article "Un-Sucking the Touchpoint," he writes:

> **A touchpoint is a point of interaction involving a specific human need in a specific time and place.†**

Jeannie Walters, a leading customer experience consultant, also advocates a broader definition. She is critical of touchpoint inventories, writing:

> **The challenge with viewing touchpoints this way is this approach often assumes the customer has a) been in a linear and direct relationship with the organization and b) reads and engages with these touchpoints in meaningful ways. In short, an examination of touchpoints is often entirely company-focused. (Sometimes, it is so company-focused the touchpoints are categorized by org chart: marketing, operations, billing, etc.).‡**

* See Christoph Spengler et al., "360° Touchpoint Management—How Important Is Twitter for Our Brand?," *Marketing Review St. Gallen* (2010).

† Chris Risdon, "Un-Sucking the Touchpoint," *Center Centre* (2014)

‡ Jeannie Walters, "What IS a Customer Touchpoint?," *Customer Think* (2013)

The notion of touchpoint visualization can even be useful beyond commercial settings that seek to optimize brand perception and profits.

Matt Sinclair, Leila Sheldrick, Mariale Moreno, and Emma Dewberry have developed a unique tool for looking at touchpoints across a broad ecosystem.§ Working in the field of *circular design*, or the creation of products beyond single lifecycles for single users, they wanted to visualize the points within an ecosystem where stakeholders can influence the product's journey to extend its life.

A touchpoint on their Consumer Intervention Map refers to an event in which a stakeholder actively and intentionally intervenes in a product's intended customer journey model. Passive touchpoints that do not involve consumer intervention are excluded (e.g., seeing an ad). Touchpoints are indicated in their appropriate phases with a system of color coding: manufacturing (orange), communication (pink), supply (blue), and usage (green). The darkness of the color shows the degree to which a brand allows consumers to intervene at this touchpoint.

Starting in the definition phase of new product development, a line connects touchpoints to describe a product's lifecycle from pre-purchase to post-purchase. **Figure 3-12** shows an example product lifecycle for an imaginary, mass-customized product, in which disposal involves extracting materials during remanufacturing and feeding them back into new product development. The approach has been validated with industry and academic experts in circular design.

Alignment diagrams, in general, reinforce an ecological view of the interaction with customers. They not only illustrate individual touchpoints but also provide an end-to-end picture of the experience. As this example shows,

§ Matt Sinclair et al., "Consumer Intervention Mapping—A Tool for Designing Future Product Strategies Within Circular Product Service Systems," *Sustainability* (2018)

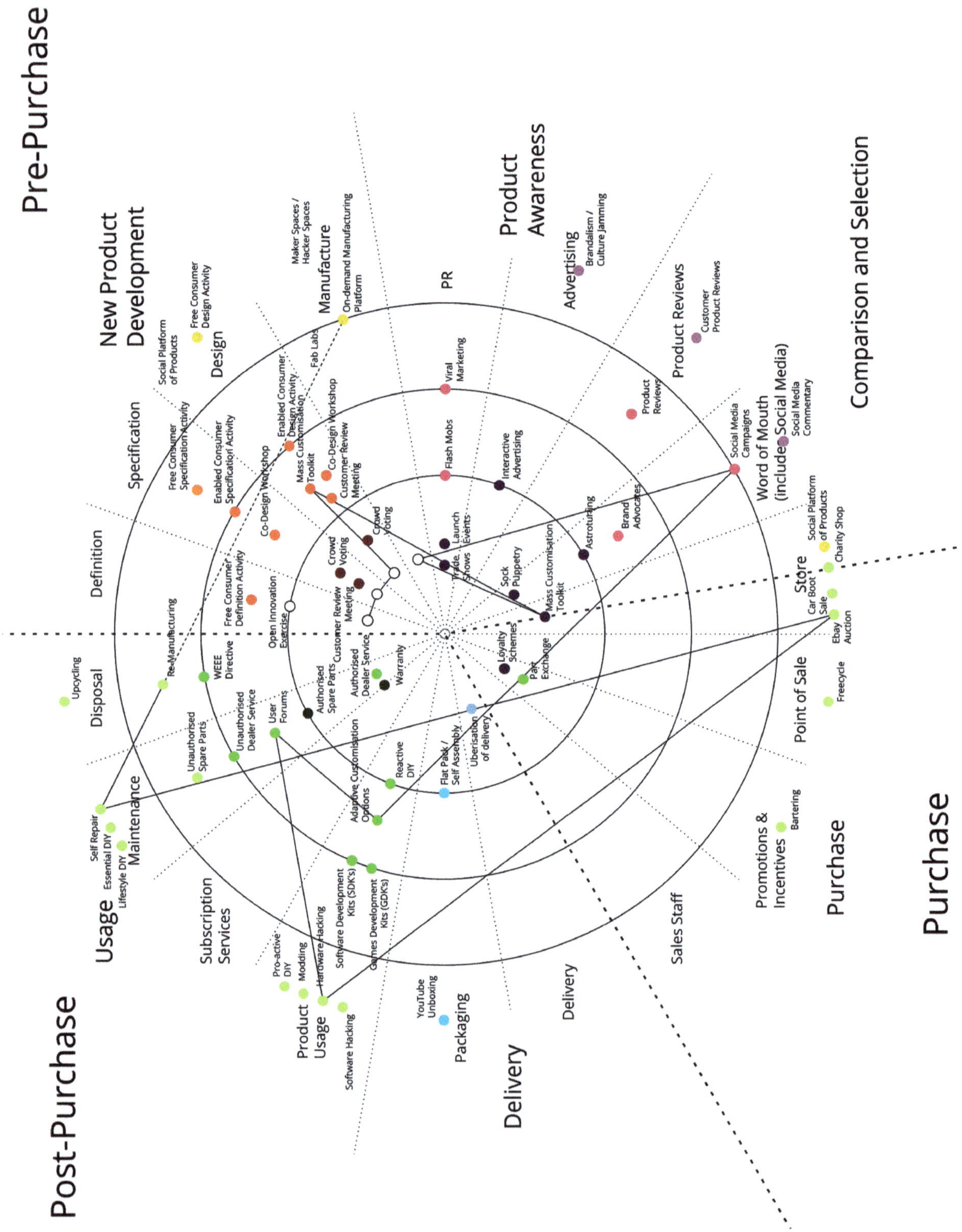

Figure 3-12. The fully populated Consumer Intervention Map reveals relationships that point to new opportunities for circular design.

mapping provides insights that go beyond delighting customers and optimizing consumption; they can drive innovation in means of production, product lifecycles, and more sustainable design.

Identifying Moments of Truth

Alignment diagrams are not just collections of touchpoints. They also provide insight for identifying and understanding critical points in the experience. Moments that matter, also called *moments of truth*, are key points in the journey that either make or break the experience.

Moments of truth can be thought of as a special type of touchpoint. They are critical, emotionally charged interactions, and they usually occur when someone has invested a high degree of energy in a desired outcome. These moments are the crux of the interaction. For example, when purchasing a new home, the selection of which property to buy will likely be a moment of truth.

The term *moments of truth* was popularized by Jan Carlzon, the then CEO of SAS Airlines, in his book of the same name. To illustrate his point, Carlzon starts his book with a story of a customer who arrived at the airport without his boarding pass. The SAS agents personally drove back to the hotel where he'd left it and delivered it to him at the airport. This left an indelible impression on the customer.

Moments of truth point to opportunities for innovation and growth. For instance, in their book *The Innovator's Method*, business scholars and consultants Nathan Furr and Jeff Dyer suggest creating what they call *journey lines*, or a brief visualization of the steps customers take. They write:

> **Create an in-depth visual portrait in which you identify pain points to understand how your customers do the job today and how they feel while doing it. Visually map out the steps customers take to achieve an outcome. It helps to assign a customer emotion to each step to identify how the customer is feeling.***

They go on to recommend looking for moments "that ignite their emotions"—in other words, moments of truth. Solutions that address these moments, they claim, are more likely to be monetizable: people are generally willing to pay for services that address critical needs. In this sense, moments of truth are points of opportunity for the organization.

Focusing on moments of truth allows you to concentrate your energy on experiences that matter. The perceived coherency of your offering is given by how you handle moments of truth. Diagrams provide insight into these points across time, allowing organizations to design a more cohesive experience and reduce transitional volatility.

Focusing on moments of truth allows you to concentrate your energy on experiences that matter.

* Nathan Furr and Jeff Dyer, *The Innovator's Method* (2014)

Aligning for Value

Business magnate Warren Buffett once said, "Price is what you pay; value is what you get." In other words, from the individual's perspective, value is a much richer, more dynamic concept than cost, involving human behavior and emotions. Value is a *perceived* benefit.

Existing frameworks help us understand the subjective nature of the concept. Marketing professors Jagdish Sheth, Bruce Newman, and Barbara Gross identify five types of customer value:*

- ***Functional value*** relates to the ability to perform a utilitarian purpose. Performance and reliability are key considerations with this type of value.
- ***Social value*** refers to the interactions among people, emphasizing lifestyle and social awareness. Peloton (*onepeloton.com*), for instance, creates community through live and on-demand fitness classes where members compete on leaderboards, share achievements, and connect with other riders to turn solitary workouts into social experiences.
- ***Emotional value*** emphasizes the feelings or affective responses a person has while interacting with an organization's offerings. For example, personal data security services tap into the fear of identity theft or data loss.
- ***Epistemic value*** is generated by a sense of curiosity or a desire to learn. This type of value emphasizes personal growth and the acquisition of knowledge. Khan Academy, for example, provides online courses that allow people to learn at their own pace.
- ***Conditional value*** is a benefit that depends on specific situations or contexts. For instance, the perceived value of pumpkins and monster costumes increases conditionally just before Halloween in the US each year.

Beyond these types, design strategist and educator Nathan Shedroff points to *meaning* as a form of what he calls "premium value."† This exceeds mere novelty and delight and looks at the purpose products and services have in our lives. Products and services that provide meaningful experiences help us make sense of the world and form part of our personal identity.

Together with coauthors Steve Diller and Darrel Rhea, Shedroff identifies 15 types of premium value in the book *Making Meaning*:

- ***Accomplishment:*** The sense of pride in achieving goals
- ***Beauty:*** The appreciation of aesthetic qualities that give pleasure to the senses
- ***Community:*** A sense of connectedness with others around us
- ***Creation:*** The satisfaction of having produced something
- ***Duty:*** The satisfaction of having fulfilled a responsibility
- ***Enlightenment:*** The gratification of learning about a subject
- ***Freedom:*** A sense of living without constraints
- ***Harmony:*** The pleasure of balance among parts of a whole
- ***Justice:*** The assurance of just and fair treatment

* Jagdish Sheth et al., *Consumption Values and Market Choices* (1991)

† Nathan Shedroff, "Bridging Strategy with Design: How Designers Create Value for Businesses" (2014)

- ***Oneness:*** A sense of unity with people and things that surround us
- ***Redemption:*** The deliverance from past failure
- ***Security:*** Freedom from worry about loss
- ***Truth:*** A commitment to honesty and integrity
- ***Validation:*** The external recognition of one's worth
- ***Wonder:*** Experiencing something beyond comprehension

Diagrams illuminate the human dynamics of value creation at all levels. When they embrace the subjective nature of value, they give organizations an outside-in view of the value they actually create. Strive to include an indication of how value is perceived from the individual's perspective.

As a class of documents, alignment diagrams allow you to visualize and locate value within your offering ecosystem. You can then ask: What is your value proposition at each point in the experience? How is the organization meaningfully unique from the customer's perspective? What meaning can you create for customers?

Summary

Historically, visual alignment has helped people make sense of the world. Take John Snow's map of cholera cases in London in 1854: he was able to literally see the cause of an outbreak by layering elements on a map. Visualizing experiences can have a similar effect on your team.

But unlike physical spaces, experiences are frustratingly intangible and broad. As the mapmaker, it's your job to frame the diagram and the experiences you'll be mapping. This includes decisions about the perspective, scope, and focus, as well as structure and use. Chapter 5 discusses initiating a mapping effort in more detail.

Touchpoints are the means by which interactions between individuals and an organization can take place. Typically, these are seen in terms of interaction with an advertisement, application, or website, or through a service encounter or phone call.

A broader definition of touchpoints, however, includes the whole context in which these interactions occur. An interaction between an individual and an organization happens at a given time and within a given environment. Organizations that design for and manage coherence across touchpoints see enormous benefits: greater satisfaction, stronger loyalty, and larger returns.

Moments of truth are critical, emotionally intense moments. They are those instances that make or break a relationship. Identifying the moments of truth points to potential opportunities for innovation.

From the individual's perspective, value is subjective and complex. There are many types of value they may consider: functional, emotional, social, epistemic, and circumstantial. Premium value goes beyond these types to include meaning and identity.

Further Reading

Jerry Angrave, The Journey Mapping Playbook *(2020)*

Angrave provides a practical, facilitation-focused toolkit for planning and running journey mapping workshops, with particular emphasis on demonstrating commercial value and building consensus for action. The book includes frameworks for prioritizing journeys, preparing sessions, and translating workshop outputs into ongoing experience programs across sectors including aviation, financial services, and manufacturing.

Lou Downe, Good Services: How to Design Services That Work *(2020)*

This guide lays out 15 essential principles for designing services that work well for users, demystifying what makes a service "good" or "bad." Based on practical experience, each chapter centers on one principle, offering concrete guidance for building better service delivery. A practical resource for both practitioners and nonpractitioners, it is the first book to describe what constitutes a good experience and provide actionable methods for designing one.

Mads Soegaard, "Top Tips to Create Effective Journey Maps," IxDF *(2025)*

Soegaard provides comprehensive guidance on creating effective journey maps through detailed exploration of experience maps, CJMs, and service blueprints. The article covers research methodology, workshop facilitation, and practical techniques for translating insights into actionable improvements, drawing from IxDF's journey mapping curriculum and industry expert contributions.

Stephanie Walter, User Journey Mapping *(2022)*

Walter provides a concise, practical guide to user journey mapping with emphasis on research methodology, workshop facilitation, and effective application of maps. The book covers map types, how to conduct user research for mapping, and how to use completed maps to bring stakeholders together and drive product decisions.

Diagram and Image Credits

Figure 3-2: Harry Beck's London Underground map, licensed from TfL from the London Transport Museum collection

Figure 3-4: Customer journey map example by Jim Tincher at Heart of the Customer, used with permission

Figure 3-7: Example customer journey map in network form by WCIG, fair use

Figure 3-9: Diagram by Andy Polaine from the article "Blueprint+: Developing a Tool for Service Design," used with permission

Figure 3-10: Touchpoint matrix by Wolfram Nagel in Multiscreen UX Design, used with permission

Figure 3-11: 360° touchpoint matrix created by Accelerom AG (*accelerom.com*), an international consultancy and research firm based in Zurich, used with permission. Accelerom has been combining management practice, cross-media marketing research, and cutting-edge analysis and visualization technologies for over a decade.

Figure 3-12: Consumer Intervention Map by Matt Sinclair, Leila Sheldrick, Mariale Moreno, and Emma Dewberry, used with permission

The map is not the territory.

—Alfred Korzybski

IN THIS CHAPTER

- Overview of map types
- Customer journey maps, service blueprints, experience maps
- Other types of diagrams

CHAPTER 4

Map Types in Review

Alignment is the goal: first outside-in, then inside-across. But alignment isn't one-size-fits-all. The fundamental dimensions of mapping—perspective, scope, focus, structure, and use—can be combined in different ways depending on what you're trying to achieve. And different combinations demand different diagram types.

This book is about possibilities. It doesn't prescribe any one approach. Instead, the burden is on you, the mapmaker, to determine the goals of the effort and the experiences to diagram, then pair that with an appropriate map type. Know your options. Don't rule out any technique in advance.

Once you understand the organization's objectives and the experiences you want to map, you can select the diagram type that's most appropriate. To do so, consider the primary elements of mapping discussed in Chapter 3.

This chapter reviews key diagram types used for mapping experiences, describing each one's structure, typical uses, strengths, and weaknesses. Use this as a reference when selecting the right approach for your situation.

Comparison of Diagram Types

The big three diagram types that have emerged over the past decade are customer journey maps, service blueprints, and experience maps. Others include ecosystem models, mental model diagrams, job maps, user story maps, day-in-the-life diagrams, and workflow diagrams. TABLE 4-1 summarizes some of the common diagram types and the differences between them.

The number and types of diagrams you'll need depend on the factors outlined in Chapter 3: point of view, scope, focus, structure, and use. Generally, there's a desire to reduce your effort as well as the number of artifacts you create, so I advise creating multiple diagrams only if necessary to illustrate significant differences.

One way to determine which type of diagram best suits your situation is to consider them along two dimensions: scope and solution-independence.

FIGURE 4-1 plots the main diagram types discussed throughout this book in a simple matrix. The intent is to show the differences between them, although there will always be exceptions in any given category. The size of each shape reflects the degree of variation within that diagram type.

TABLE 4-1. A comparison of diagram types

Type	Point of view	Scope	Focus
Customer journey map	Individual as a loyal customer, often making a purchase	Typically, from becoming aware to loyalty or leaving	Emphasis on cognitive and emotional states of the individual, including moments of truth and satisfaction
Service blueprint	Individual as the recipient of a service	Concentrated on service encounters and ecosystems, frequently in real time	Actions and physical evidence across channels; emphasis on service provision (backstage actors, processes, and workflows)
Experience map	Individual as an actor behaving in the context of a broader activity	Beginning and end are defined by the specific experience or context	Emphasis on behaviors, goals, and jobs to be done; typically includes actions, thoughts, feelings, and pain points
Ecosystem map	Multiple actors and multiple interaction points	Holistic, capturing elements of experiences across many levels of interaction	Relationships among actors, goals, content, and modes of interaction
Mental model diagram	Individual as an independent actor in the context of a broader activity	Broad, outlining elements of a fundamental activity	Centers on the reasoning, beliefs, philosophies, and emotions of the individual through the activity
Job map	Individual as an independent actor in the context of a broader activity	Can be broad or narrow; begin with a trigger, end with completion	Steps to get a job done
Day-in-the-life diagram	Individual as an independent actor in the context of a broader activity	Focused on a single day (or week)	Actions taken during a typical day or week, but with some context setting and behavioral details
Workflow or task flow diagram	Individual as a user of a given system	Focused on the detailed steps for using a system	Granular tasks and steps taken to complete a process or interact with a solution

Structure	Uses	Strengths	Weaknesses
Chronological	Used by marketing, customer experience teams, and brand managers for optimizing sales, customer relations, and brand development	Used widely; simple to understand; easy to engage others	Views individuals as consumers; often leaves out internal processes
Chronological	Used by frontline staff, internal teams, and managers to improve an existing service or brainstorm new ones	Straightforward to create and understand; good for collaboration	Lacks contextual details and emotions
Chronological	Used by product managers, designers, and strategists for product and service design improvements and innovation	Outward perspective helps build empathy and insight	Can feel abstract to some people without a concrete offering
Network or spatial displays of information	Used to gain a systemic view of relationships between multiple actors and multiple services to build strategy and innovate	Provides a strategic overview; engaging diagrams	Lack of chronology may make it hard to follow; lacks details in favor of an overview
Hierarchical	Used to develop empathy and an understanding of what's going through people's minds; helpful in finding opportunities for innovation	Normalized formats for consistency; provides deep insights into human behavior	Large diagrams can be overwhelming
Chronological	Used by strategists, innovators, and product developers to identify unmet needs and opportunities	Simple to create and understand; solution-independent	Lacks contextual details and emotional aspects
Chronological	Used by a range of people to gain empathy and a basic understanding of what customers do	Simple to investigate and create; easy to comprehend	May not reveal opportunities immediately
Chronological flow diagram	Used by product managers, designers, and developers to understand the details of a process	Highly specific and detailed	Lacks contextual cues and emotions

Diagrams toward the upper left tend to be more concrete. For example, user story maps show detailed interactions with a specific product. These are more volatile and may change with technology, but are great for illustrating an experience close to implementation.

Moving toward the bottom right, the diagrams become more abstract, dealing with broad domains. Diagrams in this quadrant are stable and foundational, and help find broad opportunities for innovation.

Typically, the more solution-independent the approach, the greater the longevity of the diagram. For example, if done properly, job maps and mental model diagrams can remain valid and stable for a decade or more. Diagrams toward the top of the chart tend to have a shorter shelf life, bounded by a short-term project.

The scope of a diagram helps determine how many will be required. In general, the broader in scope, the more holistic it is and therefore the fewer diagrams are needed. It's unlikely, for instance, that you'll need more than one ecosystem map: by definition, it shows the big picture. But creating multiple service blueprints for various customer interactions across the organization is likely.

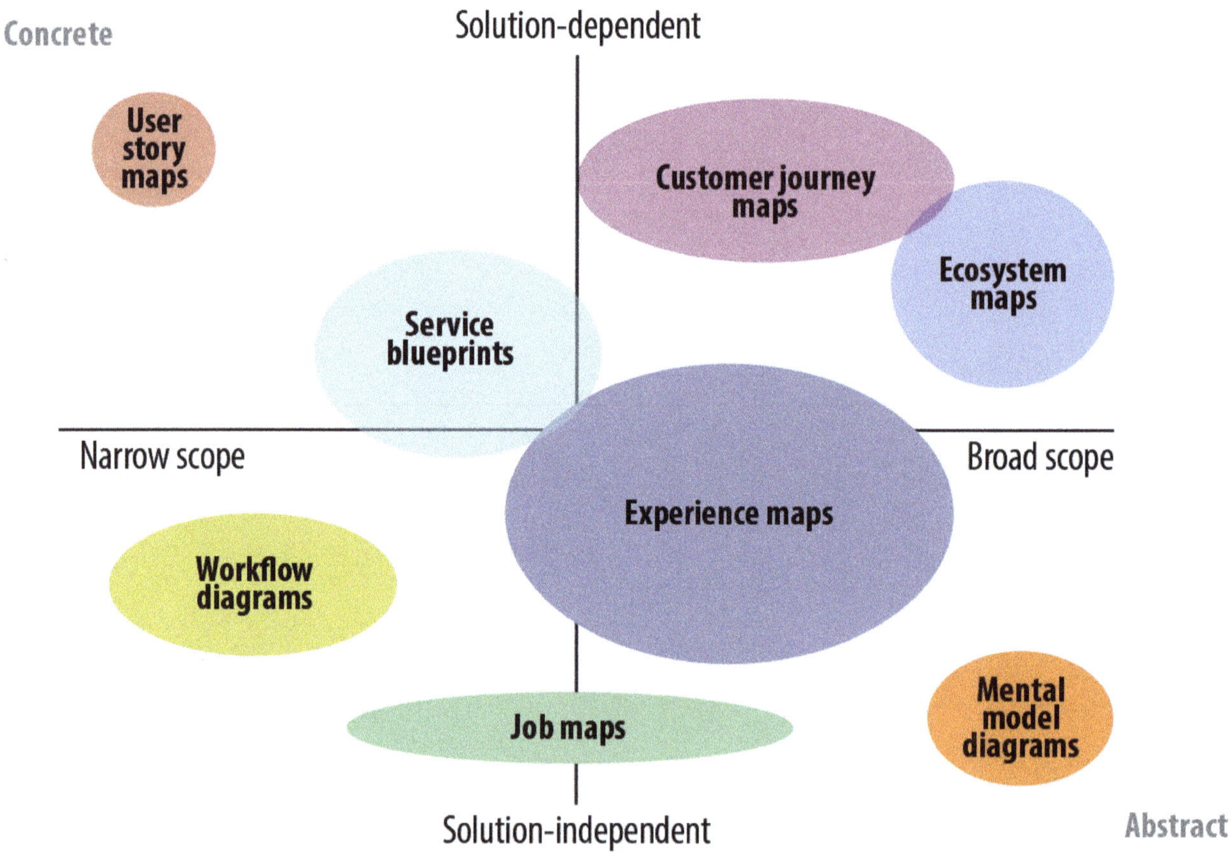

Figure 4-1. A simple matrix plotting solution independence against scope helps sort out the potential functions and purposes of different diagram types.

Customer Journey Maps

The exact origin of the term *customer journey map* is unclear. Early precursors date back to developments in the 1960s as marketers grappled to understand broad customer lifecycles.* In 1972, John Jenkins visualized one of the earliest customer lifecycles in diagram form.† But it wasn't until 2002 that customer experience pioneer Colin Shaw introduced a new type of visualization he calls *moment mapping*.‡

The contemporary style of CJMs emerged around the mid-2000s. Bruce Temkin was an early advocate for their use. In a 2010 Forrester report titled "Mapping the Customer Journey," Temkin defines CJMs as "documents that visually illustrate customers' processes, needs, and perceptions throughout their relationships with a company."§ Joana de Quintanilha and colleagues, also at Forrester, have recently updated and simplified Temkin's definition to "a customer's path and perceptions as they pursue a goal."¶

Three hallmark aspects of CJMs define the category:

Awareness

> Journey maps tell the story of how an individual comes to a particular solution. The first moment in that process is becoming aware of both their need and possible services.

Decision

> After exploring options and learning about a service, there is a point of acquisition—a decision to adopt a given solution.

Use

> The journey continues with a phase of usage, which includes things like installation or configuration, deepened learning, fixing issues, and engaging customer support. Customers decide to either stay or leave at the end of this phase.

Figure 4-2 shows an example of a CJM created by the team at Heart of the Customer that illustrates this arc. The first stage is about awareness and consideration, followed by a trial to acquire the solution, and then applying the solution. The circular shapes reflect that the journey doesn't necessarily proceed in a straight line. Emotions are plotted on a curved line, a feature of journey maps that has become standard.

Figure 4-3 is another example of a CJM, this time broader in scope. Created by Paige Roche, service design lead at Slalom, this diagram shows the end-to-end lifecycle of delivering a B2B software solution. It translated insights from interviews, onboarding pain points, and delivery challenges into a structured view that aligned cross-functional teams, identified lifecycle gaps, and served as both a diagnostic tool and an execution guide.

CJMs are a strategic tool for visualizing touchpoints so they can be managed effectively. They help answer questions such as these: How can an organization better engage customers? How might go-to-market motions be optimized? How can the product or service be improved to create more value?

The answers are less about individual touchpoint optimization and more about how touchpoints come together into a unified whole. Visualizing them in a map is key to comprehending the overall experience.

---

* Russell Colley developed a framework for evaluating advertising success in his 1961 book *Defining Advertising Goals for Measured Advertising Results* (DAGMAR for short). Robert Lavidge and Gary Steiner offered a similar model that same year in "A Model for Predictive Measurements of Advertising Effectiveness," *Journal of Marketing* (1961)

† John Jenkins, *Marketing and Customer Behaviour* (1972)

‡ Colin Shaw and John Ivens, *Building Great Customer Experiences* (2002)

§ Bruce Temkin, "Mapping the Customer Journey," *Forrester* (2010)

¶ Joana de Quintanilha et al., "What Journeys Really Are: Customers' Paths and Perceptions as They Pursue a Goal," *Forrester* (2024)

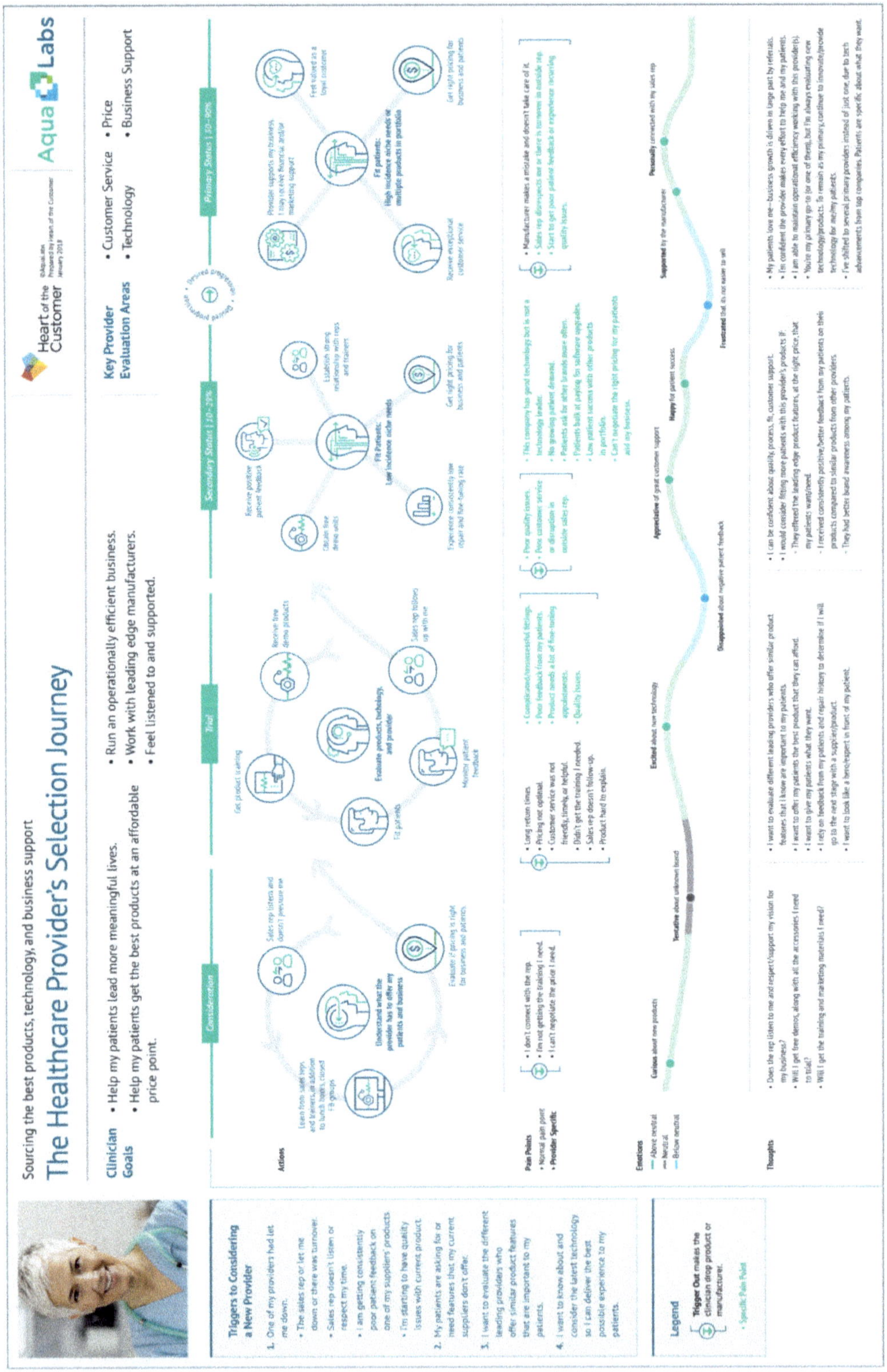

FIGURE 4-2. This diagram illustrates the basic elements of a customer journey map.

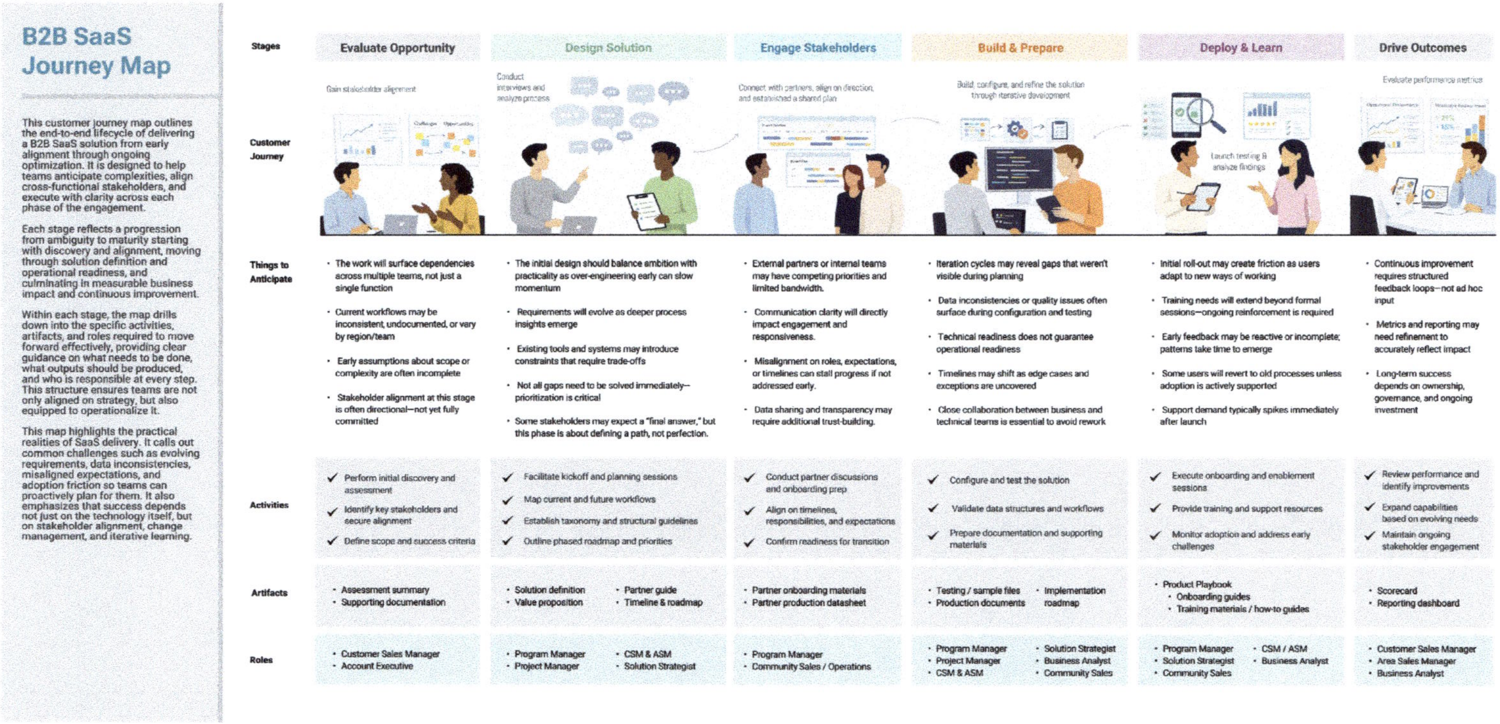

FIGURE 4-3. This customer journey map shows the complete lifecycle, from end to end.

(CJMs continued)

Strengths	CJMs view individuals primarily as consumers moving through a purchase funnel. This commercial lens is powerful for marketing, customer experience teams, and brand managers working on sales optimization, customer relations, and brand development. The format is widely used and simple to understand, making it easy to engage others.
Weaknesses	CJMs can miss the broader context of people's lives. They also typically exclude internal processes and backstage operations—that's where service blueprints excel.

Learn more:

Robert Curedale, *Mapping Methods 2* (2018)

Ray Gerber, "How to Create a Customer Journey Map," *Qualtrics* (2024)

Sarah Gibbons, "Journey Mapping 101," *NN/g* (2019)

Once you understand the organization's objectives and the experiences you want to map, you can select the diagram type that's most appropriate.

Service Blueprints

Service design can be traced back to the writings of G. Lynn Shostack in the early 1980s.* She stresses the overall importance of visualizing activities, writing:

> **The root of most service problems is, in fact, lack of systematic design and control. The use of a blueprint can help a service developer not only to identify problems ahead of time but also to see the potential for new market opportunities.†**

It wasn't until the 2000s that Mary Jo Bitner and colleagues developed a more structured and normalized approach to service blueprinting.‡ **Figure 4-4** is an example of their original format. This arrangement highlights the separation of *frontstage* interactions, which are what the individual experiences, and *backstage* interactions, which are the processes necessary to provide a service.

Modern versions of service blueprints follow the pattern they set out. **Figure 4-5** shows a service blueprint created by Brandon Schauer, previously a strategist with leading user experience design group Adaptive Path and now senior VP at climate change advocacy group Rare. It depicts the experience of a conference attendee.

* G. Lynn Shostack, "How to Design a Service," *European Journal of Marketing* (1982)

† G. Lynn Shostak, "Designing Services That Deliver," *Harvard Business Review* (1984)

‡ Mary Jo Bitner et al., "Service Blueprinting: A Practical Technique for Service Innovation" (2007)

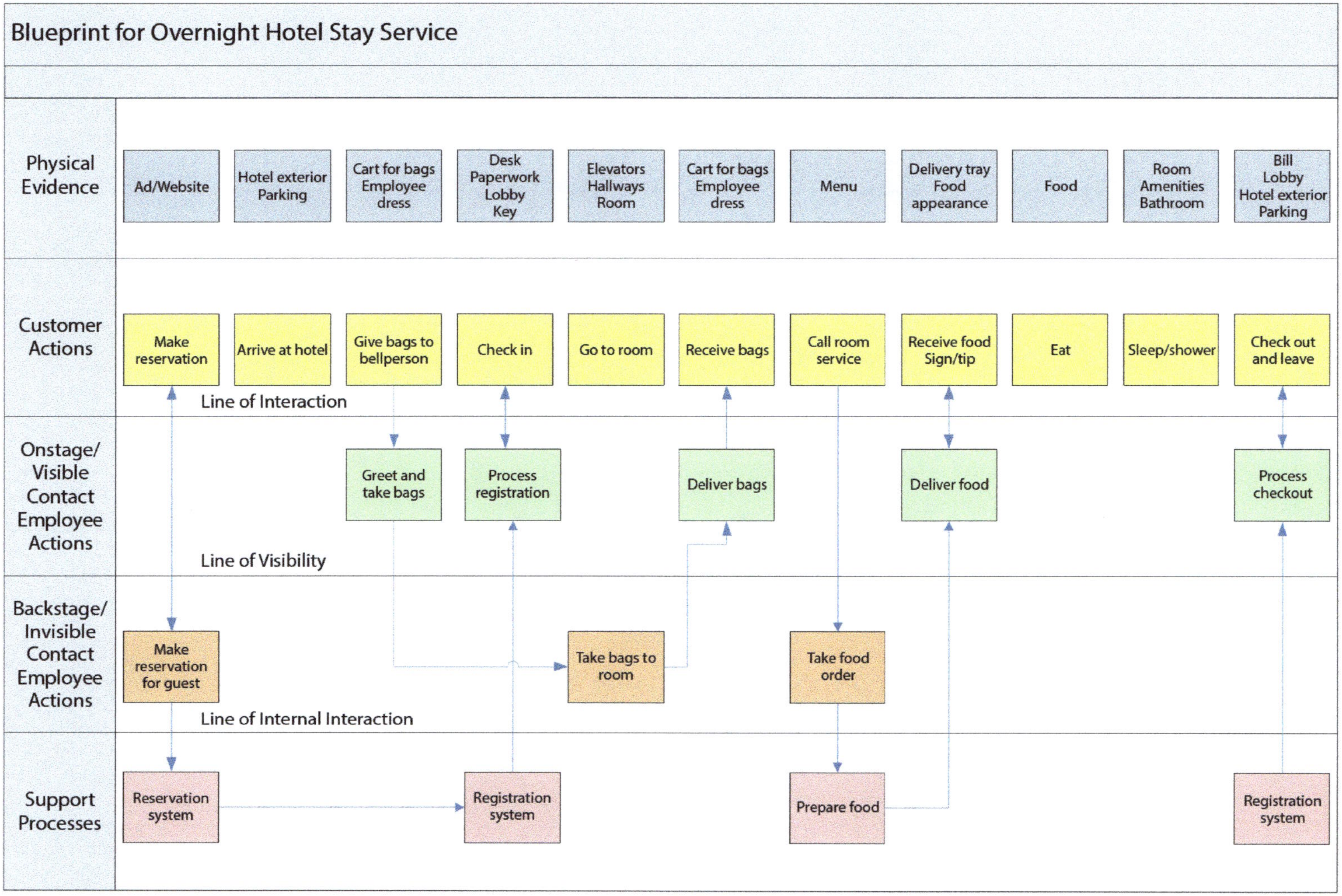

FIGURE 4-4. This diagram of a hotel service is one of the earliest examples of service blueprinting.

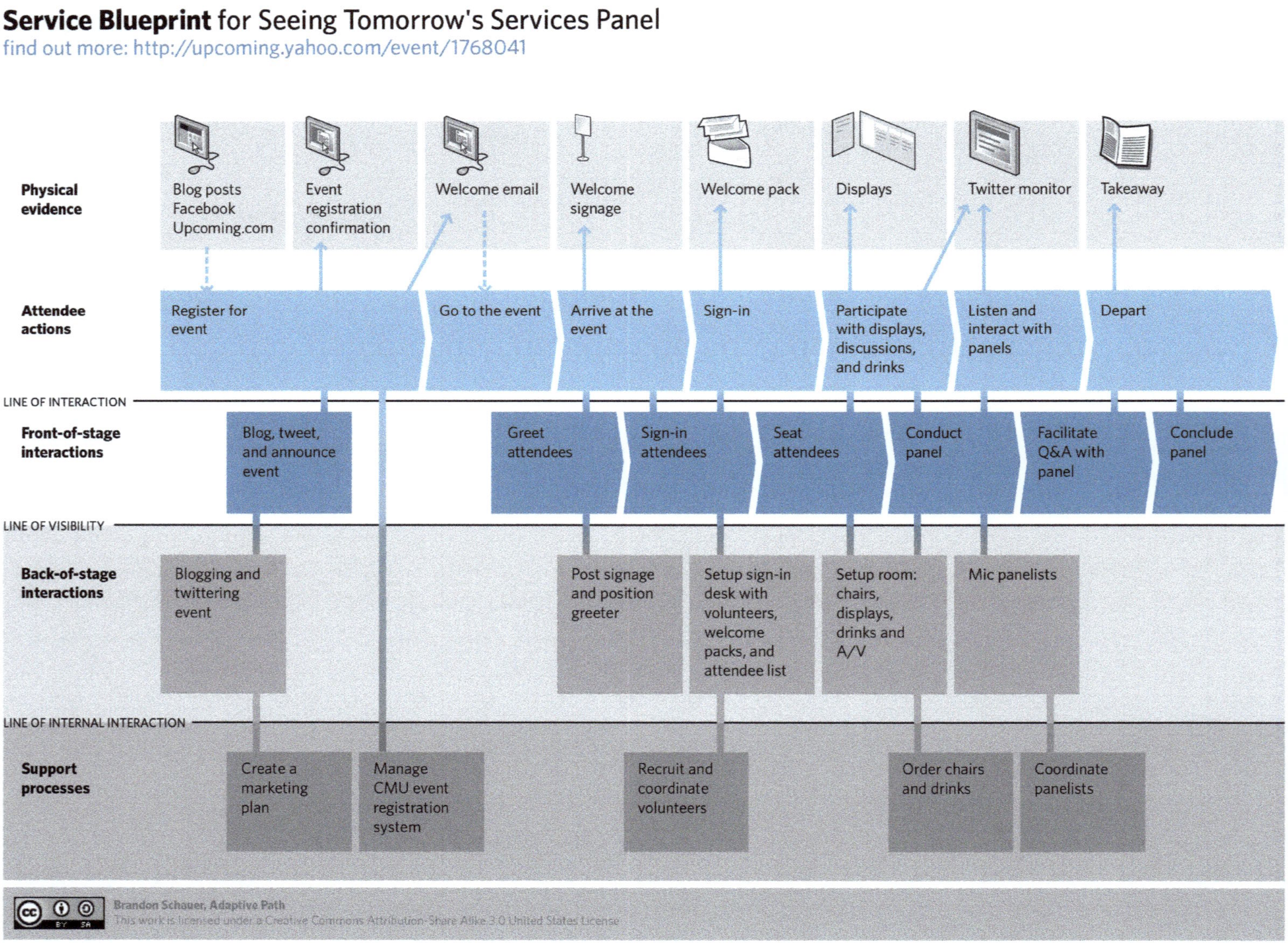

Figure 4-5. This example of a service blueprint for a conference attendee visually aligns frontstage and backstage activities.

Service blueprints typically include five key components or layers of information, reflected in **Figure 4-5**:

Physical evidence
: The manifestations of customer touchpoints, including physical devices, electronic software, and face-to-face interactions

User actions
: The main steps a customer takes to interact with the service

Onstage touchpoints
: The actions of the provider that are visible to the customer

Backstage actions
: These are the internal service provision mechanisms of the organization that are not visible to the customer but impact the experience.

Support processes
: Internal processes that indirectly impact the customer experience, including interactions with partners or third-party suppliers

Erika Flowers and Morgan Miller, founders of Practical by Design (formerly Practical Service Design), have also modified the standard service blueprinting technique. They retain the frontstage and backstage distinctions, but intentionally move away from a strict swim lane approach in favor of color-coded stacks. The columns of information can be of varying heights, saving space and facilitating online viewing.

The elements included may vary in number; they include details on relevant policies and rules, observations and facts, metrics and data, and critical moments. To engage others, you can also record open questions from the team and even start generating ideas to solve the identified opportunities. **Figure 4-6** shows an example by Flowers and Miller using this updated style of service blueprinting.

Strengths	Service blueprints offer a simple structure that makes frontstage and backstage alignment visible at a glance. They're particularly valuable for frontline staff, operations teams, and managers improving existing services or designing new ones. These diagrams require relatively light research and work well for cocreation with teams and stakeholders.
Weaknesses	Their focus on mechanics and processes means they often lack contextual details—things like "noisy waiting room" or emotional states. The term *blueprint* is misleading: these are flow diagrams, not architectural specifications.

Learn more:

Erika Flowers and Morgan Miller, *Your Guide to Blueprinting the Practical Way* (2023)

Lavrans Løvlie, Andy Polaine, and Ben Reason, *Service Design: From Insight to Implementation*, 2nd ed. (2025)

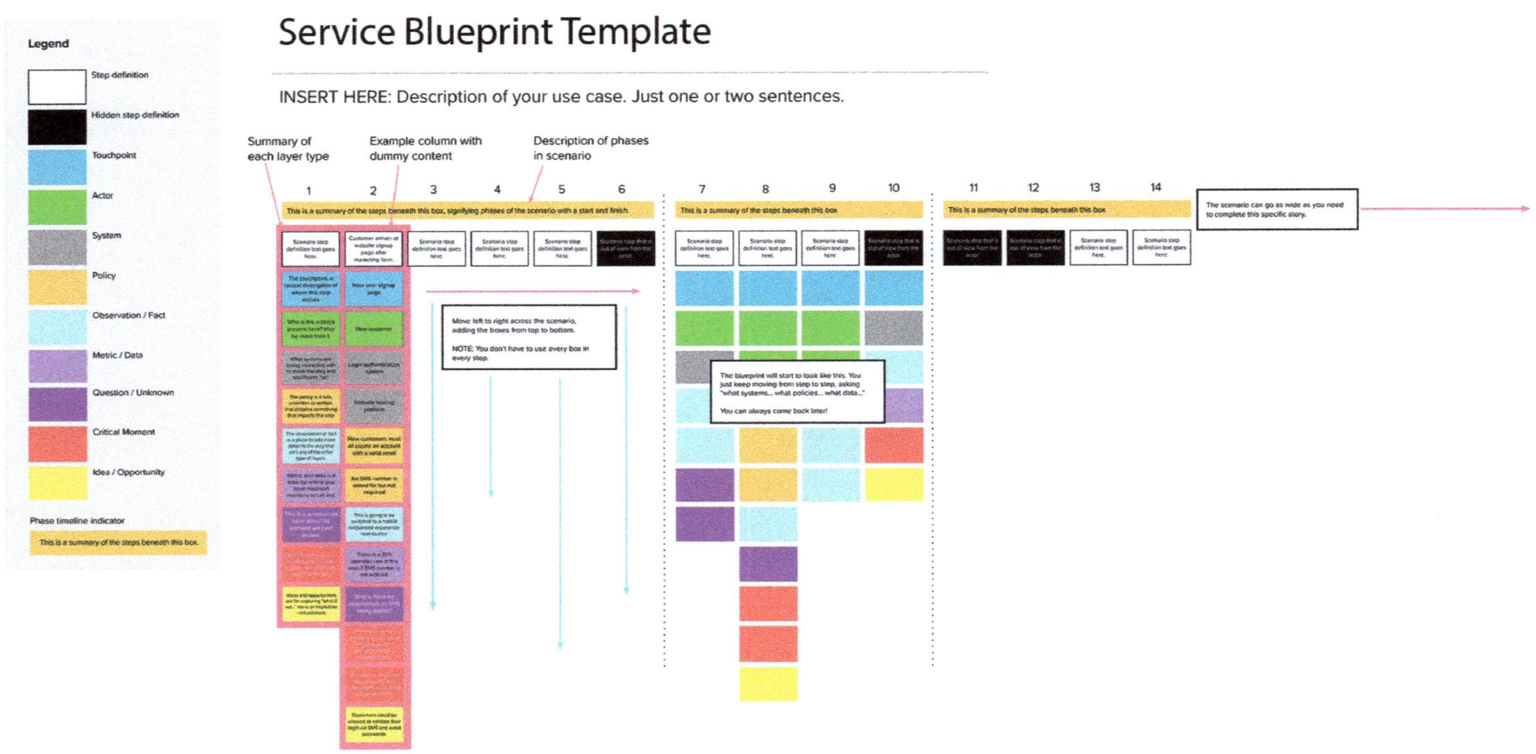

FIGURE 4-6. This practical service blueprint captures different aspects of a service in color-coded stacks rather than swim lanes.

Experience Maps

CJMs and service blueprints are tied to specific products and services. However, it's also possible to map experiences *independent* of a given product or service. In particular, *experience maps* as I define them look at the broader context of human activity, beyond the offerings of just one organization. They show the connections between people, places, and things and aid in understanding the broader context.

In other words, experience maps as defined here have a completely different point of view than, say, CJMs. Rather than seeing the individual as a consumer of a brand or offering, you can focus on their objectives and goals, regardless of the solution.

Consider the map shown in **Figure 4-7**, created by design strategist Diego S. Bernardo. His aim was to illustrate the ups and downs of growing food in the city. Negative experiences (in red) indicate reasons that someone might stop the activity. Dropout points are indicated with red lines pointing down.

The positive experiences (in blue) show the good things about growing food in the city. This diagram reminds us to look not only for pain points, struggles, and fears in an experience, but also for aspects that motivate and encourage. The loops in the diagram indicate positive feedback loops and increased engagement throughout the experience.

Overall, the diagram in **Figure 4-7** tells the story of an individual's relationship to an activity—urban gardening—not to a product, service, or brand.

Figure 4-8 shows another example of an experience map, created by Jamie Thomson of Mad*Pow. This diagram illustrates the experience of reducing cholesterol over the course of a year.

Looking at the experience in this way points to opportunities. Rather than illustrating how individuals consume a product, experience maps allow organizations to ask the question, "How do we fit into the lives of individuals?" The answers often lead to new opportunities for growth.

Strengths	Experience maps offer a fresh, outward perspective that helps product managers, designers, and strategists build empathy beyond a single brand relationship. By focusing on human activities rather than commercial transactions, they reveal opportunities for innovation and help answer "How do we fit into people's lives?" rather than "How do people fit into our offerings?"
Weaknesses	Experience maps can feel too abstract to stakeholders expecting concrete solutions or clear ROI. Without a specific product or service to optimize, some teams struggle to translate insights into action. Detailed diagrams can lead to overanalysis and "mapping overload."

Learn more:

Interaction Design Foundation, "Customer Experience Mapping"

Peter Szabo, *User Experience Mapping* (2017)

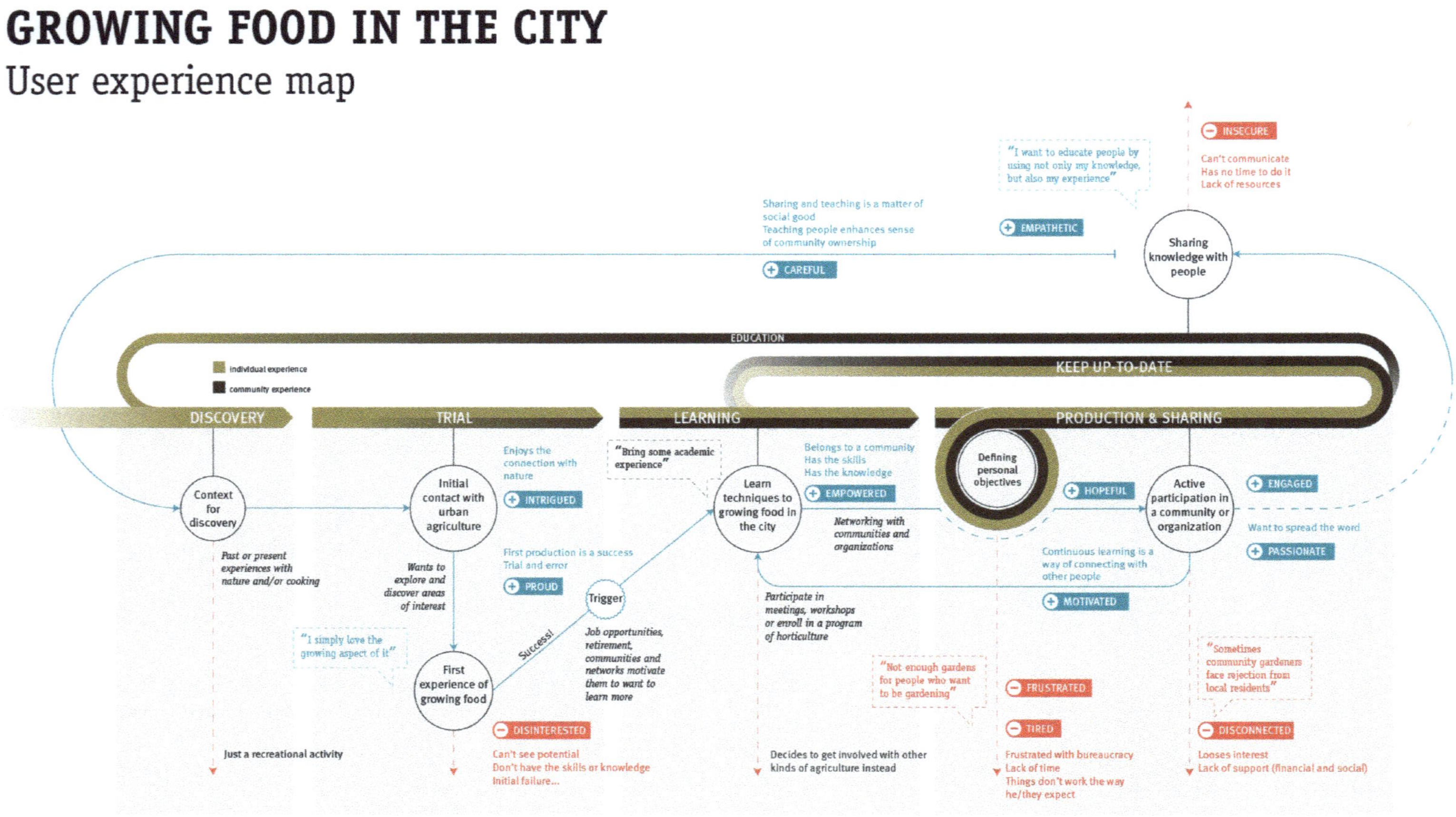

Figure 4-7. This experience map for growing food in Chicago focuses on positive and negative factors.

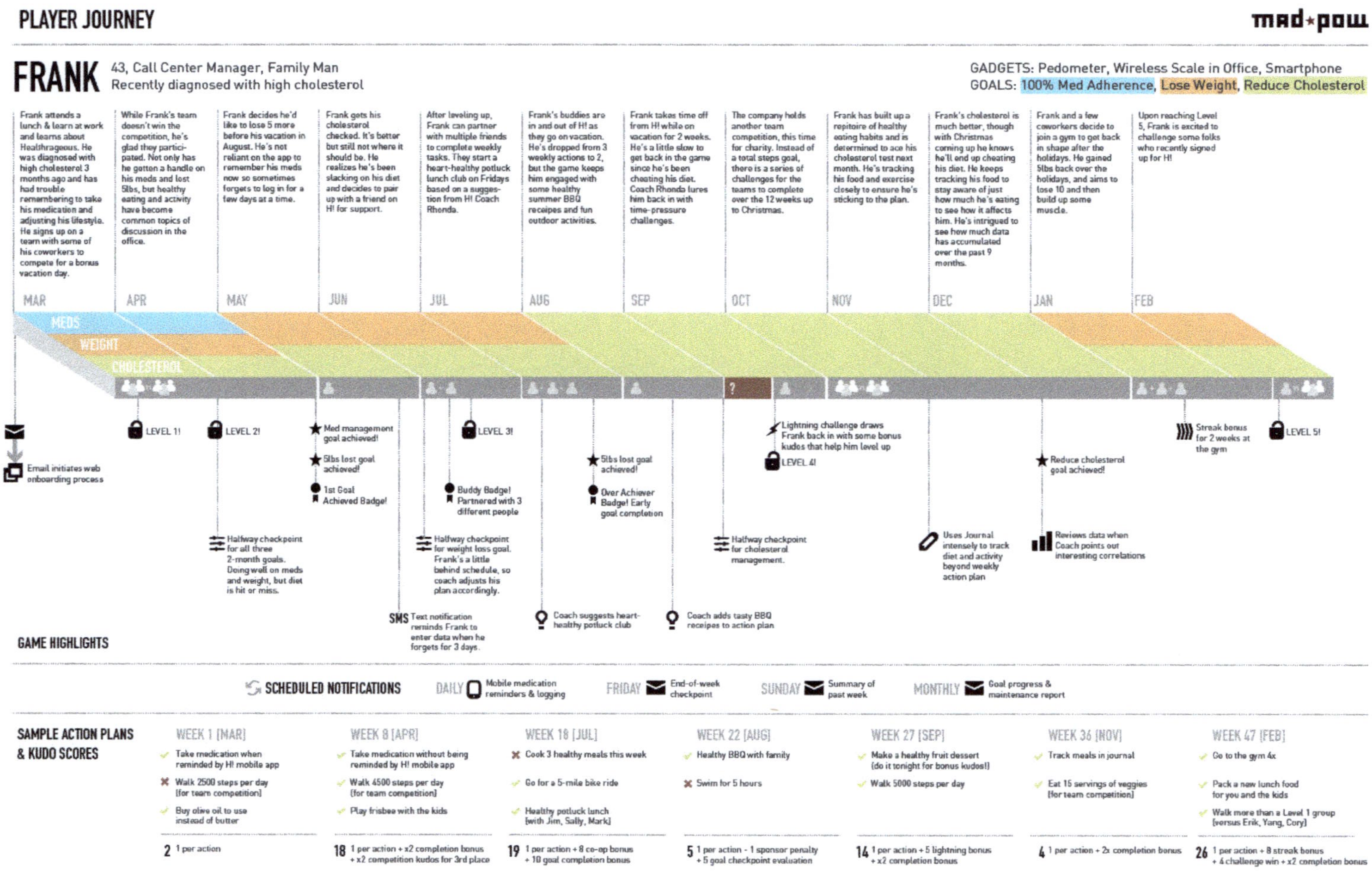

Figure 4-8. This experience map illustrates reducing cholesterol over the course of a year.

Ecosystem Models

As services and products become more interconnected, the idea of a standalone offering fades. Thinking in terms of ecosystems is the new competitive advantage. Successful organizations will be determined by how well their services fit with one another and, more importantly, how well they fit into people's lives.

Ecosystem maps favor a network-like arrangement rather than a chronological timeline. The intent is to show relationships among multiple entities that make up an experience. This embraces the complexity of modern business offerings and how they must be compatible with surrounding offerings, including those of competitors.

Ecosystem mapping applies systems thinking—viewing relationships among multiple components as a whole. According to Donella Meadows in *Thinking in Systems*, a system is "a set of elements or parts that is coherently organized and interconnected in a pattern or structure."* The relationships among elements matter more than the elements themselves. Ecosystem maps help teams identify leverage points where they can influence or impact the system to find opportunities for change and improvement.

Figure 4-9 shows an ecosystem map for car sharing from Lavrans Løvlie, Andy Polaine, and Ben Reason, found in their book *Service Design*. Each "pie slice" represents a different consideration—who, what, where, when, why, and how. The concentric circles reflect different levels of granularity. The center shows the driver-to-car relationship. Moving outward, the scope expands to include passengers, other cars, services, communities, society, and the planet. Such diagrams allow teams to see and discuss various relationships in tangible ways.

Each aspect is intentionally oversimplified to focus on connections between them rather than complexities within each. The goal is strategic insight, not exhaustive detail.

Figure 4-10 shows an ecosystem model created by service designers Paige Roche and Trevor Connolly for a large auto financing enterprise. This strategic overview of the end-to-end experience surfaced key opportunities for the lender to more effectively connect its services to both car buyers and dealers at critical moments. It served as a shared reference point for cross-functional teams across the organization, fostering both alignment and innovation.

Strengths	Ecosystem maps provide a strategic overview that helps teams see the whole system at once. The spatial arrangement reveals relationships and integration points that linear diagrams miss. These diagrams are particularly valuable for strategists and innovation teams working on XLG initiatives, helping answer the question "How do we fit into people's lives?" The network format is engaging and works well in workshops.
Weaknesses	The lack of chronology can be hard to follow for stakeholders used to timeline-based maps, making ecosystem maps harder to act on. Creating them takes significant time and research, and they intentionally lack detail. Emotions, specific touchpoints, and sequential actions are better shown in other map types.

Learn more:

Peter Jones and Kristel Van Ael, *Design Journeys Through Complex Systems* (2023)

* Donella H. Meadows, *Thinking in Systems* (2008)

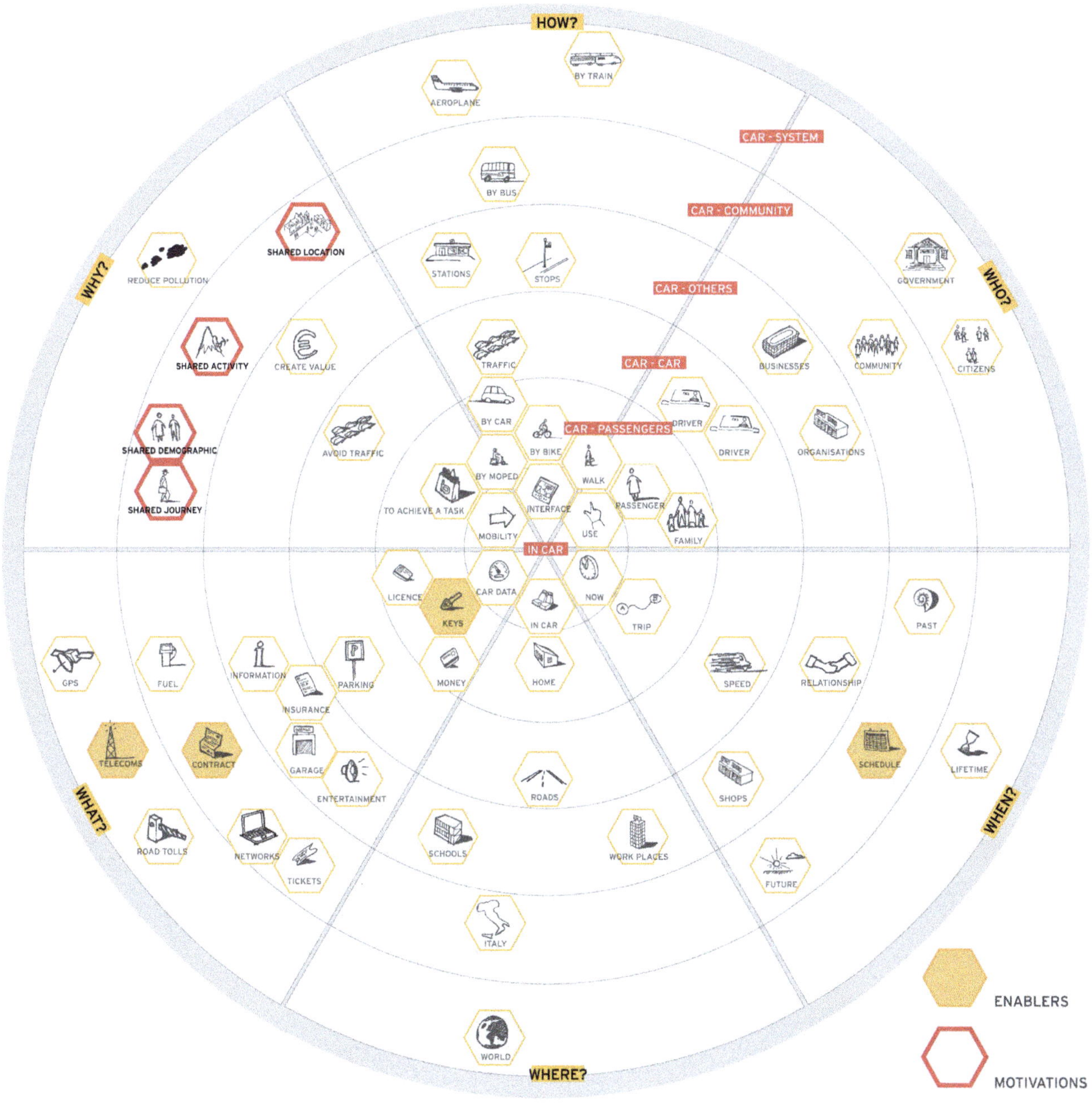

Figure 4-9. This ecosystem model for car sharing reflects interactions at different levels of granularity, from the in-car experience to cars in the community and beyond.

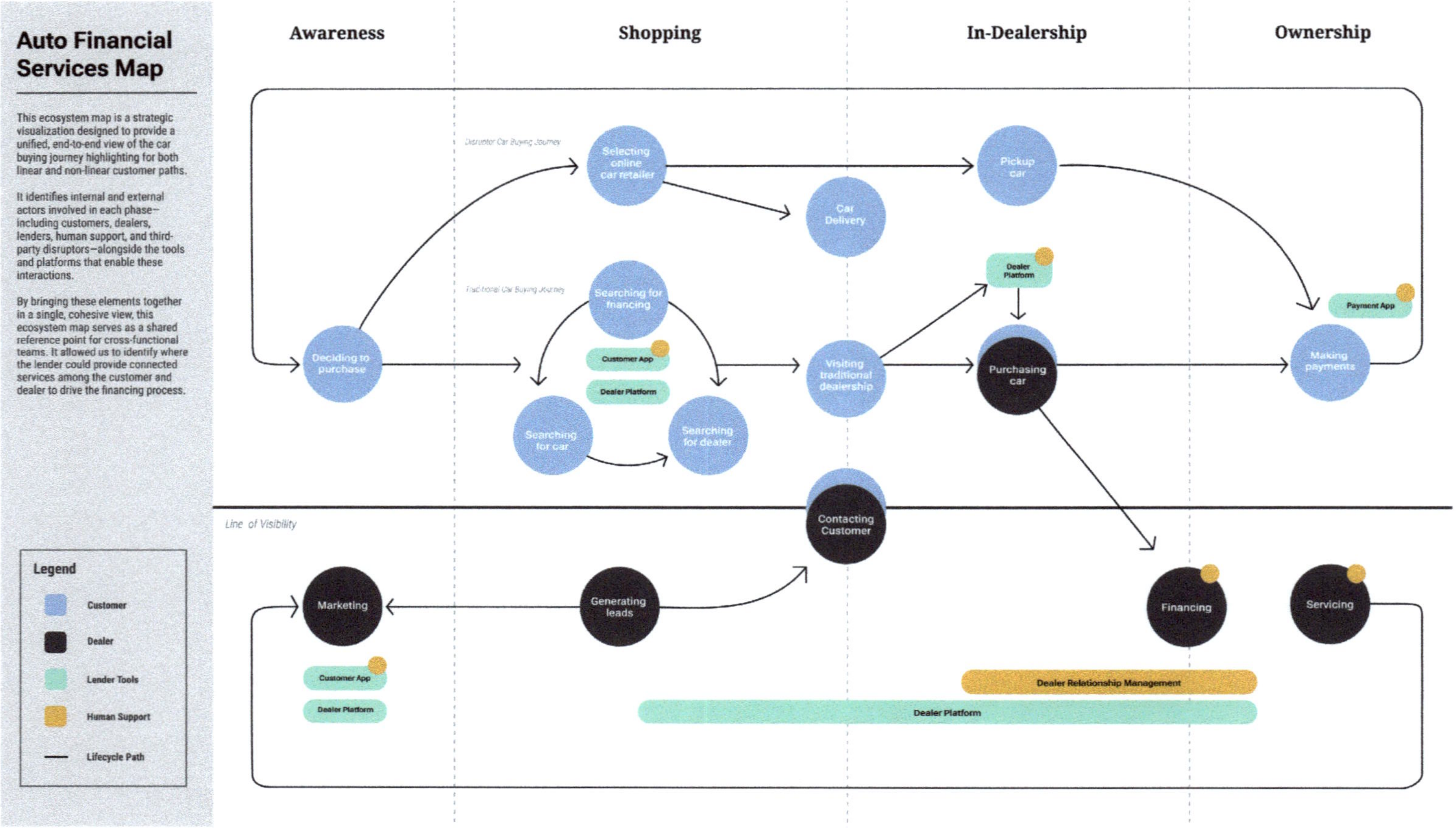

Figure 4-10. This ecosystem diagram for the auto purchasing and financing experience provides a strategic overview.

Mental Model Diagrams

Mental models describe an individual's understanding of how the world works—their frame of reality. These are cognitive constructs built on beliefs, assumptions, and past experiences. A person's mental model is a perception of how a system functions, not necessarily how it actually works. If the goal of design is to understand the mental model of the people you're designing for, visualizing it helps teams align and find better solutions.

In 2008, Indi Young published a formal method for visualizing mental models in her book of the same name. These diagrams are typically very long documents that can extend 10–15 feet across a wall when printed. **Figure 4-11** shows an example examining what goes through people's minds during and after a near-miss accident.

This part of the diagram has three basic levels:

1. ***Boxes:*** The building blocks, containing a person's thoughts, reactions, and guiding principles. Each follows a standard format: [verb] [noun] [qualifiers], written in the first person. For example: "Decide to drive home because there was nothing I could do."
2. ***Towers:*** Boxes form groups based on affinity, called *towers*. These are the areas with colored backgrounds.
3. ***Mental spaces:*** Towers form affinity clusters called *mental spaces*, delineated with dark vertical lines.

A dark horizontal line separates the mental model from *support*—the products and services that address the thought process represented within a tower. This shows alignment at work.

This approach focuses on people, not tools. For example, instead of writing "Filter image colors in Photoshop," focus on the root task: "Alter image colors" or "Improve image color." The diagrams don't reflect personal preference or opinion. You strive to capture what goes through a person's mind—their internal voice—which Young calls *thinking styles*.

Of all the diagram types in this book, mental model diagrams are the most person-focused. This provides flexibility: they can be applied to any domain or situation. They also enjoy longevity; once completed, a mental model will change only slowly, often remaining relevant for years.

Strengths	Mental model diagrams provide normalized formats for consistent results and deep insight into human thinking. They're particularly valuable for product managers, designers, and strategists seeking to understand what goes through people's minds to find opportunities for innovation. Their solution-independent nature means they remain relevant for years—properly done, they can stay valid for a decade or more.
Weaknesses	Final diagrams can be overwhelming in detail. Business leaders sometimes ask for simpler models, though that detail is also a strength for those seeking deep understanding. The lack of chronological flow can make these diagrams harder to follow than journey maps or blueprints.

Learn more:

Indi Young, *Mental Models* (2008)

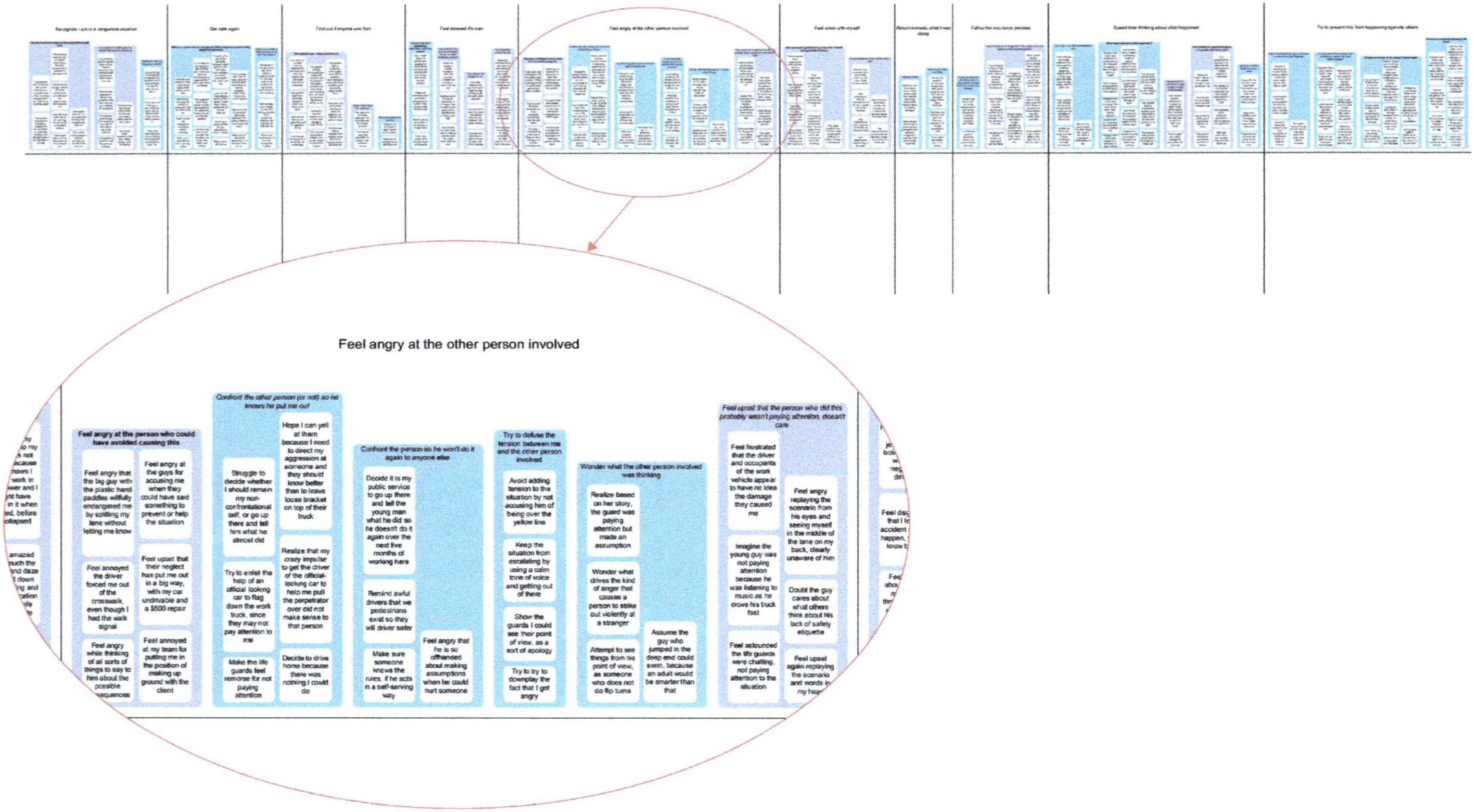

FIGURE 4-11. This is the top portion of a mental model diagram generated from primary research, describing patterns across a set of people.

Job Maps

The concept of jobs to be done (JTBD) provides a lens for understanding value creation. The framework, popularized by Clayton Christensen and Michael Raynor in *The Innovator's Solution*, is straightforward: people "hire" products and services to get a job done.

You might hire a new suit to make you look good at a job interview. You hire a messaging app to stay in touch with colleagues or friends. You hire a chocolate bar to relieve stress. These are all jobs to be done. From this perspective, people are goal-driven individuals seeking to achieve desired outcomes. Supporting those outcomes is the value organizations create.

Tony Ulwick and Lance Bettencourt at Strategyn have done advanced work applying JTBD theory in practice. They propose a model for understanding jobs as a sequence of steps, which they call *job maps*.* A job map differs from other types of diagrams in that it never refers to a brand or supplier. Instead, it maps the individual's intent and the sequence of steps for getting the job done, independent of solutions.

Figure 4-12 shows a job map for retrieving scientific information. Notice there are no references to technology or solutions, or any emotional or aspirational elements.

Because job maps are based on chronology and are solution-independent, you can use them as the basis for experience maps: create a simple job map with bare-bones steps, then arrange it in swim lane fashion and add rows for experiential and emotional aspects.

Strengths	Job maps are simple to create and understand. They're solution-independent, which gives them longevity and flexibility. They work particularly well for strategists, innovators, and product development teams seeking to identify unmet needs and opportunities for innovation.
Weaknesses	Job maps intentionally lack contextual details and emotional aspects. For holistic understanding, they need to be complemented with other research capturing aspirational, emotional, and social dimensions.

Learn more:

Jim Kalbach, *The JTBD Playbook* (2020)

Anthony W. Ulwick, *Jobs to Be Done* (2016)

Clayton Christensen et al., *Competing Against Luck* (2016)

* Lance Bettencourt and Anthony W. Ulwick, "The Customer-Centered Innovation Map," *Harvard Business Review* (2008)

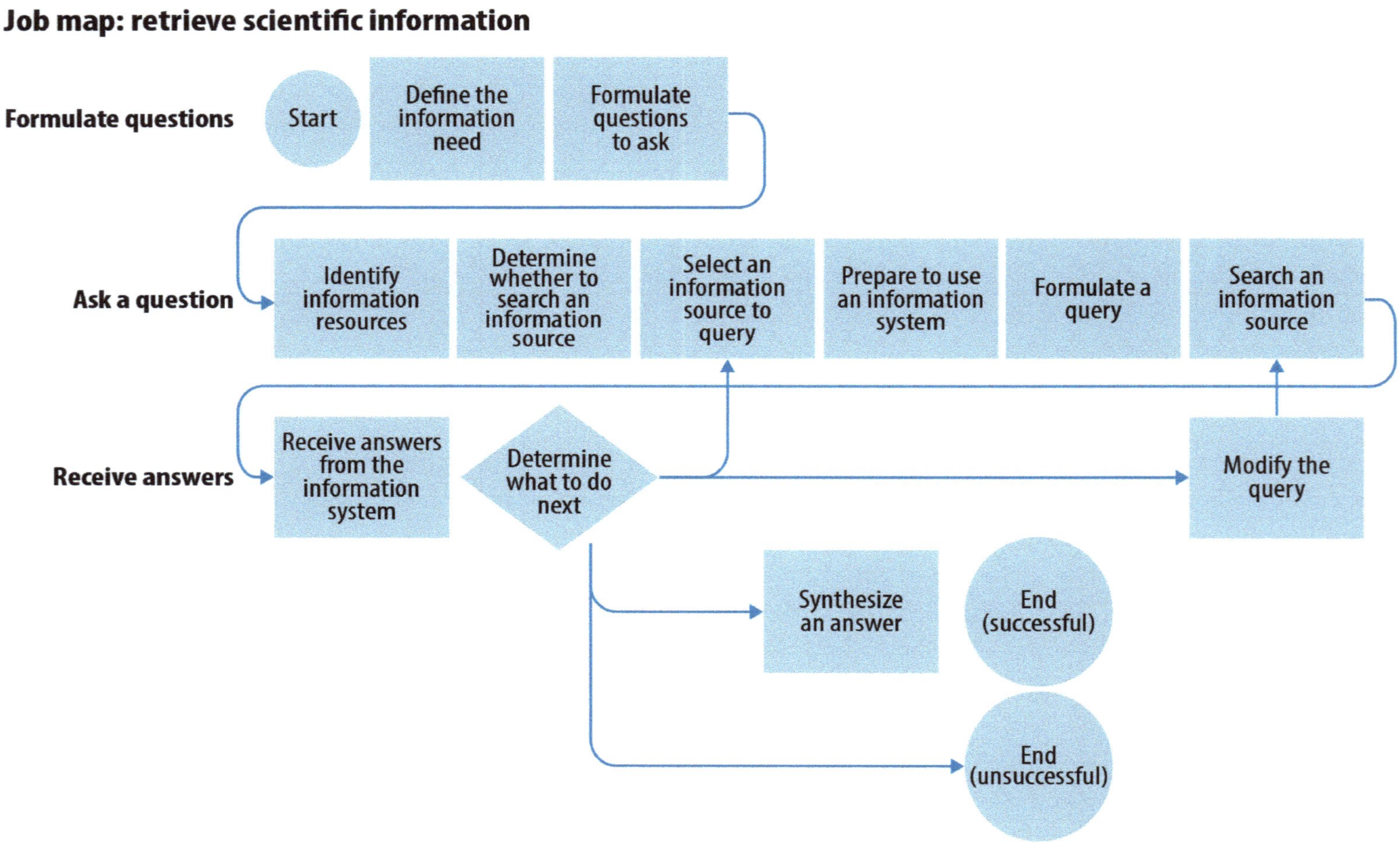

Figure 4-12. This simple job map outlines the steps involved in finding scientific information.

User Story Maps

User story maps align software development with user needs. Created by Agile coach Jeff Patton, this technique helps development teams avoid losing sight of the big picture while working on individual features.

Agile development breaks products into small chunks called *user stories*—short descriptions of features from the user's perspective, in the format "As a [type of user], I want [some goal] so that [some reason]." While this makes development manageable, teams can develop tunnel vision and lose connection to the project's overall end goal.

User story maps solve this problem by organizing user stories into a visual framework. These are the main elements:

User types
: Brief descriptions of the different roles the system serves

Backbone
: A sequence of user activities listed across the top

User stories
: Descriptions of features needed to achieve desired outcomes, typically prioritized and separated into releases

Figure 4-13 shows a classic example of a user story map created by expert Agile coach Steve Rogalsky. You can see the alignment of user activities (in orange and blue sticky notes) to planned features (in yellow).

The backbone resembles the chronology in an experience map, but user story maps lack much of the experiential detail—thoughts, feelings, context. Instead, they focus squarely on product development and release planning.

Strengths	User story maps are straightforward to create and understand. They work well for Agile teams, product managers, and developers who need to align development sprints with user needs. The visual format builds shared understanding across distributed teams and helps prevent the "Mr. Potato Head effect" where features don't fit together coherently.
Weaknesses	These maps are solution-dependent and product-specific, making them volatile—they change as the product evolves. They also lack the emotional and contextual richness of experience maps or journey maps. They're primarily useful for teams already committed to building a specific solution.

Learn more:

Jeff Patton, *User Story Mapping* (2014)

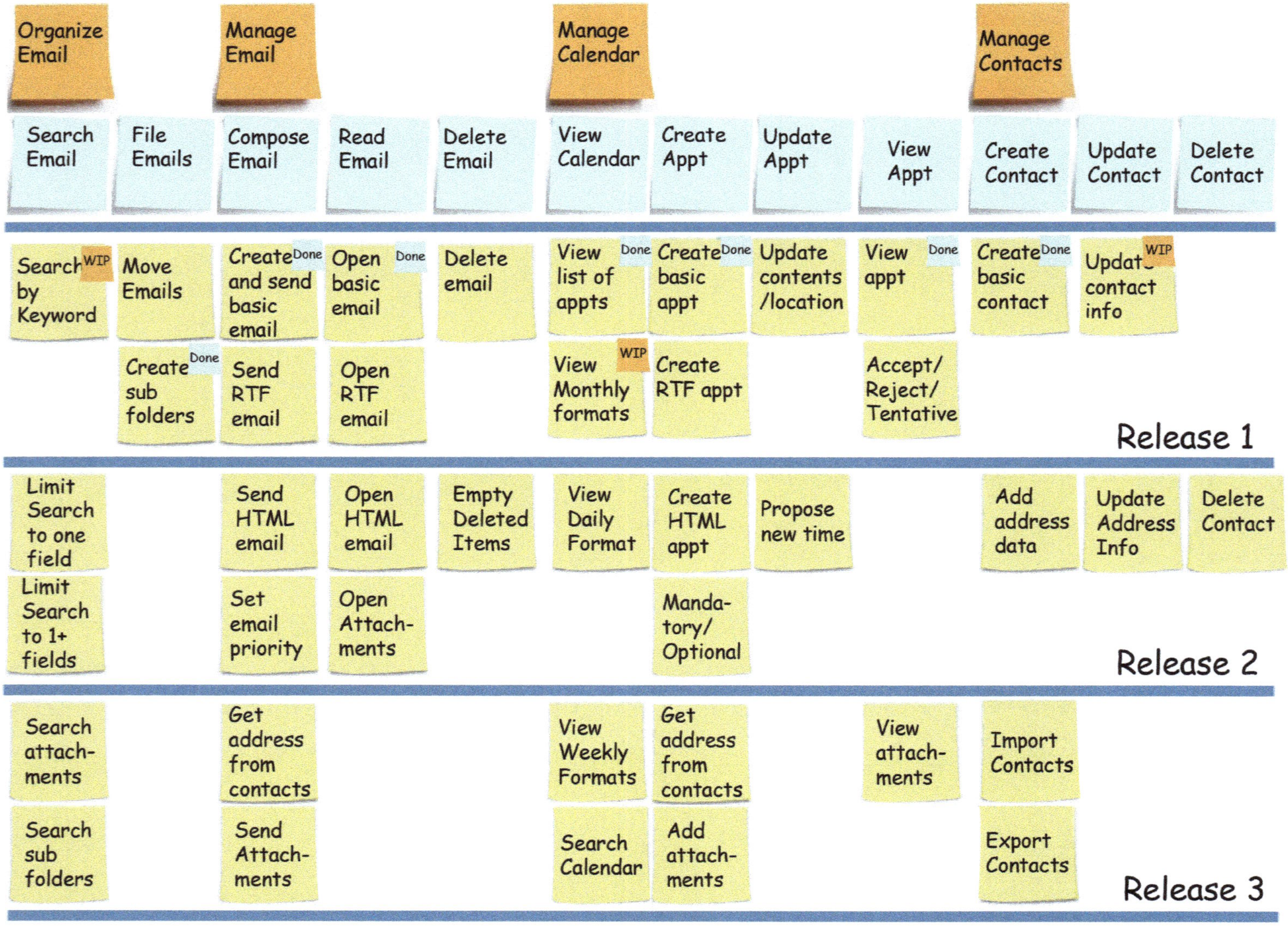

Figure 4-13. Story maps align software development tasks with the intended user experience.

Day-in-the-Life Diagrams

Day-in-the-life diagrams illustrate a typical or average day. As the name indicates, these maps show the rhythms, patterns, and states that people move through in their daily routines.

Figure 4-14 is an example created by Stuart Karten of Karten Design. It highlights the different modes of thinking an individual goes through during a day, indicated by different colors (e.g., information seeking in light blue, communicating with others in dark purple). For this reason, Karten calls this approach *mode mapping*. The line of modes extending across the diagram moves up or down to reflect positive or negative emotional states.

This approach provides a holistic view of someone's experience beyond isolated touchpoints or tasks. The diagram reveals patterns of activity, energy levels, emotional peaks and valleys, and the contexts in which people operate throughout their day.

One challenge is that when interviewing people about their typical day, you'll often get the answer "I don't have a typical day." To get around this difficulty, you can map out a typical week instead. This allows people to describe patterns across multiple days rather than forcing them to identify a single representative day. You can then form a composite—an average of typical days—based on the information they provide.

Day-in-the-life diagrams work well early in research to build empathy and basic understanding. They help teams see the broader context of people's lives before zooming in on specific moments or interactions. They're particularly useful for identifying when and where your solution fits into someone's routine, or where friction occurs.

Strengths	Day-in-the-life diagrams are simple to create and require relatively light research—often just a few interviews or diary studies. The resulting diagrams are easy to comprehend and provide essential context about when people are stressed, rushed, relaxed, or open to new experiences.
Weaknesses	These diagrams may not reveal opportunities immediately. They provide a foundational understanding rather than pointing directly to solutions. They also risk oversimplification because the "typical" day may not capture important variations or edge cases that matter for design.

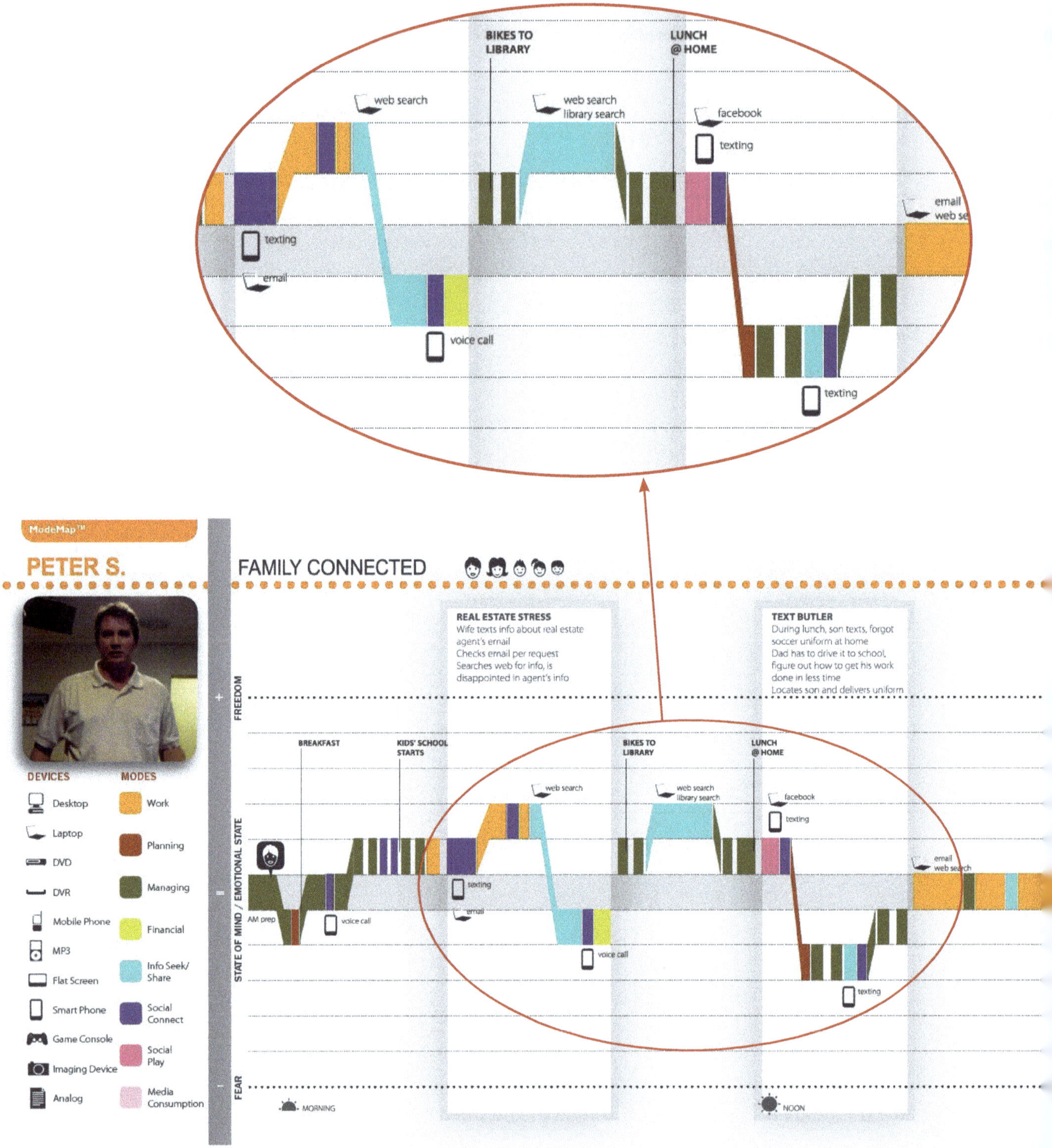

FIGURE 4-14. A day-in-the-life diagram can reflect the different physical, cognitive, and emotional modes a person goes through in a day.

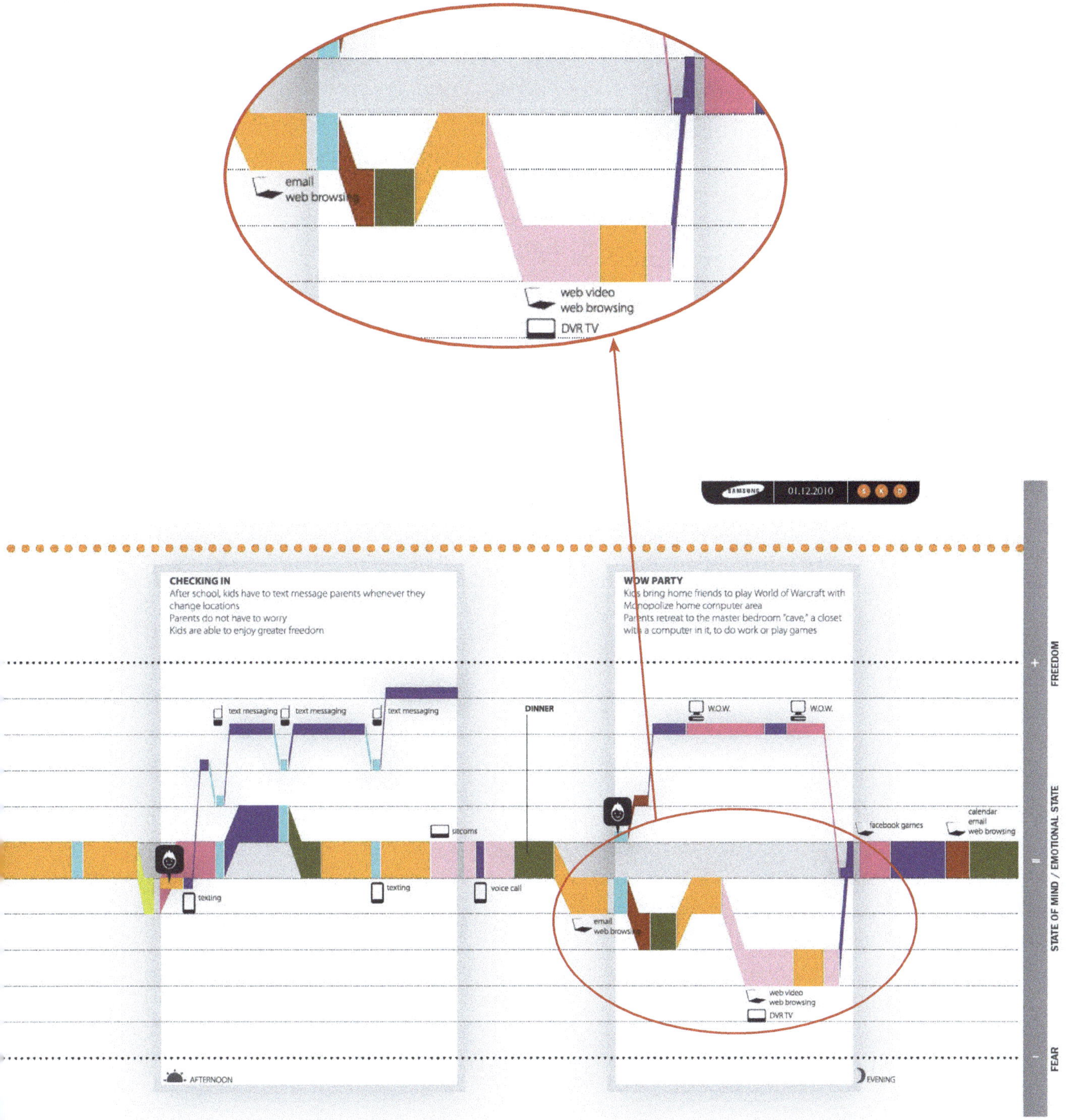
email
web browsing
web video
web browsing
DVR TV
SAMSUNG
01.12.2010
S
K
D
CHECKING IN
After school, kids have to text message parents whenever they change locations
Parents do not have to worry
Kids are able to enjoy greater freedom
WOW PARTY
Kids bring home friends to play World of Warcraft with
Monopolize home computer area
Parents retreat to the master bedroom "cave," a closet with a computer in it, to do work or play games
text messaging
text messaging
text messaging
DINNER
W.O.W.
W.O.W.
sitcoms
facebook games
calendar
email
web browsing
texting
texting
voice call
email
web browsing
web video
web browsing
DVR TV
AFTERNOON
EVENING
+
FREEDOM
=
STATE OF MIND / EMOTIONAL STATE
-
FEAR

Workflow Diagrams

Workflow diagrams break down the steps taken to achieve a goal. These diagrams focus on how a sequence of tasks fits together, often among multiple actors. They're more akin to service blueprints than CJMs.

A swim lane diagram is a specific type widely used to show workflows. It illustrates the steps of an interaction between a user and different parts of a system in a structured way. The columns or rows—depending on orientation—make up the "swim lanes," which help clarify the roles of different actors and components in an interaction.

At LexisNexis, I led an effort to map the workflow of lawyers across five international markets: France, Australia, New Zealand, Germany, and Austria. The approach in each country followed the lifecycle of a client matter from the lawyer's perspective. We wanted to understand the complex series of actions involved in completing a matter from beginning to end. After reviewing existing research and speaking with business stakeholders in each country, I conducted interviews with customers in our market. From this investigation, I created detailed workflow diagrams for each region.

Figure 4-15 shows one page from a 20-page workflow diagram. The diagrams included three types of actors: lawyers, secretaries, and other participants in the workflow. They consisted of many rows of information, seen labeled on the left side. Pain points and goals were included, as well as notes on state of mind and emotion. Personas, typical workweek charts, and org charts accompanied the diagrams to provide a more complete view of the lawyer's experience.

A related approach is task analysis, which breaks activities into discrete actions and decisions. It focuses on the cognitive and physical steps required to complete specific tasks, often at a more granular level than workflow diagrams. Business process modeling (BPM) is another variation, typically used in enterprise settings to document, analyze, and optimize organizational processes. These approaches share a common goal: understanding the detailed mechanics of how work gets done.

Strengths	Workflow diagrams are very specific and detailed, making them valuable for product managers, designers, and developers who need to understand the fine-grained steps of a process. They show multiple actors clearly, revealing handoffs and dependencies. When expanded beyond basic swim lanes, they can capture both mechanical process flow and experiential context.
Weaknesses	The detailed, process-oriented nature of these diagrams means they often lack contextual cues and emotions unless these are deliberately added. Because they're solution-focused rather than solution-independent, their longevity is limited. They can also become unwieldy for complex processes—20-page diagrams aren't unusual.

Learn more:

Maria Rosala, "Task Analysis: Support Users in Achieving Their Goals," *NN/g* (2020)

Interaction Design Foundation, "How to Improve Your UX Designs with Task Analysis" (2023)

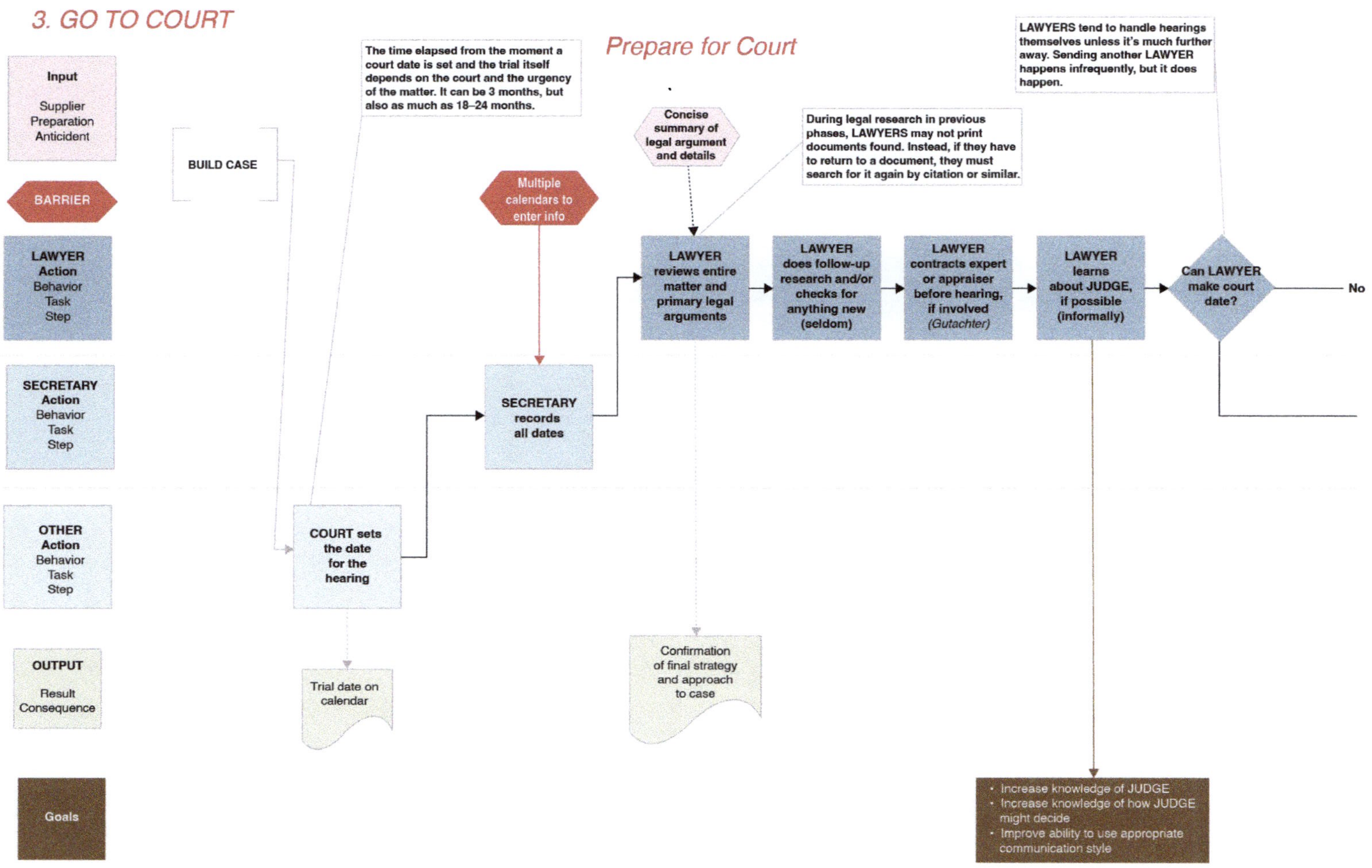

FIGURE 4-15. One page from a 20-page workflow diagram that illustrates a detailed experience.

Summary

There's no one-size-fits-all approach for creating alignment. The fundamental dimensions of mapping—perspective, scope, focus, structure, and use—combine in different ways to create distinct diagram types. This chapter provided a reference catalog of the main approaches.

The big three diagram types are CJMs, service blueprints, and experience maps:

- CJMs focus on individuals as consumers moving through awareness, decision, and use phases.
- Service blueprints align frontstage customer actions with backstage processes and support systems.
- Experience maps show human activities independent of any specific product or service.

Other diagram types serve specific purposes:

- Ecosystem maps use network arrangements to show relationships among multiple entities in a system.
- Mental model diagrams hierarchically organize what goes through people's minds during a given experience, providing deep insights that often remain valid for years.
- Job maps break down the universal stages of getting a job done.
- User story maps align software development with user needs.
- Day-in-the-life diagrams reveal daily rhythms and patterns.
- Workflow diagrams detail the mechanical steps of processes across multiple actors.

Diagrams toward the solution-independent end of the spectrum tend to have greater longevity. Job maps and mental models can remain valid for a decade or more. Solution-specific diagrams like user story maps and workflows change as products evolve but provide detailed guidance for implementation.

The number of diagrams you'll need depends on your objectives and the experiences you want to map. Generally, create multiple diagrams only when necessary to illustrate significant differences. Know your options and select the approach that makes the most sense for your situation.

Diagram and Image Credits

Figure 4-2: Customer journey map by Heart of the Customer, used with permission

Figure 4-3: CJM created by Paige Roche, service design lead at Slalom (2022), used with permission

Figure 4-4: Service blueprint example from Mary Jo Bitner et al., fair use

Figure 4-5: Service blueprint by Brandon Schauer, used with permission

Figure 4-6: Example service blueprint of a customer support scenario at Intuit, created in Mural by Erika Flowers and Morgan Miller, used with permission

Figure 4-7: Experience map by Diego Bernardo, used with permission

Figure 4-8: Experience map by Jim Kalbach and Hennie Farrow, used with permission

Figure 4-9: Ecosystem map from *Service Design* by Lavrans Løvlie, Andy Polaine, and Ben Reason, used with permission

Figure 4-10: Ecosystem model of auto purchasing and financing by Paige Roche, service design lead at Slalom, and Trevor Connolly, design director at Capital One, used with permission

Figure 4-11: Mental model diagram by Indi Young, used with permission

Figure 4-13: User story map by Steve Rogalsky, used with permission

Figure 4-14: Day-in-the-life diagram by Stuart Karten of Karten Design, used with permission

Figure 4-15: Workflow diagram by Jim Kalbach

The five-stage process for mapping experiences

PART 2
Creating and Activating Maps

A general process for experience mapping consists of five stages:

Initiate
: Chapter 5 deals with setting up a mapping initiative. Frame the effort. Get stakeholder alignment. Decide on the right scope.

Investigate
: Alignment diagrams must be grounded in evidence. Chapter 6 details techniques for research.

Illustrate
: Chapter 7 covers how to visually represent the experience. This is about creating an insightful narrative, not artistic talent.

Align
: Chapter 8 shows ways to use diagrams in workshops. Facilitate collaborative sensemaking. Build commitment to action.

Activate
: Chapter 9 introduces frameworks for translating current state insights into future possibilities. Move from understanding to innovation.

Stages 1 through 4 result in current state maps: depictions of experiences as you observe them today. The aim is to get alignment on how your team understands the experience and what problems are worth solving.

Remember: it's not about the map (noun), but the mapping (verb). Involve stakeholders throughout. Get their feedback on your initial proposal. Include them in the investigation. Create the diagram together. Come together for workshops. Don't make mapping a solitary effort.

The secret of getting ahead is getting started. The secret of getting started is breaking your complex overwhelming tasks into small manageable tasks, and starting on the first one.

—Mark Twain

IN THIS CHAPTER

- Identifying the need
- Convincing decision makers
- Deciding on a direction
- Writing a proposal
- Collaborative methods for initiating a project

CHAPTER 5

Initiate: Establishing Relevance

As experience mapping becomes more mainstream, stakeholders start asking for things like customer journey maps or service blueprints by name. In some cases, creating a map is even an expected part of a project. This is good news.

But it also makes framing the activity critical. Mapping must address a strategic imperative or fill a knowledge gap to be valuable.

Given the range of possibilities, it's up to you to define your mapping effort appropriately. Here are some key points to keep in mind:

Include others throughout.

The mapmaker plays different roles, from researcher to facilitator. But the objective is not just to create a diagram; it's to engage others in conversations and develop solutions together as a team.

Set realistic expectations about scope.

You won't design every touchpoint. Some interactions you cannot control, or simply choose not to. Mapping helps you see interdependencies and prioritize strategically.

Use AI as an assistant.

AI can generate lists of actors, create personas, and identify experiences to consider. Apply a critical eye: it's a tool, not a decision maker.

You start a mapping project as you would any other effort: by determining the goals, scope, costs, and time frame, and making them explicit. This exercise need not be lengthy or time-consuming—it may take only a single meeting—but getting off on the right foot increases your chances of success.

The aim of this phase is to make mapping relevant to the business and key stakeholders. This chapter offers a systematic approach to initiating a mapping effort, taking common pitfalls into account. It includes a range of considerations and collaborative methods to guide your process, including stakeholder mapping, value chain mapping, stakeholder interviews, and customer journey canvases. Use what fits your situation.

Start a New Project

Before embarking on a mapping project, you'll need to first determine the appropriate level of formality, then convince the decision makers to get started. Aligning with them on the intent up front ensures a positive impact.

Determine the Level of Formality

Most teams can benefit from mapping, whether the result is a hand-drawn sketch or a set of detailed, polished diagrams. Match the formality of the effort to your context before beginning to create your map.

This book describes a formal approach to mapping. External consultants working with large organizations often need this rigor. But a full-blown process may be inappropriate—startups, for instance, benefit from informal approaches.

The formality of a mapping effort can be visualized along three dimensions, as shown in **Figure 5-1**. The horizontal axis ranges from producing a single product to providing service ecosystems. The vertical axis indicates movement from the design of a single touchpoint to the design of holistic experiences. The third dimension—shown by the ovals in the middle of the graph—reflects an increase in group size.

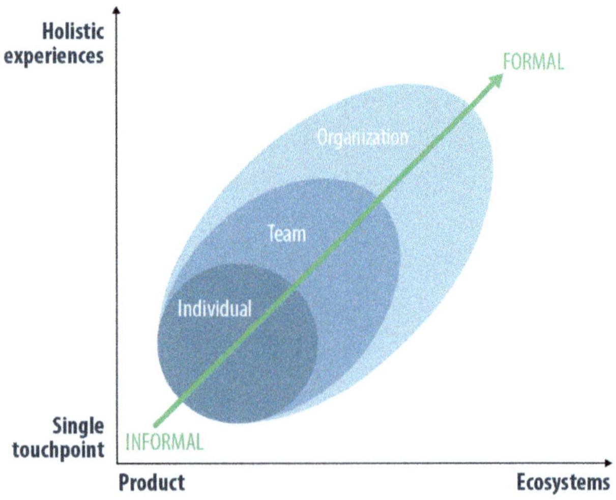

Figure 5-1. The need for models increases when entire organizations design experiences for ecosystems.

Efforts tend to become more formal as you move up and to the right in this chart. For instance, a designer working alone on a single product may not need a formal diagram, but a large team dealing with an entire service ecosystem likely would. Where your project falls on this chart determines how much effort you put into each phase outlined in this book. Do only as much work as needed.

Convince Decision Makers

Once you determine the required level of formality, you'll need to convince decision makers to support the effort. Despite the popularity of mapping, some stakeholders still don't see the benefits. If they haven't yet experienced the potential power of mapping activities, they may need some convincing. Whether you're internal or external to the organization, the arguments are similar. You'll need evidence, a champion, and ideally a pilot to demonstrate value.

Know the objections

Be ready with persuasive arguments. **Table 5-1** lists typical objections, underlying assumptions, and counterpoints. Create a similar table based on your specific situation to work through the argumentation.

Provide evidence

Know the benefits from Chapter 1, but also provide concrete evidence specific to your situation. Find examples and case studies in the literature. Forrester, for one, publishes full reports on journey mapping ROI; see the materials in the "customer experience" category on its website. Look for competitors' work by searching for their names with keywords like "customer journey map"

TABLE 5-1. Typical objections that may be raised before you get started, the assumptions behind them, and arguments you can make against them

Objection	Assumption	Argument
We don't have time or budget.	Creating diagrams takes too long and is expensive.	Mapping needn't be expensive or time-consuming. Even a formal project can be done in a matter of weeks.
Each department has its own process map.	Functional silos work efficiently individually.	Fine. But do they show interaction across channels and touchpoints? Great customer experiences cross our department lines.
We already know all of this.	Implicit knowledge is enough.	Great—then we're off to a good start. But by making that knowledge explicit, we can keep the conversations going. A map helps retain knowledge when someone leaves and orients new people.
I was in that target group. Just ask me what's valuable.	Customers are viewed from an inside-out rather than outside-in perspective.	Your input is invaluable. We want to supplement that with a grounded external perspective as well. That's where the best insights for growth and innovation are found: what we don't already know.
Marketing already does research.	Marketing and experience research are the same.	That's a good thing, but only part of the story. We need to uncover unmet needs and unexpressed feelings and show them in the context of the overall experience.

or "experience map." Showing that others are doing this goes a long way.

The most compelling evidence comes from internal success stories. If possible, point to past efforts that have proven valuable, or find others in the organization who have had success. If you can't find any examples in-house, frame your current effort as something you can showcase later.

Find a champion

Identify stakeholders who can champion your mapping effort. The more influential, the better. External consultants should look for clients with longer relationships. Internal employees should understand their organization's decision-making dynamics. A quick stakeholder analysis helps in both cases.

Run a pilot effort

If possible, run a small pilot project. Diagrams need not be complex or detailed to be effective. Again, an internal example can be more powerful than an external report or study.

Alternatively, try creating a diagram as part of another effort. For instance, if you are running a traditional usability test, add simple follow-up questions to elicit the steps in a given process. Map these together in a draft version of an experience map, and use that as a discussion point. Demonstrating value with firsthand results is often the most persuasive argument.

Create a pitch

Finally, create a succinct statement that you can easily repeat. Include the business problems you'll address. Why should a decision maker invest in a mapping effort of any kind? Here's an example pitch:

> **You'd like to grow beyond your current offerings. By mapping the entire experience, we'll quickly gain a better understanding of the needs and emotions of new markets and segments.**
>
> **Companies like Intel and Microsoft use this approach to align customer experience with business processes, creating and capturing**

value across channels while identifying opportunities that outperform competitors.

With relatively little investment, mapping provides the strategic insight we need in today's fast-changing marketplaces.

Decide on a Direction

Once you've secured buy-in, you'll need to decide on the direction of your mapping effort. The two key areas to consider are the organization's goals and which experiences to map. These inform your choice of diagram type.

Identify the Organization's Strategy and Objectives

Alignment diagrams must be relevant to the organization. They need to answer open questions or fill current gaps in knowledge. Diagrams are most effective when congruent with the organization's strategy and objectives.

Here are some questions to explore in this step:

- What is the mission of the organization?
- How does the organization create, deliver, and capture value?
- How does the organization want to grow?
- What are the strategic goals?
- What markets and segments are served?
- What knowledge gaps exist?

In many cases, the answers will come from sources inside the organization. Plan time to conduct interviews with key people to dig deeper. See "Internal Stakeholder Interviews" on page 106 for more details.

Determine Which Experiences to Map

Most organizations have relationships with multiple parties: suppliers, distributors, partners, customers, and customers' customers. To determine what experiences to map, first understand the *customer value chain*: a depiction of key actors and the flow of value to individuals.

Figure 5-2 shows a simple customer value chain for a news magazine. In this diagram, journalists provide content to the publisher, who makes money from advertisers. Stores distribute the publisher's magazine to readers, who form the audience for the advertisers. Overall, value flows from left to right in this diagram, from journalists to readers.

Figure 5-2 also indicates possible diagram types for different relationships. A *service blueprint* could map

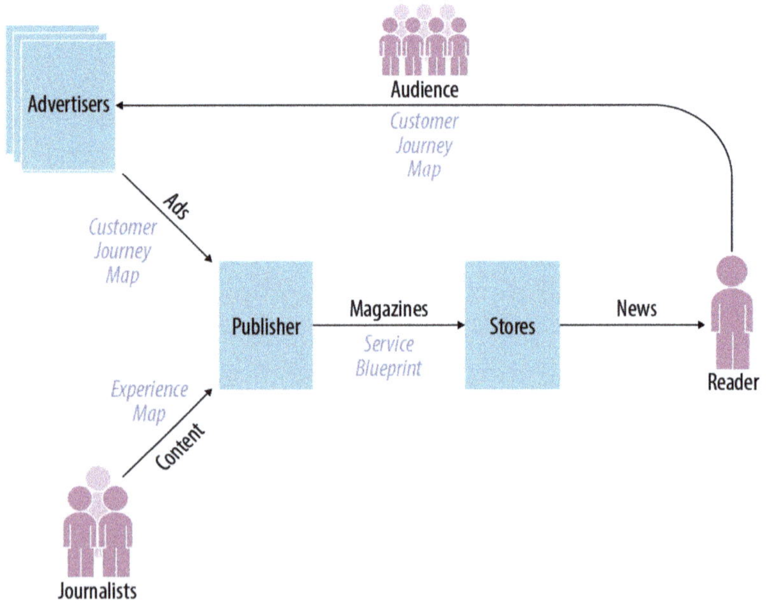

Figure 5-2. This example customer value chain for a news magazine shows the flow of value to end consumers.

publisher-to-store processes. A *customer journey map* could show the reader/advertiser experience. An *experience map* could reveal how journalists relate to the magazine's content.

Once completed, use the customer value chain to examine which relationships to map. Each relationship in this image differs—advertisers to publishers, publishers to stores, journalists to advertisers, readers to stores.

A customer value chain helps set expectations. It clarifies which experiences to map and which to exclude. See "Value Chain Mapping" on page 105 for more.

Select the Diagram Type

The diagrams discussed in this book have something in common: they all focus on value alignment. But they have significant differences as well. Understanding these differences allows you to choose the approach that makes the most sense for your situation. Know your options, and don't rule out any one technique in favor of another in advance.

Once you understand the organization's objectives and the experiences you want to map, you can select the type of diagram that's most appropriate. Refer to the detailed review in Chapter 4 to make your choice.

Showing the Value of Journey Mapping

Business stakeholders need metrics. Here's how to make the case for journey mapping with external sources and internal ROI calculations.

When building your business case, pull from recent reports by industry analysts. Forrester and Gartner are two of the most influential voices with extensive coverage of customer experience topics. Also seek out reports from leading consultancies such as McKinsey, PwC, and Bain & Company.

Search for "customer experience ROI" or "journey mapping business case" to find current data. Industry trade associations and competitors' annual reports also provide useful benchmarks.

Calculate Your Own ROI

External reports help, but nothing beats an internal case built on your own data. Stories, testimonials, and customer quotes bring the numbers to life, but most businesses want quantitative metrics to show ROI.

Table 5-2 outlines the thought process for making a compelling case. The examples in the "What to Track" column are indicative of the types of metrics you can target. Identify the metrics that make the most sense for your effort and your organization, and track them before and after implementing journey mapping initiatives.

Building Your Business Case

Overall, the process for building business metrics and finding your specific ROI follows these steps:

1. Baseline current metrics. Measure CES (customer effort score), NPS, churn, and CLV (customer lifetime value) before mapping.
2. Identify pain points. Use mapping to pinpoint highest-impact improvement areas.
3. Implement changes. Fix two or three critical friction points revealed by the map.
4. Measure improvement. Track the same metrics three to six months post-implementation.
5. Calculate ROI: (Value of Improvements – Cost of Mapping) ÷ Cost of Mapping × 100.

For example, a company spends $50,000 on journey mapping, identifies and fixes critical onboarding friction, and reduces churn by 3%. This retains $400,000 in annual revenue. ROI = 700%.

The aim is to connect journey improvements to metrics your executives already track: revenue, retention, and customer acquisition efficiency.

Table 5-2. Metrics to show ROI of customer experience

Metric	What it measures	How to measure	What to track
Customer Effort Score (CES)	How easy it is for customers to complete tasks	Survey: "How easy was it to [complete task]?" (1–7 scale)	Reduction effort score after fixing friction points, in points
Customer Satisfaction (CSAT)	Satisfaction with a specific interaction or touchpoint	Survey: "How satisfied were you with [experience]?" (1–5 scale)	Improvement in scores for specific touchpoints identified in the map
Net Promoter Score (NPS)	Likelihood customers will recommend your organization	% promoters (9–10) – % detractors (0–6)	Improvement in NPS score
Conversion rate	Percentage of prospects who become customers at key journey stages	(Conversions ÷ total visitors) × 100	Improvements at signup, purchase, or onboarding completion
Customer Lifetime Value (CLV)	Total revenue expected from a customer over the entire relationship	Average purchase value × purchase frequency × customer lifespan	Percentage increase in CLV after improving journey touchpoints
Customer Acquisition Cost (CAC) payback	How quickly you recover the cost of acquiring a customer	CAC ÷ (monthly recurring revenue × gross margin %)	Reduction in payback period as improved experiences drive faster adoption
Churn rate	Percentage of customers who stop doing business with you	(Customers lost ÷ customers at start) × 100	Reduction in churn as a percentage
Customer Health Score (CHS)	Composite score predicting customer retention and growth	Weighted combination of usage, engagement, satisfaction, and support metrics	Increase in average health score; reduction in at-risk customers
First Contact Resolution (FCR)	Percentage of customer issues resolved on first contact	(Issues resolved on first contact ÷ total issues) × 100	Reduction in FCR for savings in support costs and increase in satisfaction

Define the Effort

When the overall direction of the effort is outlined, assess the amount of time needed and approximate costs. In this step, you'll also want to ensure that you have the appropriate skills, equipment, and resources.

Estimate Duration

The time frame for mapping efforts varies greatly. It depends on the formality of the project, the type of map you're targeting, and the depth of information it contains. Small startups can create a map in hours; more formal projects might take several weeks.

Time estimates depend on the extent of your investigation and how many revision cycles and stakeholder meetings are needed.

Assess Resources

The primary resource needed for a mapping effort is staff time: someone to do the investigation, create a diagram, and facilitate workshops.

These skills are needed to complete a diagram:

- Organizing information and abstract concepts
- Collecting data and conducting primary research
- Modeling and visualizing complex information

Other project requirements include the following:

Access to internal employees

Multidisciplinary teams are ideal. Diagrams are not a give-and-go deliverable—they require active participation from people within the organization throughout the process.

Ability to recruit customers

You'll need to recruit external participants for research activities (outlined in Chapter 6).

Ability to travel

Depending on your industry and target groups, some travel may be necessary for research. Remote research is a viable option that can reduce this cost.

Transcription tools

Automatic voice-to-text transcriptions are sufficient for most mapping efforts. Teleconferencing software like Zoom provides high-quality transcriptions minutes after recording. AI services like Otter.ai and Firefly.ai do even better.

Write a Proposal

Informal efforts may not require a proposal at all. Formal projects will likely need a written statement of intent.

Keep it light. A proposal need not be time-consuming or extensive. These are key areas to cover:

Motivation

Include the reason you're embarking on the project with the organization at this time.

Aim

State the intent of the effort and the overall timeline.

Goals

List the objectives and measurable outcomes of the project.

Project participants

List everyone involved and their roles. Mention that you will need access to internal stakeholders and their involvement throughout.

Activities, deliverables, and milestones

Describe the sequence of activities and the expected outputs.

Scope

Indicate the experiences you're intending to map. You can determine these from the customer value chain, like the one shown in **Figure 5-2**.

Diagram type

Indicate your target diagram type, if known.

Assumptions, risks, and constraints

Highlight aspects of the project that may be out of your control, as well as the factors that may constrain the effort.

In total, a proposal doesn't have to be more than two pages; see the example in **Figure 5-3**.

Proposal: Acme Customer Experience Project

The Acme Corp. has successfully extended its product and service offerings over the past decade, capturing a significant market share in the process. However, the experience customers actually have with Acme has grown organically and become disjointed, resulting in declining customer satisfaction. This effort intends to align internal activities to the customer journey in order to design a more cohesive experience across touchpoints and ultimately increase customer satisfaction and loyalty.

AIM

Complete a customer journey mapping project by the end of Q1

GOALS

1. Involve stakeholders from at least 5 different departments throughout the project, from the creation of the maps to running experiments afterwards.
2. Generate and prioritze at least 100 new ideas to increase customer satisfaction.
3. Develop action plans and experiments to test 5 new services that demonstrate an increase in customer satisfaction.
4. Increase customer satisfaction scores by 5% by the end of the year.

PARTICIPANTS

- Core Project Team
  - Jim Kalbach, Project Lead
  - Paul Kahn, Designer
  - Jane Doe, User Researcher
  - John Doe, Project Sponsor
- Stakeholders
  - Sue Smith, Head of Product Development (+product developers)
  - Joe Smith, Customer Support (+customer support agents)
  - Frank Musterman, Marketing Lead (+marketers)
  - Sales and ecommerce representatives, TBD

ACTIVITIES

- Investigate: Recruit and research, internal and external participants
- Illustrate: Create customer journey map
- Align: Hold workshop and generate hypotheses
- Experiment: Run experiments to test hypotheses

DELIVERABLES

- Customer Journey Maps
- Accompanying documents, such as personas and typical day illustrations
- Catalog of prioritized ideas
- Detailed plan for experiments, included measurements of success

SCOPE

- This effort will focus on two customer personas:
  1. Our current paying customers
  2. Their customers (i.e., customers of our customers)
- The experiences should look at touchpoints from end-to-end, starting with the first contact customers have until when they decide to end the service.
- 5 hypothesis experiments with the given resources (to be confirmed depending on the nature and scope of the experiments)

MILESTONES

- Jan: Recruiting and research
- Feb: Complete journey maps and run workshops
- March: Conduct experiments to increase customer satisfaction

Figure 5-3. A proposal for a mapping project does not have to be long.

Summary

Start by framing the effort and assessing the required level of formality. Larger organizations designing holistic experiences across touchpoints need more formal efforts than individuals designing single product interfaces.

Even though stakeholders increasingly request maps by name, you may still need to overcome barriers to get started. Know the objections and be prepared with evidence to make convincing counterarguments. Identify a champion and run a pilot project. Demonstrating firsthand results goes a long way toward winning over skeptics.

The concept of alignment diagrams opens up possibilities: there is more than one way to understand experiences. Consider the organization and its goals to shape the effort for maximum impact. The key is keeping the mapping effort relevant to business needs.

Examine various relationships in the customer value chain to narrow down possibilities and set expectations. Select the most appropriate diagram type for your situation.

Use AI to speed up your work. Transcription tools help capture interviews. AI can also help map out stakeholders and develop personas or customer types.

For formal efforts, define the project in a written proposal. Work with stakeholders to refine the details and establish a well-defined plan. Informal efforts may not require a proposal at all.

Further Reading

Andrew Schall, The Persona and Journey Map Playbook *(2024)*

This step-by-step playbook provides a clear approach to creating personas and journey maps through the concept of altitudes, guiding designers in capturing user experiences at the perfect level of detail. Drawing on over 20 years of UX leadership experience at organizations like the Mayo Clinic, Citibank, and Southwest Airlines, Schall offers templates and real-world examples to create artifacts free from irrelevant attributes.

Peter Jones and Kristel Van Ael, Design Journeys Through Complex Systems *(2022)*

Focused on the design of complex systems, this book offers a concrete seven-stage process for journey creation while emphasizing the importance of problem framing, cocreation, and facilitation throughout. It includes many ready-to-use techniques and templates, available for download from *systemicdesigntoolkit.org*.

John Pruitt and Tamara Adlin, The Persona Lifecycle (2006) and The Essential Persona Lifecycle *(2010)*

This pair of books continues to serve as the standard reference on personas. At over 700 pages long, the earlier volume provides a detailed overview of persona theory and application. The second book is more practical and hands-on, showing how to create personas step-by-step.

Stakeholder Mapping

Objective	Visualize the actors and their relationships in a given network or ecosystem
Time	20–30 minutes
Participants	3–20
Materials	Whiteboard, sticky notes

For any offering or solution, there's typically a range of people whose experiences you could map. To help clarify your playing field, create a stakeholder map with potential targets and prioritize them (FIGURE 5-4). Visualizing the ecosystem of actors in a given field helps align the team on where to focus attention—and where not to.

How it works:

1. Name the area of interest you're operating in. This often corresponds to your industry, like "real estate," "education," or "healthcare."
2. Generate a list of stakeholders by role or function. Avoid naming individual people and stick to actor types. Use AI tools to complement the team's list.
3. Arrange the stakeholders to show the relationships between them.
4. Label the connecting arrows and add other details for more clarity.
5. Discuss the relationships and prioritize the roles to focus on.

Example:

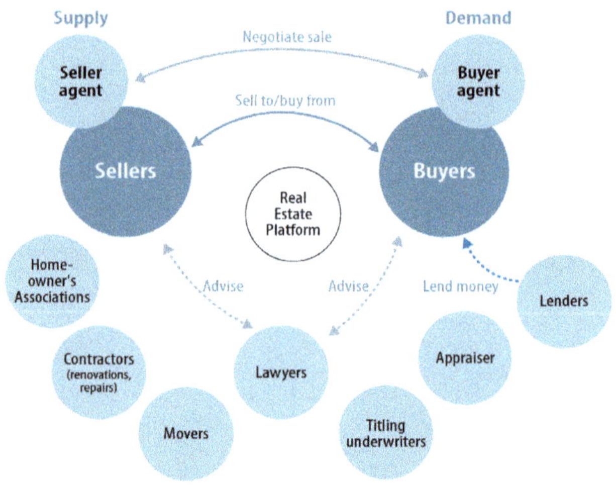

FIGURE 5-4. This is an example stakeholder map for "buying and selling a new home."

Learn more:

LUMA Institute, "Stakeholder Mapping"

Rikke Friis Dam and Teo Yu Siang, "Stakeholder Mapping: The Complete Guide to Stakeholder Maps" (2022)

Value Chain Mapping

Objective	Illustrate the flow of value from provider to consumer in a basic diagram
Time	30–60 minutes
Participants	3–20
Materials	Whiteboard, sticky notes

A variation on stakeholder mapping, value chain mapping focuses on the flow of value from providers to consumers (**Figure 5-5**). This is particularly helpful in B2B settings, where there may be many different types and levels of stakeholders to consider (e.g., from buyer to installer or admin to end user).

How it works:

1. Place the provider on the left (often your organization or offering).
2. Show suppliers and inputs to the provider.
3. List all the downstream customers and types of customers.
4. Use the diagram to facilitate a conversation around which stakeholders and which experiences matter the most.

Example:

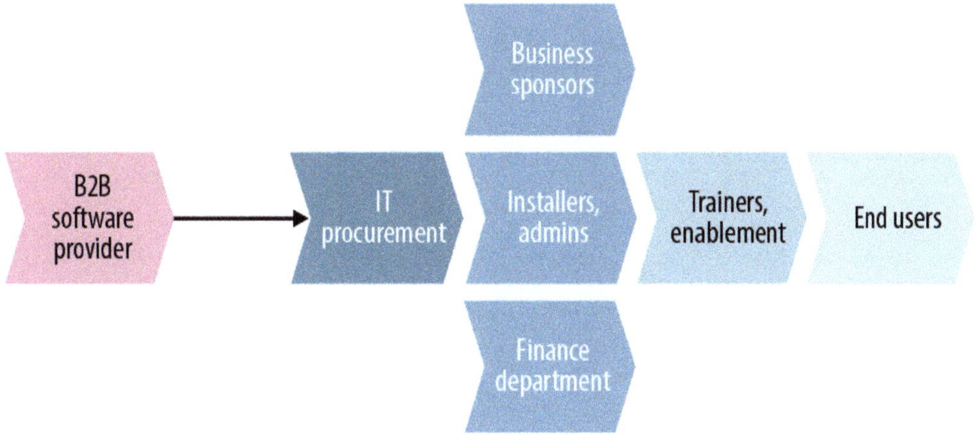

Figure 5-5. This is an example of a simple value chain map for a B2B provider.

Internal Stakeholder Interviews

Objective	Understand and align with different internal stakeholder perspectives before a project begins
Time	15–30 minutes per interview
Participants	1–2 interviewers + 1 stakeholder
Materials	Note-taking, recording

Improving the customer experience obviously requires deep knowledge of the people you serve—but it also requires a thorough understanding of the organization and how it seeks to grow and improve (FIGURE 5-6). To frame a mapping project, conducting a handful of internal stakeholder interviews is recommended. Do these in pairs to make the process more collaborative.

How it works:

1. Identify the best people to speak with. Prioritize them by importance, insights, and ability to recruit others.
2. Schedule short meetings. The interviews can be 30–60 minutes, conducted in person or virtually. Plan for 5–10 interviews, depending on the scope of your project.
3. Use open questioning to guide the conversation. The goal is to explore and learn, not to take a quantitative poll. Cover three key areas: role and function, touchpoints, and experience.
4. Have participants sketch as they talk. Use a blank template of a typical journey structure to guide the conversation and have stakeholders fill in the blanks.
5. Compare themes across interviews, looking for commonalities and differences. Pay special attention to gaps in knowledge about customers to inform your investigation.

Learn more:

Sarah Gibbons, "Stakeholder Interviews 101," *NN/g* (2022)

Dan Brown, "The Delicate Art of Interviewing Stakeholders," *Medium* (2018)

Example:

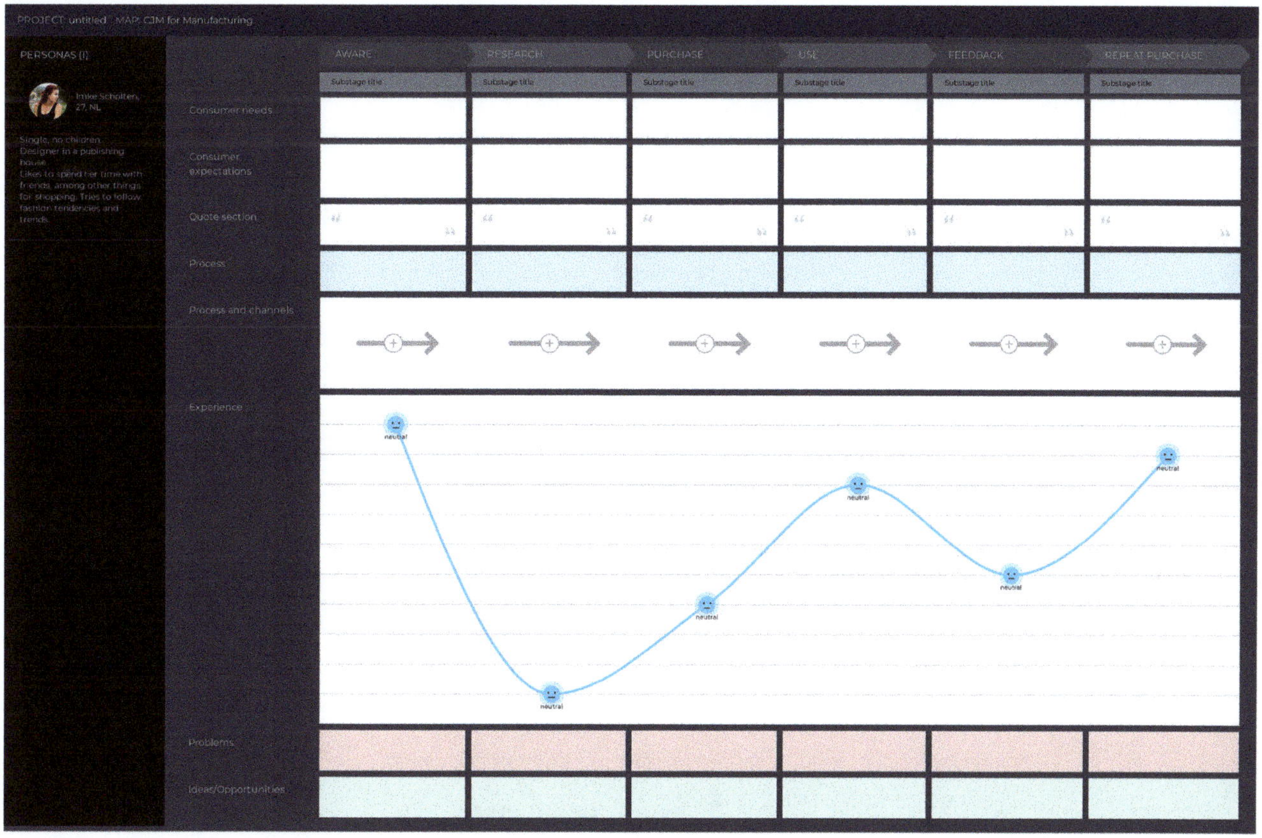

FIGURE 5-6. A simple mapping template can be used to gather existing knowledge about an experience.

Journey Canvas

Objective	Explore various aspects of a customer journey as a team to make assumptions about strengths and weaknesses
Time	1–2 hours
Participants	3–12
Materials	Journey canvas template, whiteboard, sticky notes

The customer journey canvas, created by Marc Stickdorn and Jakob Schneider, allows for team input into the mapping process (**Figure 5-7**). This simple tool visually lays out a customer's experience across various facets of information. In a workshop setting, using this canvas is more about surfacing team assumptions and exploring aspects of the experience than it is about creating a validated artifact.

How it works:

1. After defining the goals and agenda of the session, introduce a persona and a specific experience to focus on.
2. Share any available research or insights.
3. As a team, use sticky notes to list the high-level stages of the customer journey in the center of the canvas.
4. Move around the canvas to complete the other sections with the corresponding information.
5. Note any gaps in knowledge and unknowns to research further, as well as the strengths of your current service and potential customer pain points.

Learn more:

Joana de Quintanilha et al., "The Customer Journey Mapping Canvas," *Forrester* (2025)

Canvanizer, "Create a New Customer Journey Canvas"

Example:

Figure 5-7. A customer journey canvas allows the team to explore various aspects of the customer experience.

Diagram and Image Credits

Figure 5-6: Blank journey map template from UXPressia, used with permission

Figure 5-7: Customer journey canvas by Marc Stickdorn and Jakob Schneider, Creative Commons Share Alike

You can observe a lot just by watching.

—Yogi Berra

IN THIS CHAPTER

- Reviewing existing information
- Interviewing internally
- Creating a draft map
- Contextual inquiry and analysis
- Quantitative research
- Collaborative methods for research

CHAPTER 6

Investigate: Grounding in Reality

Just over two decades ago, Bain & Company uncovered a remarkable gap. Surveying 362 firms, it found that 80% believed they delivered a superior customer experience. Yet only 8% of customers felt that way.* The disconnect made waves.

In my experience, that gap hasn't closed much. Most companies still misunderstand what customers actually experience. Sure, they may have detailed data, comprehensive purchasing statistics, and other voice-of-the-customer (VoC) metrics, but they fail to understand core experiential aspects—emotional states, needs, motivations—at a deeper level.

Peter Drucker recognized this back in the 1950s. He wrote: "The customer rarely buys what the company thinks it sells.... Nobody pays for a 'product.' What is paid for is satisfaction."†

These days, we equate Drucker's "satisfaction" with the customer experience of getting a job done. But that's a messy business. People's behaviors are often irrational; they act on emotions and subjective beliefs. These are harder to understand and quantify and are generally not part of the business vernacular.

As a result, many organizations have a low appetite for understanding the customer experience as a whole. They may be willing to spend tens of thousands on market analysis reports, but getting out, speaking with customers, and observing them directly receives little attention.

Creating diagrams of experiences breaks this pattern of organizational navel-gazing. It shifts the mindset from inside-out to outside-in. It gets at the *why* of customer behavior, favoring understanding over measuring, quality over quantity.

It all begins with investigation. Research is necessary to inform your effort and provide confidence in your model of the experience. It's typically eye-opening—a healthy reality check for everyone involved, even if only incremental.

People use products and services in unintended ways. They find hacks and workarounds. In doing so, they may fabricate their own satisfaction. Mapping is about uncovering the value customers *believe* they are getting.

Of course, these days the use of AI accelerates and enhances the investigation stage of mapping—but it doesn't replace it entirely, for a few reasons. First, you need real-world context to discern whether AI output is valid. Second, AI excels at identifying common patterns but mostly reflects what is already known. Genuine fieldwork remains essential for uncovering the edge cases

* James Allen et al., "Closing the Delivery Gap," Bain & Company (2005)

† Peter Drucker, *The Practice of Management* (1954)

and lived nuances that no model—including AI—can reliably predict.

For instance, on a project I worked on for an educational testing service, my research found educators doing extra calculations by hand on paper. Adding an online mechanism for these calculations was simple, but the need had not been identified until we observed it. With proper investigative research, we were able to uncover opportunities not visible in other data.

The aim of this phase is to make sure your insights are grounded in reality. This chapter covers the main steps of investigation in mapping an experience. Although there is a logical sequence to follow, you may find yourself moving back and forth between these activities fluidly. The process is typically more iterative than linear.

Investigation is collaborative. Three methods anchor this phase: research debrief sessions guide teams in synthesizing findings from customer interviews, proto-personas offer a quick way to collaborate on creating user personas, and the empathy map exercise creates awareness of customers' situations and needs.

Think of your team as detectives during this phase. You'll piece together clues gathered from a range of sources and map them on a timeline to draw conclusions. You'll need to zoom in to see the details and zoom out to see the bigger picture at the same time.

Thin Data Versus Thick Data

When mapping experiences, it's useful to distinguish between thin and thick data. *Thin data* includes analytics, surveys, usage logs, and other quantifiable traces that reveal patterns but rarely explain why they occur. *Thick data*, rooted in ethnographic tradition, captures context and meaning through close observation. As cultural anthropologist Clifford Geertz described in his concept of "thick description," this approach helps us see the intentions and cultural cues beneath surface behavior.*

Tricia Wang revived this distinction for modern organizations, arguing that big data often strips away essential context. As Wang notes in her TEDx Talk: "I see organizations throwing out data all the time because it didn't come from a quant model or it doesn't fit in one.... [T]hick data can help us rescue the context loss that comes from making big data usable."† In this sense, thick data fills in the gaps that quantitative methods and dashboards simply cannot reach.

Generative AI tools and journey management systems can process vast amounts of thin data quickly, even generating early drafts of maps or hypotheses. These tools are valuable for spotting patterns and accelerating synthesis, but they reflect what the system already knows. AI cannot reliably surface the unexpected behaviors, emotional nuances, or environmental details that emerge only through real human interaction.

For organizations seeking customer centricity, thick data is essential. Fieldwork—interviews, shadowing, contextual inquiry—provides the depth needed to interpret experiences accurately. Thin data reveals correlations; thick data uncovers causation. These deep stories are the foundation of meaningful, human-centered experience maps.

* See Clifford Geertz's landmark essay "Thick Description: Toward an Interpretive Theory of Culture" in *The Interpretation of Cultures: Selected Essays* (1973).

† See Tricia Wang's 2016 TEDxCambridge talk "The Human Insights Missing from Big Data," based on her article "Why Big Data Needs Thick Data," *Ethnography Matters* (2013).

Review Existing Sources

As a starting point, take advantage of existing sources of information. These might include the following:

- Direct feedback sources (emails, calls, social, reviews, NPS)
- Formal research (market research, ethnographic studies, usability testing)
- Secondary sources (industry reports)
- Internal sources (stakeholder interviews)

Review insights for patterns. First consolidate findings across sources, then make conclusions based on the group's insights.

Consolidate Findings

You probably won't find a single existing source of information about the end-to-end customer experience. Most industry reports and whitepapers focus only on slices of an overall experience. Even companies with large in-house research teams may have extensive qualitative and quantitative research repositories but still lack a comprehensive view of the end-to-end journey.

Instead, you'll have to sift through the available sources and identify the relevant bits. This is a bottom-up process that takes patience and tolerance for irrelevant information—like a detective. Common generative AI tools, such as ChatGPT, can help sift through existing information and surface elements relevant to your mapping effort. Instruct the AI to identify the facets of information central to the mapping effort, defined when determining the focus of the diagram (see "Focus" on page 42).

To help organize existing data—whether extracted manually or with the help of AI tools—use a common format to review findings across source types. Use a simple progression of three steps to arrange findings:

1. ***Evidence:*** Note relevant facts or observations without judgment. Include direct quotes and data points.
2. ***Interpretations:*** Explain potential causes: why did people behave or feel this way? Consider multiple interpretations.
3. ***Implications:*** Determine the impact on the customer experience, including emotional factors motivating behavior.

Consolidate the insights from each source into a single table. This will help you sort through various information types and normalize findings for comparison across sources. **Table 6-1** shows an example consolidating insights from two different source types for a fictitious software service.

These days, VoC platforms have market listening capabilities built in, allowing existing insights to be queried at any time or on an ongoing basis. Medallia Experience and Qualtrics XM Discover are two of the leading solutions at the time of writing, geared toward large enterprises. Many others exist with varying capabilities. Most rely on AI to synthesize large amounts of data ingested from various sources and identify patterns that can inform mapping efforts.

You can also use general-purpose AI tools like ChatGPT. Enter a batch of NPS comments and prompt the tool to categorize insights. Supply existing categories if you have them, or ask it to uncover themes from the data. Remember that AI may not fully grasp context or nuance. Treat its output as a tool to assist human analysis, not replace it.

Table 6-1. Consolidating evidence from two existing sources of information for a fictitious software service

Source 1: Email feedback

Evidence	Interpretations	Experience implications
Many emails indicate trouble with installation: e.g., "After going through the instructions and process several times, I gave up."	People lack the skills and knowledge to complete the installation process and get frustrated. People don't have the time or patience to read the instructions carefully.	Installation is a problematic phase in the journey.
There were frequent questions about having admin rights to install the software: e.g., "I got the message 'Please contact your IT admin' and didn't know what to do."	For security reasons, many companies don't allow employees to install software. It may be difficult or time-consuming for employees to contact an IT admin.	For users without admin rights, installation ends their experience: it's a showstopper.
Some emails praised customer support: e.g., "The customer service agent I spoke with was really knowledgeable and helpful!"	People like to be able to speak with a "real" person. People feel like they are getting personal attention with live agents.	Customer support is a positive aspect of the current experience.

Source 2: Marketing survey

Evidence	Interpretations	Experience implications
Respondents indicated that the top ways of becoming aware of the magazine are as follows: • Social media (62%) • Web searches (48%) • Word of mouth (19%) • Ads (7%)	Customers seek input from others in their decision to purchase our software. Advertisements may not be as effective as previously assumed.	Social media plays the largest role in becoming aware of our service.
64% of customers indicated they regularly switch between a computer and mobile device while using our service.	People have a need to use the software on the go.	Customers experience our software across devices.
A majority of customers indicated installation was difficult or very difficult.	Installation is not straightforward for most users. Instructions for installation are not easy to follow.	Installation is a source of frustration.

Make Conclusions

Next, collect all the experience implications in a separate list and group them by topic. Here's what that would look like for the example data in **Table 6-1**:

- Installation is a problematic phase in the journey.
- For users without admin rights, installation ends their experience: it's a showstopper.
- Customer support is a positive aspect of the overall experience.
- Word of mouth plays the greatest role in becoming aware of our service.
- Customers experience our software across devices.
- Installation is a source of frustration.

The patterns that emerge will help bring your investigation into greater focus. Some of your findings from this exercise will be straightforward and not need much validation. Other points you uncover may reveal gaps in knowledge. For example, from this list, it's apparent that frustration during installation is emerging as a theme. But you may not know *why* this is the case and need to further research the causes of this frustration.

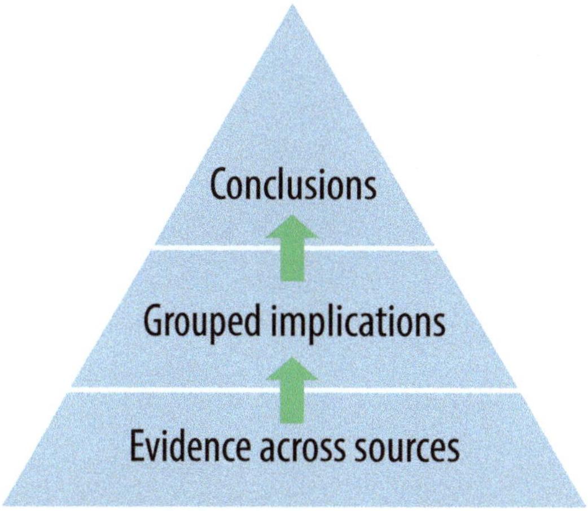

Figure 6-1. Comb existing sources for evidence, group the implications for the customer experience, and make conclusions.

Overall, the process is grounded in evidence, moving from individual facts to broader conclusions (**Figure 6-1**). Breaking down findings in a common format enables you to compare themes across different sources.

Mapping is all about finding real-world patterns and arranging them visually. This step need not take long. Depending on the number of sources to review, completion may take only a day (or less). Try distributing the review of sources across several members to work even quicker. Then come together and discuss the key findings in a brief meeting.

Reviewing existing sources of information not only informs the creation of a diagram but also sets up your research agenda for the following steps in this investigation phase. You'll have a better sense about what to ask in your next stages of research, starting with internal stakeholders.

Create a Draft Model

At this point, you should be able to draft an initial diagram to serve as a preliminary model of the experience. Consider it a "hypothesis map" to be validated with further research. See "Hypothesis Map Workshop" on page 160 to make it a team activity.

Generative AI tools can help define the primary structure of a draft model. Try a prompt like this:

> **I work in the field of [your field] and would like to create a service blueprint for interacting with the service department for [your product or offering]. Generate a chronological list of the steps involved, the frontstage actions the customers take, key questions the customers have at each stage, and the backstage actions the provider takes. Show the output in simple plain text I can copy and paste into a digital whiteboard.**

Creating an early draft diagram will guide your investigation by identifying gaps in knowledge and other research questions.

Create Personas

Personas are narrative descriptions of user archetypes that reflect common patterns of behavior, needs, and emotions (**Figure 6-2**). They make target groups easier to understand and relate to.

Personas based only on demographics fall short. Instead, focus on customers' jobs to be done and pain points. What are their goals and objectives? What questions do they have? How do they feel? Centering personas on these aspects makes them more useful and less controversial.

Personas keep users front of mind. Keep them short—a page or two at most.

AI helps create personas quickly. Unlike traditional personas based on static assumptions, AI-generated personas can draw on large volumes of real-world behavioral and qualitative data, reducing bias and providing a more realistic picture of customers. What once took weeks can now be done in minutes. Of course, AI can hallucinate and produce inaccurate results. Be aware of the limitations of AI-generated personas, and plan to validate them through real-world research.

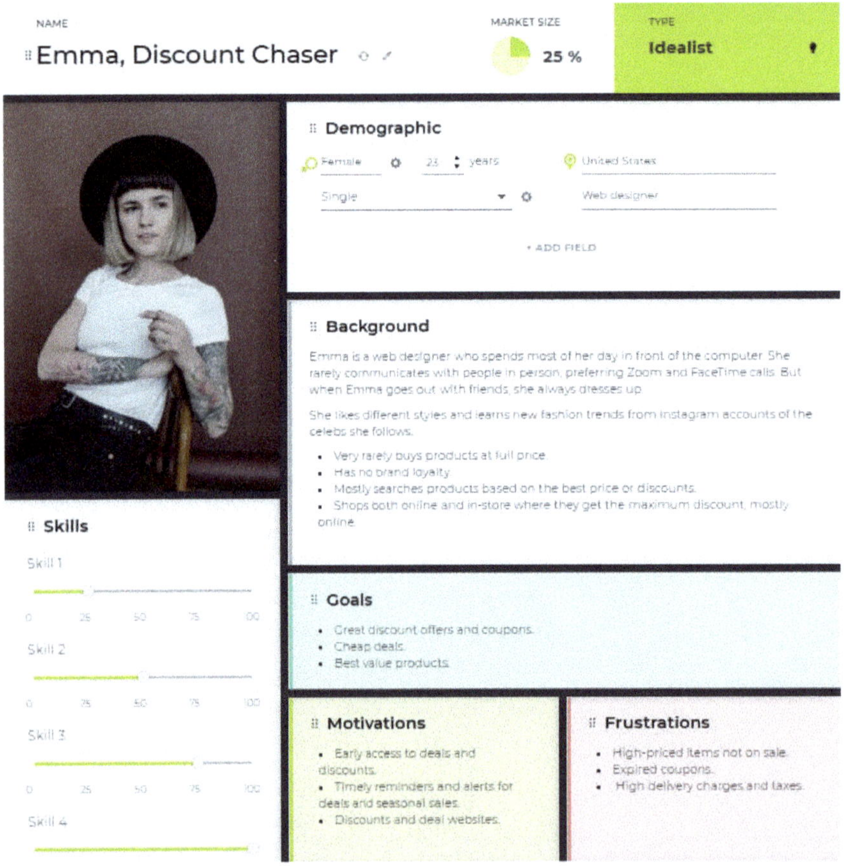

Figure 6-2. A persona shows various facets of information in a single overview.

Personas are often paired with maps of an experience. **Figure 6-3** shows a customer journey map created by Jim Tincher, founder of Heart of the Customer, with the persona integrated at the top.

Creating personas is not creative writing; it should be evidence-based. However, there are also quick ways to make the process collaborative. *Proto-personas* (also called hypothesis personas, lean personas, or assumption personas) allow teams to reflect on what they already know about customers. Empathy maps provide a team exercise for exploring different aspects of the people you serve. You'll find descriptions of both in "Proto-Personas" on page 130 and "Empathy Map" on page 132.

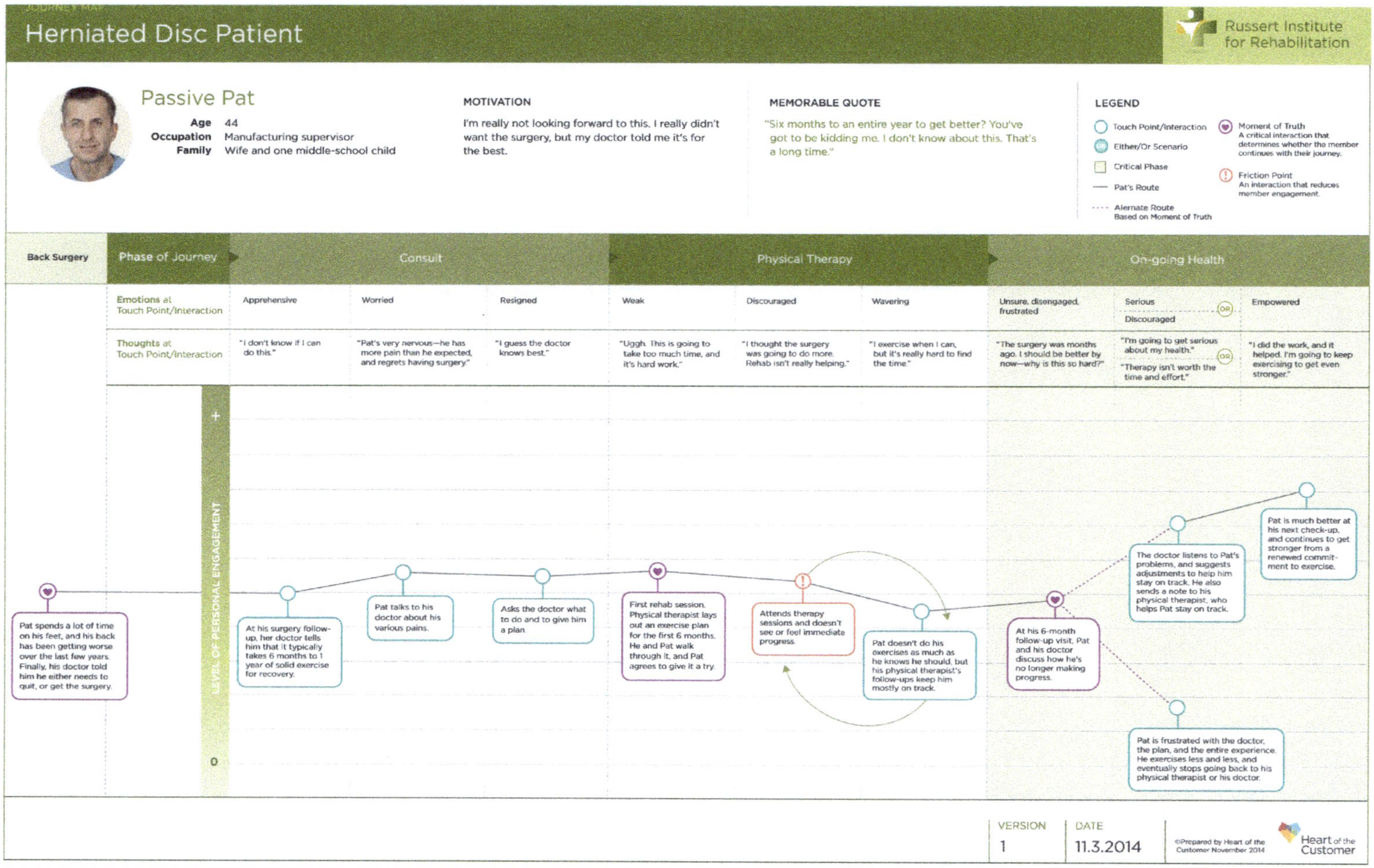

Figure 6-3. Diagrams often include a persona at the top, as seen in this example of a customer journey map.

Compile a Touchpoint Inventory

After you have an initial framework for your diagram, take inventory of current touchpoints. In this case, I'm using the word *touchpoint* to indicate the ways customers can interact with you. This usually centers on channels, devices, and points of service.

One way to create a touchpoint inventory is through a simulated walkthrough. Step through the actual customer experience yourself: sign up, purchase, use the product, and contact support. Capture screenshots of digital interactions, photograph physical artifacts such as packaging and mail, and document person-to-person interactions. This firsthand experience—sometimes called *mystery shopping*—reveals gaps and inconsistencies that are often invisible in internal documentation.

Beyond a simple list, visualize touchpoints to show which appear in each channel. **Figure 6-4** shows an example touchpoint inventory from author and service design expert Chris Risdon. This was a precursor to the more detailed Rail Europe map shown in Chapter 12. Each touchpoint is described with text, but you can also include screenshots or photos for higher fidelity.

The draft diagram and touchpoint inventory will help you understand the domain within which you are working. This will guide future research. Keep in mind that mere inspection of existing touchpoints will not provide a complete picture of the customer experience. For that, you need to do research with actual customers.

Conduct Research Externally

Research for alignment diagrams typically focuses on qualitative interviews and observations. The draft diagram you cocreated with the team helps identify assumptions and open questions about the individual's experience. Structure your research to fill in the gaps in your knowledge.

Rely on expert researchers to conduct interviews if you're new to the technique. It takes skill to be able to drive a conversation and get the data you need. Find practitioners within your company or through external agencies to help you get the necessary qualitative insights.

Conducting interviews and observations on location is the gold standard for this type of research. Face-to-face interaction allows you to see participants' environments firsthand. Remote interviews by phone or via teleconferencing software is a viable option that also yields quality insights.

This section outlines a formal approach for field research, with onsite interviews and observations. Remote interviews follow a similar pattern but involve less direct observation.

AI-Driven Research Inputs

Before or alongside field research, AI tools help you develop early hypotheses about the customer experience.

Synthetic interviews let you use large language models to "interview" simulated user types. You'll get directional signals about motivations, pain points, and expectations—typically enough to shape your research questions. AI-generated personas work similarly, pulling from

Rail Europe Touchpoints by Channel

Channels / Stage	Research & Planning	Shopping	Booking	Pre-Travel (Documents)	Travel	Post-Travel
Website	Maps Test intineraries Timetables Destination Pages FAQ General product & site exploration	Schedule look-up Price look-up Multi-city look-up Pass comparison	Web booking funnel - Pass - Trips - Multiple Trips	Select document option (from available options) - station e-ticket - home print e-ticket - mail ticket	Contact page for email or phone	
Call Center	Order brochure Planning (Products) Schedules General questions	Site navigation help	Automated booking payment Cust. Rep booking Site navigation help	Call re: ticket options Request ticket mailed Reslove problems (info, pay-ment, etc.)	Call with questions regarding tickets General calls re: schedules, strikes, documents	
Mobile	Trip ideas	Schedules	Mobile trip booking		Access itinerary Look up schedules Buy additional tickets	
Communication Channels (social media, email, chat)	Chat for web nav help	FB Comparator Email questions Chat for website nav help	Chat for booking support	Email confirmations Email for general help Hold ticket	Ask questions or resolve prob-lems re: schedules and tickets	Complaints or compliments Survey
Customer Relations						Request for refund, escelation from call center.
Non-REI Channels	Trip Advisor Travel blogs Social Media General Google searching	Airline comparison Kayak Direct rail sites	Expedia		Travel Blogs Direct rail sites Google searches	Trip Advisor Review sites Facebook

Non-linear, no time restrictions · *Linear process* · *Non-linear, but time based*

FIGURE 6-4. Take inventory of existing touchpoints to understand the current experience.

behavioral data, support logs, or analytics to create representations of user segments.

Think of these as scaffolding. They give you a draft view of the experience that real interviews will confirm, contradict, or enrich. You can run synthetic interviews at scale to compare how different user types might behave, spotting potential patterns before you talk to anyone.

These techniques can strengthen in-person research, but they don't replace it. Use them to start with clearer hypotheses. Your final map must ultimately be grounded in input from real people.

Field Research

One of the best techniques for investigation is contextual inquiry, a qualitative method formalized by Hugh Beyer and Karen Holtzblatt in their book *Contextual Design*. This involves visiting participants on location, in the context of their experiences.

While AI can accelerate analysis and identify patterns, it doesn't eliminate the need for direct customer interaction. Real-world fieldwork reveals hidden unmet needs and validates AI-generated hypotheses. Even with AI support, plan on conducting four to six interviews per customer segment.

Full-blown contextual inquiry can be time-consuming and isn't always appropriate. However, understanding its principles is valuable for effective field research for mapping efforts.

On-site interviews and observations typically last one to two hours. Longer sessions are possible but are typically not needed. To gather feedback more rapidly, send several teams into the field simultaneously, then debrief together at the end of the day.

Field research can be broken into four steps: preparing, conducting the interview, debriefing, and analyzing the data. Each is outlined next. Refer to the resources at the end of the chapter for more in-depth discussions on research techniques.

Prepare and recruit

Interviewing participants on location adds complexity to preparation. Pay attention to these key areas:

Recruiting criteria
: Determine who you need based on the information gathered during the initiation phase (see Chapter 5) and project framing. Use a screener to confirm that participants match your target profile.

Participant briefing
: Set expectations clearly. Confirm that you can interview the participants on-site with minimal interruptions and that audio recording is acceptable.

Incentives
: On-location participation typically requires greater incentives than surveys or remote interviews.

Scheduling
: Allow enough travel time between interviews. You'll typically manage only two to three on-site interviews per day.

Equipment and materials
: Prepare thoroughly. Bring your discussion guide, recording equipment (a mobile phone works well for basic audio), notepad, camera, business cards, and incentives. See "Interviewing Tips" on page 121 and the resources at the end of this chapter for additional guidance.

Don't underestimate recruiting time. Consider using a specialized recruiting agency to reduce the burden.

Conduct the interview

Since you'll be on location, don't overwhelm participants with observers. Research in pairs—no more than two people at a time. More researchers create an unnatural atmosphere that affects participant behavior and insights.

Determine clear roles for each researcher. One is the primary interviewer; the other observes and takes notes. Maintain these roles, allowing the lead researcher to build rapport and steer the conversation. The observer may ask questions at the end or when invited.

An interview has four parts:

1. ***Greet the participant.*** Explain who you are and set the stage for the interview. Keep this brief. Confirm it's OK to record before starting the audio. Have the participant introduce themselves and describe their background as it relates to the study.
2. ***Lead the conversation.*** Use a discussion guide for open questioning with naïve curiosity. Assume a master–apprentice relationship: the interviewee is the master, and you're the apprentice learning from them. Don't instruct or correct them, even if their behaviors seem inefficient.

   Learn what they actually do, not what they think the "correct" way might be. Make the interview about their experiences, not your organization. Focus on understanding the current experience and avoid projecting future solutions.

   When asking broad questions, you may get "it depends" responses. Ask about the most common or typical situation to get concrete details. A particularly useful approach is the *critical incident* technique:

   a. ***Recall a critical incident:*** Have the participant remember an event that went particularly badly.

Interviewing Tips

- ***Create a rapport.*** Establish a bond with the participant and try to gain their confidence.
- ***Avoid yes-or-no questions.*** Strive to ask open-ended questions that keep the participant talking.
- ***Follow the conversation.*** Use eye contact and affirmative gestures, such as nodding and feedback, to show you're actively listening. Agree with them when appropriate (e.g., "Yes, I can see how that could be frustrating for you").
- ***Listen.*** Let the participant do most of the speaking. Do not lead participants or put words in their mouths. Follow their line of thought and use their language.
- ***Dig deep.*** Try to understand participants' underlying beliefs and values. They may not offer this information immediately. Probe further with simple follow-ups like "Why do you think that is?" and "How do you feel about that?" A pregnant pause or repeating their last word (e.g., "Confused?" or "Frustrated?") can encourage them to continue in their own words.
- ***Avoid generalizations.*** People often generalize when talking about their own behavior. To avoid this, ask questions like "How do you personally accomplish that task or feel when doing it?" Asking them to recall a specific instance can also keep interviewees from overgeneralizing.
- ***Minimize distractions.*** People may get calls or be interrupted during the session. Try to restore focus on the interview as quickly as possible.
- ***Respect participants' time.*** Be sure to begin on time. If the interview starts running late, acknowledge that fact and ask if it's OK to continue.
- ***Go with the flow.*** The setting may not be what you expected and may not offer the best conditions for interviewing. Try to make the best of suboptimal situations.

b. ***Describe the experience:*** Ask them to describe what happened, what went wrong, and why. Be sure to ask how they felt at the time.

c. ***Explore the ideal:*** Ask what they think should have happened, to reveal their underlying needs and expectations.

The critical incident technique avoids generalizations and provides deep insight into motivations and philosophies. It helps bridge the gap between what people say they do and what they actually do.

3. ***Make observations.*** Take advantage of being on-site. Note the physical arrangement of the space, what artifacts are present, and how participants interact with them. Capture photos, screenshots, and videos as the interview unfolds. Always ask permission first.

   Consider asking participants to sketch diagrams of their work or activities. This often sparks new conversations and insights, but it can also be intimidating, depending on the nature of the field they are in. Use this technique carefully.

4. ***Conclude.*** Summarize the main points to confirm your understanding. Keep this short. Ask follow-up questions for clarification and invite any final thoughts. Keep recording during this wrap-up; people often add important details they previously left out, even while walking to the door.

   Give participants their incentive. Be sincere and appreciative—it's your way of saying thank you. Ask if you can contact them later for follow-up questions or clarification.

Debrief

Schedule time to debrief immediately after each session or at the end of each research day. Review notes with your interview partner, complete and complement each other's understanding, and capture initial observations.

For a collaborative method for creating a comprehensive team synthesis of all research findings, see "Research Debrief Session" on page 128.

Analyze the data

Qualitative research uncovers tacit knowledge—a clear strength of the approach. However, the data you collect doesn't come organized. You'll be left with a wealth of unstructured notes, photos, and recordings to work through. Don't be daunted. Let the overall story of the interaction, defined in the Initiate stage, guide your analysis.

Diagrams of current experiences are aggregate pictures of the people and organizations you are investigating. You won't be able to create a map from just one interview. When synthesizing the data you've gathered, seek out the common patterns.

From each interview, extract relevant findings and group them by theme. Then align those conclusions into a sequence for your diagram. **Figure 6-5** shows the progression from unstructured texts to common themes to sequences of experiences.

Informal analysis

Informal analysis involves comparing notes from interview sessions, along with other artifacts, such as photos. This means laying out findings and insights visually to identify themes and find patterns. A debrief is a powerful way to begin finding patterns as a team in a collaborative working session.

Whiteboards provide space to collect insights across interviews and interviewers. Colocated teams may prefer physical sticky notes and whiteboards for face-to-face discussion. Digital whiteboards help distributed teams collect insights across locations and maintain a persistent workspace.

Alternatively, you may start analyzing data in a simple spreadsheet. **Figure 6-6** shows a spreadsheet used to capture research findings. This is a modified version of a data collection sheet I used on a past project investigating a chronic illness. It allowed multiple people to contribute independently.

Formal analysis

A more formal analysis requires full transcripts of audio recordings for each interview. A 60-minute interview may yield 30 pages of transcribed text.

Use AI for speech-to-text transcription. Modern tools like Otter.ai transcribe calls and recordings instantly, though the resulting text may require manual cleanup. Conference call software such as Zoom provides built-in transcription capability.

Once you have the transcripts, use qualitative text analysis tools to comb through them. MAXQDA is great for academic coding. Modern tools such as Dovetail and Reframer from Optimal Workshop offer simpler online solutions. Reading coded passages for a particular theme allows you to draw grounded conclusions about the experience. Compare themes with your research questions and incorporate findings into the draft map.

AI greatly accelerates the coding process, but you should manually code at least a few transcripts before relying on AI. This deepens your understanding of insights, builds empathy, and sharpens your ability to judge AI outputs as relevant or hallucinatory.

Prompt AI tools to look for the facets of information you intend to include in the diagram. This is where your definition of the map's focus, as described in Chapter 3, comes into play. These machine-generated structures aren't final, but they offer a helpful starting point for researchers to refine through a human-centered lens.

AI can help you compare insights across multiple interviews, surfacing common motivations, contradictions, or themes that might be missed when reading manually. It can also spot gaps or suggest follow-up questions for your next round of research by identifying patterns and inconsistencies and pointing to hypotheses worth testing. This makes interview cycles more efficient, allowing you to move into mapping with clearer direction and stronger evidence.

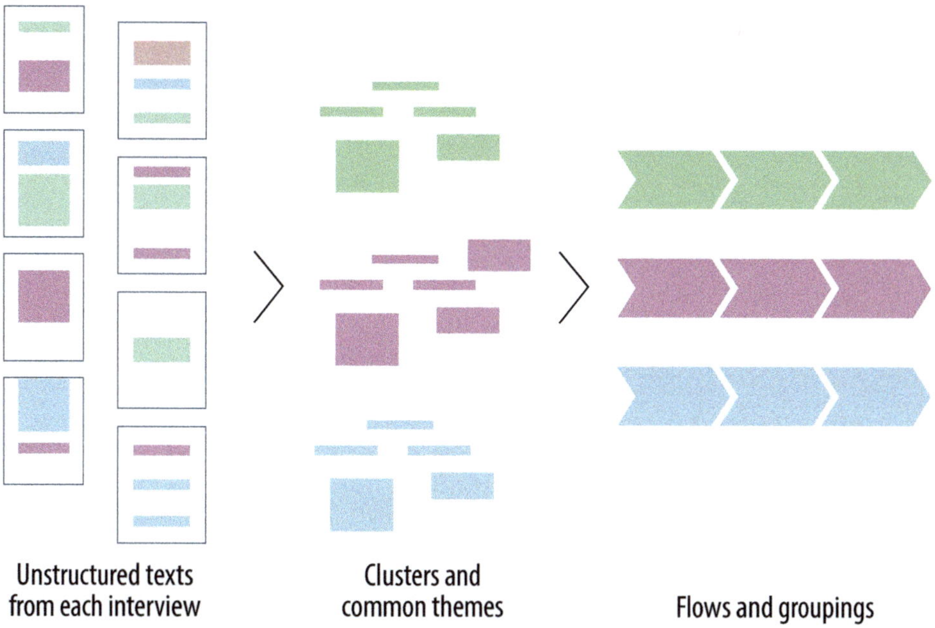

Figure 6-5. During analysis, you'll move from unstructured texts to clusters, and then to the sequences that form the diagram.

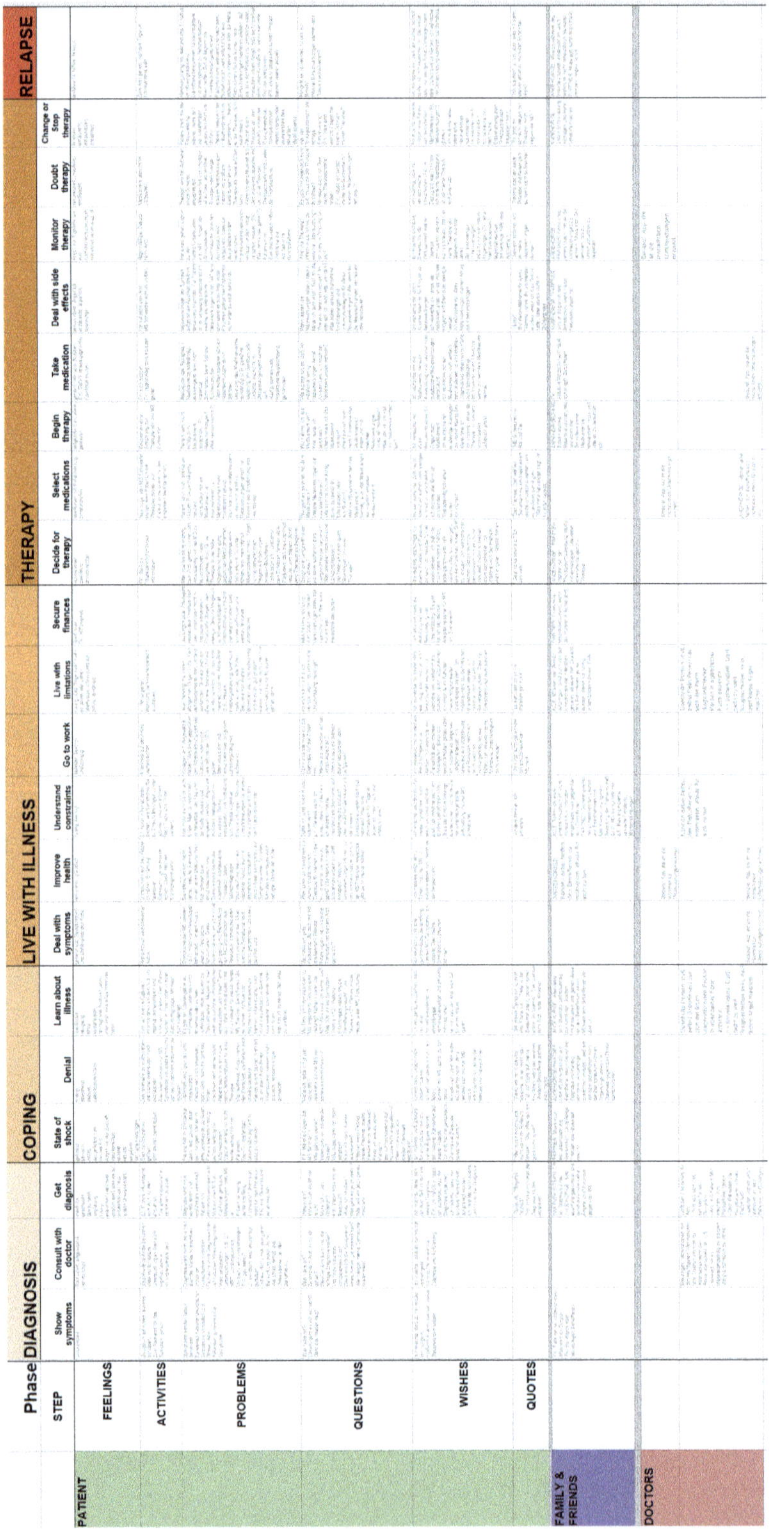

FIGURE 6-6. Use a simple spreadsheet for an informal analysis of your research.

Perform Quantitative Research

When creating an alignment diagram, surveys are the primary tool for gathering quantitative data. Although they are less commonly used when creating maps, they allow you to measure the same aspect across phases or touchpoints.

At a basic level, you want to understand what types of experiences people are having. For instance, a question might list touchpoints and ask respondents to select the ones they encounter. This lets you calculate the percentage of people who encounter a given touchpoint.

Questions using scales are more powerful. They allow you to measure aspects such as these:

- The frequency with which phases or steps are experienced
- The importance or criticality of a given touchpoint
- Satisfaction at each touchpoint or phase

When designing surveys, use a consistent scale throughout. If you ask participants to rank satisfaction on a scale of 1 to 5 for one question, don't switch to a different scale for the next.

Creating a bespoke survey can be challenging. Consider using a standardized survey instead. For instance, instruments such as the Software Usability Measurement Index (SUMI) and System Usability Scale (SUS) have been validated over decades for software and web applications

Other sources of quantitative information include the following:

Usage metrics

Electronically enabled services—everything from online software to computer chips in cars—can capture actual usage data. Web analytics and software telemetry allow for very detailed measurement of how systems are used.

Call center reports

Most call centers record the volume of calls and general traffic patterns. There is often a quantitative classification of call types as well.

Social media monitoring

Quantitative measures of social media activity, such as traffic from different platforms or the volume of hashtag use or mentions, can be included in a diagram.

Industry benchmarks

Depending on the sector and industry you are working in, benchmark data may be available. This will show how your current service compares to others in the same field.

As you collect data from these sources, consider how to incorporate them into your diagram. Rely on internal or external experts to help you manage quantitative data analysis. Many approaches depend on the type of diagram you're creating, its structure, and its depth. Chapter 7 discusses specific ways to represent quantitative information in alignment diagrams.

Journey management platforms are particularly geared toward incorporating quantitative data into the mapping process.

Summary

An experience is constructed in the mind of the perceiver. It's not something an organization owns. To map experiences, an investigation from the perspective of the individual is necessary.

Begin by assessing existing sources of information: email feedback, phone calls, blog comments, social media activity, marketing studies, industry reports. Extract relevant information that can inform diagram creation. AI tools can help surface patterns, summarize large bodies of text, or highlight emerging themes.

Create a touchpoint inventory of existing physical, digital, and person-to-person interactions. Note the channel and means of interaction, and collect images of each touchpoint. AI can assist in organizing touchpoints or detecting inconsistencies.

Create a draft diagram together with the project team and stakeholders. This provides an initial picture of your current understanding of the experience. It also provides an overview of knowns and unknowns, which guides subsequent research. In some cases, this may be all that is needed for your team to get aligned.

Interview people within the organization. Target a mix of roles across functions and levels, including frontline personnel; service desk agents and call center workers often have clear perspectives on the client experience.

AI can help prepare interview guides by analyzing existing sources and highlighting gaps.

Synthetic users and AI-driven interviews offer quick, directional inputs early in the mapping process. They help explore motivations and pain points, clarify assumptions, and draft initial hypotheses—always as a complement to, not a replacement for, real human research.

Conduct field research to fill in gaps in knowledge and deeply understand the experience from the individual's point of view. Go to the locations where participants interact with the service. Engage them in interviews and observe their surroundings. Remote research using teleconferencing tools speeds up the process but loses the richness of face-to-face interaction.

Surveys and questionnaires validate assumptions and provide quantitative data. The results can be included in alignment diagrams for greater impact. AI helps cluster responses and detect sentiment patterns to support synthesis.

All this data needs to be analyzed and reduced to key points. Only then can you draw a map of the experience with confidence. AI can assist with pattern recognition and draft synthesis, but the final meaning-making remains a human task. The next chapter discusses how to turn your research findings into a map.

Further Reading

Michele Hansen, Deploy Empathy, *2nd ed. (2025)*

Hansen's practical guide teaches the skill of interviewing customers through empathetic questioning, providing ready-to-use scripts and specific phrases for discovery, retention, and cancellation conversations. This updated and expanded edition includes guidance on using AI in customer research, a customer interview workshop guide, and additional analysis methods with worked examples. Grounded in JTBD methodology, the book demonstrates that empathy is a learnable skill, offering clear frameworks for understanding hidden customer needs, desires, and processes to build products customers love.

Hugh Beyer and Karen Holtzblatt, Contextual Design *(1997)*

This is the original landmark book that introduced a formal technique for contextual inquiry to the design community. It's thorough and well structured, with step-by-step guidance on the process. The first part discusses interview and inquiry techniques in detail. The latter parts outline a method for translating findings into concrete designs. This is a highly recommended book that everyone should read. See also Karen Holtzblatt, Jessamyn Burns Wendell, and Shelley Wood's *Rapid Contextual Design* (2004).

Tricia Wang, "Why Big Data Needs Thick Data," Ethnography Matters *(2013)*

In this article, Wang introduces the notion of thick data, or qualitative ethnographical descriptions, to contrast with the quantifications of big data. With a hat tip to Clifford Geertz's concept of thick description, thick data focuses on emotions and motivations within context to reveal new patterns and explain why people behave as they do.

Steve Portigal, Interviewing Users, *2nd ed. (2023)*

This updated edition of the acclaimed classic dispels the myth that interviewing is trivial, taking readers on a detailed journey into interviewing techniques. Recognized expert Steve Portigal covers research logistics, goal setting, and asking questions, as well as remote interviewing and addressing personal bias. With practical frameworks for mapping human behavior, amusing anecdotes, and tips from practitioners, the book demonstrates that teams that meet their customers face-to-face create better experiences.

Research Debrief Session

Objective	Identify patterns in findings across interviews
Time	90–120 minutes (best within 24 hours of interviews)
Participants	5–12, including stakeholders and interviewers
Materials	Whiteboard, sticky notes, photos, and notes from field research (printed or displayed)

After conducting customer interviews or field research, teams need to synthesize findings while insights are still fresh (**Figure 6-7**). A research debrief workshop brings researchers and stakeholders together immediately after fieldwork to share observations, identify patterns, and extract key themes. The session—in person or remote—creates shared understanding across the team by having everyone hear the same stories directly from researchers.

How it works:

1. Share individual observations. Have each researcher present highlights from their interviews, including key observations, memorable quotes, or surprising findings, while others listen and make notes.
2. Post observations on the wall, using sticky notes. Include pain points, emotional reactions, and contextual details, focusing on the strongest emotions, which are likely clues for moments of truth (see Chapter 3).
3. Cluster related observations. Working together, group similar observations into clusters.
4. Name the themes. For each cluster, agree on a descriptive label that captures the essence of the pattern. These are your key themes.
5. Map themes to journey phases. Arrange them along a timeline, or map them to your hypothesis map phases.
6. Identify implications and next steps. For each major theme, discuss what it means for your mapping effort. What needs to be reflected in the map? What gaps in knowledge remain? What should you investigate further?

Learn more:

Erika Hall, *Just Enough Research* (2013)

IDEO, "Synthesis," in *The Field Guide to Human-Centered Design* (2015)

Mads Soegaard, "Top Tips to Create Effective Journey Maps," *IxDF* (2025)

Example:

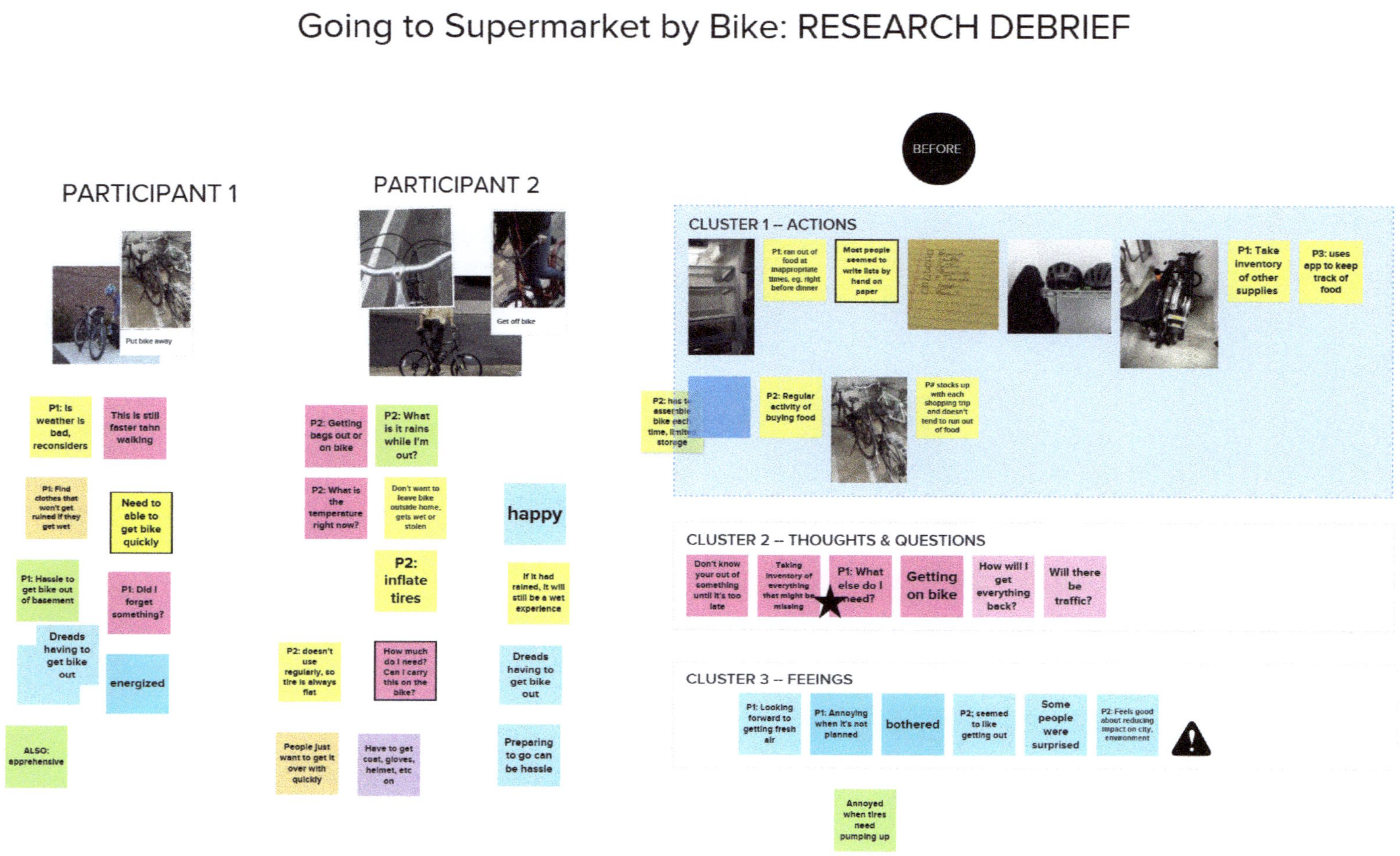

FIGURE 6-7. Mural (mural.co) is a good online tool for debriefing after interviews.

Proto-Personas

Objective	Collaborate on creating a set of low-fidelity personas as a team to better empathize with customers
Time	1–2 hours
Participants	3–12
Materials	Whiteboard, sticky notes

Proto-personas are a quick, team-based version of formal user personas (**Figure 6-8**). They are created fast, focusing on aligning the team. Also called lean personas, hypothesis personas, or assumption personas, these artifacts require subsequent validation.

How it works:

1. Identify key customer types to focus on, e.g., from a stakeholder map.
2. Fill out a simple template. Lean personas typically include four categories of information: a name and image, basic demographic details, behaviors and actions, and needs and pain points.
3. Discuss each persona and compare them if there is more than one. Identify the top needs and emotions that should be addressed.
4. Update and validate personas through real-world research.

Learn more:

Paul Boag, "Functional Personas with AI: A Lean, Practical Workflow," *Smashing* (2025)

Maddie Brown, "Personas Are Living Documents: Design Them to Evolve" *NN/g* (2023)

Sebastian D'Amore, "Boost Empathy Quickly with Proto-Personas," *Mural* (2016)

Example:

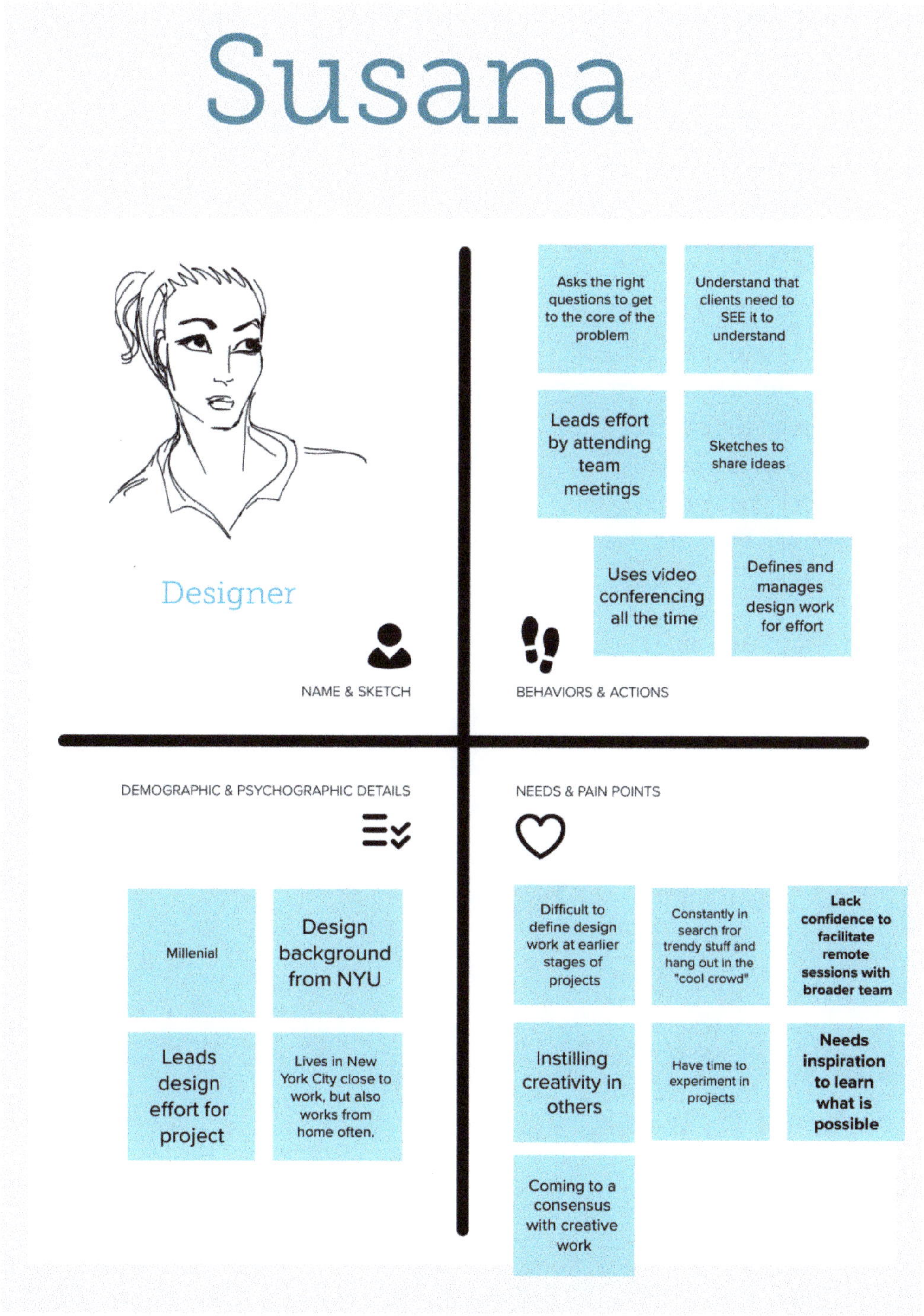

Figure 6-8. A simple proto-persona can be created on a digital whiteboard.

Empathy Map

Objective	As a team, share knowledge and insights about a given persona or customer type
Time	15–30 minutes
Participants	3–20+
Materials	Empathy map template, whiteboard, sticky notes

Created by Dave Gray and the folks at XPLANE, an empathy map is a collaborative visual tool used to represent a team's current understanding of what a customer thinks, feels, says, and does (**Figure 6-9**). A simple chart with several quadrants is all that's needed to allow teams to contribute. Use it as a warm-up for a meeting or workshop to keep the customer top of mind.

How it works:

1. Identify a persona or customer type to focus on. With larger teams, split participants into breakout groups to focus on different customers.
2. Work individually for a few minutes to fill out the quadrants of the empathy map. Strive to base insights on existing research.
3. Review everyone's contributions and discuss for clarity. Deduplicate similar concepts and add more as the conversation unfolds.
4. Reflect on the insights and draw conclusions. If in breakout groups, reconvene the entire team and have each group present its map to the others.

Learn more:

Tim May, "The Empathy Map: A Human-Centered Tool for Understanding How Your Audience Thinks," *XPLANE blog* (2021)

Dave Gray and Sunni Brown, *Gamestorming 2.0* (2025)

Example:

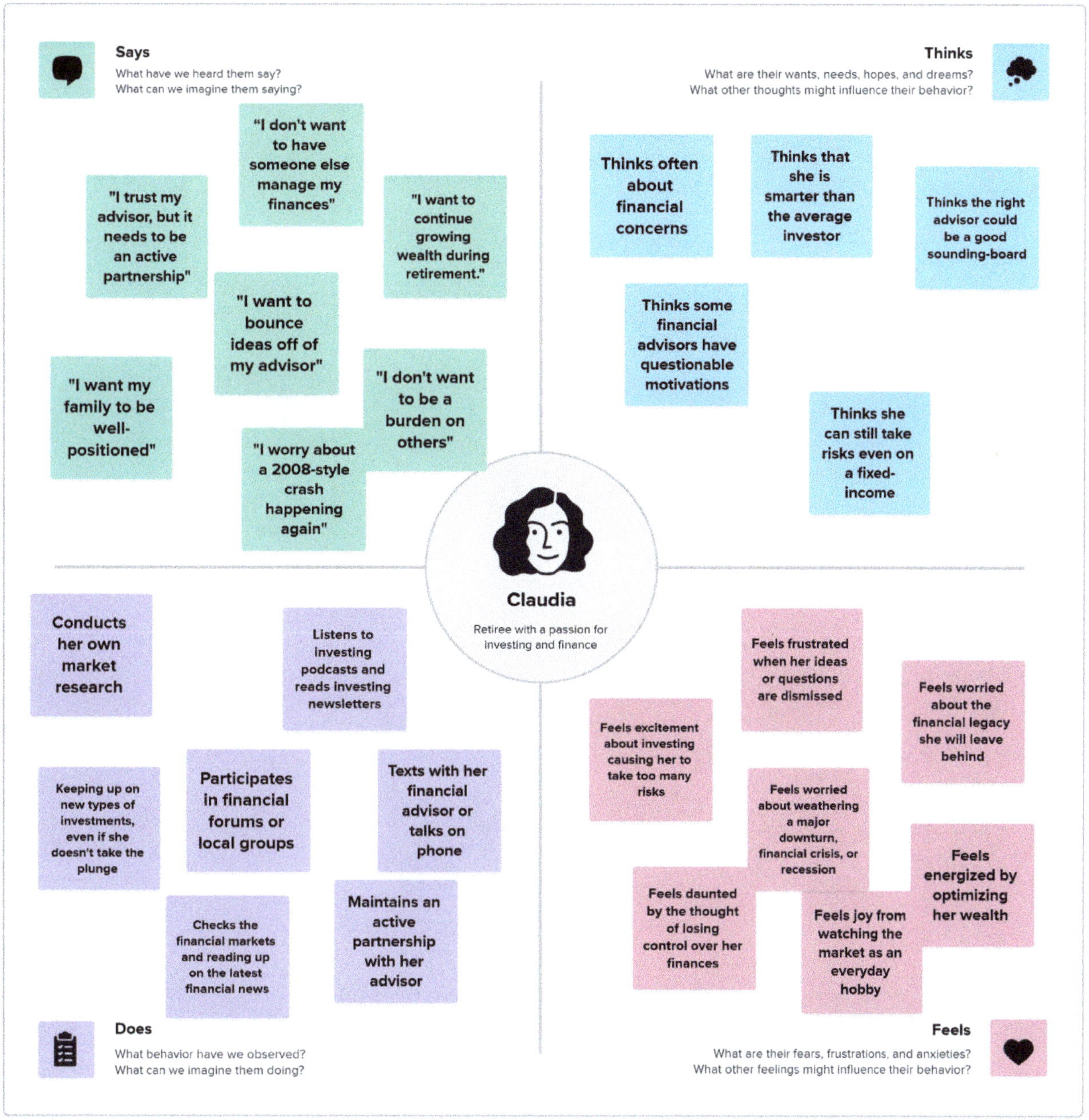

Figure 6-9. An empathy map represents insights about a customer type or persona.

Diagram and Image Credits

Figure 6-2: Example persona from UXPressia (see Anastasia Schebrova, "Creating a Persona—a Step-By-Step Guide with Tips and Examples"), used with permission

Figure 6-3: Customer journey map created by Jim Tincher of Heart of the Customer (*heartofthecustomer.com*), used with permission

Figure 6-4: Touchpoint inventory created by Chris Risdon, appearing in his article "The Anatomy of an Experience Map," used with permission

Figure 6-6: Example of an online spreadsheet for data collection in Google Sheets, modified from the original version

Figure 6-7: Example research debrief analysis by Jim Kalbach, created in Mural

Figure 6-8: Proto-persona example created by Sebastian D'Amore, used with permission

Figure 6-9: Example empathy map created by Mural, used with permission

Graphical excellence is that which gives to the viewer the greatest number of ideas in the shortest time with the least ink in the smallest space.

—Edward R. Tufte, *The Visual Display of Quantitative Information*

IN THIS CHAPTER

- Layout and form of a diagram
- Consolidating the content
- Designing the information
- Tools and software
- Collaborative methods for diagramming

CHAPTER 7

Illustrate: Visualizing the Experience

"I'm not a graphic designer and can't draw. How can I possibly create a diagram?"

I get that reaction a lot in my experience mapping workshops. There's good news: mapping is not about artistic talent. It's about bringing all your findings into a single, cohesive storyline. The hard part isn't the styling; it's creating an insightful narrative of the experience.

Consider the diagram in **Figure 7-1**, created by Eric Berkman, coauthor of *Designing Mobile Interfaces*. Visually, it has very few elements, but it reveals key insights about both positive and negative aspects of service at a Starbucks coffee shop. Diagrams don't need to have elaborate graphics to be effective.

In some cases, a mere row of sticky notes on a wall may be all that's required—for instance, in a small startup where you're working closely together informally. Other times, such as if you're presenting to the CEO of a large bank on a formal project, you'll want something more polished. Regardless of the level of fidelity your illustration requires, a few principles of design go a long way toward creating a compelling visual story.

The aim of this phase is to visualize the experience so others can engage with it. This chapter discusses three interdependent factors in illustrating experiences:

1. Laying out the diagram, or determining the overall form
2. Compiling the content into a reduced format
3. Designing the information for a compelling visualization

You may move back and forth between these tasks, so be prepared to iterate. After completing this chapter, you should be able to transform the insights from your investigation into a meaningful diagram.

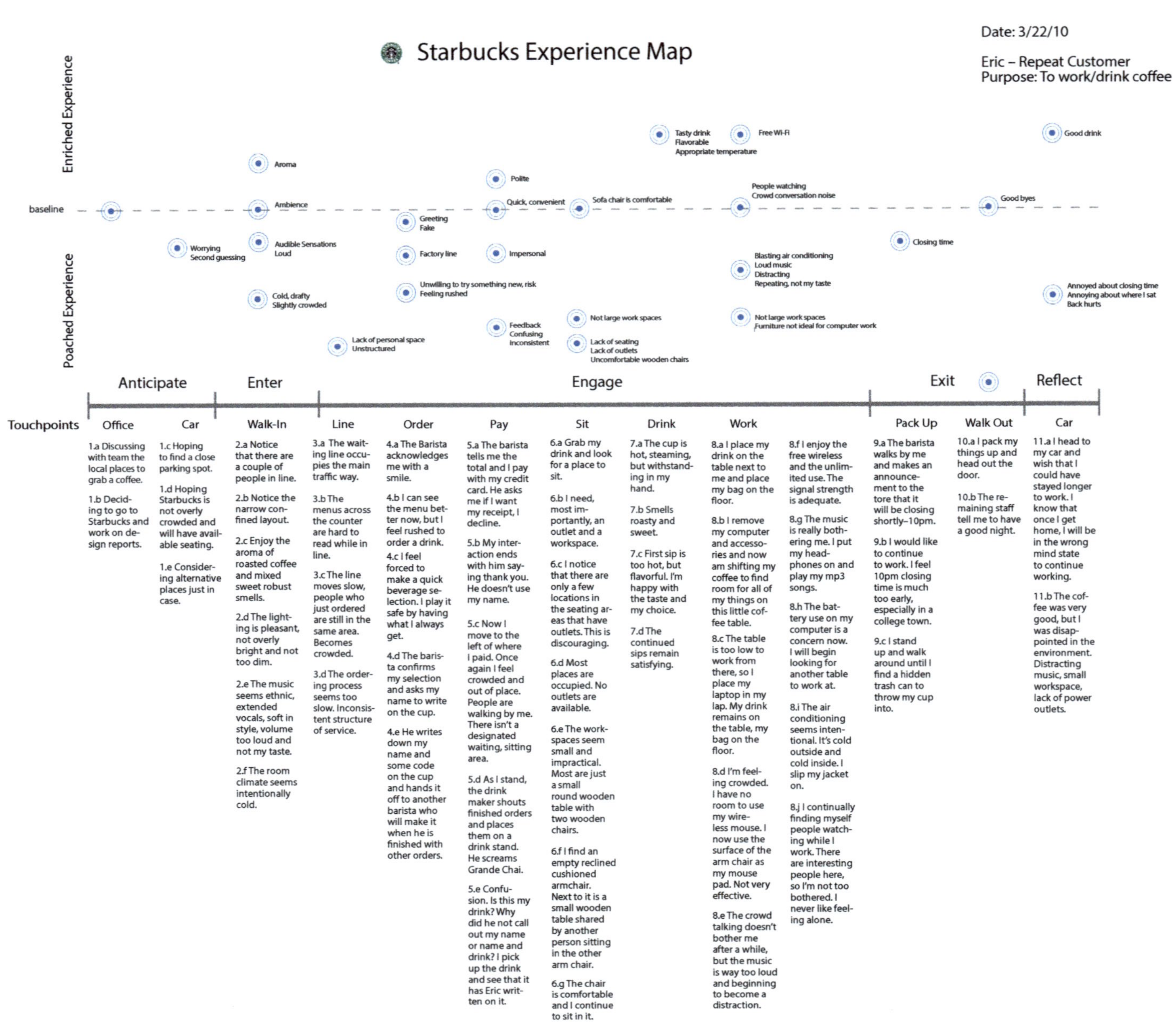

FIGURE 7-1. A simple diagram is sometimes all that is needed to provide insight.

Lay Out the Diagram

Some methods prescribe a layout in advance. Mental model diagrams, for instance, are organized hierarchically into towers, and a formal service blueprint will have prescribed rows of information by default. Otherwise, the layout and structure of the diagram are up to you, the mapmaker.

I recommend a simple table or timeline, which is the most common layout and works in most situations. But considering alternative forms is worthwhile as well. As discussed in Chapter 3, typical organizational schemes (chronological, hierarchical, spatial, or a network) will affect the layout of your diagram. **Figure 7-2** shows some possible layouts.

Regardless of the layout you use, it's important to consider how the form of the information can enhance the overall message. For instance, Sofia Hussain, a leading design strategist in Norway, created the diagram in **Figure 7-3**. She intentionally chose a circular form to show that the success of this event planning app relies on repeat use. The form amplifies the message.

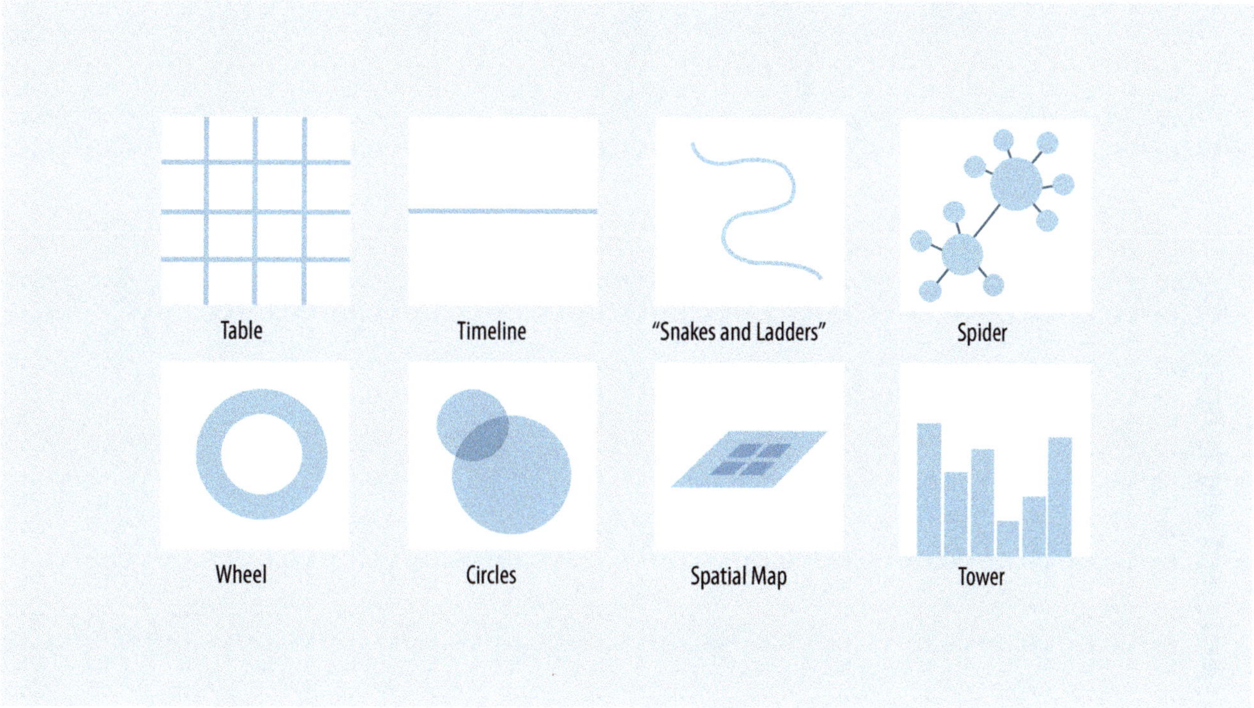

Figure 7-2. Consider alternative layouts for your diagram to enhance the storyline.

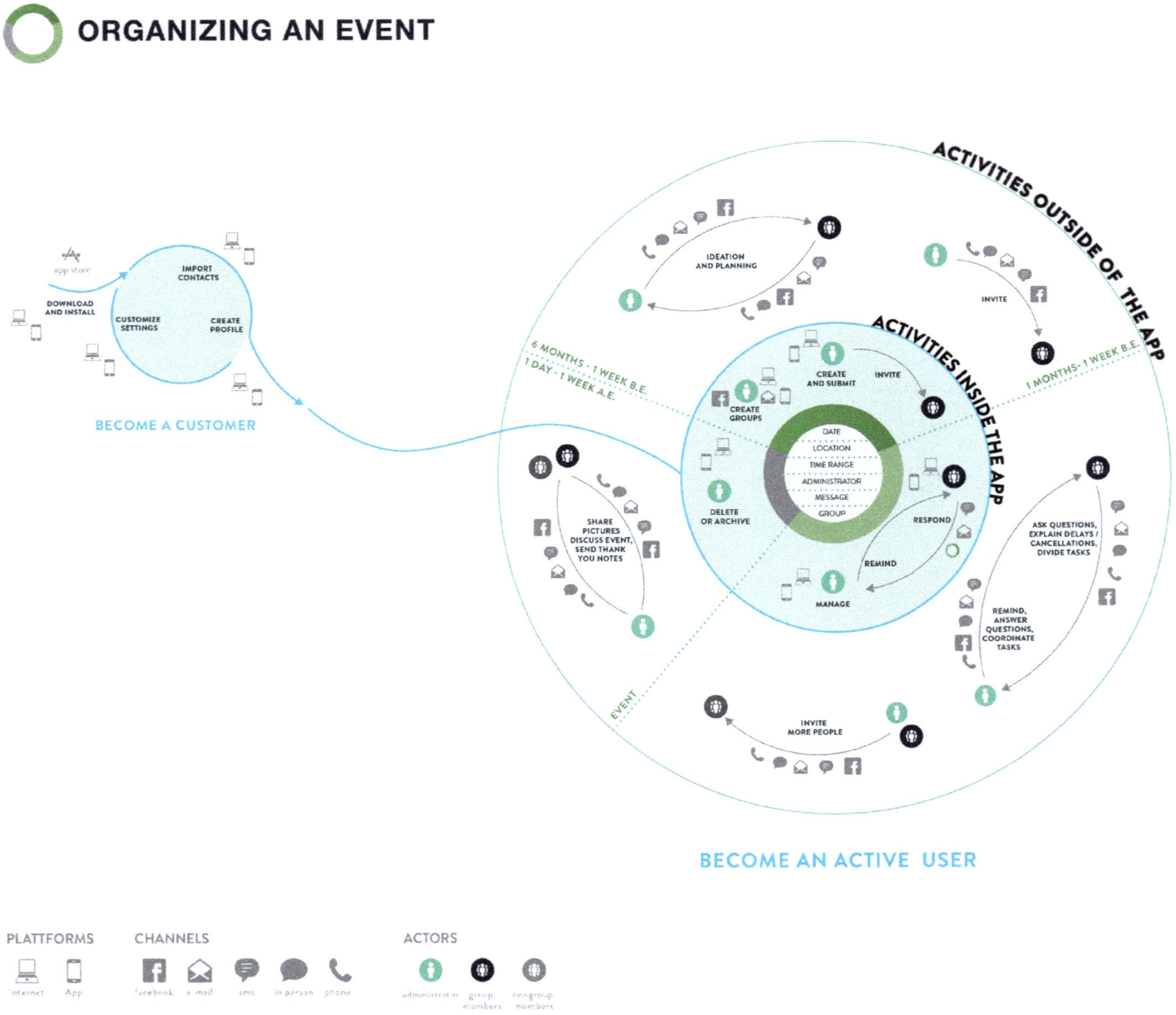

Figure 7-3. Make the shape of your diagram meaningful—for example, a circular diagram in this case reflects a desire for repeat use of an event planning app.

Display Chronology

Chronological maps are typically simple for others to grasp, but they can present a challenge: not all aspects of an experience are sequential. Some events are ongoing, some have a variable order, and others may have different subflows. When creating such a map, you may have to overcome what I call *the chronology problem*, or showing irregularities in a strict timeline. Some tactics are shown in **Figures 7-4a** through **7-4d**.

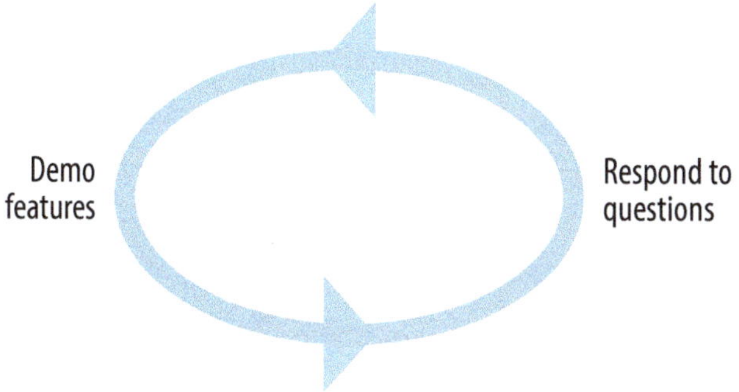

Figure 7-4a. REPEAT BEHAVIOR: Use arrows and circles to show repeating actions. For instance, during a sales call, the salesperson may alternate between demoing a product and responding to customer questions.

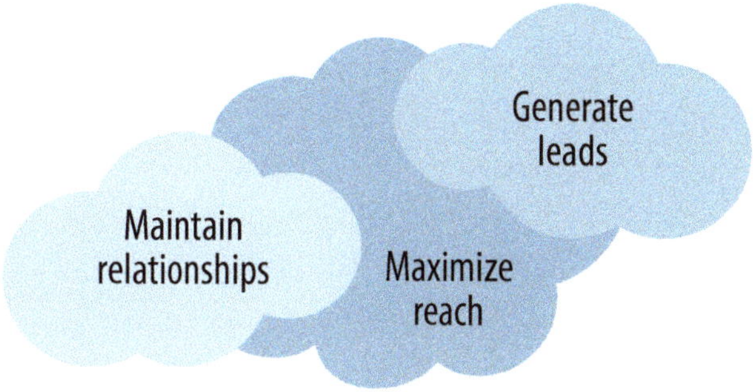

Figure 7-4b. VARIABLE ORDER: A cloudlike form can indicate that activities don't happen sequentially. For instance, a salesperson may generate new leads, maintain existing relationships, and maximize reach all at the same time.

Figure 7-4c. ONGOING ACTIVITY: Indicate the first time that an ongoing behavior occurs, then show that it continues, to avoid repetition. For instance, a salesperson may continually look for new leads.

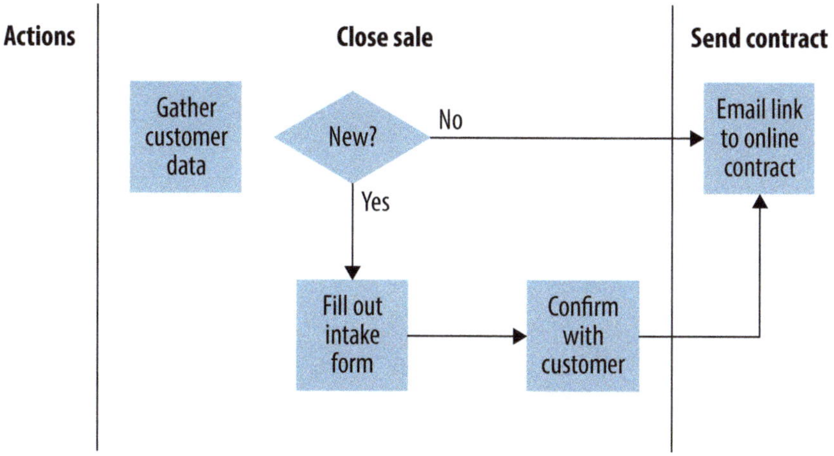

Figure 7-4d. ALTERNATE FLOWS: You may come across distinct subflows in the experience. Insert a decision point if needed, but keep these to a minimum to avoid overcomplication. For instance, a salesperson may have distinct activities based on the customer type.

Compile the Content

At this stage in the overall process, the aim is to map the current state of an experience. Mapping future states and coming up with solutions come later, as outlined in Chapter 9.

Reduce the data you've gathered to the most salient points, and look for patterns. Work both from the bottom up and from the top down, alternating between the two (**Figure 7-5**). Start by clustering and grouping findings repeatedly until you've reduced your research to just key insights. At the same time, work from the top down using your draft map to help direct your consolidation.

Be prepared to shift things around. Your goal is first to create a prototype of the diagram, taking qualitative and quantitative information into account.

Qualitative Information

A majority of information used to describe experiences is qualitative—rich descriptions of the *why* and the *how*, rather than quantitative data about *how many*. Here are some guidelines for determining the primary qualitative elements to include:

Create phases, categories, and divisions.

Determine the major "joints" of the model you're creating. Generative AI tools can help provide options quickly. In chronological maps, this means creating phases: e.g., *Become Aware*, *Purchase*, *Use*, *Get Support*. There are typically anywhere from 4 to 12 phases. For spatial maps and hierarchical diagrams, you need to create categories. Try to find what feels natural for you and for stakeholders. Keep in mind that the labels should be formulated from the perspective of the individual, not the organization. For instance, if you're mapping the experience of getting a new job, the first phase should be *Start Search* (what the individual does), not *Recruit* (what the organization does).

Describe the experience.

Decide what aspects of the experience to show. Core elements include actions, thoughts, and feelings. Consider ways to make the description as rich as possible. For instance, you can include direct quotes from customers or photos from your investigation. It's up to you to determine what is most relevant for your given effort. The aim is to demonstrate what is valuable both to the customer and to the organization through the condensed findings of your investigation.

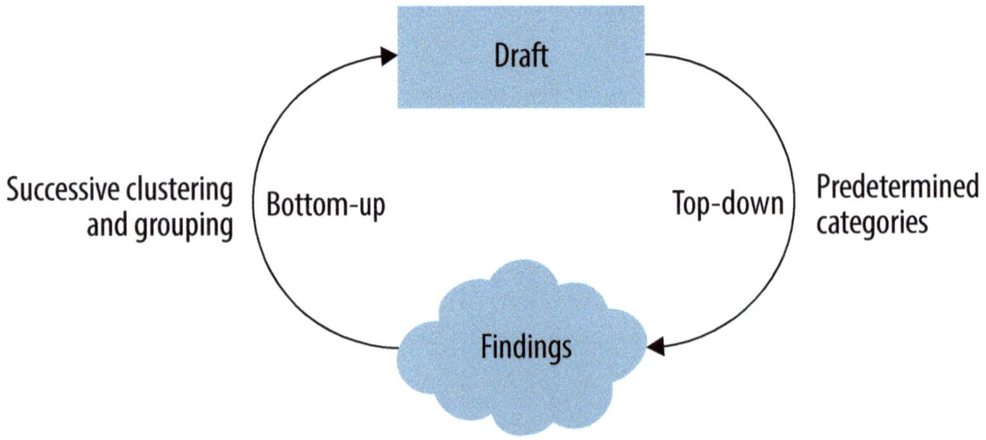

Figure 7-5. Work iteratively from the bottom up and from the top down to consolidate your research findings.

Show touchpoints.

Describe the interfaces between the individual and the organization in each phase. Think about the context of use. Remember, a touchpoint takes place within a given set of circumstances. Be sure that the information in the map surrounding the list of interfaces provides the context for each touchpoint.

Include aspects of the organization.

Indicate which roles or departments are involved at each touchpoint. Other elements you can map are the goals of the organization, strategic imperatives, and even policies. Show what is valuable to the organization.

Formatting the content is one of the trickiest parts of mapping. After being steeped in data and research, you may want to include every detail you've found. Resist this urge. Favor brevity and clarity over comprehensiveness. A map is intentionally a summary of insights for others. Too much detail can overwhelm and be off-putting to some. It takes practice to be able to express an experience in a compact form.

Table 7-1 lists a set of guidelines to follow to iteratively transform research insights into concise content for a diagram. In this table, assume you are creating a customer journey map for a software company. In the top row are two example insights that might be found from research. This isn't what gets included in the diagram; instead, the aim is to compress each raw insight down to its essence by following the process outlined here.

Note that it's important to keep the same syntax for each type of information. A cohesive system of content will make the diagram more readable and more unified. You can come up with your own patterns, but make sure you stick to the system for consistency.

Here are some formats I often use in mapping, for some of the most common information types:

Actions

Start each with a *verb*; e.g., download software, call customer service.

Thoughts

Phrase as a *question*; e.g., Are there hidden fees? Who else do I need to involve?

Feelings

Use *adjectives*; e.g., nervous, unsure, relieved, delighted.

Pain points

Start each with a *gerund*; e.g., waiting for installation, paying invoice.

Touchpoints

Use *nouns* to describe the interface; e.g., email, customer hotline.

Opportunities

Begin each with a verb that shows change; e.g., *increase* the ease of installation, *eliminate* unnecessary steps.

Table 7-1. A process for reducing raw observations into compact, well-formed statements

Guideline	Description	Example 1	Example 2
Start with insights	Start with clusters of raw observations from your research.	*Research cluster 1:* People indicated they sometimes hesitate and reconsider during the customer acquisition phase because of our premium pricing model.	*Research cluster 2:* There is a clear pain point around deploying the solution, primarily due to a lack of necessary technical knowledge.
Use natural language	Use language that reflects the individual's experience in terms they would use.	People reconsider when making a purchase because they may be nervous or anxious about the high cost.	Users struggle to install the software for the first time if they don't have the required technical skills.
Keep voice consistent	Rewrite the insights in either the first or third person—pick one and don't mix voice.	I reconsider when making a purchase because I'm anxious and nervous about the high cost.	I struggle to install the software for the first time because I don't have the necessary technical skills.
Omit pronouns and articles	To save space, omit articles and pronouns, which are implied.	Reconsider when making a purchase due to anxiety and nervousness over high cost.	Struggle to install software for first time without necessary technical skills.
Focus on the root cause	Reduce the information to reflect underlying motivations and emotions.	Feel anxious and nervous when making a purchase due to high cost, and then reconsider.	Struggle during installation due to lack of necessary technical skills.
Be concise	Rewrite the descriptions to use as few words as possible. Use a thesaurus if needed.	Feel anxious during purchase about cost, and then reconsider.	Struggle during installation due to lack of technical skills.
Use abbreviations sparingly	Abbreviations can be OK if they are widely used and accepted.	Feel anxious during purchase about cost, and then reconsider.	Struggle during installation due to lack of tech skills.
Rely on the context of the map	Some information can be inferred from its position. Rely on the row and column headers if you have a table-like diagram.	Anxious about cost *(for the Purchase column and Feelings row)* Reconsider *(for the Purchase column and Actions row)*	Struggle due to lack of tech skills OR Lack tech skills *(assuming an Installation column and a Pain Points row)*

Quantitative Information

Including quantitative content adds validity. Consider how to incorporate metrics, survey results, and other quantitative data into your diagram. **Figures 7-6a** through **7-6d** show some of the options.

1. Word of mouth (48%)
2. Web searches (26%)
3. Internet ads (19%)
4. TV ads (7%)

Figure 7-6a. SHOW NUMBERS AS TEXT: Include numbers and figures to show absolute values. For instance, you may have quantitative data on how people find your service.

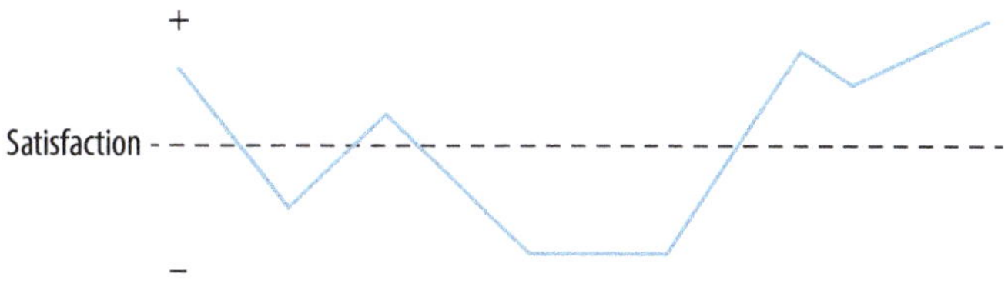

Figure 7-6c. PLOT VALUES ON A GRAPH: A simple graph shows the rise and fall of a given measure across a diagram. For instance, you may have quantitative data for customer satisfaction at each touchpoint in a journey.

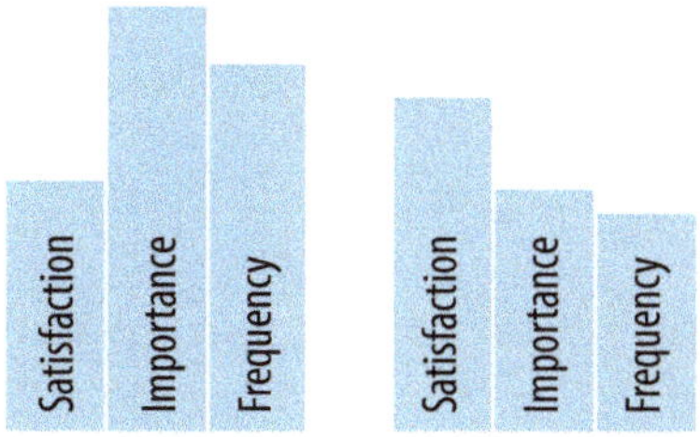

Figure 7-6b. USE BARS TO SHOW AMOUNTS: Vertical bars show relative quantities. Absolute values can be included in text if needed.

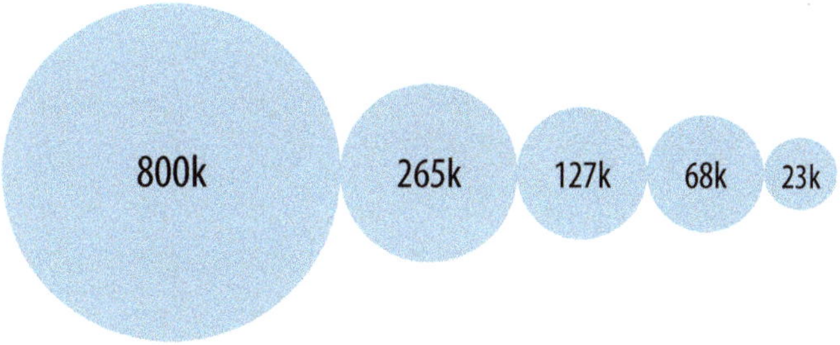

Figure 7-6d. USE SIZE TO INDICATE QUANTITY: It's also possible to show quantity with the size of a shape. For instance, this example could be used to indicate the number of customers who move through a typical purchase funnel.

Design the Information

People like information that is rich in presentation. Content that is presented with color, texture, and style has relevance to our lives and our work.

The visual presentation of a diagram influences how others understand the information. Strive to create a consistent visual language that enhances your overall message. What insights should be highlighted? What are the key messages you wish to communicate? How can you make the diagram approachable, aesthetically pleasing, and more compelling?

Even if you're not a graphic designer, you can make some basic decisions to help the clarity of the diagram. Stay true to these principles:

Simplify
: Avoid frivolous and decorative graphics. Strive for efficiency in display.

Amplify
: The design should amplify the goals of the project and expectations of sponsors.

Clarify
: Strive to be as clear as possible.

Unify
: Use consistency to create a cohesive visualization.

The key aspects to pay attention to are typography, graphics, and visual hierarchy, as discussed in the following sections.

Typography

Typography refers to the selection of letterforms and the general design of text. Since experience maps are generally heavily text-based, the typography of your diagram is paramount to facilitating its practical use.

Typographical options can overwhelm. Let function and purpose guide your choice. When in doubt, favor legibility and intelligibility over flair and expression. Consider typeface, size and width, case, and bold and italic styling (**Figures 7-7a** through **7-7d**).

Graphic Elements

After you've compiled the content, you need to consider how to represent it visually. Graphic elements play an important part; you may not be able to create the graphics yourself, but being aware of a few basics will help you plan and critique the outcome.

Show relationships with lines

Lines are a principal means of creating visual alignment. They have four primary functions in alignment diagrams: dividing, containing, connecting, and showing paths.

Be careful of unnecessary lines. If every cell in a table-like diagram has a line border, for instance, the overall diagram can feel visually heavy. As a general rule of thumb, use as few lines as possible, and only where they add meaning.

Serif

The quick brown fox jumps over the lazy dog.	Times New Roman
The quick brown fox jumps over the lazy dog.	Georgia
The quick brown fox jumps over the lazy dog.	Courier

Sans Serif

The quick brown fox jumps over the lazy dog.	Arial
The quick brown fox jumps over the lazy dog.	Verdana
The quick brown fox jumps over the lazy dog.	Trebuchet

Figure 7-7a. SELECT A TYPEFACE: Typefaces have two major categories: serif and sans serif. Typically, diagrams use a sans serif typeface for the bulk of the information, though you may encounter serif typefaces as well. It's best to use only one or two typefaces in a diagram.

Different font widths

The quick brown fox jumps over the lazy dog.	Verdana
The quick brown fox jumps over the lazy dog.	Frutiger
The quick brown fox jumps over the lazy dog.	Frutiger Condensed
The quick brown fox jumps over the lazy dog.	Arial
The quick brown fox jumps over the lazy dog.	Arial Narrow
The quick brown fox jumps over the lazy dog.	Franklin Gothic
The quick brown fox jumps over the lazy dog.	Franklin Gothic Condensed

Figure 7-7b. CONSIDER FONT SIZE AND WIDTH: You will be motivated to use a small font size to get more information into the diagram. Avoid making the text so small it can't be read. Instead, work with the content to reduce it to its most meaningful essence.

Also, be aware of the overall width of the font you're using. For instance, Verdana is a very wide font and not recommended. Instead, try a condensed or narrow font. Pair these with their regular versions for greater consistency.

All caps: full sentence vs. short label

✗ THE QUICK BROWN FOX JUMPS OVER THE LAZY DOG

✗ CONTACT CUSTOMER SUPPORT FOR HELP

✓ BECOME AWARE

✓ DECIDE

Figure 7-7c. PAY ATTENTION TO CASE: Generally, longer texts are harder to read in capital letters than in mixed case. They will take up more space as well. Single words or short phrases, however, such as the title of a phase in a journey, may work well in uppercase. Use all caps sparingly to add emphasis or show differences.

Different font styles for emphasis

The quick brown fox jumps over the lazy dog.	Frutiger
The quick brown fox jumps over the lazy dog.	Frutiger Ultra Black
The quick brown fox jumps over the lazy dog.	Frutiger Light Italic

Figure 7-7d. EMPHASIZE WITH BOLD AND ITALIC STYLES: Use bold and italics to help distinguish different information types, but do so sparingly. Generally, the information will be more readable if you keep the same weight and style. A mix of bold and italics can get messy quickly.

Convey information with color

Color is more than just decoration. It helps create a sense of priority and facilitates understanding. **Figure 7-8** illustrates two key uses of color in experience mapping:

- *Color coding* allows viewers to visually connect individual facets of information across the diagram, even when they're not on the same line of sight. This is crucial for creating a sense of visual alignment. For instance, pain points or moments of truth may use a consistent color throughout the diagram.

  Note that colorblind viewers may not be able to distinguish colors well, and also that colors have different meanings in different cultures.

- *Background regions* can also be indicated with color. This avoids unnecessary use of lines. For instance, I like to use different shades of the same color to distinguish larger phases of a journey. This helps guide attention by creating natural sections of focus.

Using too many colors can have diminishing returns. Use color purposefully for emphasis, and be sure to make it consistent.

Add icons for efficiency

Icons not only communicate a great deal of information in a small amount of space, but also add visual interest. Typical icons found in experience maps include people, physical evidence of touchpoints, emotions, and moments of truth (see **Figure 7-9**).

You can take many directions, with near-endless variation (e.g., solid backgrounds versus outlines only, as seen in the first row of **Figure 7-9**). Decide on a style and keep it consistent throughout the diagram.

Not all information types can be neatly represented using icons. In addition, icons can carry different meanings in different cultures. Consider how you might express the idea or concept you want to represent with as little bias and as few cultural implications as possible. If there's a chance of ambiguity, create a key to explain the icons.

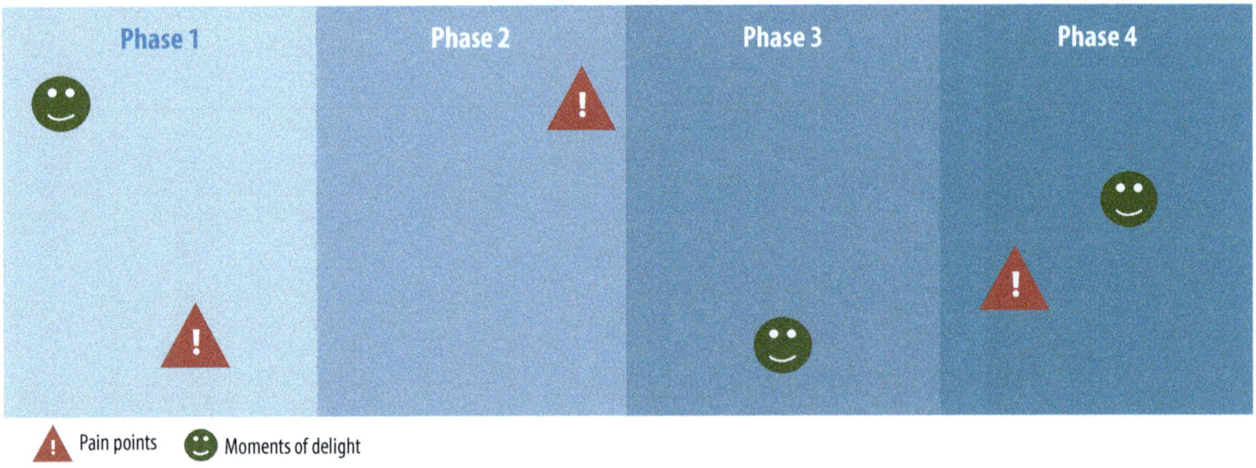

Figure 7-8. Information can be conveyed with color.

Also keep in mind that if you use too many icons, the diagram will be difficult to comprehend; readers will constantly have to refer back to the key to understand the information. Aim to present the content in such a way that it can be read without reference to a key or further explanation.

The Noun Project (*thenounproject.com*) is a website that aggregates icons and symbols from contributors around the world. The images are readily accessible for use, either in the public domain or with a Creative Commons license. It's a great resource for icons that can help you achieve consistency in your diagrams.

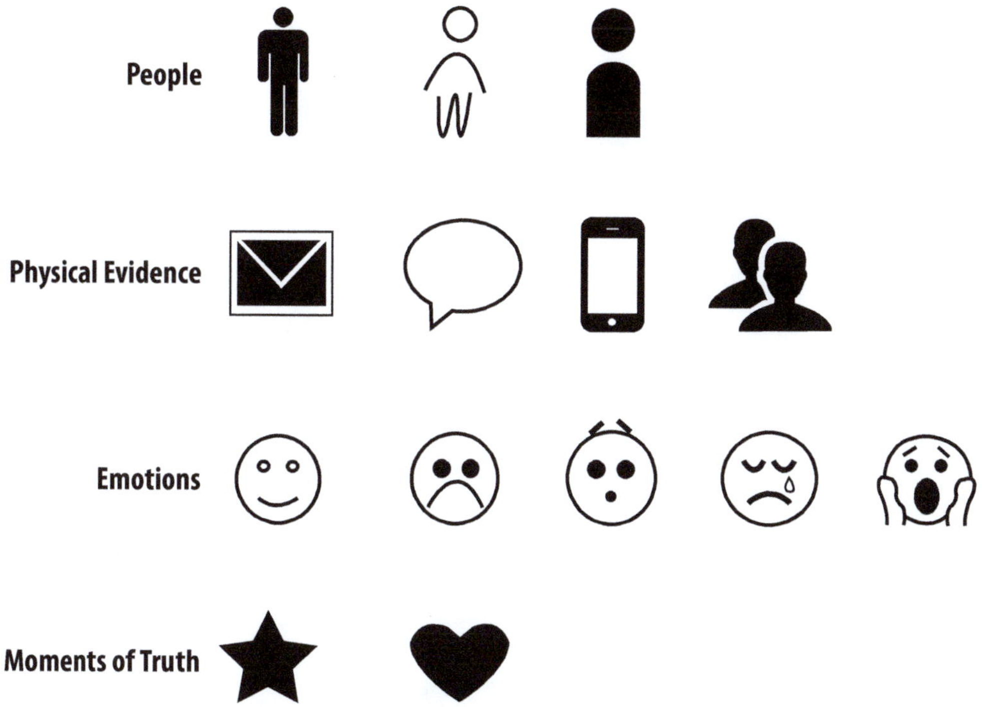

Figure 7-9. Add icons for efficiency.

Visual Hierarchy

Not all information in a diagram is of equal importance. Create a visual hierarchy to direct how the eye perceives the experience you're mapping. As illustrated and explained in **Figures 7-10a** through **7-10d**, techniques for this include good alignment, different visual weights for emphasis, layering, and avoiding chartjunk.

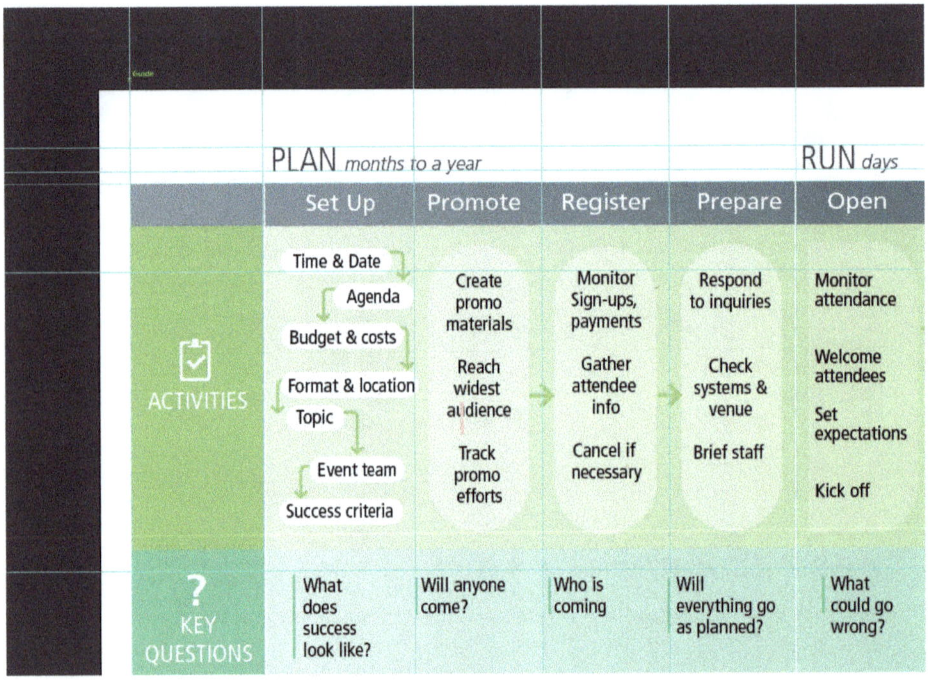

Figure 7-10a. ALIGN ELEMENTS: Visual alignment is critical in a diagram. A grid—an invisible structure of equally spaced lines to which elements are justified—creates clear lines and guides readers' line of sight vertically and horizontally. Strive for alignment even if you are using a spreadsheet or mapping sticky notes on a wall.

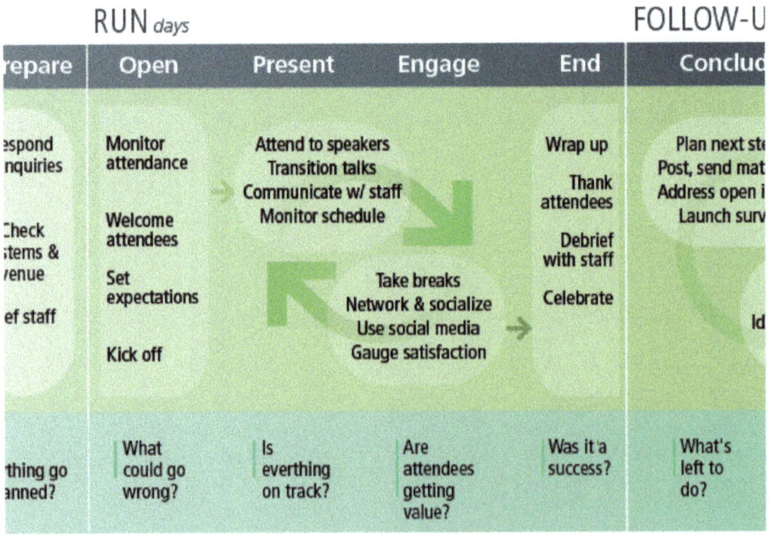

Figure 7-10b. CREATE EMPHASIS: The weight and size of both text and graphic elements provide focus and differentiation. For instance, in this image, the phase headers ("RUN," "FOLLOW-UP," etc.) are larger than the rest of the text, creating a sense of hierarchy. Arrows of different sizes are also used to represent different aspects of the experience.

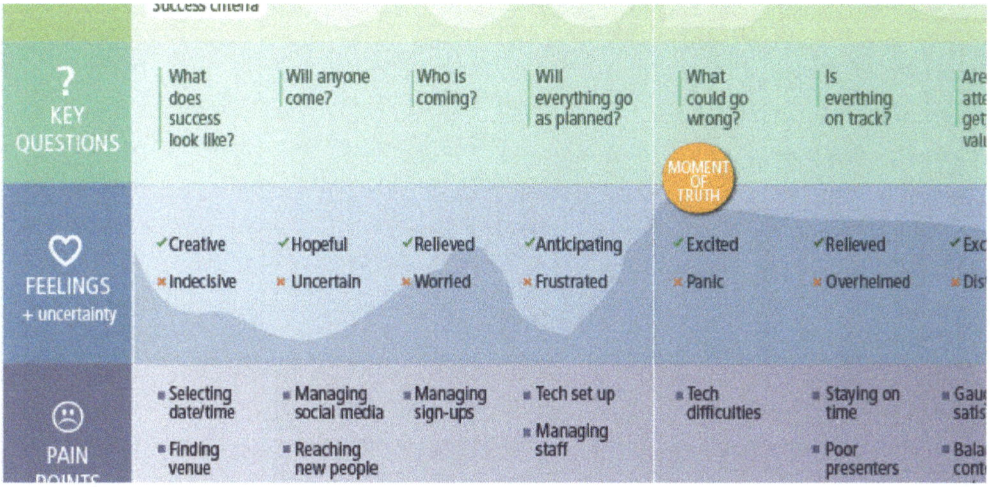

FIGURE 7-10C. LAYER INFORMATION: Make some elements stand out more than others by layering different text sizes and shading. In this example, "uncertainty" is indicated through background shading, and specific emotions are shown as positive or negative, all within a small space on the diagram.

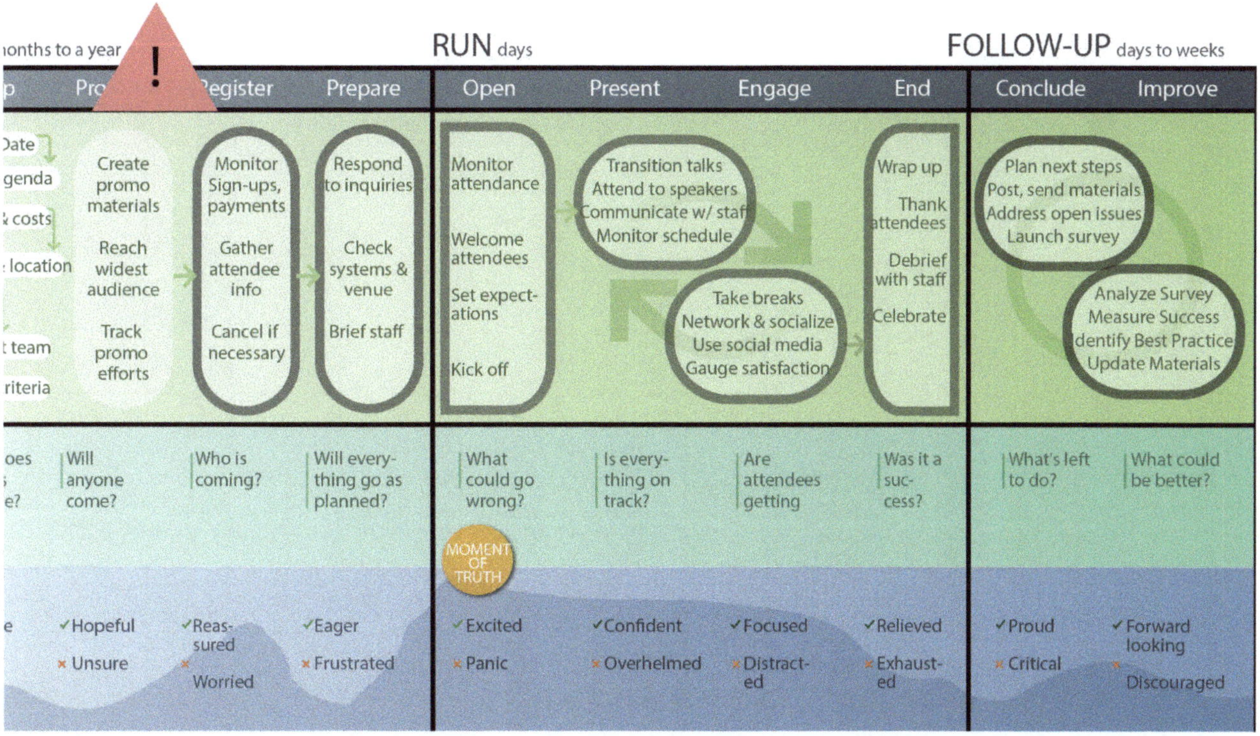

FIGURE 7-10D. AVOID CHARTJUNK: *Chartjunk*, a term coined by information design expert Edward Tufte, is anything unnecessary in an information display. Make every mark count.

Example Diagramming Process

The process of illustrating an experience in a single diagram is iterative. The insights you'll map drive the visualization, and the visualization will impact the form of those insights.

Figure 7-11 shows an example draft diagram for organizing a conference event, in this case completed in a simple spreadsheet. It reflects a first pass at consolidating the research observations to include in the map. Thought has been given to the chronological phases, the wording and formatting of text, and the balance of content in general.

The next step is to add a more visually compelling narrative. **Figure 7-12** shows an updated version of the draft diagram created by design leader and startup advisor Hennie Farrow.

Various aspects of design come together in **Figure 7-12** to guide the audience through the experience in a more engaging and compelling way:

Typography

In addition to a regular font (Frutiger), this diagram also uses a condensed font (Frutiger Condensed) to make the best use of space. All capitals are used for the phase names and row headers for emphasis and to set them off from other text. The text has even size and weighting for the most part, with bold and italics used sparingly for emphasis.

Hierarchy

Horizontal and vertical alignment creates a sense of rows and columns across the diagram. Different background shadings set the row and column headers and the phases at the top off from the main content of the map.

Event Organizer

	BEFORE THE CONFERENCE				DURING THE CONFERENCE				AFTER THE CONFERENCE	
	Plan	**Promote**	**Invite Attendees**	**Prepare**	**Initiate Event**	**Start Main Presentations**	**Engage Audience**	**End Event**	**Follow-Up on**	**Improve Event**
ACTIONS	· Set budget, costs · Determine topic · Create agenda · Set date and time · Set success criteria · Figure out reporting	· Create materials · Reach widest audience · Decide where, when · Cross promote · Track data on promotion · (Re-)evaluate promotion	· Maintain contact lists · Figure out who to invite · Create calendar entry · Send save the date notices · Send invitations and follow-up reminders	· Co-create materials · Organize materials · Make materials accessible · Discuss handoffs · Check equipment	· Show up early · Go over ground rules · Communicate time · Monitor attendance · Greet audience	· Welcome attendees · Give overview, timings · Set expectations · Instruct attendees on environment, tools	· Integrate social media · Gauge attentiveness · Take breaks Network	· Wrap up · Thank people · Stay for questions · Debrief · Plan next steps	· Address unanswered questions · Send out materials · Collect feedback · Launch survey	· Analyze survey results · Review metrics, compare to goals · Gauge effectiveness · Update materials
THOUGHTS	Who is this for? Will they come? What does success look like?	Who do I target? How do I best promote? Is promotion effective?	Who am I attracting? What are their needs? Will everything go as planned? Will I remember everything?	Will anyone come? What does success look like? How do I best promote? Is promotion effective?	Who is signing up?	Will everything go as planned? Will I remember everything?	Is the audience engaged? Are they getting their money's worth?	Was it well-received? A success?		
FEELINGS	creative indecisive	hopeful uncertain	relieved worried		MoT! excited panic (high uncertainty)	relieved overwhelmed	relieved exhausted	forward looking discouraged	proud	
PAIN POINTS	· Figuring out when to schedule an event	· Determining social media channels · Managing social media promotions · Unprofessional looking material	· Having to reschedule the event · Updating meeting details, agenda, etc.	· Locating materials · Consolidating materials · Setting up hardware · Coordinating staff	· Unexpected technical difficulties	· Unexpected technical difficulties	· Maintaining focus · Gauging attendee understanding		· Lack of time to follow-up right after	· Lack of motivation to update materials · Lack metrics collected · Inability to show effectiveness of event
OUR GOALS	· Maximize reach to the widest audience	· Maximize reach to the widest audience	· Maximize the number of people that attend · Increase the likelihood that the right people attend	· Increase the likelihood audience will be engaged · Maximize professional appearance	· Increase the likelihood of a smooth start	· Increase the likelihood that attendees have a positive experience · Maximize utilization of time while not "on stage"	· Maximize audience engagement · Reduce the likelihood that attendees get distracted	· Maximize overall satisfaction	· Maximize the length of the relationship with attendees	· Increase the quality of future events · Maximize buzz around the event and topic
CURRENT SATISFACTION		7.1 / 10	4.2 / 10		8.2 /10	6.5 / 10	5.5 / 10		8.7/10	

Figure 7-11. Before adding graphic detail, find the right layout and consolidate the insights from your investigation into a draft diagram.

Content

Syntax is used consistently—for instance, verbs for the phases and activities, and adjectives for feelings. The voice is consistent as well.

Graphic elements

Color is used to distinguish the different facets of information in the rows. The first column with the row labels has darker backgrounds, providing depth to the overall diagram and giving that information priority.

Icons are added for visual interest. Each information type also includes a unique element to help provide a sense of cohesion. For instance, the organizational goals have arrows to show the desired direction of the outcome, pain points have a square bullet, and key questions have a line. The moment of truth in this experience is indicated with a graphic element in the middle.

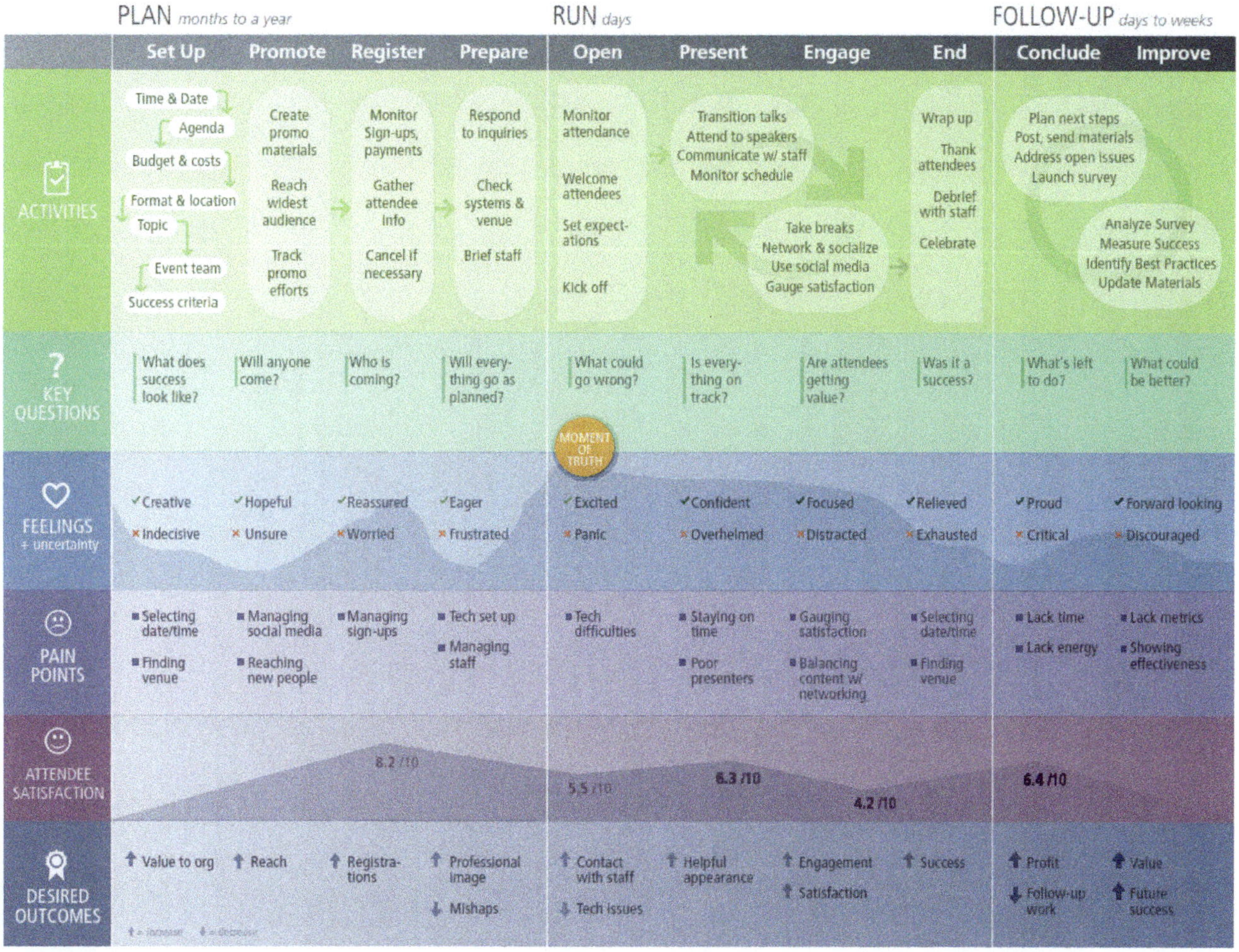

Figure 7-12. Use visual design elements to tell a more compelling story and guide your audience through the experience.

Showing Your Emotions

Emotions play a critical role in the experiences we have. Some description of the individual's emotive state of mind is necessary when mapping experiences, but emotions aren't easy to represent in a diagram.

The simplest approach is to indicate emotions with text. It's also possible to show emotions with icons of facial expressions. **Figure 7-13** shows a simple but highly effective diagram created by Craig Goebel for Intuit.

Notice how the emotional journey in **Figure 7-13** is plotted on a line that moves up and down with the different states of feeling. This is a common approach that has emerged over the past few decades. **Figure 7-14** is an early example from a 2004 report by Ed Thompson and Esteban Kolsky titled "How to Approach Customer Experience Management"; it's an excerpt from a diagram assessing the experience of business passengers on a major US airline.

One problem with the plotted-line approach is that it suggests some kind of quantification. However, rarely is

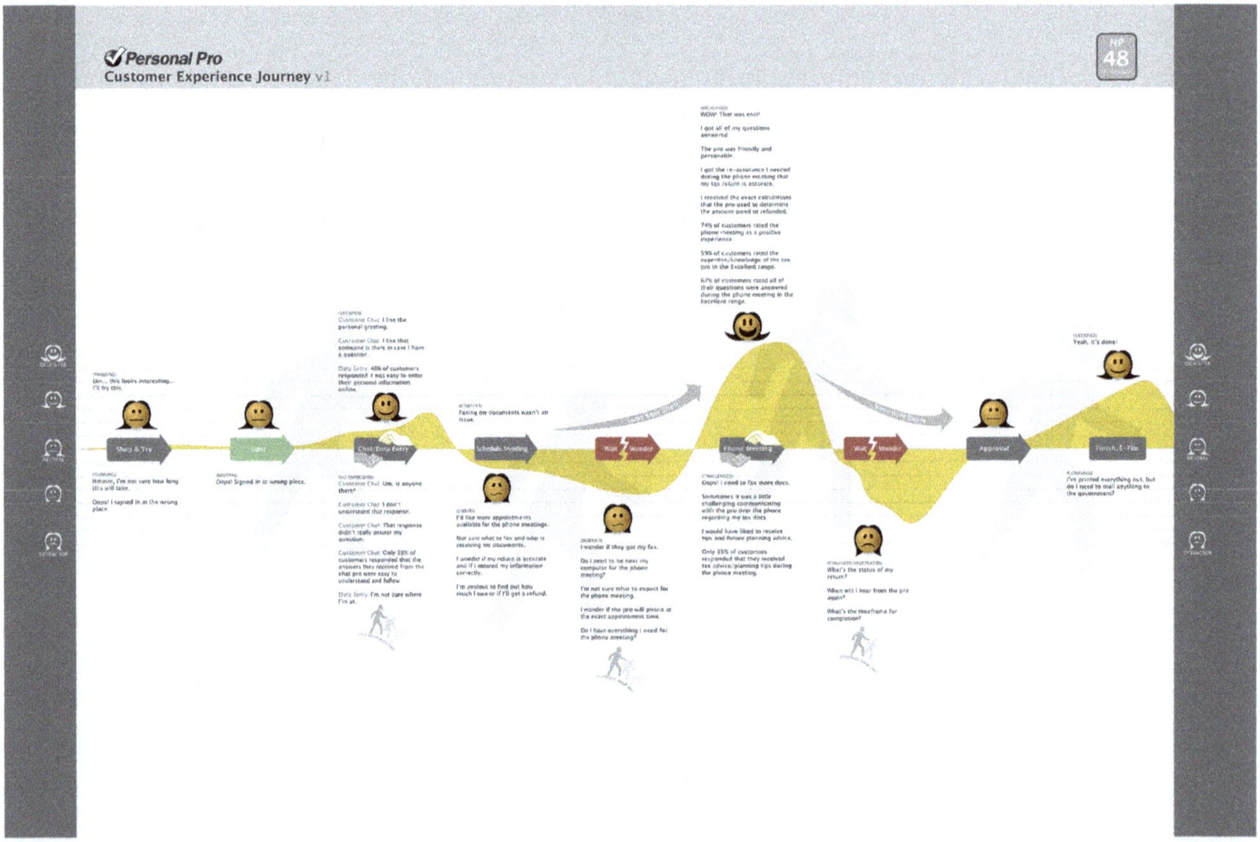

Figure 7-13. This journey map created by Craig Goebel consists primarily of emotional states shown with icons plotted on a curve.

this information derived from quantitative investigation—typically, it's estimated intuitively. Be careful what you communicate and how.

What's more, the plotted-line approach oversimplifies the emotions. It's unusual for us to have just one emotion at a time. For example, when checking out of a hotel resort after a two-week vacation, you may be *delighted* with the service but *sad* to leave or even *anxious* about going back to work on Monday—all at the same time.

An approach that I typically take focuses on a range of possible emotions by indicating the most prevalent positive and negative emotion at each phase of the experience. The Feelings row in **Figure 7-12** is an example of this: notice that the curved line specifically reflects "uncertainty," which drives a lot of the emotions uncovered during research.

Understanding and representing emotions is a challenge. Consider the trade-offs you'll have to make and how best to characterize the emotional aspects of the experience you're illustrating.

Mapping Tools

You can use a range of tools and software to illustrate a diagram, depending on your skills and needs. For informal efforts, a simple whiteboard with sticky notes may suffice. In other cases, you may want to create a more polished diagram to formally present to clients and stakeholders.

This section reviews some of the options that are available for different skill levels, from spreadsheets and slide decks on the low end to more specialized diagramming tools. I recommend using one of the many purpose-built online tools or a digital whiteboard for most of your work. You may need a more powerful graphics program for more polished and highly detailed maps.

For-Purpose Mapping Applications

Various web-based tools are designed specifically for mapping experiences. They offer the benefit of easy sharing and high portability. Many have evolved from simple online map creation tools into journey management

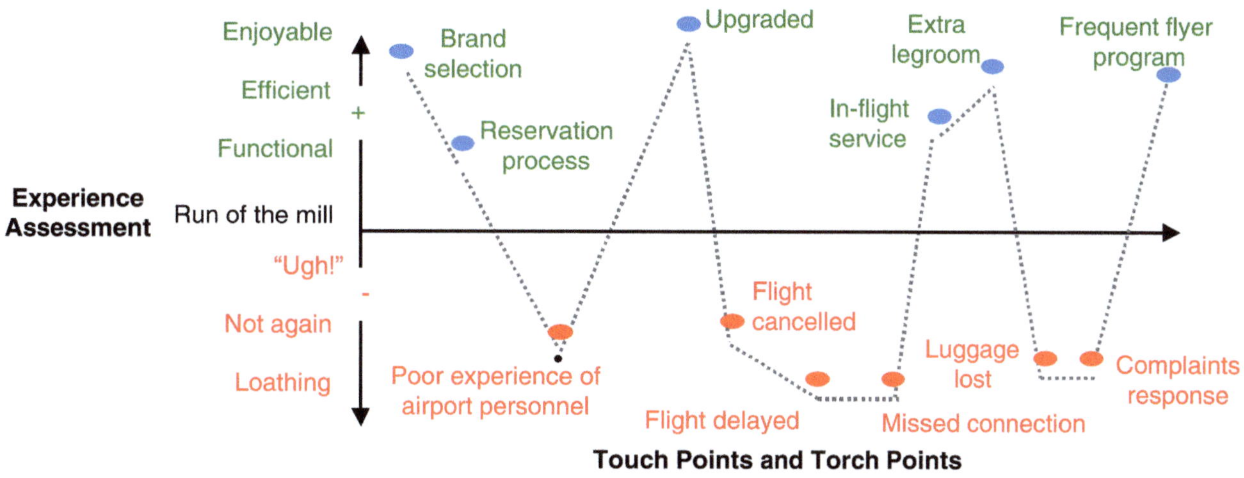

Source: Gartner Research (October 2004)

Figure 7-14. The idea of plotting emotional highs and lows is common in mapping and appeared as early as 2004.

platforms, which we'll explore in Chapter 10. At the time of writing, these are some current options:

- UXPressia (*uxpressia.com*)
- TheyDo (*theydo.com*)
- Smaply (*smaply.com*)
- JourneyTrack (*journeytrack.io*)
- Cemantica (*cemantica.com*)
- cxomni (*cxomni.net*)

Several of these tools provide AI capabilities to accelerate initial map creation—a key advantage of for-purpose tools over general diagramming software. UXPressia, for instance, can generate draft maps from text descriptions or persona profiles. TheyDo can analyze interview transcripts and feedback to automatically extract insights and build journeys. Some tools even generate custom storyboard visuals for each stage.

These AI features can't replace actual customer research, but they significantly reduce the time from data to draft, allowing teams to focus on refinement and action rather than starting from scratch.

Whiteboards

For a more lightweight option, online whiteboards such as Mural (*mural.co*) and similar tools work well for all aspects of the mapping process. Their flexibility and large canvas area allow for the creation of detailed

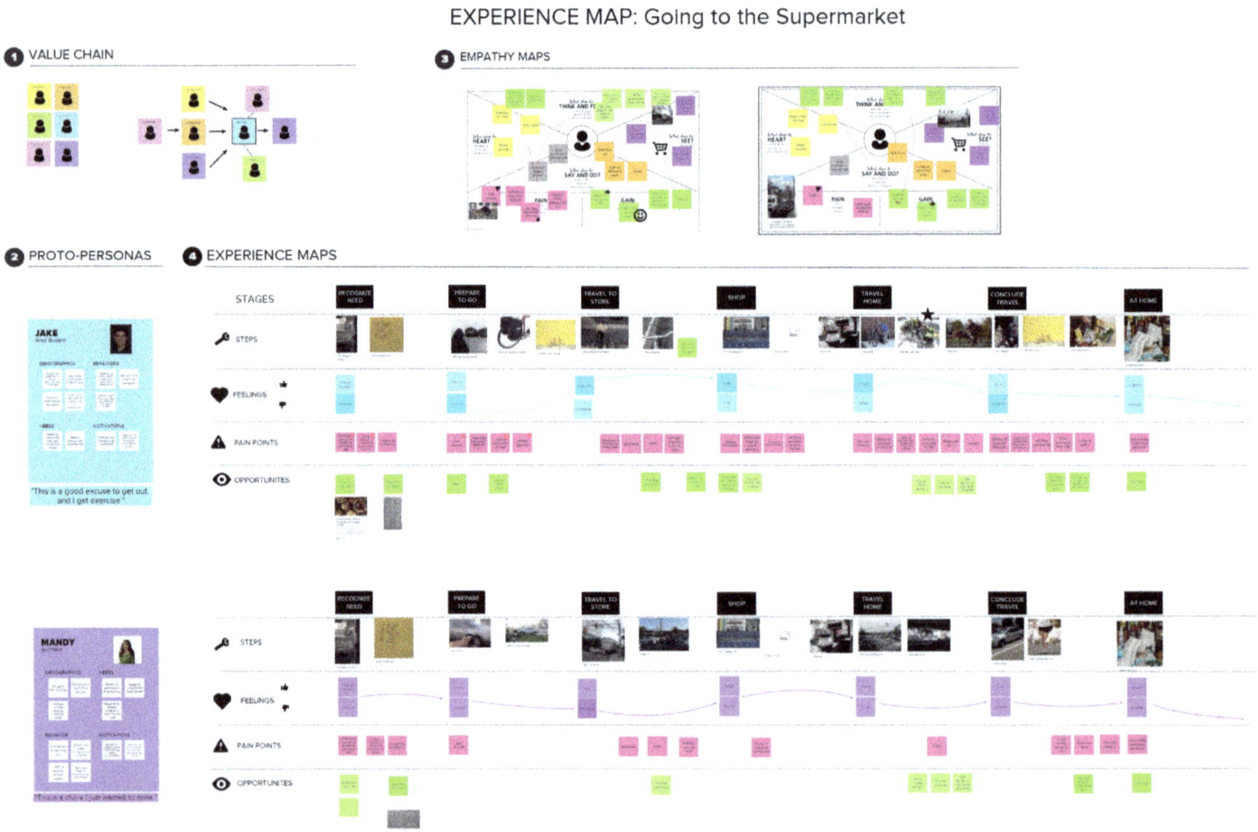

FIGURE 7-15. Mural allows for several mapping activities and a comparison of different experiences to be completed in one place.

diagrams. A key advantage of mapping in an online whiteboard is the ability to collaborate directly around the diagram; you can move from mapping to workshop in the same space.

Figure 7-15 shows a mapping exercise I completed using Mural. Note that multiple collaborative activities are included in one diagram: value chain mapping, personas, empathy maps, and experience maps. The large canvas also allows for a direct comparison of two different experiences—in this case, going to the supermarket by bicycle and by car.

Graphics Applications and Diagramming Tools

Diagramming tools such as Visio, Signavio, and Lucidchart offer a middle ground between whiteboards and graphics applications. Originally designed for flowcharts and process diagrams, they can be adapted for experience mapping.

For an even more polished and professional map, you can turn to formal graphics applications. Figma offers a powerful browser-based design environment. Adobe Creative Cloud—in particular, Illustrator (shown in **Figure 7-16**)—is also widely used. These programs require training and practice to use effectively.

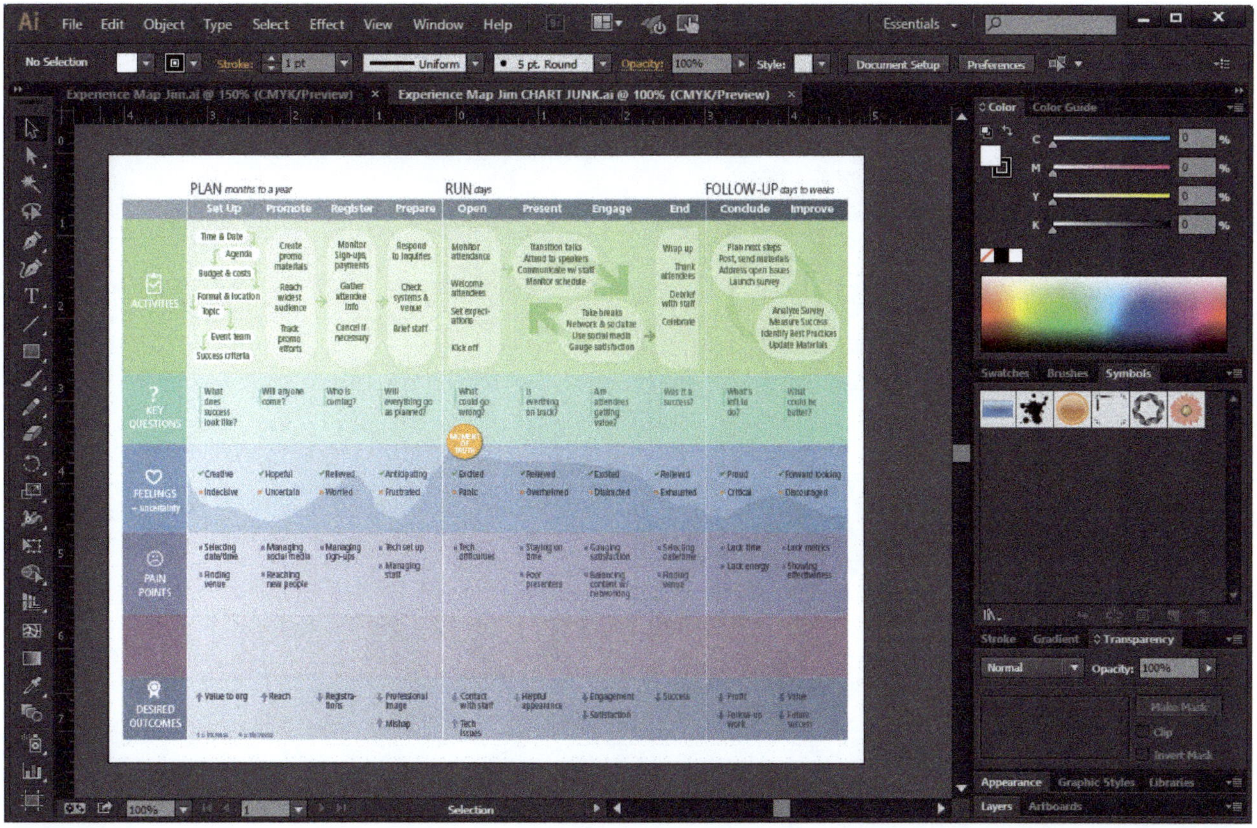

Figure 7-16. The map example in **Figure 7-12** was created with Adobe Illustrator.

Summary

The goal at this stage in the process is to assemble the insights from your investigation into a single diagram. Mapping an experience not only captures a great deal of information in a compact space, but also provides a compelling form of storytelling that stakeholders want to engage with.

The shape of your diagram conveys meaning. A chronological diagram typically takes the form of a table or timeline, but you can use alternatives as well, such as circular layouts, spider-like networks, and "snakes and ladders." Consider how the form of the diagram amplifies the overall message.

Getting the content to fit in a condensed format is challenging, commonly requiring an iterative process of clustering and grouping, then clustering again. Your goal is to reduce the information to representative, aggregated behavior for the target group. Thinking from the top down helps with this process. Use the form and structure of your diagram to guide you in compiling the content.

It's important to understand the basics of information design and the importance of visualization, even if you are not a graphic designer. Typography is critical, since much of the diagram is text. Graphic elements add visual interest and efficiency. Lines, shapes, icons, and colors enhance comprehension.

Visual hierarchy also plays a role. Not all elements are of equal importance. Use layering and different sizes to bring some aspects to the foreground and push others into the background. If you need to hire a graphic designer, you should be able to discuss these basics with them.

A variety of tools are available for illustrating diagrams. Spreadsheets and basic diagramming tools provide an easy starting point and quick results. High-end graphic applications can produce polished maps, but require expert skills to use effectively. There are more and more online tools available, including dedicated mapping solutions and multipurpose whiteboarding platforms.

Further Reading

Robert Bringhurst, The Elements of Typographic Style, *3rd ed. (2008)*

> This attractive, extremely well-written book is considered by many to be a "bible of typography." The illustrations and examples included are impeccable and engaging. There is a wealth of practical information, including a review of selected font specimens and a thorough glossary. This volume is a timeless reference to own.

Edward Tufte, Envisioning Information *(1990) and* Visual Explanations *(1997)*

> Tufte is the leading thinker in information design. These two books are a few of his many tomes outlining fundamental principles of information design. Understanding these concepts helps greatly in creating alignment diagrams.

Visual Critique Session

Objective	Evaluate and improve the visual design of a draft experience map to ensure that it communicates insights effectively to its intended audience
Time	60–90 minutes
Participants	4–8 people, including the map creator(s), a facilitator, and reviewers with diverse perspectives
Materials	Draft map (projected, printed large format, or shared screen), sticky notes, whiteboard

A structured review process helps refine the visual design and clarity of your experience map before wider distribution. This collaborative critique focuses on whether the map is scannable, is readable, and effectively highlights key insights, rather than debating content accuracy.

How it works:

1. Set the context. The map creator explains the purpose, intended audience, and key messages. Clarify that this session focuses on visual design and communication, not necessarily content validation.
2. Do a silent review. Have participants examine the map individually, noting what draws their eye, what's confusing, and what works well.
3. Conduct a guided critique. Work through design dimensions systematically: first impressions, visual hierarchy, readability, consistency, and clarity. Focus on whether the map communicates key insights effectively at a glance.
4. Prioritize and plan. Identify the top three to five changes that will improve clarity and effectiveness. Assign responsibilities and a timeline for revisions.

Learn more:

Adam Connor and Aaron Irizarry, *Discussing Design* (2015)

LUMA Institute, "Critique"

Hypothesis Map Workshop

Objective	Create a preliminary experience map based on team assumptions and identify research questions
Time	90–120 minutes
Participants	5–12 stakeholders representing different functions (product, marketing, sales, support, operations)
Materials	Whiteboard, sticky notes, prepared template or framework (optional)

For any mapping effort, begin by surfacing what you already know and what you don't. A hypothesis map workshop brings stakeholders together to create a preliminary diagram based on current assumptions about the customer experience (FIGURE 7-17). The workshop produces a draft map that serves as a "straw man" for discussion and validation. It can be done in person, or just as effectively in a remote session.

How it works:

1. Frame the effort. State the mapping scope, identify the primary customer type, and clarify whether you're mapping the current or future state.
2. Define the chronological structure. Use sticky notes to identify the main phases of the experience (typically about four to seven phases), and arrange them in sequence from left to right.
3. Map assumed customer actions. For each phase, write out what customers do—one action per sticky note. Use their language to maintain a clear customer perspective.
4. Add detail. Capture what customers are thinking, how they're feeling, and what questions they have at each stage, using different-colored sticky notes.
5. Identify touchpoints. Document where customers interact with your organization, including channels, tools, and both intentional and unintended touchpoints.
6. Surface unknowns and assumptions. Mark areas of uncertainty or disagreement, list explicit assumptions, and prioritize the research questions you most need to validate.
7. Put it to use. Use this hypothesis map to structure your research plan, focusing interviews and observations on validating or correcting your team's assumptions. As research findings come in, update the map to reflect reality rather than assumptions.

Learn more:

Kate Kaplan, "How to Run a Journey-Mapping Workshop," *NN/g* (2020)

Example:

Figure 7-17. A hypothesis map can be created during a cocreation workshop.

Diagram and Image Credits

Figure 7-1: Customer journey diagram for Starbucks created by Eric Berkman, used with permission

Figure 7-3: Diagram created by Sofia Hussain, appearing in her article "Designing Digital Strategies, Part 1: Cartography," used with permission

Figure 7-12: Experience map for organizing a conference created by Hennie Farrow with Jim Kalbach

Figure 7-13: Journey map created by Craig Goebel (*linkedin.com/in/craiggoebel*), used with permission

Figure 7-14: Excerpt from a diagram appearing in Ed Thompson and Esteban Kolsky's Gartnér research report "How to Approach Customer Experience Management," used with permission

Figure 7-15: Screenshot of experience map by Jim Kalbach, created in Mural

Figure 7-17: Photo by Martin Ramsin, cofounder and CEO of CareerFoundry (*careerfoundry.com*), used with permission

Visualizations act as a campfire around which we gather to tell stories.

—Al Shalloway

IN THIS CHAPTER

- Using diagrams to gain empathy
- Envisioning possible solutions
- Making ideas concrete
- Running an alignment workshop
- Collaborative methods for alignment

CHAPTER 8

Align: Making Sense Together

I'm lucky: throughout the majority of my career, I've had the fortune to come into direct contact with the customers of the companies I worked for. I've observed hundreds of people at their workplaces or in retail stores or in their homes, across many industries. I've seen what they experience in context. This is a privileged position.

Ideally, everyone in an organization would have first-hand contact with customers. But for many, this type of exposure is limited. Even frontline personnel, such as customer support center agents, may see only a small portion of the experiences customers have. Anecdotes come in without context.

A broader picture is needed to connect the dots of varying perspectives about the customer experience across the organization. Diagrams provide such a view. But creating a diagram is not the ultimate goal. Rather, it is a means to engage others in a conversation. It's your job to make that happen.

Having secured buy-in, done your research, and created your map, you have to take the story of what customers actually experience back to the organization. At this point, your role switches from mapmaker to facilitator. The aim is to get alignment on the current state of the customer experience and how your organization comprehends it. If the team members don't agree on where they are now, how can they agree on the best future direction?

Your diagram will help calibrate a common understanding. This phase makes experience improvements actionable for your team. While you certainly want the map to be based on valid evidence, the real magic happens in the shared act of sensemaking, problem framing, and cocreation. The journey is the destination.

An *alignment workshop* is an event that brings stakeholders together to focus on the experience from the outside in. This session can be held in person or remotely.

This chapter outlines the three stages of the workshop, shown in **Figure 8-1**:

1. ***Empathize:*** Gain a shared understanding of the individual's experience from an outside-in perspective.
2. ***Envision:*** Find opportunities and imagine future solutions.
3. ***Express:*** Articulate ideas quickly and get initial feedback.

The next chapter discusses how to run experiments and, more broadly, mobilize teams to action.

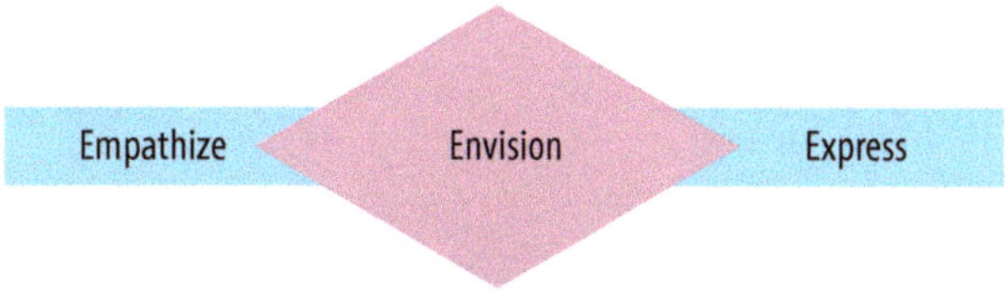

Figure 8-1. Alignment workshops focus on empathizing with customers, envisioning solutions, and expressing ideas.

Empathize: Build Shared Insight

It's not enough that *you* empathize with the experiences people have. You need to ensure that others gain that same deep insight. Strive to spread empathy throughout the organization. The empathy discussed here is rooted in comprehension—seeing the world through someone else's eyes.

Resist the urge to jump to a solution. Instead, begin by simply grasping the current experience. Identify the customer pain points that matter most, then frame the challenge for the team to move forward.

Understand the Experience

The first step in the process is examining the current experience. Assessing how well you support that experience will help you identify opportunities to create unique value.

To kick off the workshop, review the findings from your investigation together as a group. Make the diagram the focal point. Complement it with other artifacts you've created, such as personas.

You can also play audio or video clips from interviews to highlight a specific state of mind or pain point, or have other researchers tell stories from the field that bring the experience to life. Provide a rich description of the world as you've observed it in a way that is relevant to the organization.

After setting the stage, have the workshop participants engage with the diagram. Display it prominently so a group of people can stand around it (**Figure 8-2**). For in-person workshops, large printouts work well. In remote settings, rely on a digital whiteboard that everyone has access to. The aim is to immerse the team in the details of the experience by examining the map together. If the diagram has many sections, break the team into groups and have each one read through a different part.

The workshop is not a presentation for passive consumption. Participants should be active contributors. Prompt the group with directed thought exercises. For instance, have them identify moments of truth and discuss the relative importance of each touchpoint. You can use several techniques to engage them from the start:

Mark up the diagram.

Invite people to comment on, correct, or add information directly to the diagram. **Figure 8-3** shows a service blueprint marked up with participant feedback and comments written during a remote workshop. This gives participants a sense of ownership of the diagram and invites them to contribute to it.

Figure 8-2. Display the diagram prominently, in a large format, so people can gather around it.

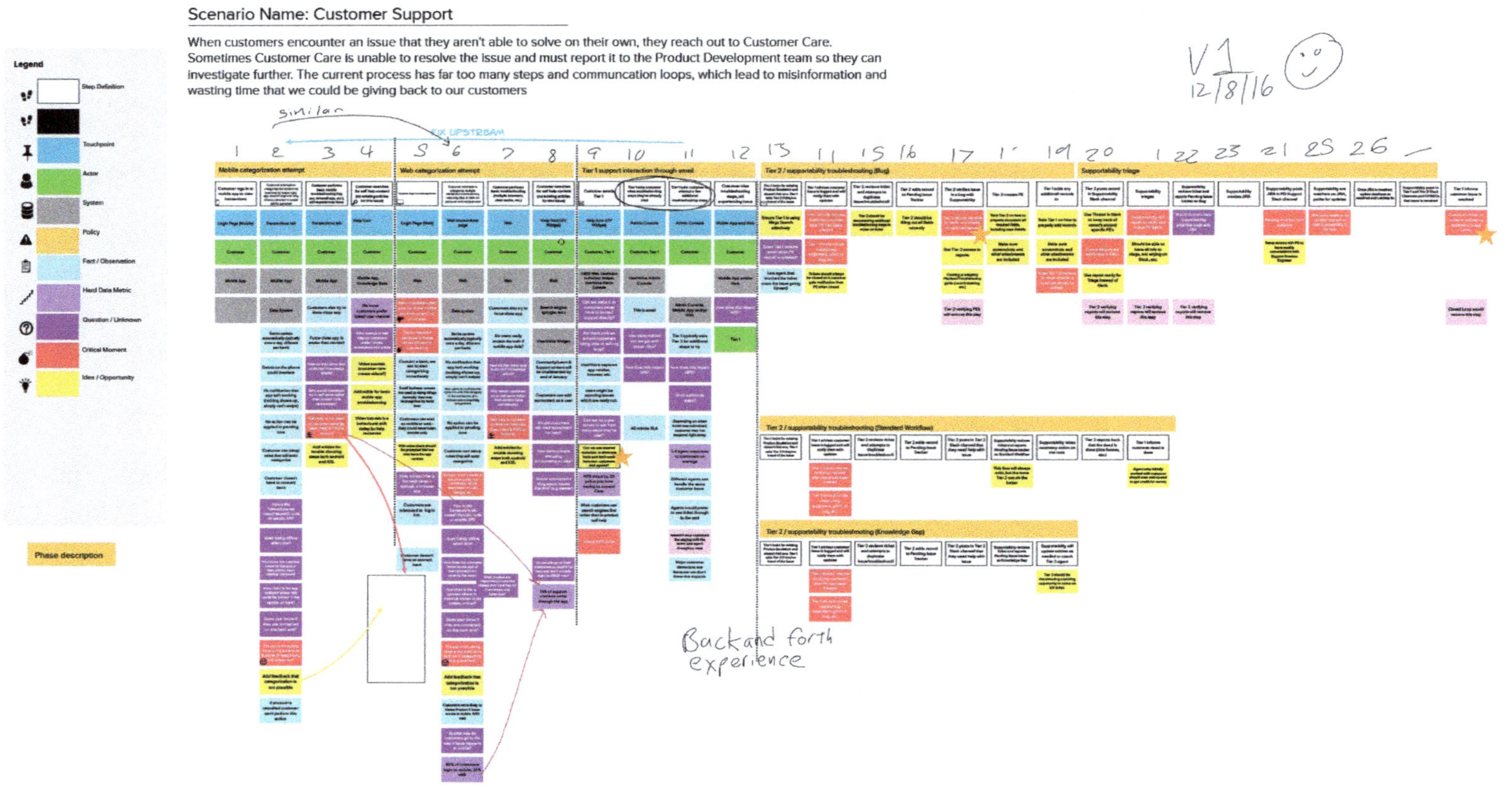

Figure 8-3. Invite everyone in the workshop to contribute to the diagram, whether in person or in a remote session.

Tell stories.

Have everyone in the group recount stories from the field research or their own interactions with customers. What have they heard people saying at each stage in the experience? What evidence can they add? Use this opportunity to continue sharing insights within the team.

Role play.

Consider role playing as a way for participants to deepen their understanding of the experience. This may not work for experiences that have discontinuous steps or hidden cognitive aspects, but it's an effective way for people to walk in the shoes of the customer—almost literally.

Empathy doesn't come from the diagram itself, but from the conversations that create a deeper understanding of the experience. As the facilitator, you have to ensure that a meaningful dialogue happens.

Identify Opportunities

Maps of an experience tell a story in a way that helps you uncover opportunities for improvement and innovation. But answers don't magically pop off the map. The sensemaking activities described here reveal the underlying issues and opportunities that matter, which often are not directly represented in the diagrams themselves:

Identify moments of truth.

Collectively identify the points in the experience that are most important to the people you serve. Give everyone some colored dot stickers, and have them indicate the most critical moments. Discuss the areas that got the most votes.

Vote on the importance to the organization.

Look at what's valuable to the organization. Give everyone a dot to vote on the most important points in the experience.

Rate your own performance.

One of my favorite activities to run is to ask the workshop participants to rate how well their product or service supports customers at each stage. School grades provide a familiar scale that most can relate to, or you can devise a simple scoring system (1–5 or similar). If you're working in multiple groups, compare the ratings after you come back together.

For instance, **FIGURE 8-4** shows ratings from two separate groups working on the same section of a diagram. The scale was 1–6, with 1 being the best

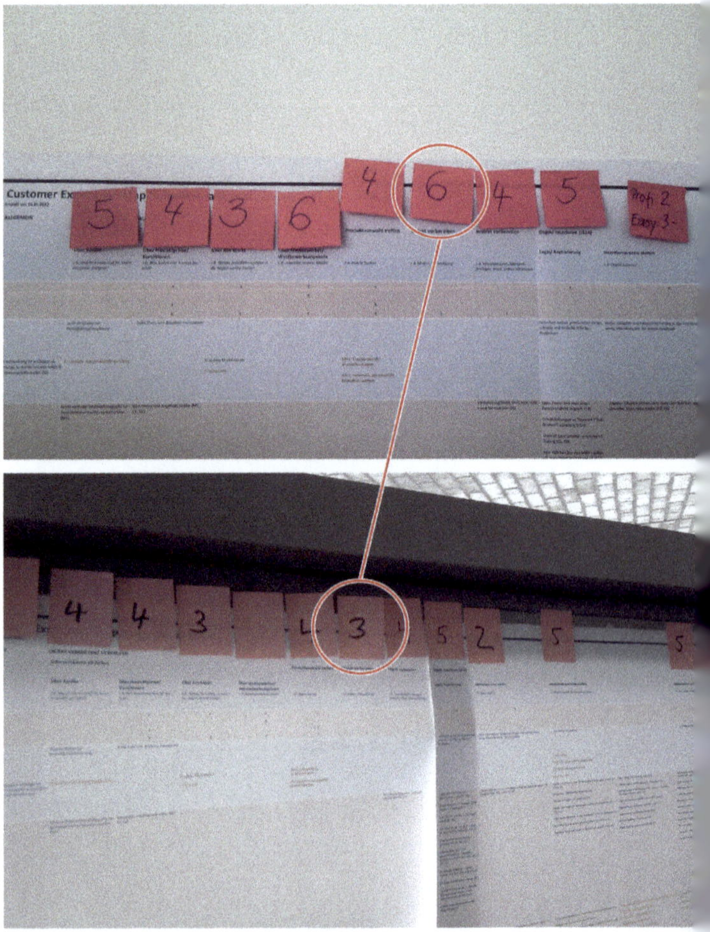

FIGURE 8-4. In this example, rating performance reveals a discrepancy between two workshop breakout groups, leading to a conversation to harmonize the differences.

score and 6 the worst. The scores between breakout groups diverged: for one section, one group gave it a 6 while the other gave it a 3.

Members of the team who gave the lower rating were closer to customer feedback and had insight that the others didn't. The ensuing conversation was enlightening for the whole group, building both empathy and consensus.

Identify pain points.

These activities serve to align different views on the optimal points of intervention. Strive to make opportunities explicit by highlighting some or all of the following aspects:

- ***Weaknesses:*** Look for points of failure. How can you better support users? When are their needs least satisfied?
- ***Gaps:*** Find where no support is offered. What pain points are not addressed? What moments of truth are potentially overlooked?
- ***Effort:*** Identify the points where people have to expend the most energy to get to the next step. Where is there the most friction in the experience?
- ***Competitors:*** Look at what other providers are doing at each step in the journey. Where are you underperforming? When do competitors provide satisfaction?

Table 8-1. Types of barriers that prevent individuals from getting value*

Barrier	Example	How to identify
Access: Some experiences are limited to specific times or places, or they pose physical or cognitive barriers.	Videoconferencing (Zoom, Google Meet) made remote medical consultations accessible during the pandemic, removing geographic barriers to healthcare.	Look at the instances in which an individual is not able to consume a product or service at all. Are they locked out of getting value?
Skill: People may lack the ability to perform a necessary task.	AI writing assistants (ChatGPT, Grammarly) removed the skill barrier of professional-quality writing.	Many steps in a process is a sign that skill may be a barrier. How can you make it simple enough for anyone to do?
Time: Interacting with a product or service may simply be too time-consuming.	Digital document signing (DocuSign) reduced contract processing time from days to minutes.	Look for high dropout rates in a process and assess whether lack of time is the root cause. What can you do to shorten the process?
Money: People may lack the financial means to afford a product or service.	Streaming services removed cost barriers through subscription models.	Identify points where a service has high costs. Ask how you might offer that same service for free.
Effort: Certain aspects of the experience create friction.	Before Uber came along, getting a taxi was hit-or-miss, and payment required people to fumble through their wallets for cash.	Look for ways to reduce the customer's time to task completion and remove friction.

* This table is adapted from *The Innovator's Guide to Growth* by Scott Anthony et al. (2008). See their book for more on barriers to innovation.

Remove barriers.

A particularly good way to spot opportunities for innovation and improvement is to look at what's holding people back in their current experience. Identify the obstacles to getting the jobs done at each stage in the diagram. **Table 8-1** summarizes key types of barriers to overcome, with examples and tips on how to identify each type.

Visualizing opportunities directly on the map allows the team to take a step back and consider them in the context of the organization's offering. For example, you can add a star or other icon to the most impactful points of intervention. Broader patterns will typically emerge. Prioritize the customer pain points that the team should focus on moving forward.

Frame the Challenge

Before launching into ideation, explore the challenge and frame it clearly. A couple of activities can help the team deepen their understanding quickly:

Make it worse.

A fun exercise for exploring opportunities is what I call *make it worse*, also known as *reverse brainstorming*. At each of the pain points you identified, ask: "How might you exacerbate the problem?" The answers may lead to laughter, but this exercise helps teams better understand the underlying causes and nuances of the customer's pain points.

Ask "What if?"

Continue exploring by asking "What if…?" questions. These questions help frame direction by introducing constraints or inversions: What if we eliminated a step? What if we focused on one specific channel? What if we served only our most demanding customers? Putting such constraints on the team's focus encourages deeper exploration of the problem space.

Create "How might we" statements.

After some exploration, you'll want to create "How might we" (HMW) statements. As the name indicates, each begins with a positive invitation to ideate:

- *How* indicates finding concrete solutions.
- *Might* indicates we don't know and have the humility to explore options.
- *We* indicates it's a team activity.

Seeding ideation with clear statements focuses the team on finding a specific solution. The language used is important: starting questions with "How might we…" provides a sense of safety for exploring a range of options together without fear of failing. It's an admission that the team doesn't have the answers from the outset but is committed to finding them together.

Prioritize opportunities.

With multiple options to follow, the team needs to focus its energy. Not every opportunity deserves equal attention. Use dot voting to identify which HMW statements resonate most strongly with the group. The goal is to identify the top two or three that will frame your ideation efforts in the Envision phase.

Envision: Explore Possibilities

In my experience, diagrams inspire ideas very quickly. Typically, workshop participants are teeming with ways to improve and innovate. It's your job as the facilitator to direct their attention and focus this energy. You'll help participants follow two motions: diverging and exploring many options, then converging on a direction or concept.

Diverge: Generate Ideas

At this point in the session, participants move from seeking to understand the current experience to envisioning possible solutions. The process is one of "going wide" in terms of ideas and concepts. This mode of working is commonly called *divergent thinking* (**Figure 8-5**). The aim at this stage isn't to decide on a single solution or direction to follow, but to explore the art of the possible.

To set the right expectations with the team, communicate the rules of divergent thinking:

Go for volume.

Aim to cover a breadth of ideas. Keep the details to a minimum at first. Avoid filtering ideas as you go.

Withhold judgment.

Create a safe place for people to be creative. Participants should be comfortable contributing ideas, even unformed ones.

Build on ideas.

Get the group to say "Yes, and..." instead of "But..." to ideas as they emerge. Find the underlying value of ideas and build on that.

Find alternatives.

Try to come up with variations and alternatives to initial ideas. Don't discard them too soon.

Encourage crazy ideas.

Refrain from self-censorship during ideation. There will be plenty of opportunities to prioritize and evaluate ideas later.

Be visual.

Work on whiteboards or flipcharts to map out ideas as they come. Uncover new relationships and connections as you brainstorm. For instance, Crazy Eights is a popular approach to visual brainstorming: create a grid of eight squares and have participants quickly sketch ideas in each box (**Figure 8-6**).

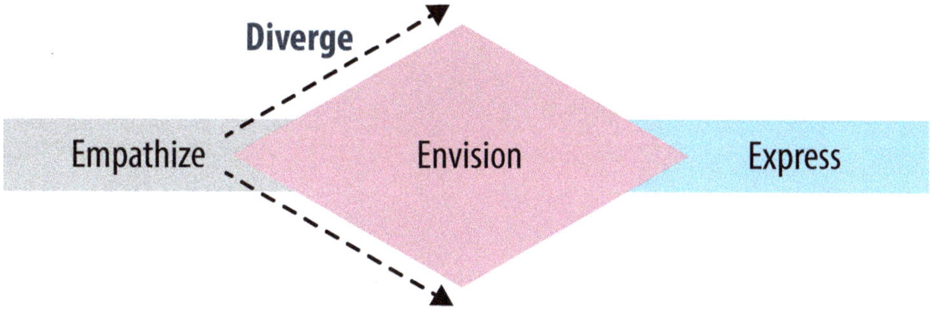

Figure 8-5. Begin by exploring different ideas with divergent thinking.

Figure 8-6. Visual brainstorming with the Crazy Eights technique for rapid thumbnail sketches.

The intent is to protect ideas in their infancy. Create an environment that embraces a range of possibilities, and encourage participants to recombine ideas into innovative ones. After collecting initial ideas from the group, conduct directed exercises to support this. "Challenge Industry Assumptions" on page 181, "Creative Matrix" on page 182, and "Group Brainwriting" on page 184 discuss techniques that work particularly well with mapping.

Converge: Prioritize Concepts

By this point in the alignment workshop, the team should have generated a lot of ideas. That's just the first step. Don't end there. Instead, integrate evaluation activities directly into the workshop—in other words, switch from divergent thinking to convergent thinking (**Figure 8-7**).

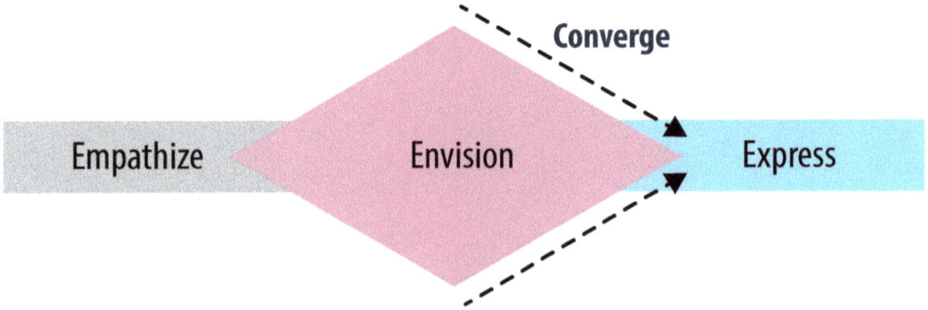

Figure 8-7. After divergent thinking, converge ideas into concepts and prioritize them.

Use the Importance/Difficulty Matrix for an initial prioritization, as shown in **Figure 8-8**. On one axis, consider how easy an idea is to implement (its difficulty). On the other axis, consider its importance for the individual's experience. Use the map and your identification of opportunities to help assess impact.

The aim is to sort the output of ideation into these quadrants. After sorting, you can then do subsequent prioritization within each quadrant.

Additionally, when the difficulty of an idea is high (i.e., that concept is harder to implement), you can find ways to move it up the matrix by either changing it to be easier to implement, considering alternative ways to implement it, or both.

Figure 8-9 shows an example of a prioritization matrix from a workshop I once conducted. We used a window for the matrix grid. We quickly identified five high-impact ideas that the engineering team could implement immediately—literally the next day—with no extra funding or resources.

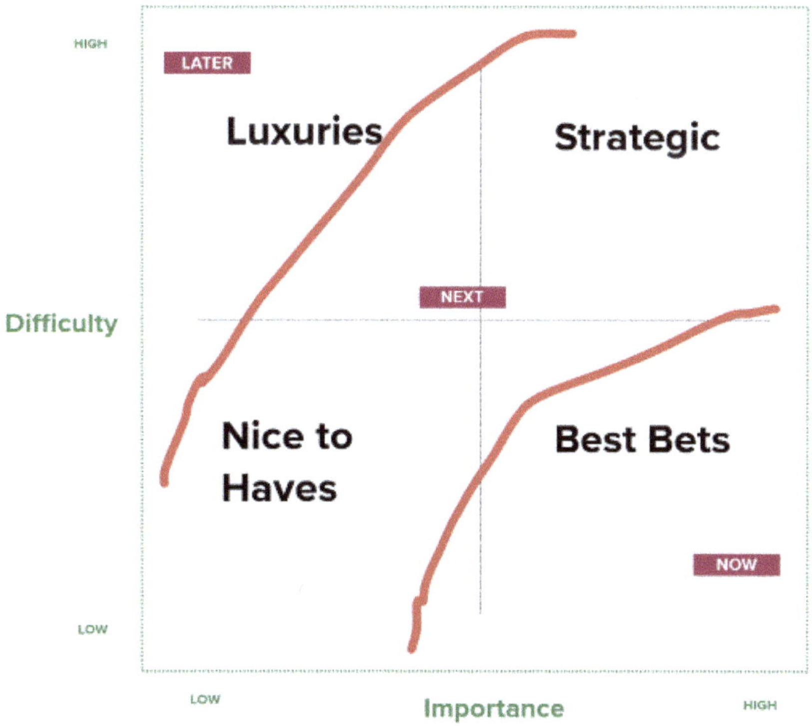

Figure 8-8. A simple prioritization scheme looks at importance and difficulty in a single matrix.

Figure 8-9. Prioritization of ideas by feasibility and value to the customer can be done on a simple grid.

Express: Make Ideas Concrete

Innovation often comes without epiphany. Don't expect to be able to recognize an innovation as such immediately. You'll have to first develop your ideas iteratively. Focus on lightweight artifacts that represent each concept, but leave them open to interpretation and learning.

After selecting ideas to move forward with, quickly articulate the details of each concept and test them for rapid feedback.

Articulate Concepts

Within just a few hours, you can create representations of your leading ideas for evaluation. The resulting artifacts will help "debug" your thinking and can prove or disprove the value of an idea quickly. Here are a few techniques:

Write scenarios.

Write out the details of a concept in prose, and let others read and critique it. Be as specific as possible about the anticipated experience. Even the simplest of concepts can easily lead to multiple pages of text.

Create storyboards.

Represent the intended experience in a series of graphic panels, then critique the idea as a group. See "Storyboarding" on page 186 for more details.

Draw a flowchart.

Express your idea as steps in a flowchart. This will help you make connections and see all the moving parts at once.

Sketch ideas and wireframe solutions.

Draw rough images of the product or service to share with others. Create simple versions of screens that outline the proposed interaction (**Figure 8-10**).

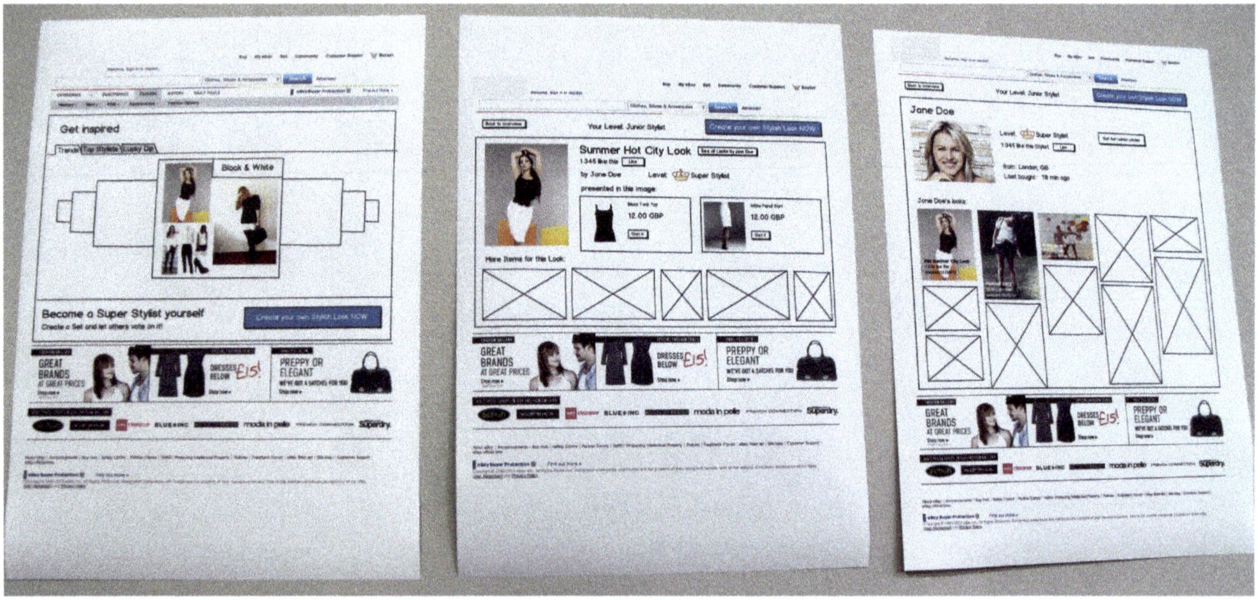

Figure 8-10. Wireframes created during an alignment workshop quickly bring ideas to life.

Build a low-fidelity prototype.

Modern prototyping tools make it easy to create testable concepts within minutes (**Figure 8-11**). Design tools like Figma allow quick interface mock-ups. AI-powered tools such as Google Stitch, v0, Bolt, and Lovable can generate working prototypes from text descriptions. Even tools like ChatGPT or Claude can produce functional HTML prototypes during a workshop session. This space is evolving rapidly, so explore current options.

Be careful about moving into high-fidelity prototypes too quickly. Keep the level of fidelity aligned with your level of certainty. Show just enough to get feedback on a key flow.

It's sometimes possible to prototype physical products in a day-long workshop. For instance, in one workshop I conducted, we tested an idea for improving the shipping experience for a large ecommerce website. We went to the local postal supply store, bought a box with the approximate dimensions we needed, and mocked it up to look like we had envisioned it. This was then used to get immediate feedback from potential customers.

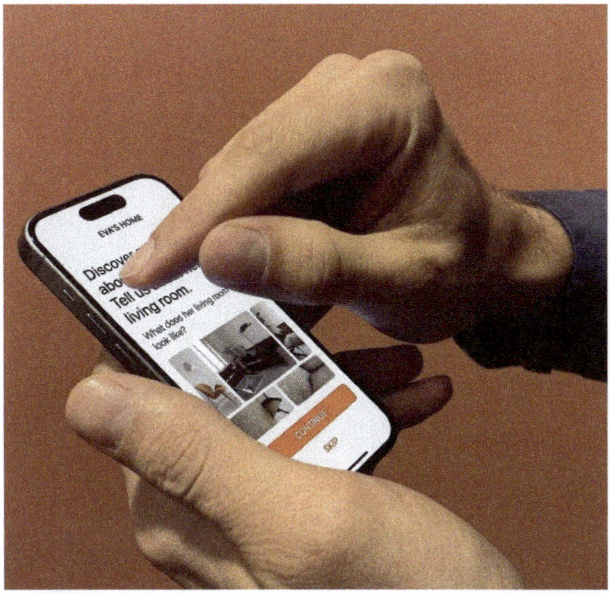

Figure 8-11. Modern tools allow for rapid prototyping, even within the span of a single workshop.

Get Feedback

Get feedback on your concepts as quickly as possible, even during the workshop. This will not be controlled, rigorous research, but instead serves as a quick way to validate your assumptions about an ideal solution. Does your concept address the problem in the right way? Are you moving in the right direction?

To refine your evaluation with feedback from potential end users, try some of these lightweight techniques:

Hallway testing

Get feedback from people close by who are not part of the workshop. Colleagues in other departments, for instance, can provide quick initial reactions to your concepts. In remote settings, have colleagues who weren't workshop participants give feedback via teleconferencing.

Online tests

Many online services provide feedback on concepts and prototypes—for example, UserTesting.com. You'll usually get results within a matter of hours.

Focus groups

Recruit people in advance of the workshop to give direct feedback. Present the concepts to a small focus group of two or three people and watch how they react.

Think-aloud testing

Ask participants to think aloud in moderated sessions as they interact with your prototype or artifact. As with focus groups, you'll have to recruit participants in advance. **Figure 8-12** shows a think-aloud test during a workshop I once led. The tests were conducted in a separate room, viewable by the workshop team via video camera.

Hold team discussions on the feedback you gather. Decide whether changes are needed or if the concept should be discarded entirely. Either way, be sure that you integrate the learning from the evaluation rounds into your thinking.

The overall aim at this point is to first understand the problem you are solving, then—using the artifacts created in the workshop (storyboard, diagrams, concepts, etc.)—get rapid feedback on the concepts you've come up with. You want to have confidence that you're solving the right problem before developing a full-fledged solution.

Figure 8-12. Test concepts during an alignment workshop for immediate feedback from potential solution users.

Running an Alignment Workshop

Diagrams don't provide answers; they foster conversations. As the facilitator of the workshop, it's your job to make those conversations happen. Whether in person or working with a remote team, your role begins with careful preparation, then moves into moderating the session, and continues with a strong follow-up.

Prepare

Organize the alignment workshop well in advance. In many organizations, getting people to commit for a whole day or multiple days is difficult. Include the workshop in your initial proposal, and schedule the event early on—even before you've started creating the diagram. The workshop is part of the mapping process.

An alignment workshop can be conducted in person or with distributed participants. I recommend avoiding a mix of remote and in-person participation: it's very difficult to balance the interaction in a hybrid situation. Either all in person or all remote is best.

Think about the environment you're creating for the discussion. For in-person workshops, it's preferable to secure a space outside of the normal workplace to avoid distractions. I prefer an oversized room to allow for a lot of movement.

In-person sessions can typically be scheduled for an entire day or even span multiple days. For remote workshops, consider splitting the workshop into smaller chunks of time; for example, instead of one eight-hour session, schedule two four-hour sessions on consecutive days for better engagement. You can use a similar approach for colocated teams, breaking the session into smaller segments and using a digital whiteboard so teams can see each other's input

Plan for breaks, catering, and social activities. For instance, planning a lunch outside of the workshop room can refresh participants and help keep them focused in the second half. Good facilitation also involves having the right tools, materials, and workflow. Consider all the details that go into creating the workshop experience for the group.

The alignment workshop is an inclusive activity, so plan to invite a range of stakeholders with different functions in your organization. The aim is to get broad buy-in and input from diverse perspectives, including industry experts from outside the organization. From this standpoint, remote sessions are advantageous because they typically open up participation to colleagues who might not be able to travel. Groups of 6–12 participants work best. Larger groups are possible but require more planning and preparation.

> *The alignment workshop is an inclusive activity, so plan to invite a range of stakeholders with different functions in your organization.*

Assign roles and clarify what's expected from everyone up front. This is particularly important for remote sessions. Some key roles are as follows:

- ***Facilitator:*** This is the person moderating the workshop, who ideally is also the mapmaker. Co-facilitators may help guide the session.
- ***Breakout group leaders:*** If you plan to break out into smaller groups, enlist one person per group to keep the discussion moving and the team on task.
- ***Decision makers:*** Include senior stakeholders to be able to make business decisions, as well as to serve as a tiebreaker if needed.

- *Designers:* Include designers and others who can help articulate concepts.
- *Industry experts:* Consider introducing outside voices into the workshop, and point out their roles to everyone else in advance.
- *Test moderator:* Include someone who can moderate user tests, if needed.
- *Contributors:* This encompasses everyone else in the group.

Plan an agenda for the workshop to mirror the desired shape of the interaction, as outlined earlier in this chapter. It's OK to improvise and go off schedule, but having an agenda will help keep the session on track. When working with distributed teams, consider how you can have work done asynchronously both before and after the real-time session to maximize the efficiency of your time together.

Keep the desired outcomes of the session in mind to guide the flow: understand the experience (Empathize), explore solutions based on the insights you prioritize (Envision), and select a concrete concept to pursue moving forward (Express). The key is to move through all three modes of working during the session to ensure you'll meet your goals. **Figure 8-13** shows what a day-long workshop might look like at a high level.

I recommend holding a short call a week before the alignment workshop to kick off before the session begins. Distribute materials, introduce everyone to one another, and set expectations during the call to get some of the housekeeping out of the way in advance. Assign pre-work to accelerate the agenda of the main session and get people thinking about the topic before they show up.

Longer sessions across multiple days are also possible and start to resemble what are called *design sprints*. See "Condensed Design Sprint" on page 214 for more details.

Run the Workshop

Once the group is assembled, clarify the expectations. Review the flow of the workshop again with the team and be sure to let them know that follow-up work will be required. The conversation does not end with this workshop; it's ongoing.

Start with a warm-up exercise, then focus on the experience represented in your diagram. The map should be the centerpiece of the session. Follow the format outlined in this chapter, moving from empathizing with the experience to exploring concepts to expressing them.

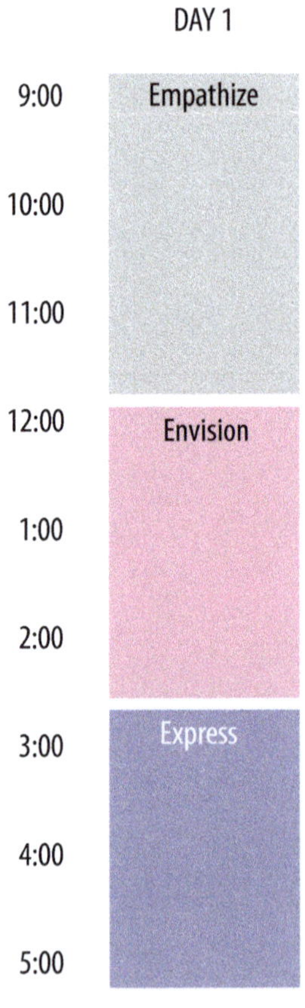

Figure 8-13. This example shows how the flow of a one-day workshop moves through the three phases of interactions, including the time to plan follow-up experiments.

The group of people you bring together may never have worked together before. For in-person sessions, include an event like a sit-down meal. When working remotely, schedule a team-building exercise into the agenda. It's important for continued collaboration that people get to know one another on a personal level. This helps build trust and respect, which goes a long way toward the success of the effort.

Follow Up

An alignment workshop is a creative endeavor that results in actionable outcomes. Alignment activities do not end with the workshop. Make sure you keep the momentum going after the session has ended. Consider ways to continue working with the team, and share the results of your effort:

Get feedback on the session.
: Follow up with a brief survey on the mapping effort and the workshop. The intent is to learn how you can improve this type of effort in the future.

Update the diagram.
: Take the feedback you get from the session and update the diagram. Include the additions and comments others made, as well as outcomes.

Distribute materials.
: Collate the output of the workshop and distribute it to others who didn't participate. Schedule a meeting to present the results to others.

Make the diagram visible.
: Create different forms of the diagram and make them visible. Print out large copies for the office space. Create flyers or handouts of the diagram that colleagues can keep by their desks. Integrate it into presentations and other documents internally. If working online, distribute a PDF of the diagram or link to your map throughout communications with the team.

You also need to ensure that the planned experiments are actually conducted, as discussed in the next chapter. Keep the momentum going with an action plan and assigned owners for each experiment. Hold weekly check-ins to track progress if needed.

Summary

A diagram is a means to an end—to get team alignment around the experience. But diagrams don't provide the answers; instead, they spark conversations. They are like campfires that people gather around to share stories and to make sense of the experiences they create.

At this stage, your role switches from researcher and mapmaker to facilitator. The goal is twofold: align the internal perspective of the organization to the outside world, and use that insight to generate new ideas. In an alignment workshop, you'll alternate between three modes of activity: empathizing, envisioning, and expressing.

Think of a diagram as a prototype of an experience. It allows team members to put themselves in the customer's shoes and empathize with them. First, read through the diagram together and assess your performance at each stage to find opportunities for improvement and innovation.

Envision possible solutions, and then select and represent ideas with the most potential. This can be done quickly with scenarios, storyboards, and wireframes. Use these artifacts to get input from others.

Finally, express concepts to make them concrete and iterate. A wall full of sticky notes does not go far enough. Strive to represent ideas and make them as tangible as possible.

Even within a single-day workshop, you can run lightweight tests. Invite a few outsiders to critique storyboards and sketches, for instance. Iterate as many times as possible, and plan to continue iterating after the workshop. If you're working with a remote group, break the session into smaller chunks and do testing or get customer feedback in between your meeting times.

Running a workshop requires careful planning. And alignment doesn't stop with the diagram or with the workshop. After you generate excitement, consider how to keep the momentum going. The next chapter discusses how to move into planning and eventually development.

Further Reading

Dave Gray and Sunni Brown, Gamestorming 2.0 *(2025)*

Gamestorming is an indispensable collection of activities for interactive workshops. This updated and expanded edition presents a range of activities and exercises, with tips on how to run them effectively. The introduction gives one of the best descriptions of workshop formats and designs I've seen.

Marc Stickdorn, Markus Edgar Hormess, Adam Lawrence, and Jakob Schneider, This is Service Design Doing *(2018)*

Drawing on decades of combined experience, the authors provide a hands-on guide to applying service design methods in organizational contexts, with detailed facilitation guides, case studies, and collaborative exercises. The companion website includes a range of methods and team exercises suitable for use with mapping efforts. See also the precursor to this book, *This is Service Design Thinking* (2012), by Marc Stickdorn and Jakob Schneider.

Kate Kaplan, "How to Run a Journey-Mapping Workshop," NN/g *(2020)*

This clear and concise article offers a wealth of practical advice based on a real-world example of a mapping workshop. It includes concrete activities and methods for getting groups to engage with the diagrams.

Joran Slane Oppelt and Geoffrey T. Nelson, Facilitation: A Human-Centered Guide to the Art of Collaboration *(2023)*

This fully illustrated resource on facilitation presents a comprehensive view of the practice. The book includes contributions from experts and covers everything from the history of facilitation to practical tools such as scripts, templates, checklists, and virtual facilitation platforms like Mural.

Mark Tippin and Jim Kalbach, The Definitive Guide to Facilitating Remote Workshops *(2019)*

I coauthored this free ebook with my colleague at Mural, Mark Tippin. It's a practical guide based on our experience helping and observing dozens of teams working remotely. Distributed team collaboration demands remote facilitation skills. Though pre-pandemic, the principles outlined here remain highly applicable. Download the PDF at *mural.co/ebook*.

Rate Your Performance

Objective	Assess how well an organization supports customers at each stage in a journey
Time	30–60 minutes
Participants	3–20
Materials	Experience diagram, whiteboard, sticky notes

Using an experience map as a mirror, teams can honestly assess their current performance at each stage of the journey (**Figure 8-14**). This method transforms the map from a descriptive tool into an evaluative one, surfacing strengths, weaknesses, and gaps. This is one of my go-to methods to use with mapping that has proven successful time and time again.

How it works:

1. Orient the group to the diagram. Have someone read the main chronology and the basic steps aloud. Ask if there are questions, or missing information that should be included.
2. Review the diagram. Stage by stage, have the team go through all the information in the map.
3. Assess performance. Give the group a rating scale—e.g., 1–5 or school grades (A, B, C, D, F). Ask: "How well do we support customers at each stage?" Rate individually first, then discuss the ratings to arrive at agreed scores.
4. Identify strengths and weaknesses. Step back and look for patterns. Where did everyone agree on strengths? Where are common weaknesses? What further information is needed?
5. Create "How might we" (HMW) statements. For key pain points and opportunities on your map, rephrase them as HMW questions, like "How might we make onboarding feel less overwhelming?" Then, assign breakout groups different statements and have them brainstorm ideas, e.g., with a Creative Matrix (see "Creative Matrix" on page 182) or brainwriting.

Variations:

1. Vote on the moment of truth or the biggest pain point.
2. Rate competitors' performance.
3. Identify the biggest gaps in your offering.

Learn more:

LUMA Institute, "Visualize the Vote"

Sarah Gibbons, "Dot Voting: A Simple Decision-Making & Prioritizing Technique in UX," *NN/g* (2019)

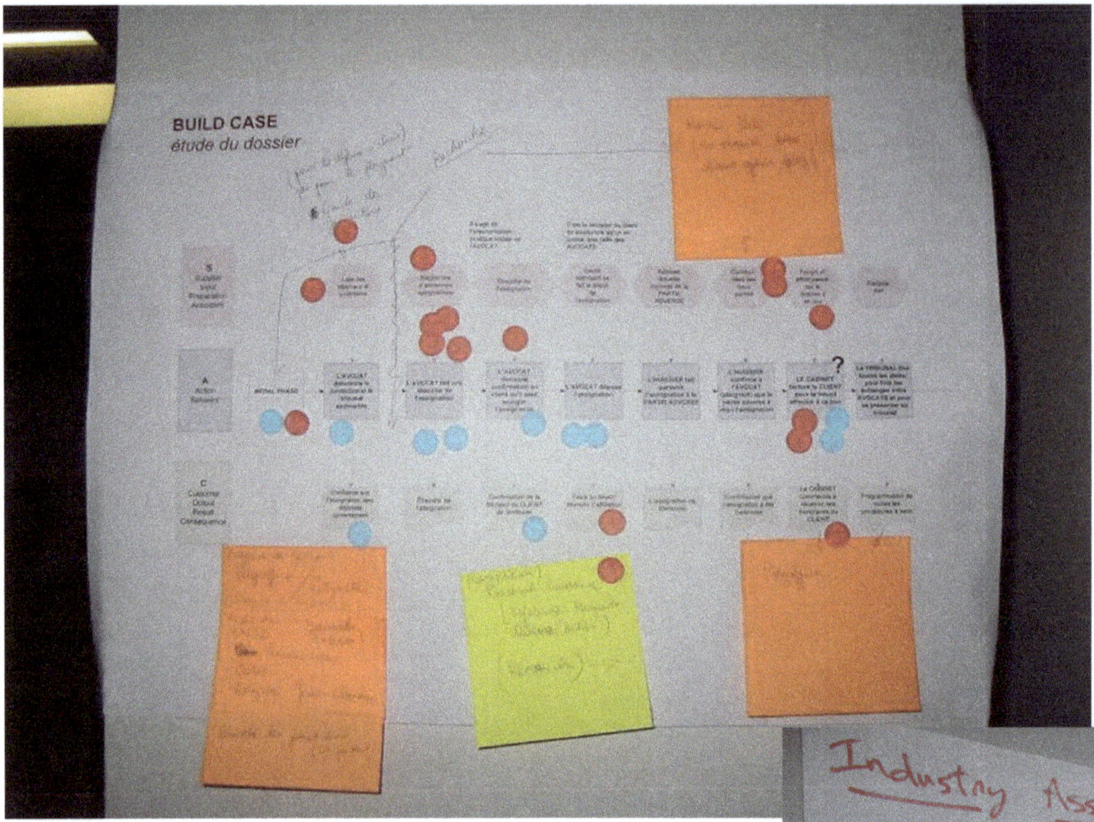

Example:

Figure 8-14. In this example from a mapping workshop, participants rated pain points in the journey and overlaid competitors' offerings for comparison.

Example:

Figure 8-15. Challenge industry assumptions in a workshop.

Challenge Industry Assumptions

Objective	Identify and challenge industry assumptions to uncover opportunities for differentiation and innovation
Time	30–60 minutes
Participants	5–15
Materials	Experience map, whiteboard, sticky notes

To go beyond finding incremental improvements, you have to be ready to challenge industry assumptions (**Figure 8-15**). Use the map to uncover the unspoken assumptions at each stage. By surfacing and deliberately inverting these assumptions, teams can identify opportunities for disruptive innovation that fundamentally change the game.

How it works:

1. Generate assumption statements. Individually, complete this sentence: "Everyone in [industry] knows that [assumption]." Use the phases of the experience map to prompt thinking. Go for volume—about five statements each.
2. Share and prioritize. Review all the assumption statements and group similar ones. Use dot voting to identify three to five of the most relevant assumptions.
3. Invert the assumptions. For each prioritized assumption, ask: What if we did the opposite? What if this element was eliminated? What conventions can we break?
4. Evaluate the possibilities. Review the inverted assumptions. Which feel promising? Which align to customer pain points? Identify the top two or three.
5. Create "How might we" statements for each inverted assumption. Use these as input into ideation, e.g. with a Creative Matrix (see "Creative Matrix" on page 182), group brainwriting, or open brainstorming.

Learn more:

Luke Williams, *Disrupt* (2011)

For alternatives, see also the Alternative Worlds (discussed in Chapter 9) and SCAMPER methods.

Creative Matrix

Objective	Generate a large number of diverse ideas quickly by exploring intersections between categories
Time	30–45 minutes
Participants	6–20 (working in teams of 3–5)
Materials	Large poster or digital canvas, sticky notes, pens

Constraints spark creativity. When ideation feels too open-ended or teams fall into conventional thinking, a structured grid can unlock novel combinations. The Creative Matrix creates deliberate collisions between categories to generate unexpected solutions at their intersections.

How it works:

1. Set up your Creative Matrix. The columns and rows of the matrix are variable (**Figure 8-16**). For mapping, combinations of the following typically work well:
   - *Columns:* Key journey stages, HMW statements, or personas/customer types
   - *Rows:* Resources, technologies, or barriers to overcome
2. Populate the matrix. After deciding on the column and row labels, brainstorm ways to address the issues implied at the intersection of each.
3. Find patterns and themes. Look for commonalities that can be combined into overarching solution concepts to address customer pain points.
4. Share concepts. Review the generated ideas, select the most promising, and integrate them back into a future state journey map, showing how these solutions improve the experience.

Learn more:

LUMA Institute, "Creative Matrix"

Example:

Figure 8-16. You can use this simple Creative Matrix template to brainstorm across multiple pain points (column headers) and solution types (row headers) at once.

Group Brainwriting

Objective	Generate diverse ideas by having teams sequentially build upon each other's work
Time	60–90 minutes
Participants	9–15 (working in groups of 3–5)
Materials	Experience map, whiteboard, sticky notes in four different colors

Brainwriting (also called *Round Robin*) generates fresh ideas through group authorship. As concepts pass from group to group, they evolve in unexpected ways. This method works particularly well with experience maps because breakout groups can build on one another's thinking at different stages of the journey.

How it works:

1. Generate initial concepts. Each group works on a different section of the experience map, or a different experience entirely. Using one color of sticky notes, they brainstorm new, ideal steps and/or solutions for their assigned area. Using another color, they add comments to clarify their concepts.
2. Rotate and question. Groups rotate to a new map. They read the steps and comments from the previous group and then use a new color to pose questions about each step: What's unclear? What might not work? What's missing?
3. Rotate and ideate. Groups rotate again to a map they haven't seen. After reading the steps, comments, and questions, they use a fourth color to brainstorm new ideas and improvements (**Figure 8-17**). Select the strongest concepts to focus on and sketch them out.
4. Present and synthesize. Groups return to their original maps to see how others built upon their work. Each presents key insights and unexpected directions that emerged from the collective input.

Learn more:

LUMA Institute, "Round Robin"

Interaction Design Foundation, "Brainwriting"

Example:

FIGURE 8-17. This section of a design map created in a workshop shows the various types of information on different-colored sticky notes.

Storyboarding

Objective	Visualize how a new concept plays out in a customer's experience
Time	45–60 minutes
Participants	3–8 per storyboard
Materials	Template with 6–10 blank rectangles

Walt Disney once said, "In our studio, we don't write stories, we draw them." Storyboarding brings ideas to life by visualizing people experiencing your concept in action. This method works powerfully with experience maps because it transforms abstract improvements into tangible scenarios that teams can evaluate and refine. Even primitive sketches convey a meaningful sequence of events, helping teams communicate possibilities more clearly than words alone.

How it works:

1. Select the concept. Choose an idea from the experience map to develop—typically, a solution to a pain point or an opportunity to improve a specific phase of the journey.
2. Draft the storyline. Outline the beginning, middle, and end of the scenario. Who is the main character? What is the setting? What triggers the experience? How does it resolve?
3. Draw key frames. Sketch each major step or moment in the sequence. Don't worry about artistic quality—stick figures work fine. Focus on showing what happens and how the customer experiences it. Add a brief descriptive phrase beneath each frame.
4. Review and assess. Present the storyboard to the group (**Figure 8-18**). Does the concept work in practice? Where might it break down? What's compelling? What needs refinement? Decide whether to pursue, modify, or shelve the idea.

Learn more:

LUMA Institute, "Storyboarding"

Example:

Figure 8-18. Storyboards represent ideas visually with fairly low effort to test concepts.

Pitch Presentation

Objective	Present new concepts in a persuasive format that builds support and identifies next steps
Time	45–60 minutes total
Participants	3–8 per team, plus stakeholders and decision makers as an audience
Materials	Presentation template, storyboards, timer

Ideas mean nothing without buy-in. After teams develop and storyboard concepts, they need to pitch them convincingly to decision makers and stakeholders. A structured pitch format with strict time limits forces teams to distill their thinking to its essence. This method transforms workshop outputs into actionable proposals.

How it works:

1. Prepare the pitch. Teams consolidate their concepts into a structured presentation: the name of the concept, how it works, convincing arguments and benefits, and recommended next steps. Consider using a Concept Poster format to help structure the team's thinking around their pitch (see **Figure 8-19**).
2. Present to the group. Each team delivers its pitch within a two-minute time limit. Use storyboards and visuals to illustrate the concept in action. Focus on clarity and persuasion, not perfection. For an extra twist, invite executives or business sponsors who weren't in the mapping workshop to be the audience and judges.
3. Q&A and feedback. After each pitch, the audience asks clarifying questions and provides immediate feedback. What resonates? What concerns arise? What's missing?
4. Evaluate and decide. After all the pitches, the group discusses which concepts warrant further development. Use dot voting or discussion to prioritize next steps.

Learn more:

Carmine Gallo, "The Art of the Elevator Pitch," *Harvard Business Review* (2018)

Team Asana, "15 Creative Elevator Pitch Examples for Every Scenario" (2025)

LUMA Institute, "Concept Poster"

Example:

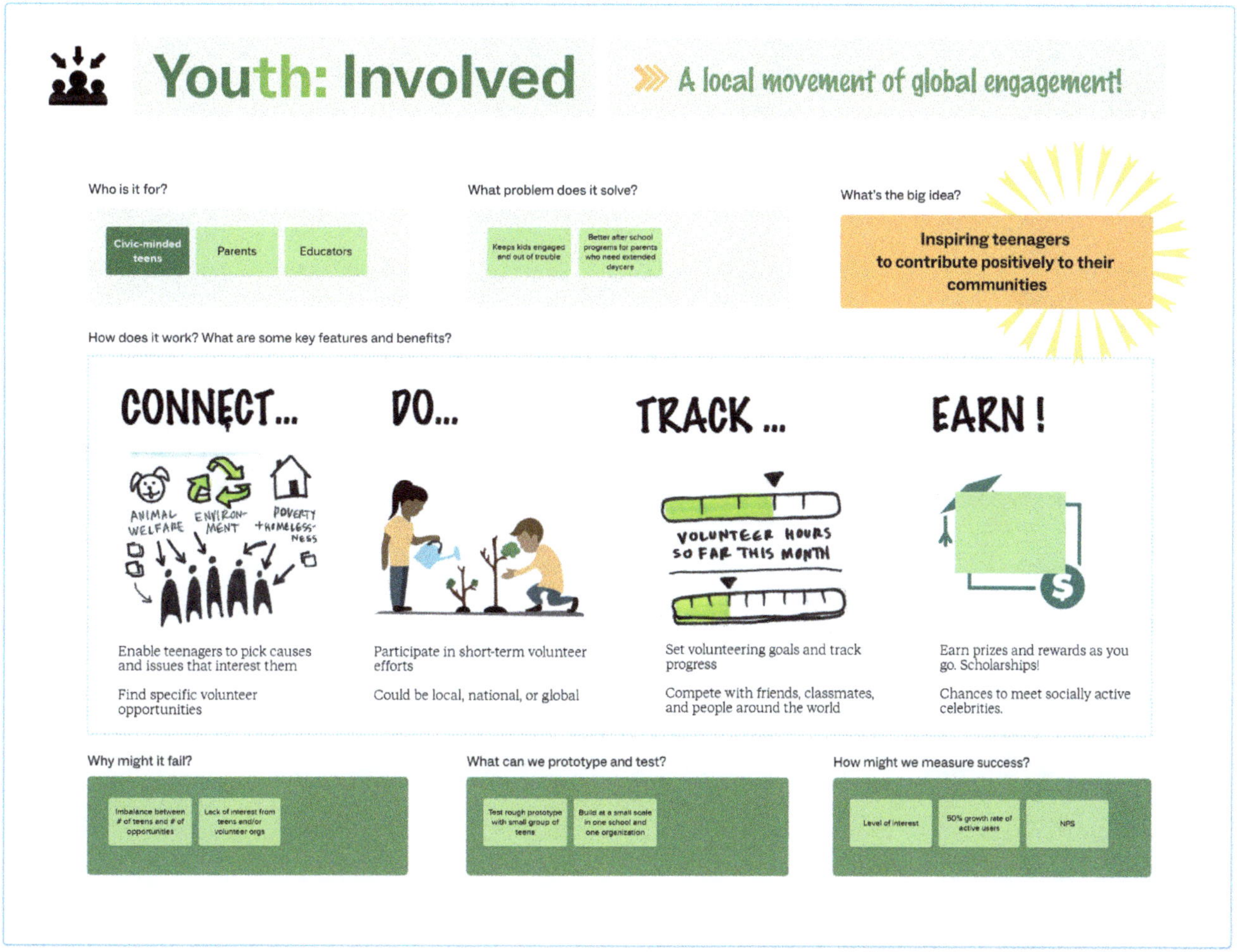

FIGURE 8-19. A Concept Poster includes structured sections to help lay out the details of a pitch presentation.

Diagram and Image Credits

FIGURE 8-2: Photo of Nathan Lucy running an alignment workshop, used with permission

FIGURE 8-3: Example service blueprint used in a workshop at Mural, used with permission

FIGURES 8-4, 8-9, 8-10, 8-11, 8-12, 8-14, 8-15, 8-17: Photos by Jim Kalbach

FIGURE 8-6: Example of thumbnail sketching with Crazy Eights by Mark Tippin, used with permission

FIGURE 8-18: Example storyboard created during a workshop by Erik Hanson, used with permission

FIGURE 8-19: Example of a Concept Poster by Mural, used with permission

If you don't know where you are going,
any road will get you there.

—Lewis Carroll, *Alice in Wonderland*

IN THIS CHAPTER

- Ideas are overrated
- Mapping future experience
- Planning experiments
- Collaborative methods for activation

CHAPTER 9

Activate: Driving Momentum and Impact

Throughout this book, I've urged you to empathize with the people you serve. The key is to view your offering from the outside in rather than the inside out. Strive to build that empathy as a team *before* conceiving new solutions.

I've experienced firsthand the trap of rushing into solutions. At one company I worked for, a small team spent two months behind closed doors developing a concept that helped people plan events, without any contact with potential customers. Anyone who did interact closely with the target could immediately see that the solution had serious flaws. It didn't address real needs or align with users' mental models. Despite the team's passion, its fully fledged product concept was doomed from the outset. The team could have spent its time more wisely by better investigating the problem first.

Once you've gained empathy and identified the right opportunities to target, you're ready to design concrete solutions to implement.

Note that I'm not advocating weeks or months of up-front research, which could be perceived as slowing things down. But as the previous chapters have demonstrated, the mapping process helps teams develop a common understanding of an individual's experience and accurately frame the problem. Once you've gained empathy and identified the right opportunities to target, you're ready to design concrete solutions to implement. This is part of your role as the mapmaker. It's not just about doing research and creating a diagram. You also have to plan for strong follow-through into the solution space.

The aim of this phase is to make your insights matter and keep the momentum going. Up to this point, this book has focused on current state visualizations—diagrams of the world as it exists today. This chapter discusses ways to make mapping actionable. First, consider how to design future experiences with techniques such as storylines and user story mapping. Then, run the experiments planned at the end of the alignment workshop (described in Chapter 8). Finally, devise ways to keep the mapping effort alive and ongoing—empathizing with customers should never end.

Envision Future Experiences

Mapping is a key way to capture observations from the real world and represent them visually. But mapping can also be a generative technique to describe the experience of new solutions, particularly in complex or overarching experiential contexts. Teams need to see the end-to-end experience so they can design products and services that fit in, even if they are not in control of all the parts. Two techniques that are useful for this are to-be mapping and storylines.

Create a Future State Map

As mentioned previously, this book focuses on current state maps: mapping an experience as it currently exists to create empathy and understanding, which leads to identifying opportunities. At some point, however, you may want to consider *future state maps*, also called *to-be maps* or *target state blueprints*.

As their name suggests, future state maps outline the experience of a solution that doesn't yet exist. Unlike current state maps, they aren't based on research. Instead, future state maps represent a vision of a potential experience and serve as a communication tool for a team building a new service of some kind.

There are a few ways to map future experiences. I typically try to avoid creating a separate diagram. Instead, it's often possible to include future experiences within the current state map—for example, at the bottom, as shown in **Figure 9-2**. This highlights the transition needed to move from the present to the future. Both cause and cure are captured in one place.

Sometimes, however, the to-be state involves a fundamentally different flow of interactions, and the chronology of steps may change as well. For instance, an as-is map of a traditional taxi experience would look very different from one of using Uber. With Uber, the payment method is set before the ride begins, the destination is given to the driver before the rider gets in the car, and tips are often given later. In cases like this, the future state is best represented in a separate diagram.

Erika Flowers and Morgan Miller demonstrate techniques for creating a separate future state map in their popular book on service blueprinting.* They point to several reasons for making a future state map:

1. You're striving to create something completely new that's never been done before.
2. The team needs to explore the feasibility of a desired experience in detail.
3. You need to align the desired experience with stakeholders and your organizational structure.

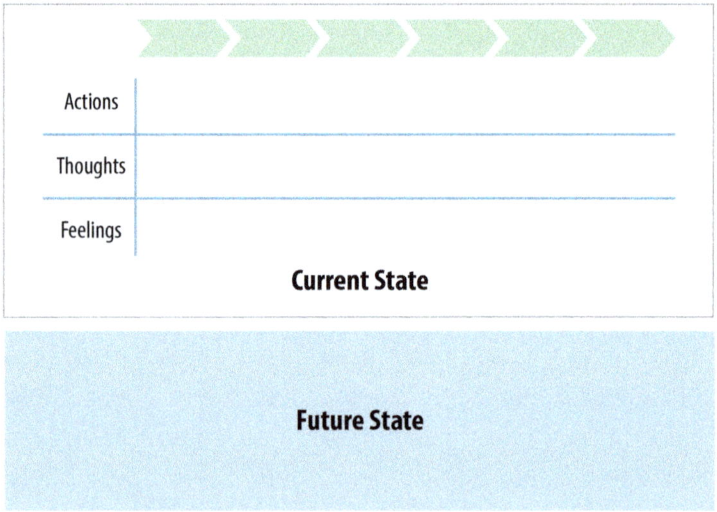

Figure 9-2. Mapping the future state alongside the current state shows the relationship between the two.

* Erika Flowers and Morgan Miller, *Your Guide to Blueprinting the Practical Way* (2023)

4. You need a thorough checklist of what to develop and how the organization will deliver the desired experience.

While research informs the creation of a future state map, the map itself is based on the team's best guess of what an ideal experience will look like. As a result, to-be mapping need not be a formal activity. In fact, a lightweight exercise can be just as fruitful. Plan a short activity with your team to envision the future experience together. See **"To-Be Mapping Exercise" on page 212** for some ideas.

When envisioning future experiences, don't just focus on ideal outcomes; also consider what could go wrong. UX strategist Debbie Levitt developed an approach called *disaster journey mapping* to identify potential risks that teams might otherwise miss.* The goal is simple: map what happens when things fail.

Levitt once worked with a beauty subscription company that sent customers sample-sized makeup products with links to purchase full-size versions. The engineering team didn't want to code the product page to display the specific shade sent in each customer's box. It seemed like a minor shortcut to them.

Levitt mapped the disaster: customer receives and loves a shade, clicks to order the full size, doesn't realize the website shows the default color instead of their sample, receives the "wrong" product, contacts support frustrated, posts an angry review, and cancels the subscription. Showing this sequence made the risk tangible. The team coded the page correctly.

Use disaster mapping sparingly—save it for situations where you spot a serious flaw others are dismissing. Map out the complete path from problem to relationship damage. Sometimes the best future state maps show what to avoid.

Align to Future Storylines

Storytelling isn't just for communicating a vision—it also helps make sense of complex problems. According to digital product strategist Donna Lichaw, author of *The User's Journey: Storymapping Products That People Love*, you can use the principles of storytelling to guide the design of products and services.

To do this, Lichaw uses a structure common to most stories called the *narrative arc* (**Figure 9-3**). This structure can be traced back to Aristotle; it's a timeless form that has been used to tell stories across cultures for thousands of years.

The elements of the narrative arc are as follows:

- ***Exposition:*** Good stories first establish the context and introduce the characters.
- ***Inciting incident:*** This is the point where something goes wrong or there is some change to the situation.
- ***Rising action:*** A good story builds over time.
- ***Crisis:*** The story rises to a point of maximum friction—the point of no return.
- ***Climax/resolution:*** The climax is the most exciting part of the story and the point at which the audience realizes that all might be well again.
- ***Falling action:*** After the climax, the tension subsides as the story moves toward its end.
- ***End:*** Any remaining conflicts are resolved, and the narrative concludes.

* Levitt's disaster journey mapping technique is also described in Stéphanie Walter's *User Journey Mapping* (2022).

In the context of mapping, the purpose of storylines is not storytelling, but designing products and services with the structure of a story in mind. In other words, apply the narrative arc to the design process itself. To do this, Lichaw recommends first mapping out an ideal journey against the narrative, then developing your product or service based on that flow.

Figure 9-4 shows an example of using a narrative arc to plan the content of a digital service. The intent is to make the user's journey into a dramatic, engaging story. The result is a strategy for content and features that meet audience needs.

Applying narrative arcs in design workshops is straightforward. Together with Lis Hubert, Lichaw describes the process in her article "Storymapping: A MacGyver Approach to Content Strategy":

1. Hold a workshop with a broad set of stakeholders.
2. Draw the user's journey as a narrative arc on a whiteboard (**Figure 9-4**).
3. Map individual pieces of content that users would need at each stage.
4. Below that, record existing content.
5. Identify gaps and weaknesses in the existing content.
6. Prioritize and plan a broader content strategy.*

Following these steps results in a content strategy with focus and meaning. It aligns teams to a common purpose and yields more engaging services.

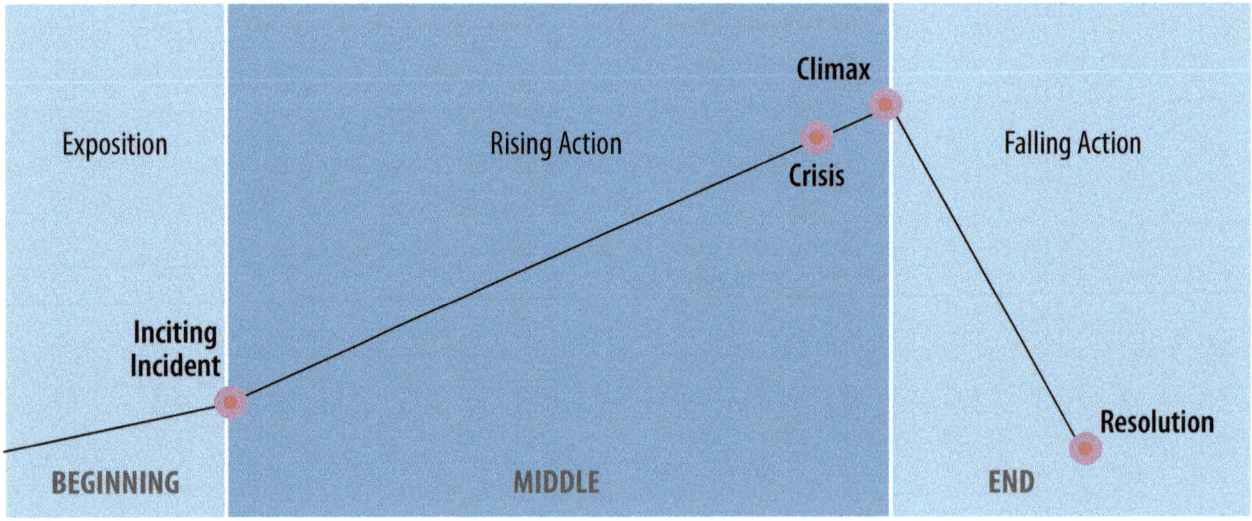

Figure 9-3. The archetypal narrative arc shows the rise in action before the resolution.

* Lis Hubert and Donna Lichaw, "Storymapping: A MacGyver Approach to Content Strategy, Part 1," *UXmatters* (2014)

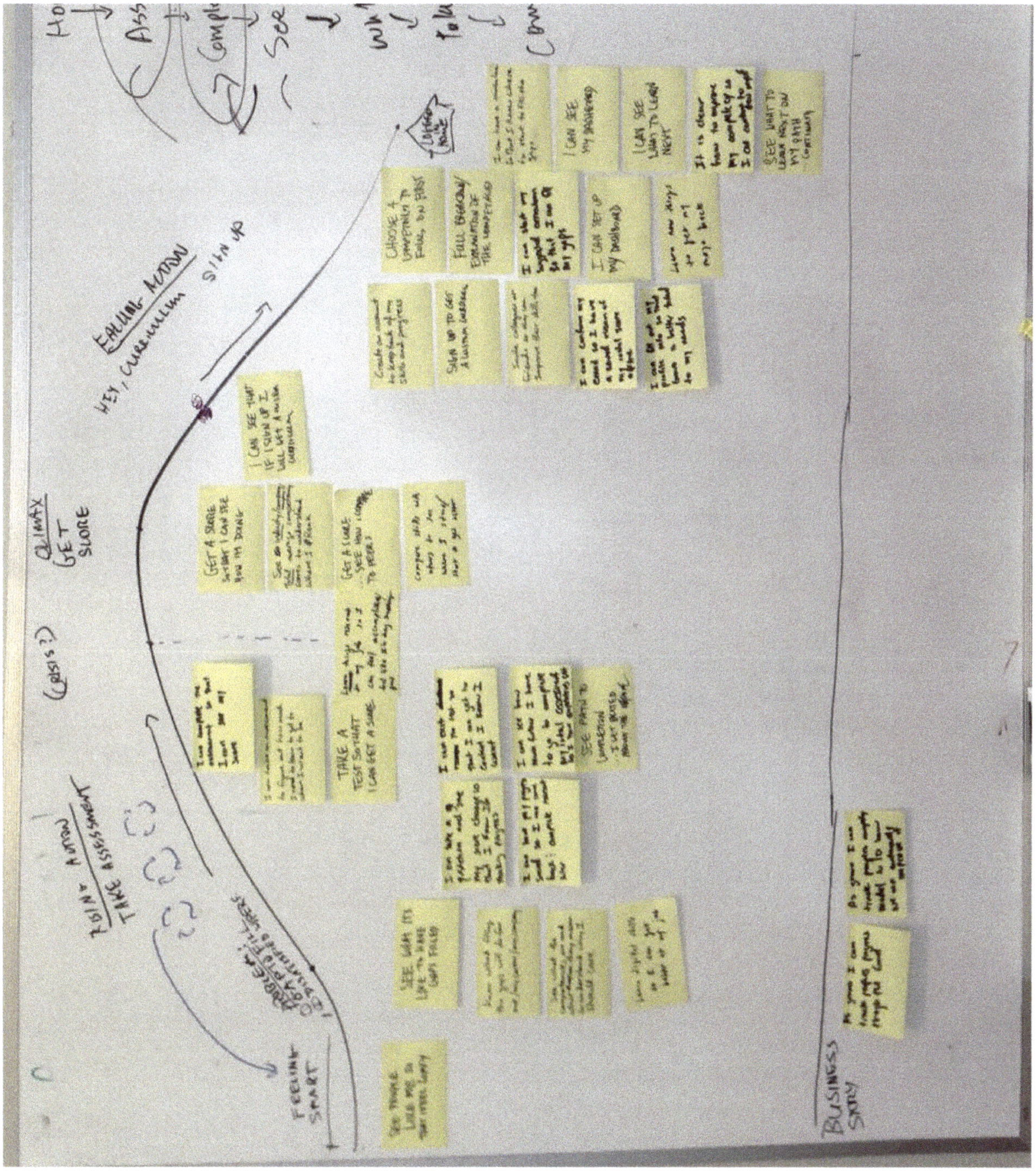

FIGURE 9-4. This example of a narrative arc and envisioned content from a workshop shows the rise of action and the resolution.

Ideas Are Overrated

Generating ideas is fun—addictive, even. I should know: working as a design lead, I've facilitated many ideation sessions in my career. You could say I'm an ideaholic.

You've probably experienced this too: a team gets together for a few hours or days to brainstorm ideas. "Go for volume," they're instructed. In the end, there may be hundreds of ideas on the workshop room wall (**Figure 9-1**). Success is tacitly measured by the number of sticky notes used.

But the volume of ideas is rarely the problem. I've never come across an organization that doesn't have enough ideas. Most are swimming in ideas they don't know how to act on and can't agree on which ones to focus on first. Yet, we continue to engage in exercises that add more to the pile.

Part of the problem is an erroneous Darwinistic view of the idea lifecycle. We assume that the best concepts will simply rise to the surface on their merit. But that's not how organizational decision making works. Natural forces within any organization act to keep ideas down. Chief among these is uncertainty, a leading idea antibody within enterprises.

Many ideas seem great at the time we have them. "This is it! We're going to save the company!" But when hard decisions need to be made, even the best ones wither quickly.

Part of the problem is that it's difficult to recognize a great idea in its infancy. We assume there will be some *aha* moment when everything just feels right. But what does innovation feel like?

History shows that many profound innovations weren't recognized as such at first. As Scott Berkun reminds us in *The Myths of Innovation*, most innovations come without epiphanies. Take the Wright brothers' first flight: only a handful of people witnessed it, and it took them six years to sell their first airplane. Or consider that it took years for 3M's low-adhesion glue to find a viable application—the product we now know as Post-it notes.

We're obsessed with the origin of ideas, but we should pay more attention to where ideas end up in organizations. The point is to set the right expectations. An idea on a sticky note is just the beginning of a long, iterative process. You won't go from sticky notes directly to implementation.

Innovation is a process of continual reinvention. Here are some simple things you can do to keep the momentum going:

Manage ideation as an ongoing project.
: Invite a project manager to your ideation session. Their primary function is to break outcomes into actionable steps and create a plan for continued development.

Aim for experiments as outcomes.
: Make experiments the result of your alignment workshop. This sets the right expectations. It also signals that more feedback from the market about the solution is needed through continued research and investigation.

Make small bets.
: Avoid aiming only for breakthrough innovations. Instead, make a lot of small bets. You don't know how big an idea will turn out to be.

Commit resources before you start.
: Get commitment for continued experimentation in advance. A cheap experiment may take only four to eight weeks and require a budget of a few thousand dollars.

Conduct cheap tests.
: Be prepared to reinvent over and over again. After getting real-world feedback, your final product may not resemble the initial idea.

Long Live Ideas!

This is not to say you shouldn't do any free-form brainstorming. Generating ideas is a healthy part of the employee experience, bringing people together and providing a safe forum to exercise creative muscles.

The point is to keep in mind that ideas themselves are overrated. Business decisions don't get made based on a sketch. Set realistic expectations, and be prepared to prove your ideas from a business standpoint if you want a chance of succeeding.

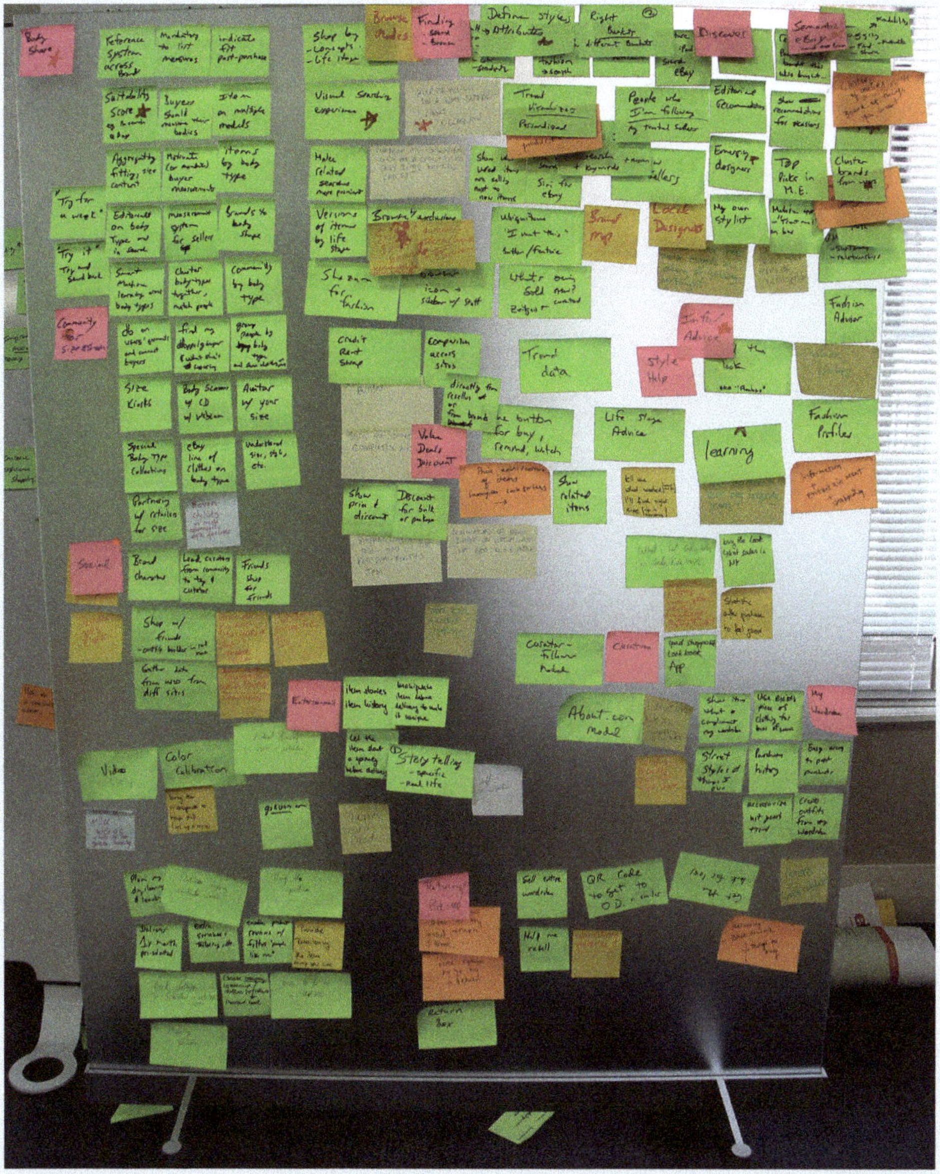

FIGURE 9-1. It's easy to generate a lot of ideas, but that shouldn't be the end of your work.

Aspire to Transform Customers

User story mapping is another useful technique for to-be mapping. As we saw in Chapter 4, this approach is an excellent way to keep development aligned with user needs. But there's another question worth asking that can take your thinking in an entirely new direction: who do we want our customers to become?

The principle is simple: products and services that merely connect, delight, and provide positive experiences don't go far enough. What's needed is a better way to envision how users may act.

Enter *The Ask*, a single question outlined by MIT professor Michael Schrage in his book *Who Do You Want Your Customers to Become?* Successful innovations, Schrage contends, don't merely ask users to do something different; they ask them to *become* someone different.

For example, George Eastman didn't just invent an affordable, easy-to-use automatic camera at the end of the 19th century; he created *photographers*. His innovation allowed everyone to do something only trained professionals could previously do.

Through the lens of The Ask, Google is not just a sophisticated search algorithm; it lets everyone become *expert researchers*. Or consider eBay as a trading platform that has created a new breed of *entrepreneurs*.

However, innovations that ask people to become something they don't want to become typically fail. Take the Segway. What did it ask us to become? A mad, helmeted scientist racing down the sidewalk? An authority figure (like a police officer) towering over other pedestrians? Or maybe just a "weirdo on a scooter" (**Figure 9-5**)? For sure, there are other reasons the Segway failed, but the underlying issue was that it asked people to adopt a lifestyle they just didn't want.

McDonald's "Super Size" campaign is another example. From a business standpoint, it was very effective: for a few extra cents in cost, customers got a good deal. But it also asked them to become *unhealthy*. That ended up hurting the company's reputation.

The Ask pairs well with mapping. At each stage, you can ask, "Who do we want our customers to become?" Then use the answers to guide future solution development, which often takes things in a whole new direction. See **"Who Do You Want Your Customer to Become?" on page 210** for more on this method.

Figure 9-5. The Segway asked us to become someone we didn't necessarily want to be.

Plan Development with User Story Mapping

Narrative arcs work well for content strategy and experience design, but software teams need a more development-focused approach to align their work with user needs. Software producers typically want to avoid creating products with seemingly random elements tacked on in unexpected places. But when teams are focusing on individual features, they can get tunnel vision and unknowingly assemble features that conflict with one another.

Agile coach Jeff Patton came up with a technique called *user story mapping*. He advises development teams to make sure everyone has a common view of the bigger picture:

> **If I have an idea in my head and I describe it in writing, when you read that document, you might quite possibly imagine something different.... However, if we get together and talk, you can tell me what you think and I can ask questions. The talking goes better if we can externalize our thinking by drawing pictures or organizing our ideas using index cards or sticky notes. If we give each other time to explain our thoughts with words and pictures, we build shared understanding.***

A strength of user story maps is that they are simple to comprehend. As described in Chapter 4, there are three main elements: user types (descriptions of roles), the backbone (a sequence of activities), and user stories (features needed to achieve the desired outcomes). The backbone is similar to the chronology in an experience map, but doesn't include experiential details, like emotions.

The process of user story mapping requires team participation, following these steps:

1. Frame the idea. As a team, discuss *why* you are building the product. Identify the problems it solves and write your responses at the top of the map.
2. Map the big picture. Illustrate the flow of the solution chronologically, including details about specific actions. If possible, include the pain points and moments of delight users have today to inform your development decisions.
3. Explore. Use the map to facilitate conversations about desired outcomes and the intended experience. Describe the features needed to support users and capture them as stories on the map.
4. Create a release strategy. Break the user stories into releases, starting with the minimum needed to achieve the desired outcome.
5. Build, measure, learn. As development progresses, track the team's learning against the user story map. Keep it in a visible place and refer back to it often.

A user story map illustrates how user stories relate to one another within an overarching model. This allows teams to grasp the system as a whole. More importantly, it aligns planning and development with actual user experiences. Ultimately, it's about developing a shared understanding of the software a team intends to build, helping guide decisions, improve efficiency, and produce better outcomes.

I once facilitated a user story mapping for a large publisher with teams spread geographically from Chicago to Dublin. We used conferencing software and a virtual whiteboard to map the user stories (**Figure 9-6**).

Don't assume that everyone has the same mental image of what a project or effort is about. Map out the solution to gain a common understanding.

* Jeff Patton, *User Story Mapping* (2014)

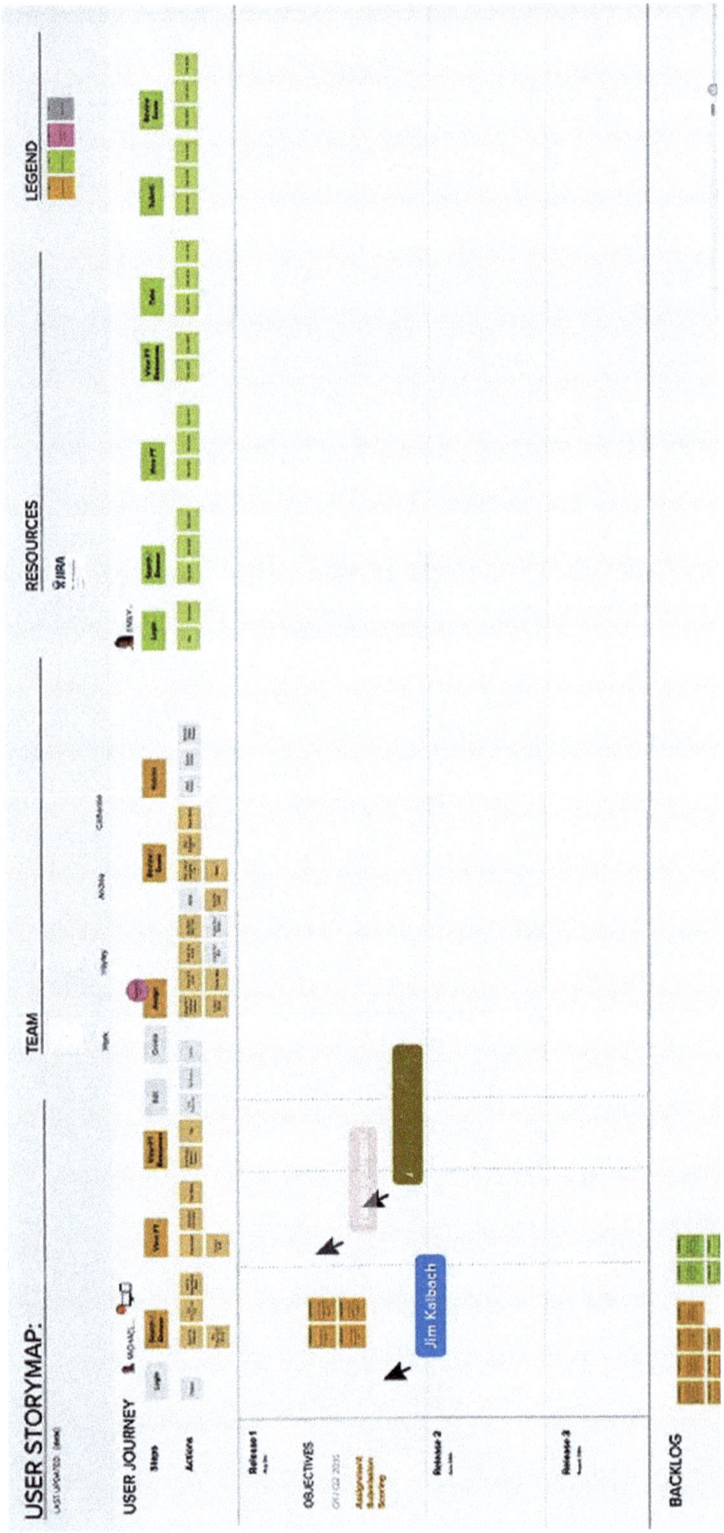

FIGURE 9-6. User story mapping can be done easily online, helping remote teams get aligned.

Run Experiments

Creating new value brings uncertainty. Although you may have gotten some initial feedback on your ideas during the alignment workshop, you still don't know how the market will react to the proposed innovation.

As discussed in Chapter 8, when you conduct an alignment workshop, it's important to set the right expectations with your team and stakeholders. The results aren't implementation-ready ideas, but hypotheses that need testing. More work is needed to flesh out your leading concepts and prove their business viability with experiments.

Start by creating explicit hypothesis statements for each concept you've decided to move forward with. Structurally, these statements have three parts:

> We believe that providing [solution, service] for [individual, customer, user]
>
> will result in [desired outcome, assumed effect],
>
> and we will know this when we see [result, measurable impact].

Notice that the hypothesis is phrased as a *belief*. You won't know the actual impact until you introduce it to the market. Also note that if there is not a measurable outcome, you don't have a testable hypothesis. Be sure to include a metric.

Next, create a plan of experiments to be conducted over the following weeks. Here are some approaches you can use to test concepts and get more clarity on the solutions:

Explanatory video
: Create a video explaining your service and circulate it online. Measure interest via traffic and response rates.

Landing page
: Create a landing page (sometimes called a *fake door* or *smoke test*) announcing the fictitious launch of your proposed service.

Prototype testing
: Simulate a functioning version of your concept. Test this with potential customers and measure concrete aspects such as task completion and satisfaction.

Concierge service
: Start with a simulated version of your service. Invite a limited set of potential customers to sign up, then provide the service manually.

Limited product release
: Create a version of your service with only one or two functioning features. Measure the success and appeal of those features.

Those familiar with Lean techniques will recognize some of these approaches. Combinations are also possible.

The key point is that you need to have prior commitment to follow through after the workshop. Enlist a champion and get sponsor buy-in for extended experimentation from the beginning of the initiative. For instance, I once conducted a multiday alignment workshop that started with exploration of an experience map. We easily generated dozens of ideas that we prioritized and narrowed down to a few that got further developed and tested quickly during the session.

One participant was a project manager, who focused on creating a project plan of experiments to be conducted. We also secured some time to continue working on the concepts afterward. So, instead of ending the workshop with only concepts and rough prototypes, we also had a plan to move forward with additional experimentation and the resources to do so.

For one of the leading concepts, the project team enlisted a professional graphic artist to create a storyboard. This was then turned into a video with a voice-over track. As the storyboard and video were developed, the original concept evolved and expanded. By simply fleshing it out, we learned and refined it.

Then we put the video on the landing page, where visitors could sign up to be notified about a beta release (**Figure 9-7**). Those who signed up were presented with a short three-question survey. Some of the parts we'd thought would be most beneficial got a cool reception from visitors to the page, while other parts we hadn't emphasized received more attention. We adjusted our priorities and modified the concept accordingly.

From these touchpoints, we measured traffic to the website over a given period of time, the number of sign-ups, and responses to our survey. We also spoke with selected individuals to better understand their motivations and what excited them about our value proposition. In the end, SnapSupport morphed into something different from its initial concept in the workshop.

The purpose of such experiments is not to launch a product, service, or feature, but to learn about which solutions address your problem best. Often, small tests provide insights that have big impacts. As facilitator, part of your job is making sure the right follow-through motions are in place.

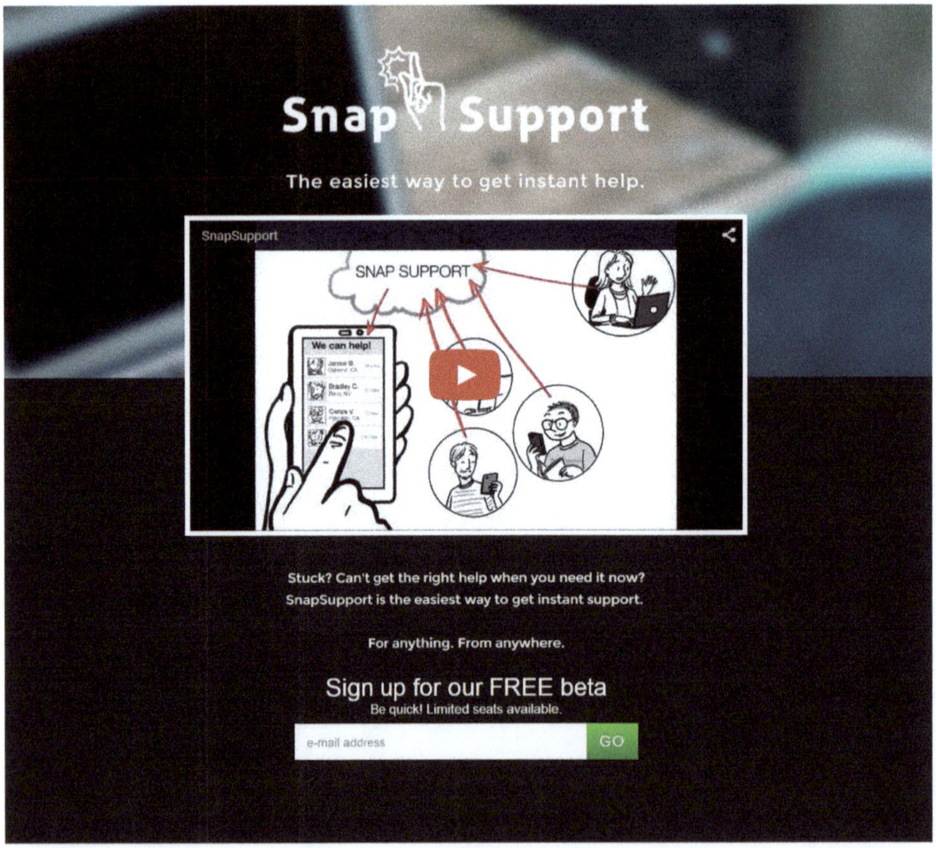

Figure 9-7. SnapSupport began as a concept video and landing page to test market reactions to the idea before a working prototype was even built.

Conduct Design Sprints

Individual experiments help you test specific hypotheses over time. But what if you need to compress the entire cycle—from mapping to prototyping to testing—into just a few days?

Design sprints are a popular format for guiding teams through a structured series of activities to design a specific solution. They focus on solving conceptual challenges before development begins. The term *sprint* is borrowed from Agile methods, which organize development work into short one- to four-week cycles. **Figure 9-8** shows the basic flow of a design sprint.

Mapping flows naturally into this process. Once you have a direction to follow from the alignment activities, you can run a design sprint to maximize agreement on a solution in a short amount of time. In fact, the authors of the book *Design Sprint*, Richard Banfield, Todd Lombardo, and Trace Wax, specifically highlight the function of current state maps in the sprint process, noting that mapping "will add context to your project and highlight opportunities you may have otherwise missed."*

There are similarities between multiday alignment workshops and design sprints. For instance, a map of the user journey is a core part of design sprints, as outlined in Jake Knapp's bestselling book *Sprint*. However, while an alignment workshop focuses on getting agreement on the right problem to solve, a design sprint aims to produce a concrete solution.

Note that a design sprint need not take a full five days. Shorter formats have become more common. For instance, I once ran a condensed design sprint over two days (**Figure 9-9**). After analyzing the current experience, the team conducted exercises to generate solutions. For each barrier identified, participants individually sketched possible solutions, photographed them, and uploaded them to a shared digital workspace (**Figure 9-10**).

Using UserTesting.com, they gathered feedback on their proposed solutions overnight. Some assumptions were validated, while others were disproven, allowing the team to iterate. The workshop concluded with a concrete implementation plan for the coming months.

Figure 9-8. Design sprints typically begin with a map of the experience to understand the context of the solutions a team will devise within the next week.

---

* Richard Banfield et al., *Design Sprint* (2015)

FIGURE 9-9. A combination of a value chain, proto-personas, and an experience map fit into one mural, as well as the results of an initial brainstorming session.

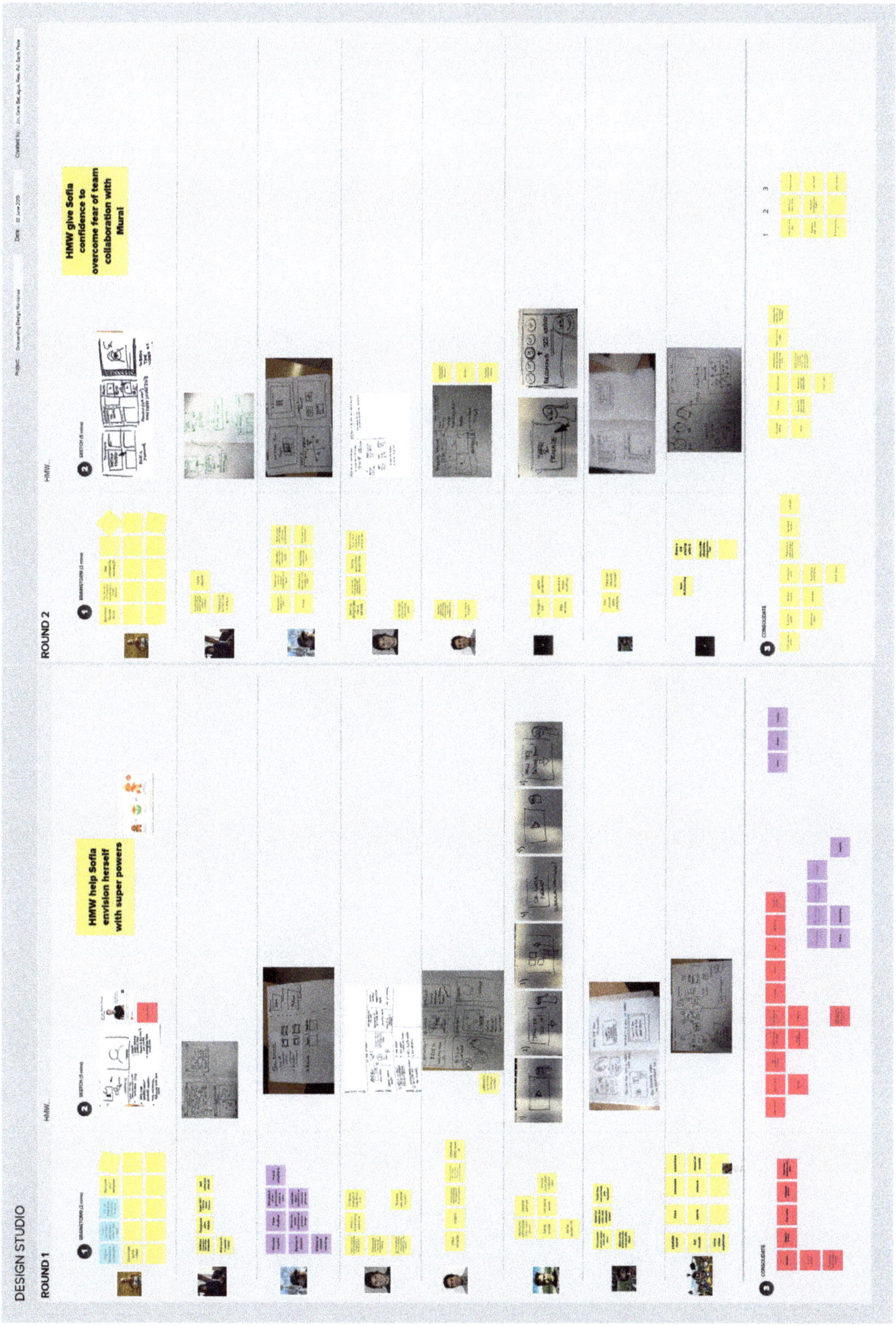

FIGURE 9-10. A condensed design sprint allows teams to quickly find solutions together.

Summary

After gaining empathy and understanding through current state mapping and identifying opportunities in an alignment workshop, it's critical to activate those insights by designing and testing concrete solutions in the market. Otherwise, the insights from your mapping effort may fall flat and fail to make the desired impact.

This chapter explored several approaches to make mapping actionable. First, envision future experiences using techniques such as future state mapping, storylines that apply narrative arcs, and user story mapping to align development with user needs. Asking, "Who do we want our customers to become?" reframes innovation around customer transformation rather than product features.

Second, run experiments to validate your hypotheses before committing significant resources. Create explicit hypothesis statements with measurable outcomes, then design lightweight tests such as explanatory videos, landing pages, prototype testing, concierge services, or limited releases. The goal is to learn which solutions best address your problem, not to launch perfect products.

Finally, design sprints provide a concentrated format for moving from mapped insights to tested solutions in just a few days. By combining mapping, sketching, prototyping, and user testing, teams can quickly validate ideas and emerge with concrete implementation plans.

Ideas are overrated—not because they don't matter, but because most organizations are already swimming in them. What's often missing is the follow-through: testing them, refining them, and committing resources to prove their business value.

Further Reading

Erika Flowers and Morgan Miller, Your Guide to Blueprinting the Practical Way *(2023)*

Flowers and Miller provide a practical, step-by-step guide to creating service blueprints, complete with templates and real-world examples. The book emphasizes accessibility and actionability, making blueprinting approachable for teams new to the method. It includes a detailed section on future state mapping.

Jeff Gothelf and Josh Seiden, Sense and Respond *(2017)*

This book advocates for outcome-focused management by building a culture of learning through rapid experimentation. The authors argue that modern business contexts demand real-time customer observation and ways of working that embrace continual change. They bridge Agile, Lean, and Design Thinking into a unified approach centered on self-guided teams and deep customer listening.

Michael Schrage, Who Do You Want Your Customers to Become? *(2012)*

This is a short ebook with a powerful message: rather than looking at who your current customers are and trying to delight them, strive to transform them—enable them to become somebody or something they currently are not. The simple question "Who do you want your customer to become?" reframes your focus to go beyond providing incrementally better services.

Donna Lichaw, The User's Journey *(2016)*

Lichaw regularly writes and teaches about storylines. This is a complete volume of the techniques she's developed over the years. You can find more information online, including articles on UXmatters (*uxmatters.com*).

Jeff Patton, User Story Mapping *(2014)*

Patton pioneered the technique of user story maps and details the approach in this book. It is well written and gets to the key points quickly. Later chapters include details on validation through Lean processes.

Jake Knapp, Sprint *(2016)*

This is the book that started the design sprint trend and continues to stand as the original source of information on the technique. See also *Design Sprint* by Richard Banfield, C. Todd Lombardo, and Trace Wax (2015).

Alternative Worlds

Objective	Explore how innovators outside your domain would approach your challenge
Time	60–90 minutes
Participants	8–30 people
Materials	Sticky notes, markers, large wall space

Creative thinkers don't conjure great ideas from nowhere; they look at common things in uncommon ways. To keep the momentum going with forward-looking solutions that emerge from an alignment workshop, engage the team with additional activities. This method asks, "What would _____ do?" The blank might be another company or brand, a well-known leader, or a public institution.

Adopting a completely different perspective can help teams break out of conventional thinking and come up with fresh ideas. For instance, if you're looking to reinvigorate a public library, you might ask: "What would Starbucks do?"

How it works:

1. Frame the challenge. State your problem or opportunity clearly and display it where everyone can see it. Use "How might we" statements.
2. Generate alternative worlds. Working individually, write innovative entities—companies, brands, people, organizations—on sticky notes. Post all the notes on a shared surface.
3. Select. Use dot voting (three dots per person) to choose three to five diverse worlds to explore. Each one should be genuinely different from your domain.
4. Understand each world. For each selected world, discuss: What are their core values? What makes them successful? What unique practices do they use? How do they treat customers?
5. Apply perspectives. Create breakout groups of three to five people and assign each one an alternative world. Ask the groups to consider: "How would _____ solve our challenge?" (**Figure 9-11**).
6. Share and synthesize. Each group presents their ideas. Look for patterns and surprising connections. Use dot voting to identify the most promising concepts. Discuss how to adapt these ideas to your context.

Learn more:

Dave Gray and Sunni Brown, *Gamestorming 2.0* (2025)

LUMA Institute, "Alternative Worlds"

Example:

FIGURE 9-11. In this example, the Olympics is used as an alternative world to explore.

Who Do You Want Your Customer to Become?

Objective	Identify aspirational customer transformations that drive breakthrough innovation
Time	45–60 minutes
Participants	5–15 people
Materials	Experience map or journey map, sticky notes

Products and services that merely connect, delight, and provide positive experiences don't go far enough. Successful innovations don't just ask users to do something different—they ask them to become someone different. This method reframes innovation around customer transformation rather than product features.

How it works:

1. Review the journey. Display your experience map where everyone can see it. Review the major phases or divisions. These natural breaks in the journey provide opportunities for transformation.
2. Pose "The Ask" at each phase (**Figure 9-12**). Moving through the journey phase by phase, ask: "Who do we want our customers to become at this stage?" Brainstorm possible people or roles—for example, an explorer, a teacher, a curator, a coach, an advocate, a creator, an investigator, a collaborator. You can also name famous figures who embody the transformation you desire (e.g., Thomas Edison, Mother Teresa, Jane Goodall).
3. Select the transformation. For each phase, agree on which transformation is most compelling and achievable, and write it clearly on the map.
4. Design for transformation. With the desired transformations identified, brainstorm how to enable them. What capabilities must customers develop? What investments in their skills are needed? What experiences would catalyze the change? Capture ideas on sticky notes and organize them by phase.
5. Assess feasibility. Review all the transformations and ideas together. Ask: Does this transformation create mutual value? Are we asking customers to become someone they want to be? Prioritize transformations that align business goals with genuine customer aspirations.

Learn more:

Michael Schrage, *Who Do You Want Your Customers to Become?* (2012)

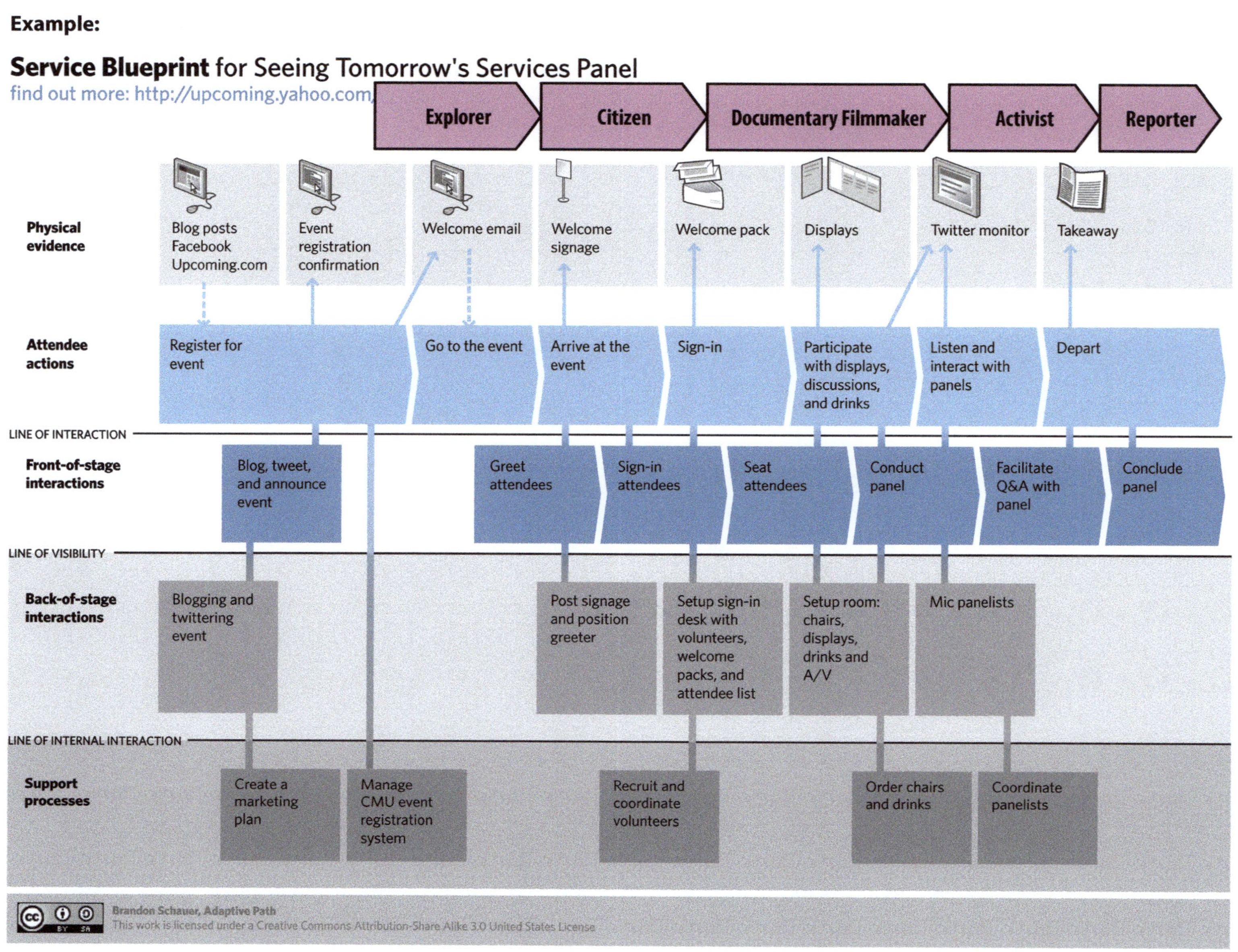

FIGURE 9-12. This example of a service blueprint shows possible responses to The Ask at each phase.

To-Be Mapping Exercise

Objective	Visualize and align on an ideal future customer experience
Time	45–60 minutes
Participants	5–12 people
Materials	Whiteboard, sticky notes

Most mapping focuses on the current state—understanding experiences as they exist today. But at some point, you need to envision the future experience you're creating. To-be mapping, also called *future state* or *target state mapping*, diagrams an intended experience that doesn't yet exist. Unlike current state maps based on research, to-be maps represent a vision that serves as a communication tool for teams building new services. IBM's Enterprise Design Thinking toolkit offers a straightforward approach to draft this vision collaboratively (**Figure 9-13**).

How it works:

1. Set up the framework. Draw four horizontal rows and label them Phases, Doing, Thinking, and Feeling. Divide the Phases row into major stages of the future journey (typically four to six phases).
2. Map the ideal experience. Working individually or as a group, fill out each row with sticky notes. Start with Doing: What actions does the customer take in each phase? Move to Thinking: What goes through their mind? Then Feeling: What emotions do they experience? Push for an ideal vision—don't let current constraints limit thinking.
3. Identify the moment of truth. Review the complete to-be map. Look for the peak emotional high point—the moment that might differentiate your solution. Mark this "magical moment" clearly. This becomes your North Star for design decisions.
4. Compare to the current state. Place your current state map alongside the to-be map. Where are the biggest gaps? What fundamental changes are required? Which pain points will get eliminated? Which new capabilities must be built? Identify your highest-priority opportunities.
5. Plan next steps. Decide whether to append the to-be vision to your current state map or keep it separate. Assign owners for key gaps. Determine which hypotheses to test first.

Learn more:

IBM Enterprise Design Thinking, "To-Be Scenario Map" (2018)

Example:

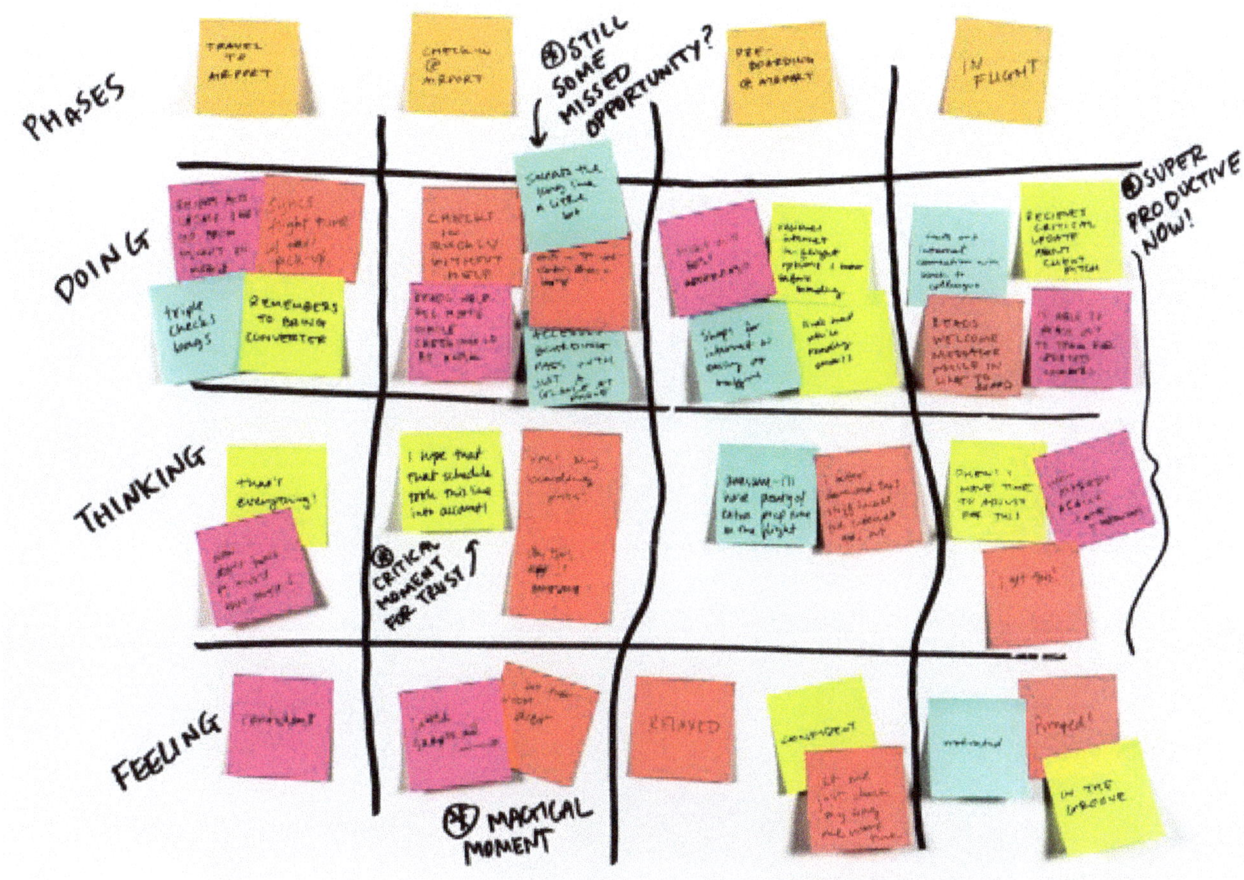

FIGURE 9-13. IBM's simple approach to to-be mapping includes identifying a target "magical moment" in the intended experience.

Condensed Design Sprint

Objective	Rapidly validate solutions through prototyping and user testing
Time	2–3 days
Participants	5–7 core team members plus facilitator, 3–5 users for testing
Materials	Whiteboard, sticky notes, prototyping tools (digital or paper), testing space

A design sprint compresses months of development into a few days. Developed at Google, this structured workshop brings together an interdisciplinary team to map challenges, brainstorm solutions, build a realistic prototype, and test it with target users. The result: crucial insights and clear direction before committing significant resources. Design sprints work powerfully with experience maps: whereas alignment workshops help teams agree on the right problem to solve, design sprints produce concrete solutions.

How it works:

1. Map and sketch (day 1). Start with your experience map to frame the challenge. Identify the target moment—the specific part of the experience you want to solve. Independently sketch solution concepts, then review the sketches together and vote on the strongest ideas. Create a detailed storyboard showing what users will experience during testing.
2. Prototype (day 1 or 2). Build a realistic facade—just enough to test the concept with users. This might be a clickable interface, a service walk-through, or a physical mockup. The prototype should feel real but doesn't need to function fully. Prepare interview questions and a testing script. If time permits, do a quick internal walk-through to catch obvious issues.
3. Test and decide (day 2 or 3). Conduct one-on-one user tests with three to five target customers. Observe how they interact with the prototype and look for patterns. Debrief as a team after each session. By the day's end, decide what to build, what to modify, or whether to pivot entirely.

Learn more:

Jake Knapp, *Sprint* (2016)

Richard Banfield, C. Todd Lombardo, and Trace Wax, *Design Sprint* (2015)

Backcasting

Objective	Create a realistic roadmap from an ideal future state back to present actions
Time	60–90 minutes
Participants	5–15 people
Materials	Experience map or journey map, large timeline template, sticky notes

Most planning starts with the present and projects forward. Backcasting flips this approach: define your desired future state first, then work backward to identify the steps needed to get there (**Figure 9-14**). This method breaks linear thinking by starting with radical possibilities rather than incremental changes. Originally developed for sustainability planning, backcasting reveals the policy shifts, cultural changes, and technological advances required to achieve ambitious goals—making it a powerful tool for mapping transformative customer experiences.

How it works:

1. Define the future vision. Describe multiple ideal customer experiences three to five years from now. Be specific and ambitious. What does the journey look like? How do customers feel? What's transformed? What new capabilities do they have? Capture the vision where everyone can see it.
2. Set key milestones. For each future vision, work backward to identify three or four major milestones along the timeline. These represent significant shifts or achievements needed to reach the vision. Place them at natural intervals (e.g., Year 3, Year 2, Year 1, Now). For each milestone, describe what must be true at that point.
3. Map required changes. Moving right to left, brainstorm what's needed to reach each milestone: technological advances, policy or process changes, cultural shifts, and new capabilities, partnerships, or resources. Organize these under the corresponding milestones using sticky notes.
4. Plan present actions. Focus on the earliest milestone and the path from now to that point. What specific actions must start today? What decisions need to be made? What resources are required? What obstacles might block progress? Create a list of concrete next steps.
5. Assess feasibility. Review the complete roadmap from the future to the present. Does the path feel realistic? Are there gaps? What assumptions need testing? Identify the highest-priority actions and potential showstoppers.

Learn more:

Peter Jones and Kristel Van Ael, *Design Journeys Through Complex Systems* (2022)

Example:

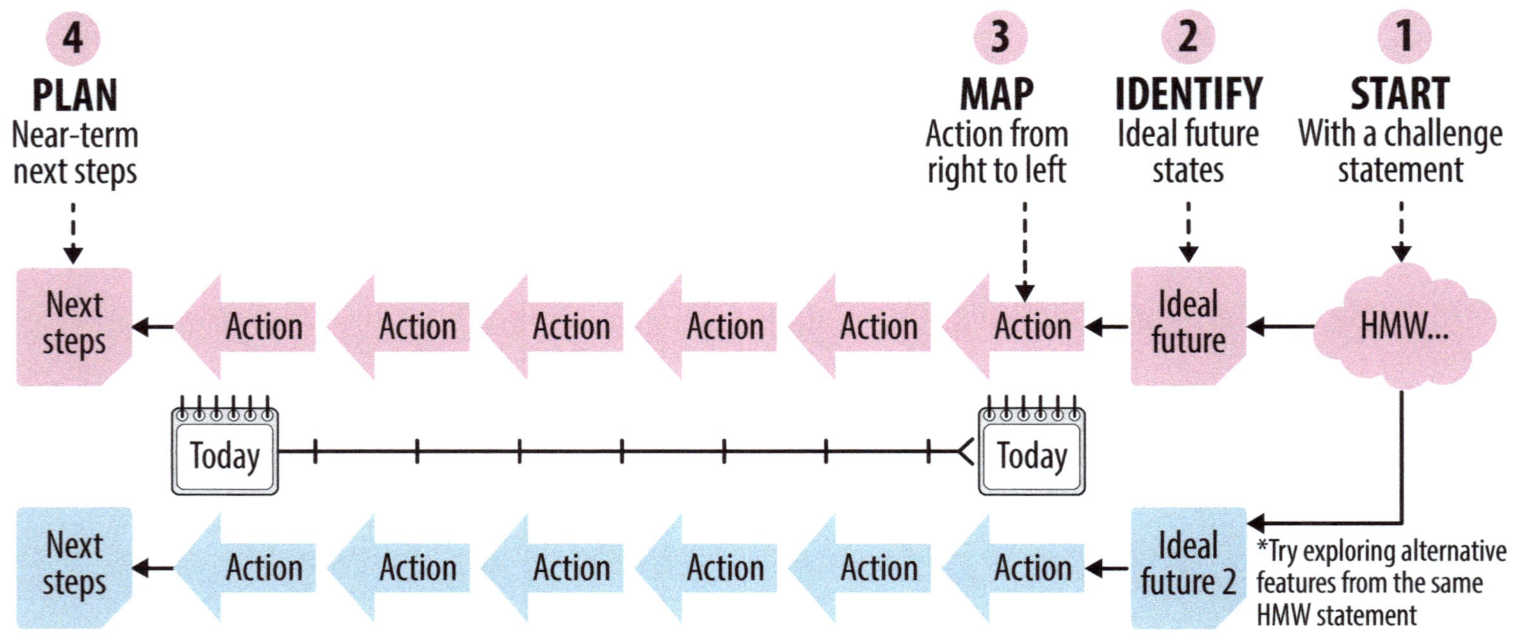

FIGURE 9-14. Backcasting works from the future state, on the right, back to a concrete near-term plan, on the left.

Hypothesis Testing

Objective	Validate solution assumptions through structured experiments
Time	30–45 minutes to create hypotheses; 2–8 weeks to run experiments
Participants	3–8 people for planning; varies by experiment type
Materials	Hypothesis template, experiment planning canvas, measurement tools

Innovation brings uncertainty. Coming out of an alignment workshop, you have promising ideas—but they're hypotheses, not proven solutions. Hypothesis testing, drawn from Lean Startup and Lean UX principles, provides a disciplined approach to validating assumptions before committing significant resources. Rather than building complete solutions and hoping they work, you design small experiments to learn quickly and fail cheaply. This method transforms sticky-note ideas into evidence-based decisions (**Figure 9-15**).

How it works:

1. Write explicit hypotheses. For each concept, create a statement: "We believe that providing [solution/service] for [customer/user] will result in [desired outcome], and we will know this when we see [measurable result]." Without measurements, you can't test the hypothesis.
2. Design experiments. Choose an experiment type, such as an explanatory video, landing page, prototype test, concierge service, or limited feature release. Match the experiment to your level of uncertainty and available time.
3. Define success metrics. Specify what you'll measure and what indicates success—for example, 100 sign-ups in two weeks, 80% task completion, or a 4+ satisfaction rating. Set thresholds in advance to avoid confirmation bias.
4. Run the experiment. Test with real target customers. Collect quantitative data and qualitative insights. Document what you learn, not just whether you succeeded.
5. Analyze and decide. Review the results against your success criteria. Decide whether to build, modify and retest, or stop. Create new hypotheses for the next iteration based on your learnings.

Learn more:

Jeff Gothelf and Joshua Seiden, *Lean UX*, 2nd ed. (2017)

Ash Maurya, *Running Lean*, 3rd ed. (2022)

Example:

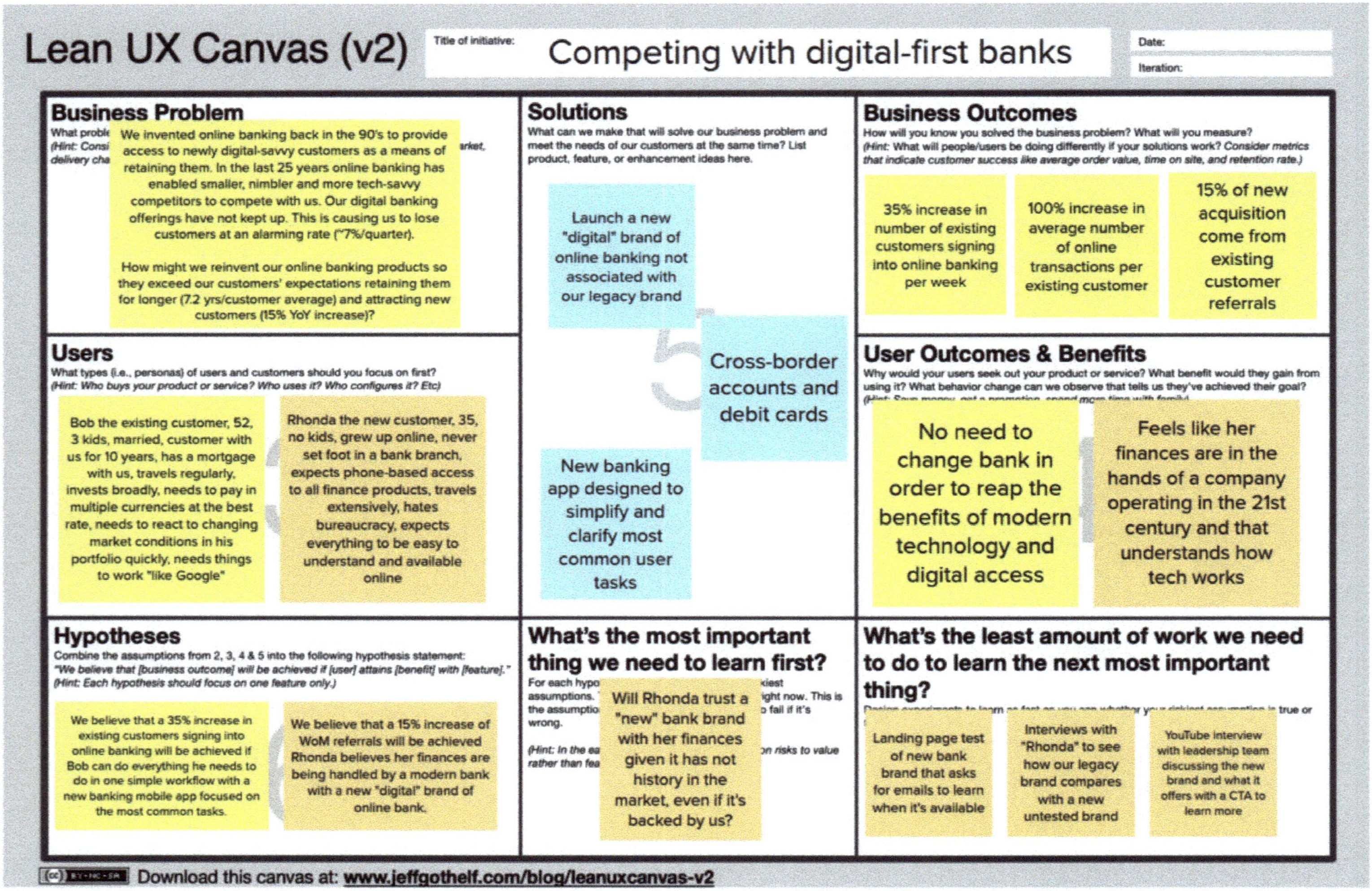

FIGURE 9-15. This completed Lean UX canvas shows the logic in arriving at testable hypotheses.

Diagram and Image Credits

Figure 9-1: Image from workshop by Jim Kalbach

Figure 9-4: Photo of storyline exercise by Donna Lichaw, used with permission

Figure 9-5: Photo by Scott Merrill (*skippy.net*), used with permission

Figure 9-6: Example of a user story map by Jim Kalbach, created in Mural

Figure 9-8: Design sprint schedule from *Sprint* by Jake Knapp, used with permission

Figure 9-9: Journey map and team brainstorming session by Jim Kalbach, created in Mural

Figure 9-10: Example of a design studio by Jim Kalbach, created in Mural

Figure 9-11: Alternative Worlds example by Mural, used with permission

Figure 9-12: Service blueprint created by Brandon Schauer of Adaptive Path, used with permission

Figure 9-13: Example of a to-be map from the IBM Enterprise Design Thinking toolkit (*ibm.com/design*), fair use

Figure 9-14: Example backcasting based on drawing originally created by Mark Tippin, used with permission

Figure 9-15: Example completed Lean UX canvas by Jeff Gothelf, used by permission

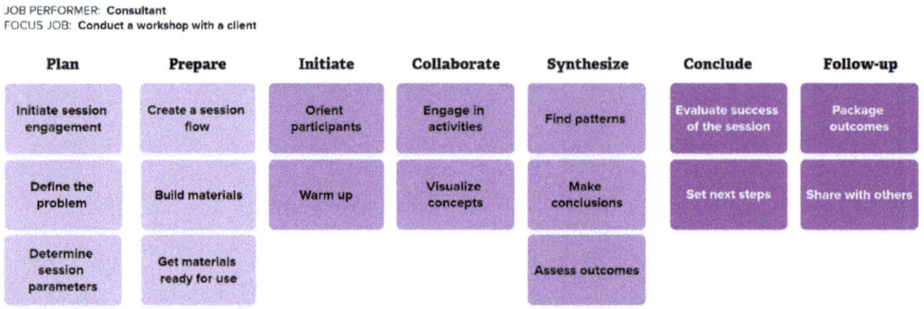

JOB PERFORMER: Consultant
FOCUS JOB: Conduct a workshop with a client
Plan
Prepare
Initiate
Collaborate
Synthesize
Conclude
Follow-up
Initiate session engagement
Define the problem
Determine session parameters
Create a session flow
Build materials
Get materials ready for use
Orient participants
Warm up
Engage in activities
Visualize concepts
Find patterns
Make conclusions
Assess outcomes
Evaluate success of the session
Set next steps
Package outcomes
Share with others

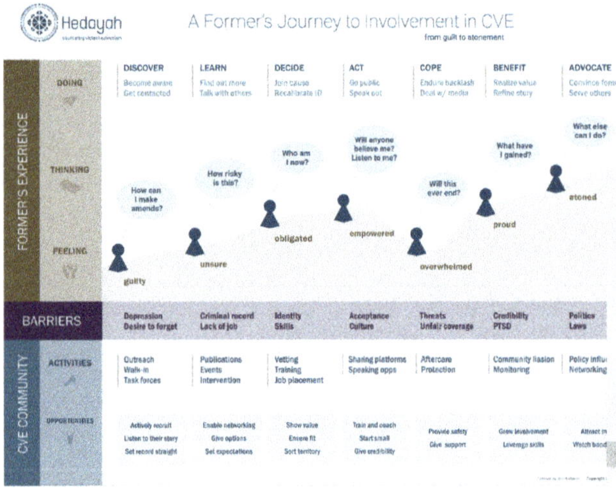

Hedayah
A Former's Journey to Involvement in CVE
from guilt to atonement
DISCOVER
LEARN
DECIDE
ACT
COPE
BENEFIT
ADVOCATE
FORMER'S EXPERIENCE
DOING
THINKING
FEELING
How can I make amends?
How risky is this?
Who am I now?
Will anyone believe me? Listen to me?
Will this ever end?
What have I gained?
What else can I do?
guilty
unsure
obligated
empowered
overwhelmed
proud
atoned
BARRIERS
Depression
Desire to forget
Criminal record
Lack of job
Identity
Skills
Acceptance
Culture
Threats
Unfair coverage
Credibility
PTSD
Politics
Laws
CVE COMMUNITY
ACTIVITIES
OPPORTUNITIES
Outreach
Walk-in
Task forces
Publications
Events
Intervention
Vetting
Training
Job placement
Sharing platforms
Speaking opps
Aftercare
Protection
Community liasion
Monitoring
Policy influ
Networking

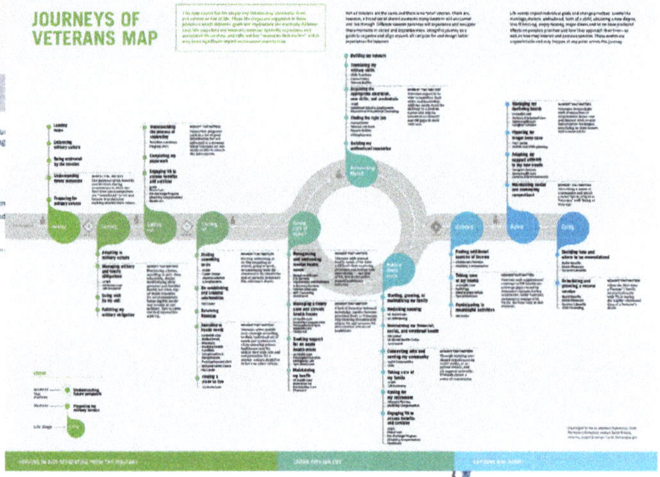

JOURNEYS OF VETERANS MAP

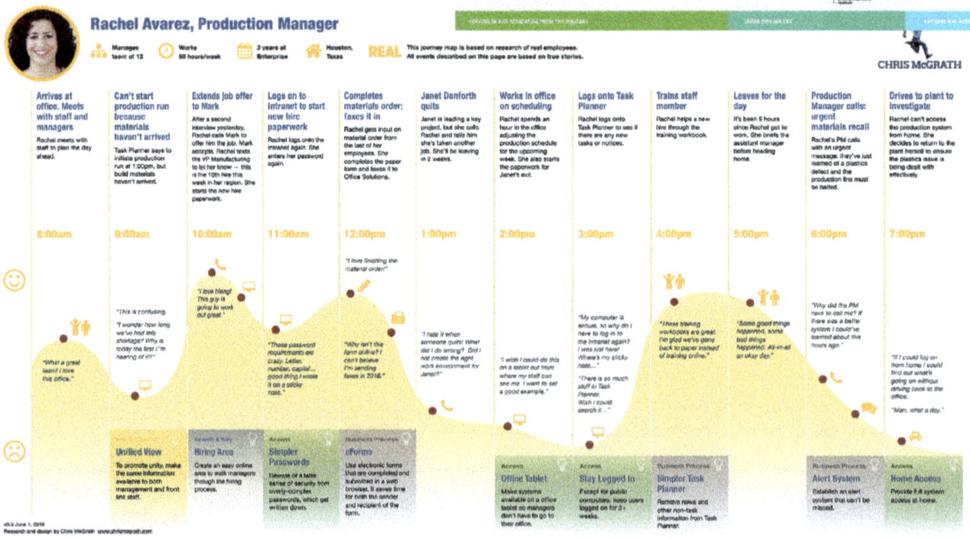

Rachel Avarez, Production Manager
Manages team of 12
Works 50 hours/week
3 years at Enterprise
Houston, Texas
REAL
This journey map is based on research of real employees. All events described on this page are based on true stories.
Arrives at office. Meets with staff and managers
Can't start production run because materials haven't arrived
Extends job offer to Mark
Logs on to intranet to start new hire paperwork
Completes materials order; faxes it in
Janet Danforth quits
Works in office on scheduling
Logs onto Task Planner
Trains staff member
Leaves for the day
Production Manager calls: urgent materials recall
Drives to plant to investigate
8:00am
9:00am
10:00am
11:00am
12:00pm
1:00pm
2:00pm
3:00pm
4:00pm
5:00pm
6:00pm
7:00pm
Unified View
Hiring Area
Simpler Passwords
eForms
Offline Tablet
Stay Logged In
Simpler Task Planner
Alert System
Home Access
CHRIS McGRATH

PART 3
Mapping in Context

Part 3 examines how mapping applies to specific strategic contexts and organizational challenges:

- Chapter 10 looks at journey management. How do organizations orchestrate experiences at scale? Today, journey managers use real-time data to coordinate diverse touchpoints. We're seeing "living maps" that update continually. Journey management shows what becomes possible when mapping is taken to scale, but for now it remains accessible to an elite few. Mapping is for everyone.
- Chapter 11 focuses on employee experience. The best way to create a great customer experience is to foster an exceptional employee experience. If you treat your employees right, they'll treat your customers right.
- Chapter 12 explores strategy mapping. Diagrams point to new opportunities. They provide a new way of seeing the market, your organization, and your position.
- Chapter 13 covers mapping for social good. The principles apply beyond commercial contexts. The key difference: optimizing for human prosperity rather than just profit.
- Chapter 14 integrates Jobs to Be Done theory with experience mapping. Understanding the motivations and context behind behavior deepens your understanding of what customers are trying to accomplish.

Mapping experiences isn't a single method. It's a way of telling the story of value alignment. There are many ways to do that. This book is about possibilities, not one specific technique.

In God we trust; all others must bring data.

—Edward Deming

IN THIS CHAPTER

- When collaborative mapping hits a wall
- Three layers: mapping, management, orchestration
- Journey management at enterprise scale
- When to use mapping versus management
- Experience as advantage
- Collaborative method for prioritizing insights and opportunities

CHAPTER 10

Journey Management: Orchestrating Experiences at Scale

In my first book, *Designing Web Navigation*, I discussed the principle of transitional volatility. David Danielson coined this term to describe the degree of reorientation a person experiences when moving from page to page on a website.* If there is too much volatility, they get lost in hyperspace.

The pattern consists of three phases: becoming accustomed to one location (habituate), forming an expectation about the next point (predict), and then adjusting to a new position (reorient). This cycle repeats with each interaction (**Figure 10-1**).

We see a similar effect on a larger scale when individuals interact with organizations. Instead of page to page, they move from touchpoint to touchpoint. At each interaction there is a reorientation period, even if brief. When this reorientation is excessive, the experience feels disjointed and even frustrating.

High transitional volatility arises from inconsistency across touchpoints. You've probably experienced this yourself. I once dealt with a credit card issue where the issuer and the bank disagreed on responsibility. As they blamed each other, I was caught in the middle, forced to bridge their internal gaps across months of website visits, calls, emails, and even faxes. The degree of reorientation at each point was high. Apparently, it was my job to figure it all out. Needless to say, they no longer have my business.

More recently, I encountered a music publishing platform that treated its online and physical CD businesses as separate entities. Trying to sort out issues across the two meant repeating myself constantly and restarting conversations with each interaction. The burden was on me, the customer, costing hours of my time.

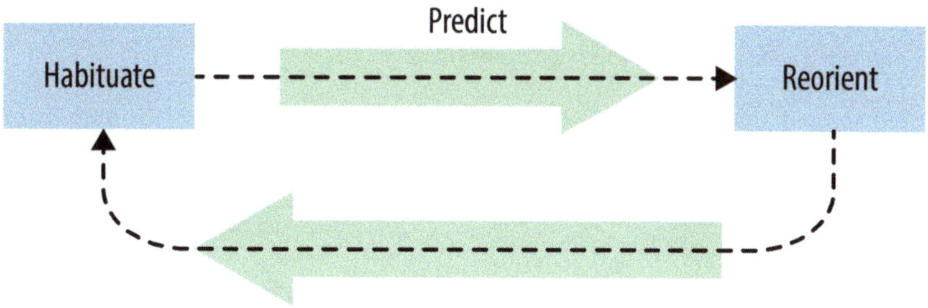

Figure 10-1. The basic pattern of transitional volatility can lead to inconsistent and unsatisfactory experiences.

* David Danielson, "Transitional Volatility in Web Navigation," *IT & Society* (2003)

The advice is clear: don't force people to bridge gaps in your offering. That's your job.

But here's the challenge: as organizations grow, these gaps emerge organically. Customers then experience a company as disconnected silos rather than a coherent whole. This organizational fragmentation represents one of the fundamental challenges that both journey mapping and journey management address. Make no mistake about it: these gaps will exist. The question is how you continually strive to address them.

This chapter describes the growing field of journey management and its complementary relationship to mapping experiences. (Spoiler alert: mapping still matters, even with journey management in the picture.) By the end, you will understand how both capabilities are essential for realizing XLG strategies.

When Mapping Efforts Hit a Wall

The pattern repeats across industries: a company gets serious about the customer experience and pulls together cross-functional teams to explore an end-to-end customer journey map. For a moment, everyone feels genuine alignment. People walk out saying, "Now we get it."

These moments matter—they create insights, quick wins, and innovation opportunities. And they certainly help build the foundation of a customer-centric culture.

But the customer journey map becomes outdated faster than anyone expected. Within months or even weeks, it's a story about what used to be true rather than what is true now.

This is where most organizations hit the wall: not in creating customer journey maps, but in keeping them alive as business conditions change. The challenge goes beyond visualizing journeys; it requires tackling the tough problem of managing them at the speed and scale modern business requires.

Insights identified in cross-functional workshops often fail to flow into the systems where teams actually work: Jira, roadmaps, budget decisions. The shared understanding created in the room on Thursday dissolves by Monday morning as everyone returns to competing priorities and departmental metrics.

For large organizations managing millions of customer interactions daily, collaborative mapping can cover only a fraction of the touchpoints in play. The method that created alignment cannot sustain it. Journey management emerged to address this gap.

From Mapping to Management

In 2025, Forrester made a significant change to its annual vendor evaluation, releasing a Wave report on customer journey management platforms instead of journey mapping platforms.* This shift reflects a move from visualization as a creative practice to an operational discipline—and a broader transformation in how organizations approach customer experience.

Journey mapping helped teams visualize experiences, build empathy, and uncover friction. It brought people together across silos in ways few other methods could. At its best, mapping was catalytic, illuminating what no dashboard could reveal.

* Joana de Quintanilha et al., "The Forrester Wave: Customer Journey Management Platforms, Q4 2025," *Forrester* (2025)

Journey management emerged to address scaling challenges. The aim is to create the infrastructure for acting on journey insights continually rather than episodically. It builds on, rather than replaces, the wide range of mapping approaches discussed in this book; both capabilities remain essential, serving different but complementary purposes at varied organizational scales and maturities.

Journey management is generally positioned as a separate function alongside journey mapping and orchestrating actions across touchpoints. I organize these into three distinct components that clarify what each does and when you need it. Undergirding each of these layers are insights and data (see **Figure 10-2**).

Mapping provides the foundation of understanding. Management creates the organizational capability to act on insights continually rather than episodically. Orchestration delivers personalized experiences at scale based on that understanding and governance. The three layers are interrelated, and it's essential to understand how they work together.

Journey Mapping Creates Understanding

Mapping helps you understand what customers experience and why. It's discovery work. Through collaboration, teams visualize the customer's experience, capturing their emotions, pain points, and opportunities. This creates shared understanding across silos and drives alignment on what matters most, helping address the gaps that create transitional volatility for customers.

Journey management platforms also begin with mapping. You need to diagram the experience before you can connect it to data. The collaborative mapping activities described in this book serve as a precursor to journey management, providing a way to model experiences before diving into analytics.

Management Provides Governance

Management is the operating system for journeys: the infrastructure that governs, updates, and aligns them with business goals over time. Where mapping creates a snapshot, management makes journeys living artifacts connected to strategy, key performance indicators (KPIs), personas, and decision-making processes.

Journey management answers questions that mapping alone cannot:

- Who owns each part of the journey?
- How do we prioritize improvements?
- What evidence justifies budget allocation?
- How do we sustain changes after they're implemented?

Effective management requires embedding journeys into how decisions are made and resources are allocated. This involves establishing regular governance rhythms, defining clear ownership, and implementing systems that keep journey insights current as business conditions change. By integrating both quantitative and qualitative data, journey management provides a living, single source of truth for the entire organization.

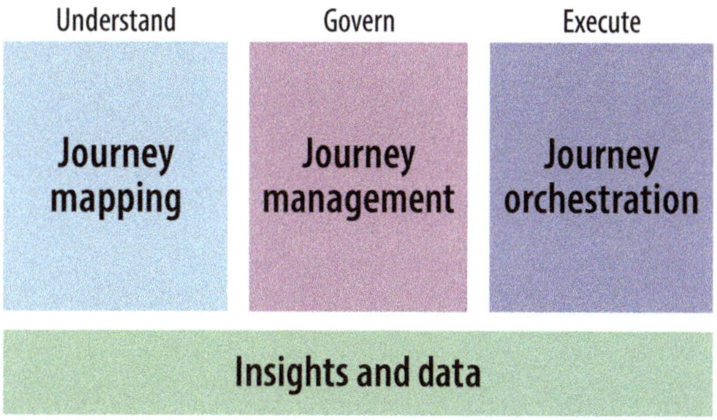

Figure 10-2. The components of customer-centric capabilities are undergirded by insights and data.

Orchestration Enables Execution

Orchestration is the real-time execution engine where triggers, decisioning, and automation come alive. When someone abandons a cart, orchestration determines what happens next and pushes the appropriate action across channels instantly. When a customer calls support after multiple failed login attempts, orchestration ensures that the agent sees the full context.

This layer coordinates multiple services and systems to deliver value in the moment. It's analogous to marketing automation, which coordinates communications at various touchpoints, but applied to the entire customer experience. Orchestration requires technical infrastructure that can manage state across distributed systems, handle failures gracefully, and route work to appropriate owners in real time.

Although similar on the surface, journey management and journey orchestration serve different purposes. Orchestration operates in real time, determining the best next actions as customers move through experiences. Journey management works with lagging data, analyzing what happened and why to expose gaps, validate improvements, and inform strategy.

Success in any of these areas depends heavily on the quality and accuracy of insights and data. Organizations often excel at one component while neglecting the others, limiting their ability to create truly exceptional customer experiences. The most mature organizations maintain capabilities across all three, applying the appropriate approach based on context, organizational readiness, and specific objectives.

Journey Management as Business Infrastructure

As journey management consultant Bill Staikos observes, "A single broken moment in a customer journey does not just reduce satisfaction. It creates work. It creates tickets. It creates refunds. It creates escalations. It creates manual overrides. It creates wasted time. It creates rework. It creates churn risk. It creates brand damage you cannot easily measure."*

This is the real tax organizations pay for journey friction: not soft metrics about satisfaction, but hard operational and financial costs that show up in support volume, margin pressure, and slower growth. These costs affect employees as much as customers, generating rework and inefficiency that compounds across the organization. (See Chapter 11 for more on the customer–employee experience connection.)

Research consistently demonstrates that the journey experience directly affects customer retention, loyalty, and revenue. For example:

- Nearly half of consumers have already abandoned brands because of poor customer experience, and 86% say they will leave a brand after just two or three poor experiences.†
- Two-thirds of customers say they find a positive experience more influential than great advertising.‡

* Bill Staikos, "Journey Management in 2026 Is Finally Becoming What We Pretended It Was," *LinkedIn* (2026)

† Emplifi, *11 Key Things Consumers Expect from Their Brand Experiences Today* (2022)

‡ Tom Puthiyamadam and José Reyes, "Experience Is Everything," *PwC* (2018)

- Modern consumers expect experiences tailored to their individual needs; 60% of consumers are likely to become repeat buyers when offered personalized experiences.*
- Omnichannel campaigns and experiences can drive nearly 500% more orders than single-channel approaches.†

Daniel Hoffman from Lufthansa Group's Digital Hangar faced a problem common to large organizations: "We realized most of our insights died in the workshop graveyard. Everything felt like a one-shot initiative. We needed a way to continuously connect insight to action."‡

The transformation started small, beginning with UX teams before getting executive sponsorship: "We introduced the platform in the UX area first. The first colleagues immediately saw a use case in their value stream. They saw their own data. They saw their own problems. That made the difference."

Research consistently demonstrates that the journey experience directly affects customer retention, loyalty, and revenue.

From there, a cross-functional working group formed across Miles and More (Lufthansa's loyalty program), Lufthansa Systems, Eurowings, and the core Lufthansa brand. What united the participants was shared frustration with the difficulty of acting on existing insights.

A critical unlock was creating a shared taxonomy. As Hoffman explains, "Product already operates this way. They call it a sequence of experiences. But because we have a common taxonomy for the universal phases, everyone can operate in the same reality."

The operational impact was immediate. Customer service teams sitting on massive volumes of help center feedback had previously tried clustering 20,000+ entries manually. With the journey management platform, they uploaded the data and got clear results in just four minutes.

This speed enabled a new workflow. Lufthansa introduced a simple threshold: when more than 200 negative feedback entries are logged for a topic in a given week, a journey-based investigation process triggers automatically. Teams investigate, derive solutions, and track outcomes over time.

The rollout now spans seven business units. Each adapts the framework to its needs, from highly digital environments to complex operational airline experiences.

Hoffman's key lesson is clear: "Talk to your way-of-working people from day one. We came from a service design and UX perspective. People asked, is this another UX tool? It was hard to say no. But this is for everyone. It is crucial that everybody is using it if you want to make real impact."

This transformation was about making journeys the system for decision making. In this sense, journey management goes beyond creating better maps. At its core, it's about using journeys as an organizing principle for data. As TheyDo CEO Jochem van der Veer told me, "We're bringing that all back together through the lens of a journey as an organizing principle for data. That's what journey management is about."

---

* Twilio, *State of Personalization Report* (2021)

† Bernard Meyer, "What We Can Learn from Omnichannel Statistics for 2022," *Omnisend blog* (2022)

‡ TheyDo, "Lufthansa Group at Forrester CX Summit: From Service Design to System of Record" (2025)

This distinction matters. Some organizations reorganize teams around journeys—an option discussed in the next chapter. Others keep their functional structure but use journeys and journey data as "the context we share across teams to make decisions." This results in a type of lattice overlaying silos rather than replacing them.

The Fundamental Data Challenge

Journey management platforms promise to connect scattered customer data into a unified view. The upshot is that journey management changes how organizations make decisions. When the journey becomes the shared reference point, teams naturally shift from optimizing their own metrics to solving customer problems that span departments.

> *Both modes of collaboration—synchronous and asynchronous—are necessary for delivering exceptional customer experiences.*

However, there's a fundamental challenge few vendors talk about openly: most organizations lack the data quality to make journey management truly work. Poor data quality sabotages the entire approach. This can stem from causes such as the following:

Fragmentation across departments
: One team logs "order_finished" while another uses "purchase_completed." These inconsistencies make it impossible to build a cohesive view of the customer journey.

Failed personalization
: Inaccurate or outdated data prevents reliable identity resolution. You end up sending a marketing email to someone who just called to cancel their subscription.

Weak measurement
: Siloed or noisy data makes it difficult to track ROI for specific touchpoints. Teams can't prove which actions actually improve the customer experience.

Operational friction
: Outdated contact information or duplicate records create direct friction for customers, disrupting what should be seamless experiences.

Openprise's 2025 State of RevOps Survey found that organizations struggling with data quality cite missing or incomplete data (93%), duplicate records (85%), and nonstandardized data (77%) as their top technical hurdles. Nearly 71% report that poor data quality negatively impacts go-to-market activities.*

The solution isn't a one-time technical fix. Data quality requires continual investment: automated validation to catch errors before they propagate, clear governance about what gets tracked and how, and tying data quality improvements directly to journey KPIs like conversion and retention.

This is why journey management platforms require dedicated data engineering resources. The platform doesn't fix your data problems—it exposes them. Organizations need the capability to continually curate, validate, and maintain data quality, or the entire investment becomes expensive shelfware displaying unreliable information.

---

* Openprise, *2025 State of RevOps Survey* (2025)

Collaboration Models: From Synchronous to Asynchronous

Throughout this book, I've emphasized collaborative sessions where diverse perspectives come together in real time. These synchronous sessions create value through immediate debate and shared discovery. The process builds alignment as much as the map itself.

Journey management works differently. It asks teams to collaborate asynchronously, working on the same journeys at different times and on their own schedules. People contribute at their convenience rather than coordinating calendars for live meetings and workshops for the ongoing optimization of the customer experience.

Journey management platforms support this through several lightweight coordination mechanisms, such as:

- *@mentions* to flag specific people for input on journey stages or insights
- *Comments* for questions, observations, or context directly on the journey
- *Assigned ownership* to clarify who maintains which journey segments
- *Reactions* to signal agreement or importance without lengthy discussion
- *Status indicators* showing what's validated versus what needs review
- *Notifications* to stay informed without constant checking

Asynchronous collaboration enables scale. Organizations can maintain hundreds of journeys with distributed ownership. Teams across time zones can contribute without scheduling overhead. Updates happen continually rather than waiting for the next workshop.

This isn't to say that journey management doesn't require synchronous collaboration. See "Importance/Difficulty Matrix" on page 240 for an example of a prioritization exercise that requires real-time debate.

Both modes of collaboration—synchronous and asynchronous—are necessary for delivering exceptional customer experiences, but they serve different purposes. Generative work, such as envisioning futures and building empathy, thrives in synchronous sessions. Summative work, like updating data, tracking metrics, and coordinating fixes, scales through asynchronous contributions. Match the collaboration model to what you're trying to accomplish and the scale at which you're operating.

Journey Management Platforms

Two complementary categories have evolved in the market: dedicated journey management platforms and broader customer experience platforms with orchestration capabilities.

Dedicated journey management platforms specialize in mapping, governing, and coordinating customer journeys across organizations. Forrester's 2025 Wave report, referenced earlier, evaluated current leading customer journey management platform vendors. They differed in focus and approach, though most offered overlapping capabilities across several categories. For example:

- ***Operational alignment:*** TheyDo emphasizes team collaboration and connecting maps directly to business initiatives.
- ***Governance and audit:*** JourneyTrack leans toward governance workflows and audit trails, making it suitable for regulated industries.
- ***Operational integration:*** Cemantics focuses on connecting journeys to operational data for continuous improvement cycles.

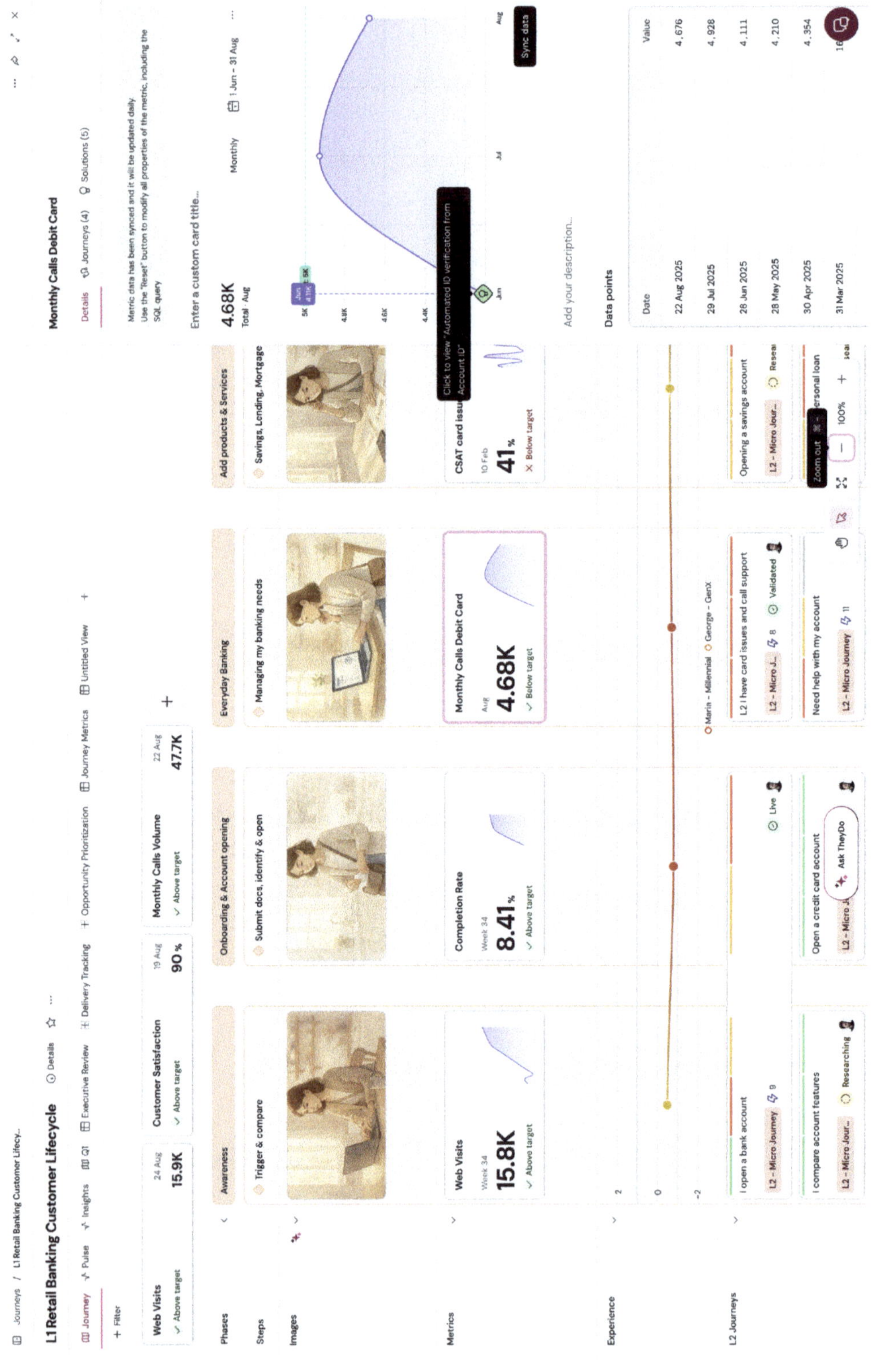

Figure 10-3. This dashboard from TheyDo shows the organization of data around the journey along the top.

- ***Service design roots:*** Smaply and UXPressia offer strong visual mapping foundations; Smaply excels at connecting journeys to internal service delivery, while UXPressia balances accessible templates with depth for mature practices.
- ***Complex B2B cycles:*** cxomni specializes in handling multistakeholder journeys and cross-organizational coordination.

These platforms turn journeys into living artifacts that connect to strategic initiatives, enable cross-functional collaboration, and provide governance structures for managing journeys at scale. Most integrate AI for pattern detection and data analysis, but human validation remains essential.

The Journey as an Organizing Structure

Journey management platforms organize around a central principle: journeys themselves become the organizing structures for customer data. For example, **Figure 10-3** shows a dashboard from TheyDo, with the journey chronology across the top serving as the backbone.* Customer feedback, operational metrics, and behavioral data are all connected to specific journey stages rather than being scattered across separate systems.

This journey-centric structure enables teams to drill down from high-level views into detailed information at any touchpoint. **Figure 10-4** shows how teams can examine unified data around a single stage: what customers experience, what the data reveals, and what opportunities exist. This real-time view is highly detailed, and much of the information links back to primary sources, allowing for further exploration.

The structure works through what platforms call an *experience taxonomy*: a shared vocabulary that connects what customers do, what they're trying to achieve, and what the organization should do about it. This taxonomy turns scattered feedback into structured, AI-ready insights.

Without this connective tissue, customer data remains fragmented across systems. With it, everything ties back to business metrics and goals, giving organizations a view of how each journey impacts outcomes. The journey structure, then, gives teams the context they need to interpret and understand the insights they've gathered.

Within journey management platforms, AI is transforming how teams interact with data by creating synthetic personas—AI-powered simulations of customer segments that can be "interviewed" as if they were real people. These "digital twins" can be brought into meetings and consulted on service improvements. Rather than just viewing dashboards, teams can now interact with customer proxies directly.

The conversation happens in the context of the journey map itself, so when a persona describes frustration at a particular stage, it's clear which touchpoint they're referencing. This makes synthetic research far more contextual than isolated data points and disconnected feedback. **Figure 10-5** shows how this might look in a journey management tool, in this case, UXPressia.

Some platforms let you query the maps themselves, asking questions like "How consistent are these three onboarding journeys?" or "What patterns appear across our B2B and B2C experiences?" The AI analyzes journey structures, identifies gaps, and can suggest updates when new research is added. This scales the work of maintaining maps without removing human judgment from the process.

* Note that I have professional relationships with several journey management platform vendors, including TheyDo and UXPressia, and have consulted with organizations implementing these tools.

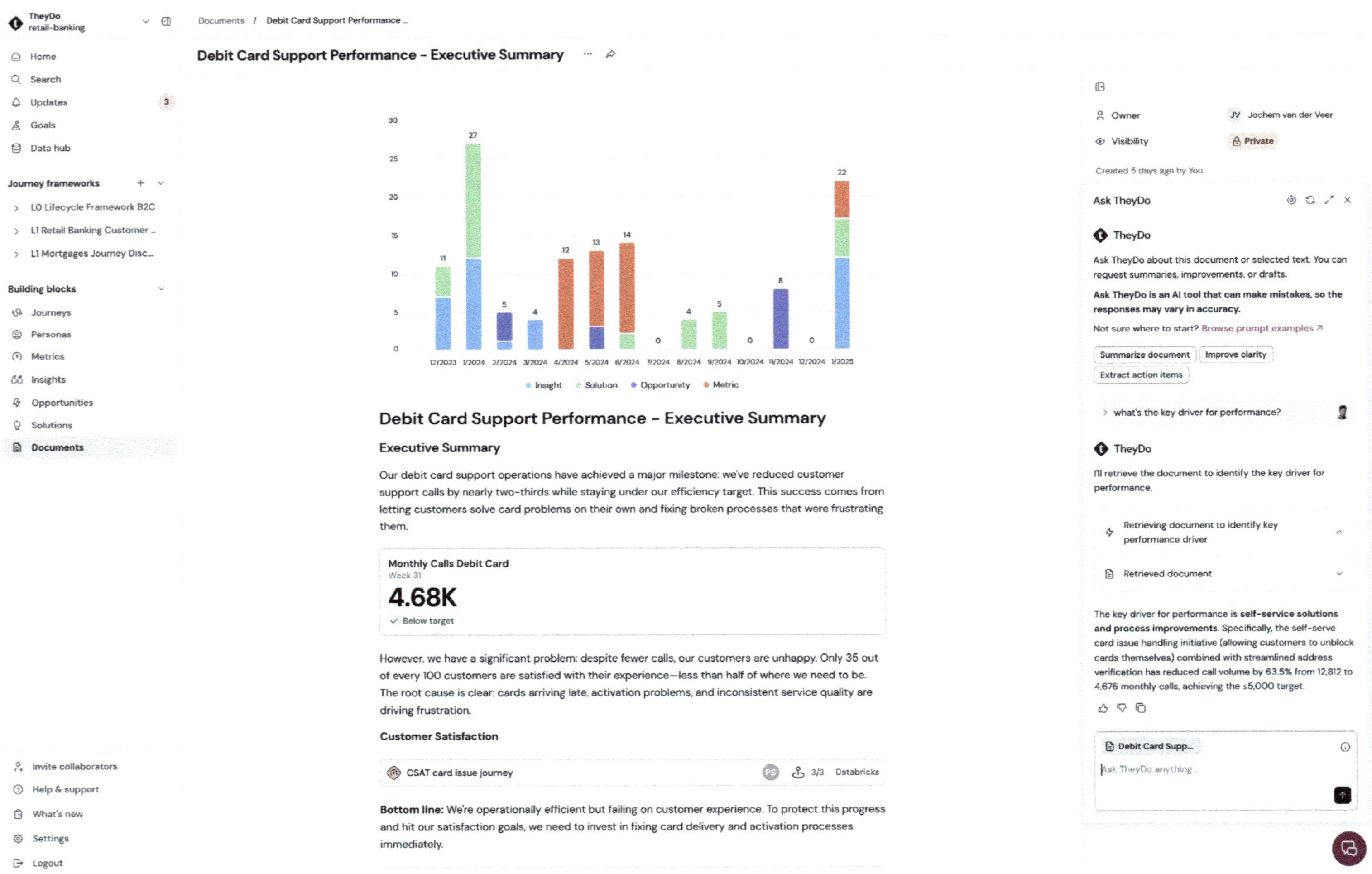

FIGURE 10-4. Detailed views within journey management platforms provide a wealth of specific data points and real-time insights.

Interviews with synthetic personas can even generate journey maps automatically. As Yuri Vedenin, CEO of UXPressia, told me: "We will never get rid of journey maps, but they will be generated automatically. On demand." This captures the likely future: AI handles the creation and updating of maps, while humans continue to rely on them as stable artifacts for alignment.

None of this works with fragmented data. AI can surface meaningful insights only when customer data lives in one organized place. Scattered spreadsheets, disconnected surveys, and siloed analytics don't provide AI enough structure to be useful. This is why the journey as organizing principle matters so much: it creates the foundation AI needs to actually help rather than just adding another layer of noise.

While synthetic personas broaden access to customer insights beyond research teams, they don't replace interviews with real customers. These personas lack contextual details: tone of voice, emotional expression, physical environment, and the unexpected tangents that reveal hidden needs. More critically, real-world interviews provide the grounding needed to judge whether AI outputs are valid. Without direct customer contact, how do you know if the synthetic responses accurately reflect reality?

Journey management platforms serve organizations that need to coordinate strategy and governance across many journeys. Mature organizations often pair them with orchestration platforms for execution and personalization. The key is matching tool sophistication to organizational readiness and genuine need, rather than adopting such a platform simply because it represents "best practice."

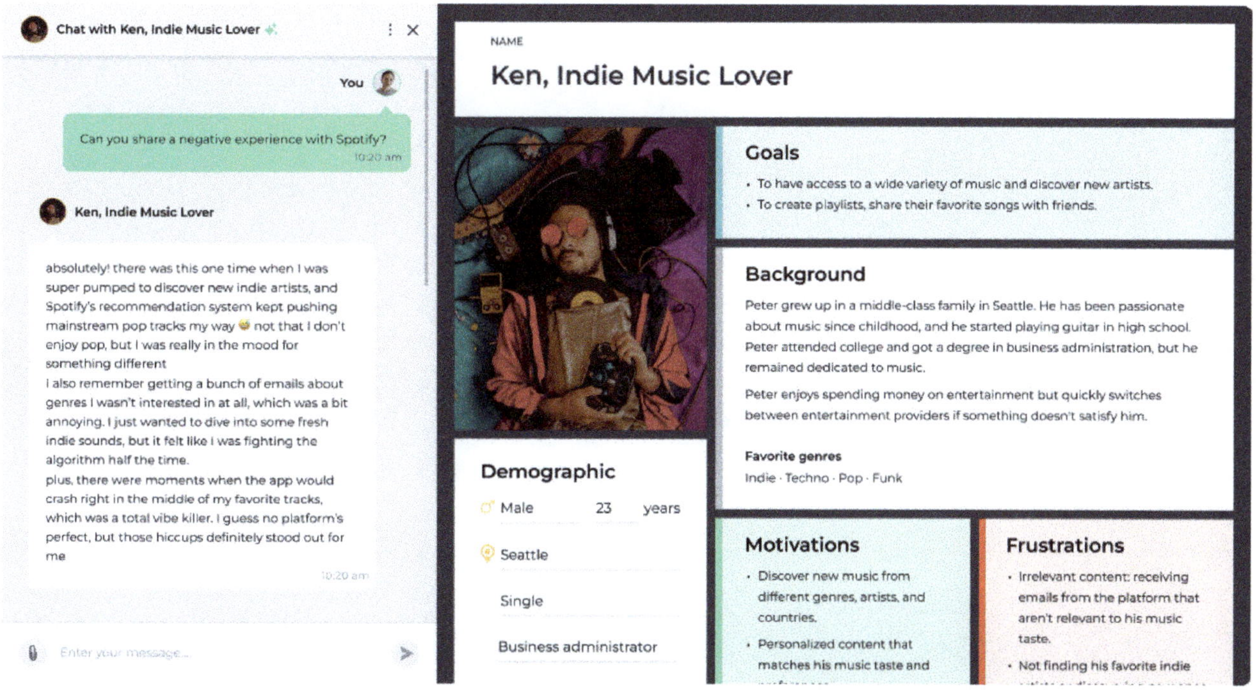

Figure 10-5. UXPressia allows teams to quickly create synthetic personas and interview them in the context of the journey.

Is Journey Management Right for Your Organization?

Journey management platforms are most useful for organizations operating at significant scale. Most teams don't need them—and that's fine. Here are some questions you can use to assess whether journey management is right for you, structured around six key readiness factors:

1. ***Complexity of experiences and channels.*** Are you managing dozens of distinct customer journeys across multiple channels (web, mobile, in-person, phone, chat, etc.)? Do experiences span multiple brands or regions?
2. ***Data availability and access.*** Do you have comprehensive data across the entire journey? This means behavioral data (clicks, transactions, usage), experiential data (surveys, feedback, support tickets), operational data (process metrics, service level agreements), and financial data (costs, revenue). If critical touchpoints lack instrumentation or you can't access data from key systems, journey management won't reliably work.
3. ***Experience types.*** What is the nature of the experience you're looking to understand? Journey management platforms aren't designed for many noncommercial contexts, such as student, citizen, employee, or partnership experiences, or other journeys that lack behavioral tracking.
4. ***Scale of experience delivery.*** Does delivering a single experience require coordination across dozens of teams and hundreds of people? Do silos create gaps that customers experience as friction?
5. ***Dedicated capacity for journey data curation.*** Do you have a customer experience team or equivalent with data engineers or insights specialists who can structure, validate, and maintain journey data over time? Like a data warehouse, journey management requires ongoing investment in people and governance.
6. ***Specific business problem with measurable impact.*** Can you articulate what journey management will solve? For example, if your goal is "Reduce know-your-customer (KYC) time from 90 to 60 days," answers like "Our customer experience function will operate better" indicate you're not ready.

If you answered no to two or more of these questions, collaborative journey mapping likely provides what you need: shared understanding, cross-functional alignment, and actionable insights without the infrastructure overhead. For the vast majority of teams, collaborative mapping provides exactly the right level of capability.

Mapping Still Matters

The most persistent criticism of journey mapping is that it's static. By the time a map is complete, customer expectations have shifted and operations have changed. How can static artifacts remain relevant in dynamic environments?

The answer: being static isn't a flaw, it's essential.

It's hard to align around a constantly shifting target. Experience maps intentionally stabilize a complex system so people can reason about it together. Stable structures help orient teams when they have more and more dynamic data and provide them with a framework to make sense of the noise.

This is precisely why modern journey management platforms continue to use maps as their primary organizing mechanism. Even the most sophisticated AI-powered systems require stable journey structures to organize and interpret data. As Yuri Vedenin, CEO of UXPressia, puts it: "Journey management is impossible without journey mapping. You can't manage something until you create it."

As discussed in Chapter 2, the value of collaborative mapping lies in its ability to help people make sense of experiences together, not necessarily in its precision. Journey management platforms promise accuracy, but when the underlying data is incomplete or dirty, they can also create a false sense of confidence. Collaborative mapping acknowledges uncertainty while enabling action anyway.

The real alternative to a static map isn't something more "dynamic." It's invisible opinions, competing metrics, and dueling anecdotes.

Dashboards don't interpret themselves—they show you *what* customers do, not *why* or *how* it feels. Numbers don't convey frustration, confusion, or delight. This is the difference between thin and thick data (see Chapter 6): thin data reveals correlations; thick data uncovers causation. You can't optimize your way to customer centricity—it requires the cultural transformation that only thick, qualitative understanding enables.

Experience maps intentionally stabilize a complex system so people can reason about it together.

AI can't create the moment when teams recognize how their work combines to create customer pain. And it certainly can't help teams develop empathy for what it's like to be on the other side of your processes.

In an era where teams are swimming in data, alignment (not more information) becomes the primary constraint. Mapping experiences remains one of the most effective ways to build that alignment capability.

When Collaborative Mapping Excels

The distinction between mapping and management is, in part, a conceptual one. Mapping is generative: forward-looking, exploratory, envisioning what doesn't exist yet. It requires diverse perspectives coming together, with value emerging from the collaboration itself. The process is the product as much as the map.

Journey management tends to be summative: analytical, measurement-based, diagnosing and optimizing what currently exists. It can be done by specialists working within platforms, with insights shared out rather than cocreated. It's expert-driven and scales through automation. Journey management excels at monitoring current experiences and reactive issue resolution: "Where is it broken? How do we fix it?"

This distinction matters for strategy. Journey management optimizes current positions but can't determine where to move next. Strategy requires making hard choices about future direction that data alone can't answer. Collaborative mapping creates the forum where those strategic conversations happen. Different organizational moments call for different approaches:

- Transformation and innovation require generative mapping.
- Optimization and scaling require summative management.

You can't buy alignment. Journey management platforms can show you problems, but they can't create the cross-functional relationships and shared understanding that enable coordinated action.

The Breadth of Mapping

While journey management platforms focus on customer interactions with existing solutions, as we saw in Chapter 4, mapping encompasses a much broader spectrum. To give just a few examples:

- Service blueprints connect journeys to backstage operations.
- Ecosystem maps reveal complex relationships across organizations.

- Mental model diagrams capture how customers think about problems.
- Job maps show the steps required to complete work independent of any solution.

Journey management platforms largely address one type of experience: the consumption journey. Customers interacting with your product or service generate behavioral data, transaction records, support tickets, and survey responses. These data streams feed the platform.

But many experience types discussed in this book fall outside this scope. Student, citizen, supplier, partnership, and community experiences often operate without the behavioral tracking that journey management requires. And the data that does exist is unlikely to be structured or captured in a way that supports journey management. A university knows when students register for classes but typically doesn't track the emotional journey of choosing a major. A city knows when citizens pay parking tickets, but it can't realistically capture the experience of navigating bureaucracy to open a small business.

While journey management platforms focus on customer interactions with existing solutions, mapping encompasses a much broader spectrum.

Future experiences compound this limitation. To-be maps describe what does not yet exist. They require imagination, not data analysis. Journey management platforms excel at optimizing current experiences but can't design fundamentally new ones. By definition, future state maps must be created manually and remain "static" until the experience exists and generates data.

This is why mapping's scope remains broader than management's. Journey management focuses on an important but narrow slice of experience work: optimizing existing customer journeys at scale, typically in commercial settings. Mapping spans the full spectrum.

Accessibility and Scale

Finally, the cost of journey management is prohibitive to most organizations. Implementation requires months of taxonomy development, data integration across enterprise systems, change management consulting, and dedicated platform administrators. Success demands executive sponsorship, cross-functional coordination at scale, and organizational maturity that takes years to build.

Global enterprises with dedicated customer experience teams can leverage these tools effectively, but startups bootstrapping their way to product/market fit typically cannot. Neither can most small businesses, project teams, or design agencies doing discovery work.

For most organizations, collaborative journey mapping remains the most accessible, highest-impact practice for becoming customer centric. It doesn't require IT approval, procurement cycles, or data integration projects. It requires a room (physical or virtual), diverse perspectives, customer research, facilitation skills, and a commitment to act on what you learn.

Journey management platforms are powerful tools for organizations that can leverage them, but collaborative mapping remains essential for the vast majority of organizations seeking to become more customer-centric with the resources they have. It continues to spread precisely because it is an accessible alternative that works at a human scale.

Experience as Advantage

The people you serve don't care about your org chart. They experience your company as one entity, regardless of its internal structure. When customers must navigate your organizational complexity to solve their problems, you've made your internal convenience their burden.

This is where journey management creates strategic advantage at scale. When you can measure which journey improvements drive retention, identify friction that causes churn before it happens, and coordinate fixes across departments, experience becomes a measurable growth lever. Journey management turns XLG from aspiration into operational reality with clear ROI.

Customers represent neutral ground and provide a shared reference point that cuts across organizational boundaries. Every silo can find meaning and purpose in customer outcomes without territorial defensiveness. This creates a foundation for cross-silo collaboration based on shared value rather than forced coordination.

The people you serve don't care about your org chart. They experience your company as one entity, regardless of its internal structure.

Customer obsession becomes the shared language that makes cross-silo collaboration essential. Success requires embracing the paradox of silos: preserving their benefits for scalability and specialization while building effective cross-functional mechanisms for customer value creation.

Journey management and orchestration represent more than operational efficiency. They're fundamental to XLG strategy. As discussed in Chapter 1, XLG means using superior customer experiences as the primary driver of business expansion, rather than relying solely on sales and marketing spend.

Most organizations that master both technical coordination and organizational coordination respond faster to market changes, deliver better experiences, and drive better outcomes. They compete on the experience itself, not just product features or price.

Organizations need both capabilities: generative mapping for envisioning futures, building empathy, and creating strategic vision; summative management for optimizing present experiences, quantifying impact, and coordinating at scale. Success requires orchestrating both technology and human networks to deliver superior customer experiences. The foundation remains human connection, collaborative sensemaking, and the shared understanding that mapping provides.

Use the customer perspective to your advantage. When internal debates stall, return to what customers actually need and experience. That's the ground everyone has to stand on together.

Summary

Customer experiences span organizational boundaries, but companies operate in functional silos. This creates transitional volatility, where customers experience disconnected touchpoints rather than a coherent whole.

Collaborative mapping creates alignment but struggles to sustain it at enterprise scale. Journey management emerged to address this gap, providing infrastructure to manage journeys continuously across millions of customer interactions.

This chapter presented a three-layer framework for journey management:

- Mapping creates understanding through collaborative visualization.
- Journey management provides the governance to transform journeys into living artifacts connected to strategy and business outcomes.
- Orchestration enables real-time execution and personalization.

Journey management connects four data types: operational, financial, behavioral, and experiential. Together, these enable organizations to answer questions that drive resource allocation. But journey management also requires significant infrastructure, including dedicated data engineering, organizational governance, and continual investment in data quality. Most organizations lack the data consistency and accuracy these platforms demand.

The shift from point-in-time mapping to managing journeys over time also changes how teams work together. Mapping thrives on synchronous collaboration, where diverse perspectives come together in real time. Journey management, by contrast, enables asynchronous coordination through platform features, allowing distributed teams to contribute on their own schedules.

Even with journey management, however, collaborative mapping remains essential. It serves generative purposes such as envisioning futures, building empathy, and creating strategic vision. Future state maps require imagination, not data analysis.

Journey management serves more summative purposes: optimizing experiences, quantifying impact, and coordinating at scale. Its scope is also narrower. Journey management platforms focus primarily on customer consumption journeys with behavioral tracking, leaving many experience types outside their reach.

Another limitation is that because these platforms demand significant investment, months of implementation, and dedicated teams, they're accessible to relatively few organizations. For most, collaborative mapping provides exactly the right capability without the additional infrastructure overhead.

Many organizations have a place for both collaborative mapping and journey management. The overarching aim is to build a customer-centric culture where shared insights become a unifying force to drive XLG.

Further Reading

Qualtrics, "The Complete Guide to Customer Journey Management" *(2023)*

This useful resource details what customer journey management is and provides links to a range of related pieces.

Jeannie Walters, Experience Is Everything *(2026)*

A leading voice in customer experience for decades, Walters provides a holistic framework for experience as a mindset, strategy, and discipline. The book introduces journey mapping as a strategic problem-solving tool and demonstrates how to align experience goals with business outcomes. While not a journey management playbook, it establishes the strategic foundation any journey management effort requires: without a cohesive strategy, formal initiatives will likely fail.

Greg Kihlström et al., Customer Journey Management & Orchestration *(2026)*

This book is a concise, practical guide for moving beyond static journey maps toward scaled orchestration across touchpoints. The authors argue that most enterprises don't lack customer data or tools; rather, they struggle to translate customer signals into consistent decisions across marketing, sales, service, and digital channels. This playbook aims to help organizations implement journey management and next-best-action frameworks without adding unnecessary operational complexity.

Chris Risdon and Patrick Quattlebaum, Orchestrating Experiences *(2018)*

This book makes end-to-end service design actionable with a wealth of examples and hands-on, practical techniques. While creating a diagram plays a large role in the process, the authors' approach looks far beyond mapping and into the complexity of aligning modern organizations. This is a highly recommended resource.

Diagram and Image Credits

Figures 10-3 and **10-4**: Screenshots from the TheyDo journey management platform courtesy of Jochem van der Veer, used with permission

Figure 10-5: Screenshot from UXPressia courtesy of Yuri Vedenin, used with permission

Importance/Difficulty Matrix

Objective	Prioritize journey insights and opportunities for action
Time	30–60 minutes
Participants	3–10
Materials	Whiteboard, matrix template, sticky notes

Making thoughtful decisions about which insights to act on is challenging but essential. When you're dealing with various opportunities identified through journey management and differing priorities across stakeholders, a simple 2 × 2 matrix helps establish what to focus on first (**Figure 10-6**).

Plotting insights along two dimensions—importance and difficulty—makes tensions between these opposing forces visible. This gives participants the opportunity to express options, surface assumptions, debate options, and align on a course of action. Listen carefully to every point of deliberation. This isn't a scientific cost/benefit analysis—it's a tool to facilitate discussion and align the team on priorities.

How it works:

1. Prepare the matrix. Draw a large quad chart. Label the horizontal axis Importance (or Impact) and the vertical axis Difficulty (or "Cost to Execute").
2. Gather insights. Collect opportunities and pain points identified from your journey management system. Write each on a separate sticky note.
3. Plot items horizontally for Importance. Define this axis as either importance to the customer or importance to the business (pick one or the other). As a team, discuss each item's importance and position items relative to one another in a single row along the bottom of the horizontal axis.
4. Plot items vertically for Difficulty. For each item, discuss the difficulty of implementing a solution. Move the items upward on the matrix accordingly, maintaining their relative location on the horizontal axis. Give each item its own distinct place on the scale.
5. Set priorities and determine next steps. Look for related groupings within quadrants and decide which items to tackle first. Items toward the lower right (high importance, low difficulty) are your best bets to start with now. Items near the middle can be planned next. Items with high importance and high difficulty are strategic investments worth planning for later.

Learn more:

LUMA Institute, "Importance/Difficulty Matrix"

Sarah Gibbons, "Using Prioritization Matrices to Inform UX Decisions," *NN/g* (2018)

Example:

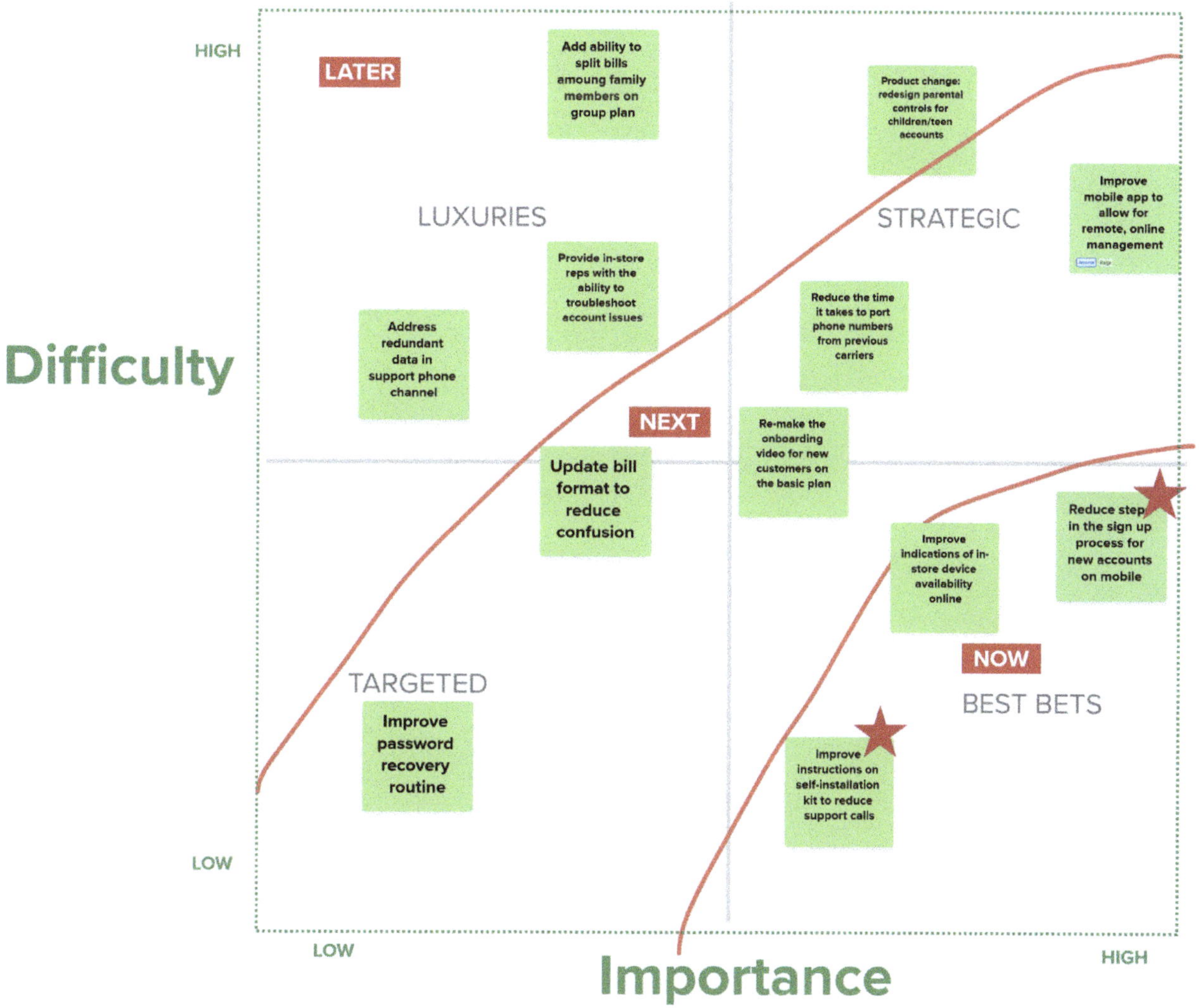

FIGURE 10-6. Plotting pain points and opportunities on an Importance/Difficulty Matrix enables you to prioritize which to tackle first.

What employees experience, Customers will. The best marketing is happy, engaged employees. Your Customers will never be any happier than your employees.

—John DiJulius, *The Customer Service Revolution*

IN THIS CHAPTER

- The employee experience and why it's important
- Mapping the employee experience
- Aligning the customer experience to the employee experience
- Organizational design and customer experience
- Collaborative method for aligning customer and employee experience

CHAPTER 11

Mapping the Employee Experience: Aligning Inside

There was a deli around the corner from my previous home in Hamburg, Germany, that sold quality meats and specialty items. I used to stop in every so often to get products that were otherwise hard to find. But the service was often rude and abrupt. I sometimes felt nervous interacting with the servers, who might get annoyed if I asked about the different types of salami they had (as if I should already know all the subtleties).

My wife worked in the area and knew a lot of the neighborhood businesses. When I brought up the abrasive service I had experienced, she immediately said, "Not surprising: the owners are exactly like that too. They are difficult people to deal with." And to be sure, the deli had high employee turnover.

The point is that organizations are often mirrors of the customer experiences they deliver. If employees are treated poorly behind the scenes, how can they be expected to provide good service to customers? If management sets a bad example for interacting with employees, why should employees act any differently toward customers?

Computer scientist and programmer Melvin Conway observed that the solutions organizations produce reflect their own communication structures. Dubbed *Conway's law*, this insight highlights the power of organizational design: how a company operates is as important as what it produces.

The growing adoption of AI in organizations only heightens the need for human-centricity. As J. P. Gownder and colleagues point out in a report from Forrester:

> **Today's AI remains intimately tied to human users, whose experience with the technology will be a principal determinant of its success or failure. Framing AI as a tool that builds new opportunities for employees in their jobs, lives, and future careers can help. And designing a human-centric culture of AI to reinforce positive practices, beliefs, and behaviors will drive both employee experience and business success.***

The report recommends highlighting resources and artifacts that employees can "see," like videos and conference calls. We can add diagrams and maps to the list as well.

Focusing on the employee experience drives not only better customer experiences but also durable AI adoption and culture transformation.

---

* J. P. Gownder et al., "Ground Your Workforce AI Strategy in Human Experience: Put Employees at the Center of Your AI Efforts to Drive Business Success," Forrester (2025)

This chapter discusses the concept of internal alignment through the lens of employee experience. As the *customer experience* becomes increasingly imperative for business growth, the *employee experience* will also become critical for success.

Said another way, the path to becoming more customer-centric is to be more employee-centric, by creating a great employee experience. The two experiences are inextricably linked. Mapping heightens alignment along both dimensions, helping to intentionally coordinate them.

What Is Employee Experience?

Employee experience is a relatively new focus area for many organizations. It goes beyond smooth onboarding, proper workplace setup, and free perks. It's about more than employee satisfaction and even more than employee engagement.

Instead, employee experience encompasses the sum of the experiences—thoughts, actions, and feelings—that an employee has with an organization over time. It's about how they understand and internalize the organization's vision and strategy, as well as the behaviors they exhibit in working toward the company's mission and how they're set up to support customers.

In many ways, managing the employee experience is an extension of existing functions such as HR or people operations. Its scope is broader, representing a modern way to manage the workforce through the lens of the overall experience.

Employee experience also overlaps with the notion of company culture, but there are some important distinctions. Culture consists of the tacit beliefs, values, and collective assumptions of a group. Employee experience is how employees live that company culture over time.

Ultimately, considering the employee experience is an explicit recognition that employees have the freedom to change jobs. While this is often easier said than done, even if unsatisfied employees don't actually leave, organizations still face costs from disengagement, quiet quitting, and eventual turnover when opportunities do arise.

An enlightened organization strives to create a sense of belonging, so people want to join its cause and stay engaged. Employee experience is about the purpose that comes with employment, which can be a motivating force as strong as (or stronger than) money alone.

With this in mind, a holistic set of contributing factors emerge. These include the following:

- Physical and digital spaces, including tools and equipment
- Internal systems, capabilities, and support
- Flexibility, autonomy, and transparency
- Feeling valued and having a sense of agency
- Coaching and mentorship on the job
- Personal and career growth opportunities
- Teamwork and social aspects of work
- Workflow and processes
- Passion for the brand
- Diversity and inclusion
- Health and physical well-being
- Emotional and psychological well-being

Variations exist from organization to organization, and perspectives may shift over time. For example, a startup may emphasize brand passion and workflow more than a large corporation, which might focus on coaching and career development.

Jacob Morgan, the author of *The Employee Experience Advantage*, offers a practical way to grasp employee experience as a whole. He compartmentalizes the key aspects into three categories:

Cultural environment

This is the biggest and perhaps most important contributor to the employee experience. A range of factors are at play here: a sense of purpose, the perceived value of employees in the organization, diversity and inclusion, fair treatment, growth and mentorship, well-being, and more.

Technical environment

The software and hardware employees use make up the technical environment. Availability and consumer-grade options are key factors in providing a great employee experience, as well as alignment of employee needs and business requirements.

Physical environment

This refers to where employees work, including in offices and remote or at-home settings. Flexibility and multiple workspace options are key factors when considering the physical employment environment. Morgan points to a desire to bring friends to work as a sign of a good physical environment.

A good employee experience is not just a nice-to-have, but an imperative for growth.

The point is that employee experience is multifaceted, shaped by multiple characteristics simultaneously. However you visualize it, the most important thing to remember is that a good employee experience is not just a nice-to-have, but an imperative for growth.

Morgan's research demonstrated that organizations that invested most heavily in employee experience were:

- Over eleven times more likely to appear on Glassdoor's "Best Places to Work" list
- More than four times more likely to feature on LinkedIn's list of North America's "Most InDemand Employers"
- Twenty-eight times more likely to be listed among Fast Company's "Most Innovative Companies"
- Twice as likely to be named by Forbes as one of the "World's Most Innovative Companies"
- Twice as likely to appear in the American Customer Satisfaction Index*

Additionally, Morgan notes that "experiential organizations had more than four times the average profit and more than two times the average revenue. They were also almost 25 percent smaller, which suggests higher levels of productivity and innovation."

This message is not necessarily new. As early as 1999, Joseph Pine II and James Gilmore showed that we had entered a new era they dubbed the "experience economy."† We are evolving toward an age of networked enterprises, in which the traditional hierarchies of the corporation will be supplanted by self-organizing systems collaborating on digital platforms.

As discussed in Chapter 1, XLG recognizes that distinctive customer experiences drive measurable business results. If customer experience is the engine of growth, then employee experience becomes a strategic imperative. The two are inseparable: employees create the experiences that customers value, and those experiences in turn drive retention, expansion, and advocacy.

The bottom line is that *how* a company works is as important as *what* it produces. This includes everything

---

* Jacob Morgan, *The Employee Experience Advantage* (2017)

† B. Joseph Pine II and James H. Gilmore, *The Experience Economy* (1999)

from recruiting to org charts to collaboration to culture. With so many factors to consider, the concept of experience becomes a unifying force. In other words, viewing the customer experience without considering the employee experience misses half of the equation.

Mapping the Employee Experience

Organizations concerned with employee experience don't want to just observe and report on it; they want to actively shape it. As with any experience, we can map employee experience as a sequence of interactions that unfold over time. Logically, creating a diagram is a key first step in facilitating a dialogue with an actionable outcome.

The process for creating an employee experience map is the same as for creating a customer experience map. This means we can apply everything we know about diagramming customer experiences to understanding and mapping the end-to-end employee experience.

After determining who will be on the team running the mapping process, begin by defining the point of view, scope, and focus. Decide which employee experience to map. Not everyone (for instance, executive management versus individual contributors) will have the same experience. Start by identifying the perspective most relevant to the problem you are trying to solve.

Be aware that this task can quickly become complex. For example, you may want to consider freelancers and how they fit into the organization in relation to the employee experience. While it can be tempting to exclude external contractors from the scope of your map, they affect the experience of full-time employees. And as the gig economy grows and organizations increasingly rely on freelancers to scale, aligning them with the organization becomes critical.

After defining whose experience to map, scope the experience. **Figure 11-1** is an example of an employee experience map provided by UXPressia, an online mapping tool. It's nearly identical to a customer journey map in form and format.

In this case, the scope of the diagram is broad—from recruiting to career development. This high-level view could help an organization prioritize which aspects of the overall employee experience it might seek to improve first. For example, addressing issues during recruiting could have a downstream effect on later stages. From this diagram, it's also clear that onboarding is a weak spot relative to other phases.

It's also possible to zoom in and map just one section, such as the period from searching for a job to completing a trial phase of employment. At any point in the overall journey, you can drill down further and map the experience in more detail. Be sure to set the right level of granularity and scope the effort to address your team's most important questions.

Figure 11-2 is a day-in-the-life map Chris McGrath created for an employee at his digital transformation consultancy, Tangowork. The top of the diagram shows the employee's workflow across a single day. The middle section includes common thoughts, along with emotional highs and lows. At the bottom, in the colored boxes, are concrete tactics to address the employee's pain points.

While such a narrowly scoped view may lead only to local, tactical solutions, mapping at this level still contributes to a more fulfilling employee experience. These granular views can ladder up into a broader picture of the overall experience employees have.

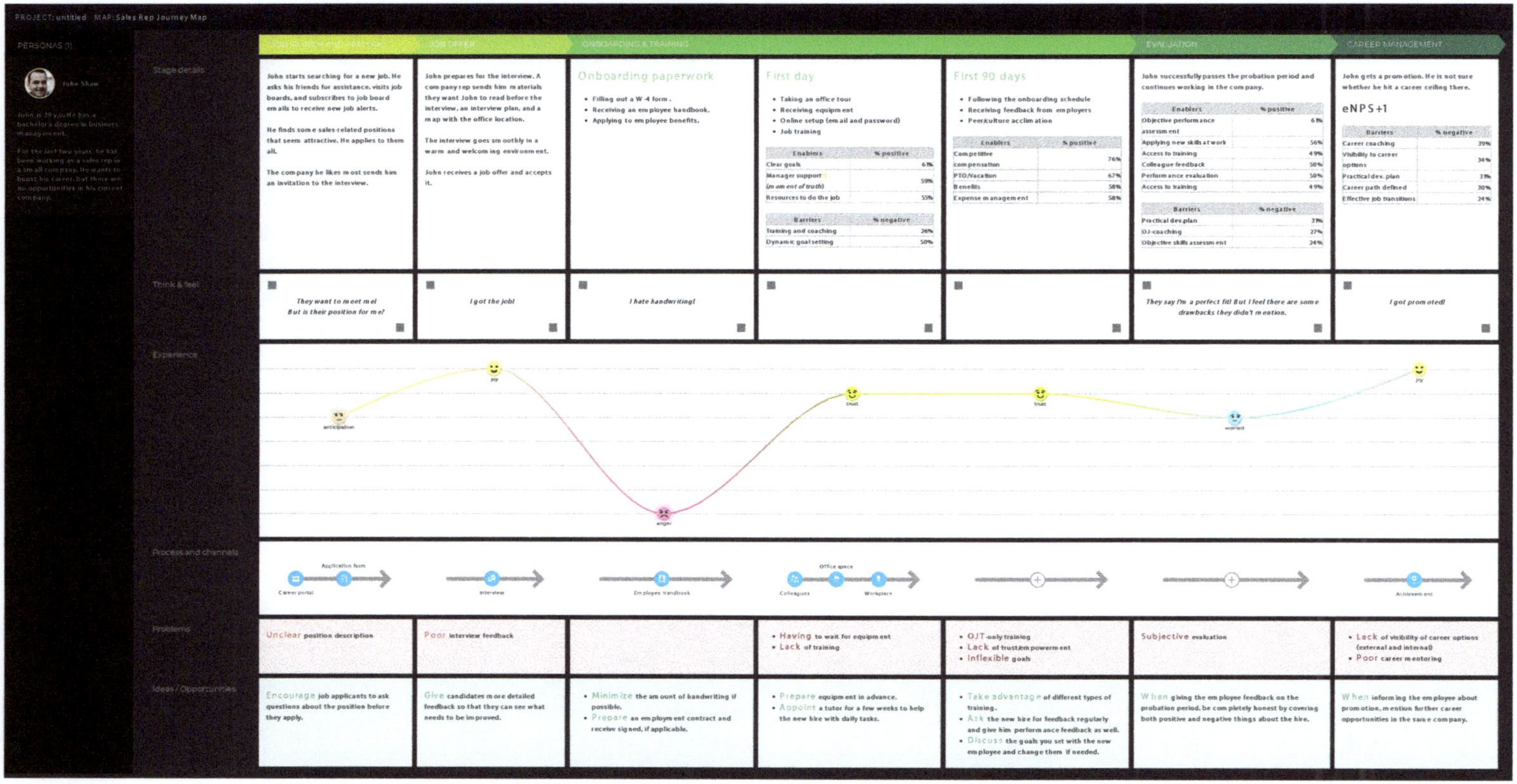

FIGURE 11-1. This end-to-end experience map shows the many touchpoints employees have with an organization, from the job search to career management.

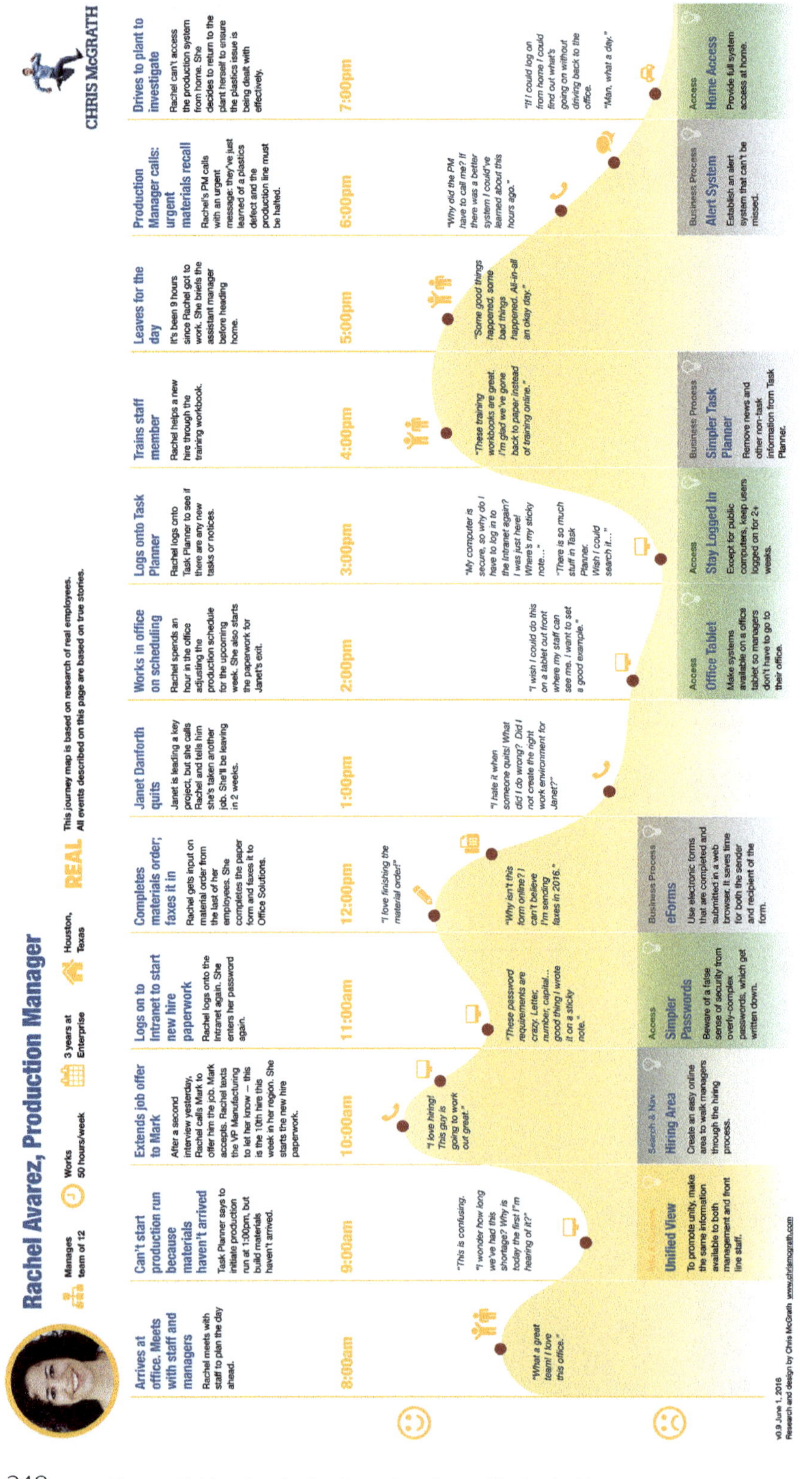

FIGURE 11-2. An employee experience map can take a day-in-the-life format rather than mimicking a customer journey map.

Figure 11-3 illustrates the approach taken by Rafa Vivas, creative director at XPLANE, a leading visual business consultancy. XPLANE's template for an employee experience map positions common stages of employment along the top, from discovery and onboarding to work, rewards, and eventually exit. The rows illustrate the touchpoints employees have with internal people, tools, and systems. The map also tracks the emotional curve and specific needs, concluding with a layer of insights and opportunities. Overall, this reflects alignment across multiple aspects of employment and points to actionable outcomes for improvement.

After defining the cornerstones of the mapping effort, use data from existing and prospective employees to research the experience. Follow the steps for the investigation stage outlined in Chapter 6. Then illustrate the experience, as outlined in Chapter 7. The aim is to tell a story that reflects the insights you gathered from your investigation in a way that is clear and accessible to others.

Aligning the Employee Experience to the Customer Experience

I like to think of the relationship of customers to employees as a single ecosystem. *How* companies provide value to customers these days is as important as the offering itself. The key is to view employees as endpoints in the value creation process: their experience is as important as the resulting customer experience.

Frontstage employees, such as sales representatives and customer support agents, may have direct contact with customers. But backstage employees, such as product developers and HR, also play a role: they either support the people who interface with customers or interact with customers through the offering itself. Everyone in an organization ultimately contributes to the experience delivered to the customer.

Figure 11-4 shows a conceptual model for how the employee experience and the customer experience are connected through direct and indirect relationships.

The point is that companies must be concerned with developing the infrastructure that supports experience, both inside and outside the organization. To be customer-obsessed, you also have to be employee-obsessed.

Brand leadership expert Denise Lee Yohn discusses the importance of this type of alignment. She points out that the biggest challenge in becoming a customer-centric company is creating a structure that enables customer centricity. Yohn approaches customer experience through the lens of a brand and relates employee experience to company culture. In her book *Fusion*, she uses the metaphor of nuclear fusion, writing:

> **When fused, the two nuclei create something entirely new. In the same way, you can unleash great power when you fuse together your organization's two nuclei: your culture—the way people in your organization behave and the attitudes and beliefs that inform them (i.e., "the way we do things around here")—and your brand or brand identity, how your organization is understood by customers and other stakeholders.***

If the customer experience is the brand in action, the employee experience is the company culture in action. In other words, if the brand represents a company's overall posture in a market, the customer experience is how people perceive it over time while interacting with the company. Likewise, while culture is the attitudes and

* Denise Lee Yohn, *Fusion* (2018)

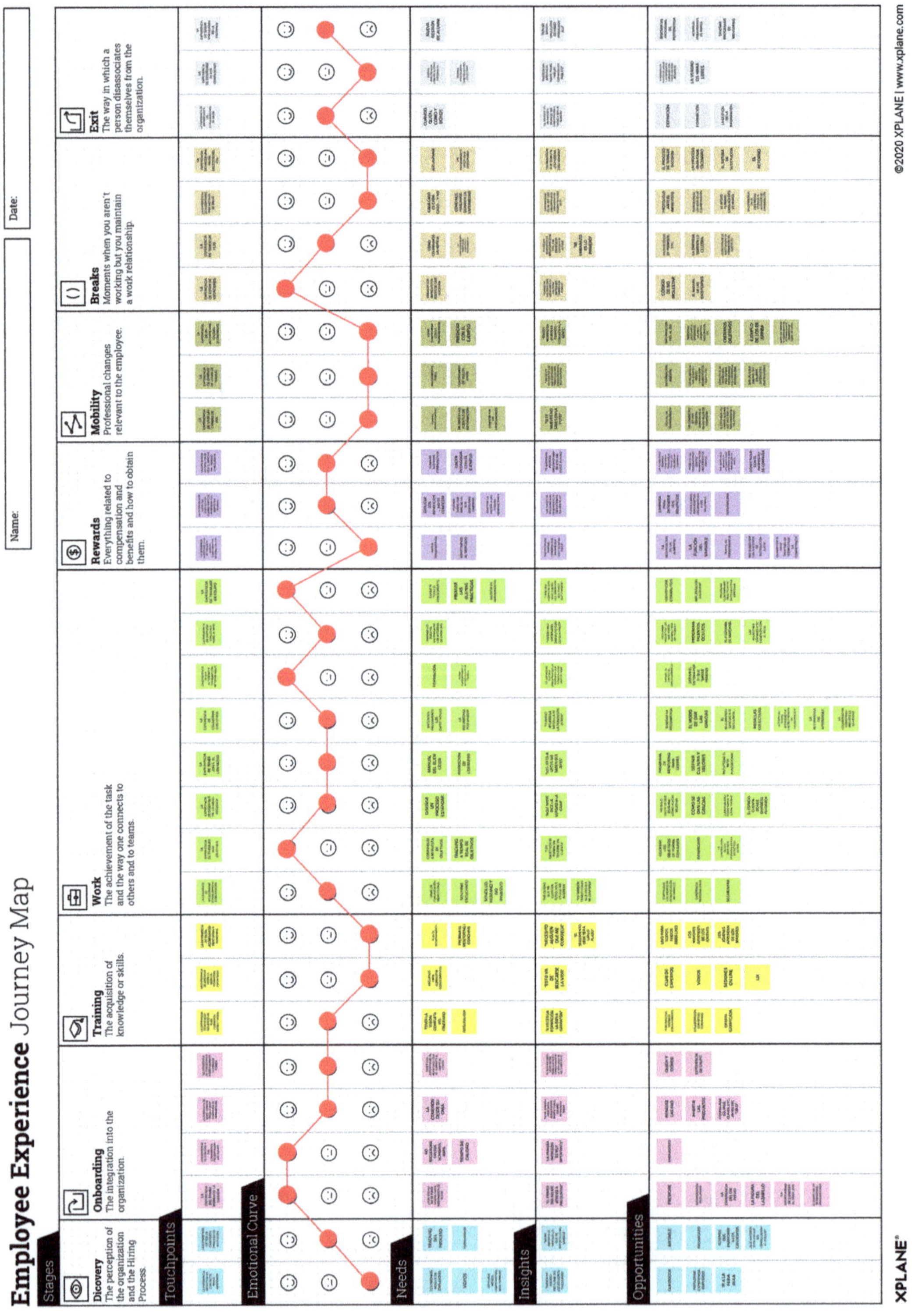

FIGURE 11-3. Using a common template enables consultants at XPLANE to map different employee experiences consistently.

beliefs of a company, the employee experience is how employees live that culture from their perspective while on the job.

Many companies have explicitly made the connection between customer experience and employee experience in the manner that Yohn recommends. For instance, former Southwest Airlines CEO Herb Kelleher made the chain reaction an explicit part of his leadership philosophy. As he often commented in blog posts and interviews: "You put your employees first. If you truly treat your employees that way, they will treat your customers well, your customers will come back, and that's what makes your shareholders happy."* The magic formula breaks down to: Happy Employees = Happy Customers = Increased Business/Profits = Happy Shareholders.

Customer journey maps typically begin with the first point of contact, continue through purchase, and extend into a long-term relationship with a brand. However, if we focus on just the customer experience, we miss half the story. What traditional customer journey maps don't show is what's beneath the surface: the massive amounts of employee activity that go into creating a customer experience (see **Figure 11-5**). Evaluating both the customer and employee sides provides a complete picture, which is critical to understanding the full breadth and depth of the journey.

Consider the visualization technique developed by Seema Jain, a sales innovation leader at Salesforce. It's a simple, straightforward approach to mapping both the employee experience and the customer experience in a single overview.

To ensure an outside-in perspective, first map the customer journey. Then map the employee journey below it, directly aligning to the phases. This visual alignment makes it easier to compare and contrast the two. Teams

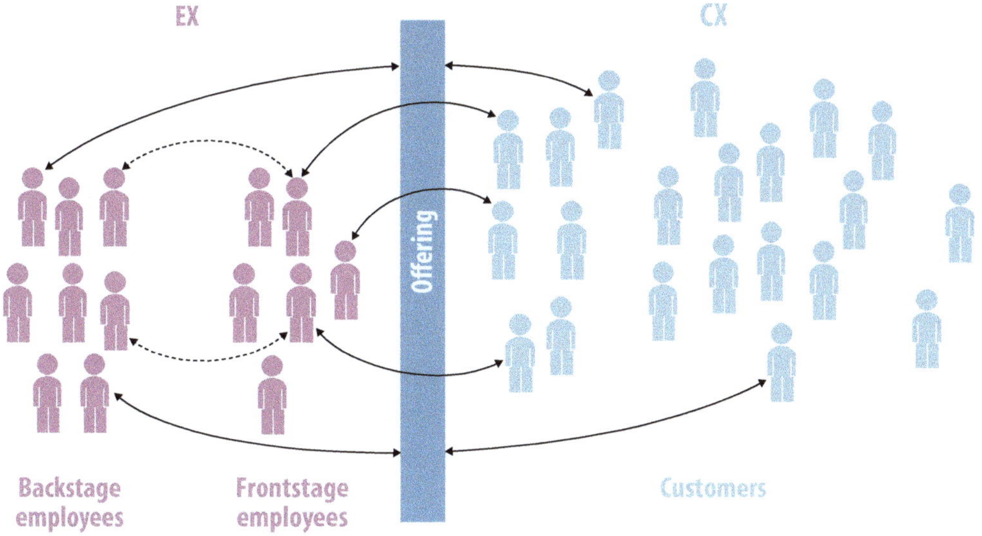

Figure 11-4. View the customer experience and employee experience as a single ecosystem.

* Herb Kelleher, as quoted in Chuck Lucier, "Herb Kelleher: The Thought Leader Interview," *strategy+business* (2004)

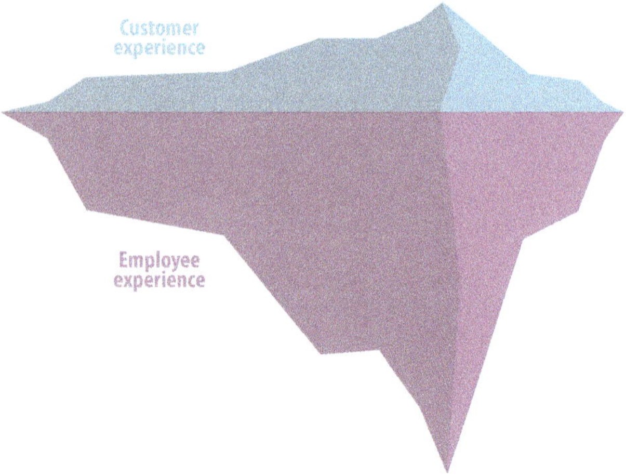

Figure 11-5. The customer experience is the tip of the iceberg above the employee activity necessary to create that experience.

can then evaluate where the gaps and opportunities lie and prioritize improvements. **Figure 11-6** shows an example of such a combined customer and employee experience diagram.

Jain explains that in workshops with a range of stakeholders, this approach supports strategic conversations about how to align employee work to better support the desired customer experience outcomes.

Illustrating a similar relationship between the customer experience and the employee experience, James Womack and Daniel Jones describe an approach they call *lean consumption*. In a *Harvard Business Review* article, they discuss the potential for positive business returns and increased value creation for both sides of the equation:

> **Companies may think that they save time and money by off-loading work to customers, making it the customer's problem to get the computer up and running, and wasting the customer's time. In fact, however, the opposite is true. By streamlining the systems for providing goods and services, and making it easier for customers to buy and use them, a growing number of companies are actually lowering costs while saving everyone's time. In the process, these businesses are learning more about their customers, strengthening consumer loyalty, and attracting new customers who defect from less user-friendly competitors.***

To visualize lean consumption, Womack and Jones recommend mapping the steps customers go through to consume products and services. The actions of the provider's employees are also included and carefully coordinated with the customer's actions. They call these diagrams *lean consumption maps*.

Figures 11-7 and **11-8** are lean consumption maps created by service design and business consultant Pete Abilla. They compare the before and after states of a service encounter for a yearly car inspection and registration in the United States.

The bar chart shows that the initial process takes the customer a total of 210 minutes, with touchpoints across two providers: the auto mechanic and the Department of Motor Vehicles (DMV). After combining inspection and registration at Jiffy Lube, a national chain of service stations, the process is reduced to just 65 minutes.

From a lean consumption perspective, the imperative for service providers is clear: don't waste the customer's time. Making their experience as lean as possible improves satisfaction and loyalty. This in turn affects the employee experience, as employees are able to complete their work more efficiently and satisfactorily, which impacts the bottom line of the business.

---

* James Womack and Daniel Jones, "Lean Consumption," *Harvard Business Review* (2005)

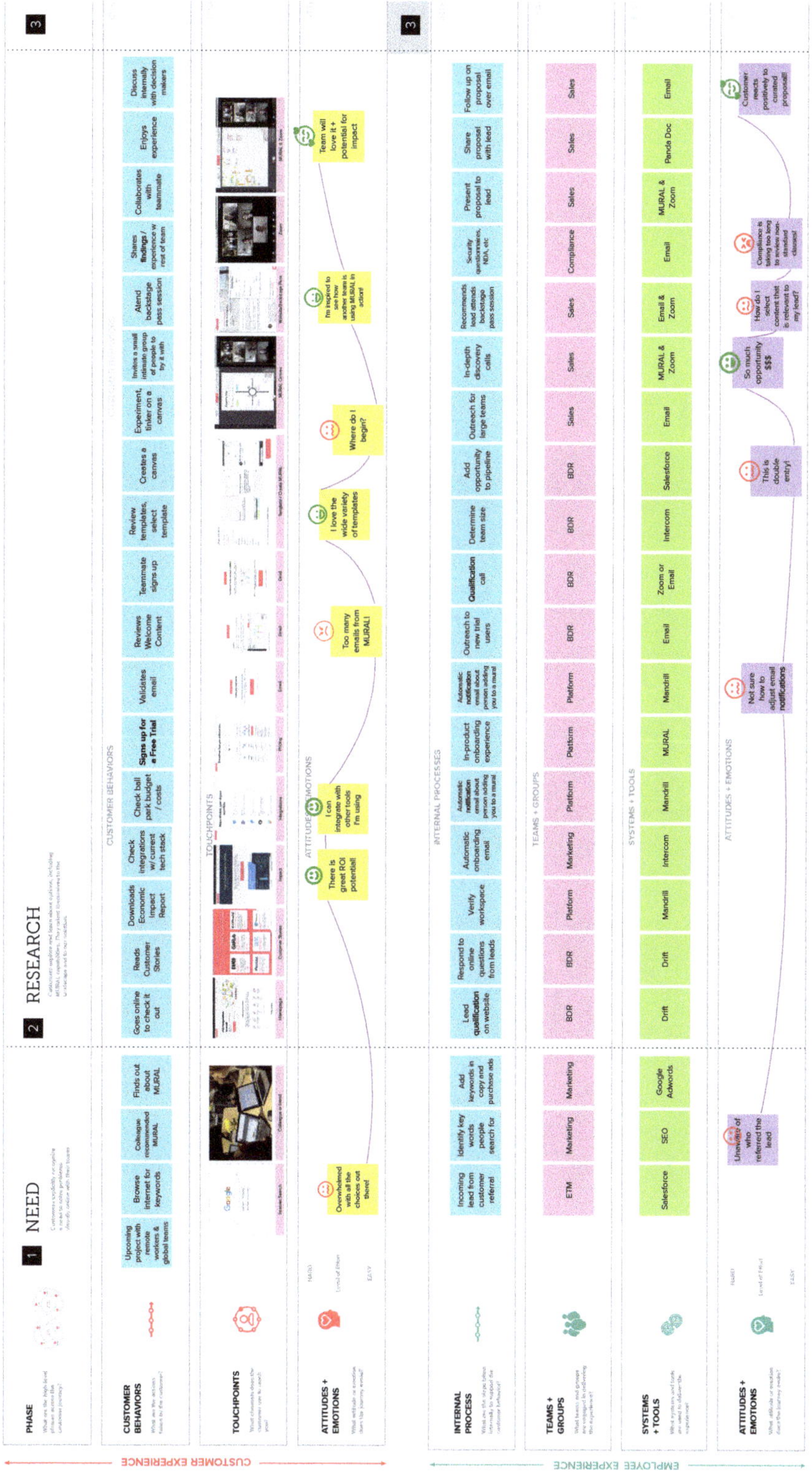

Figure 11-6. Align the customer experience with the employee experience in a single diagram to identify opportunities for improving both.

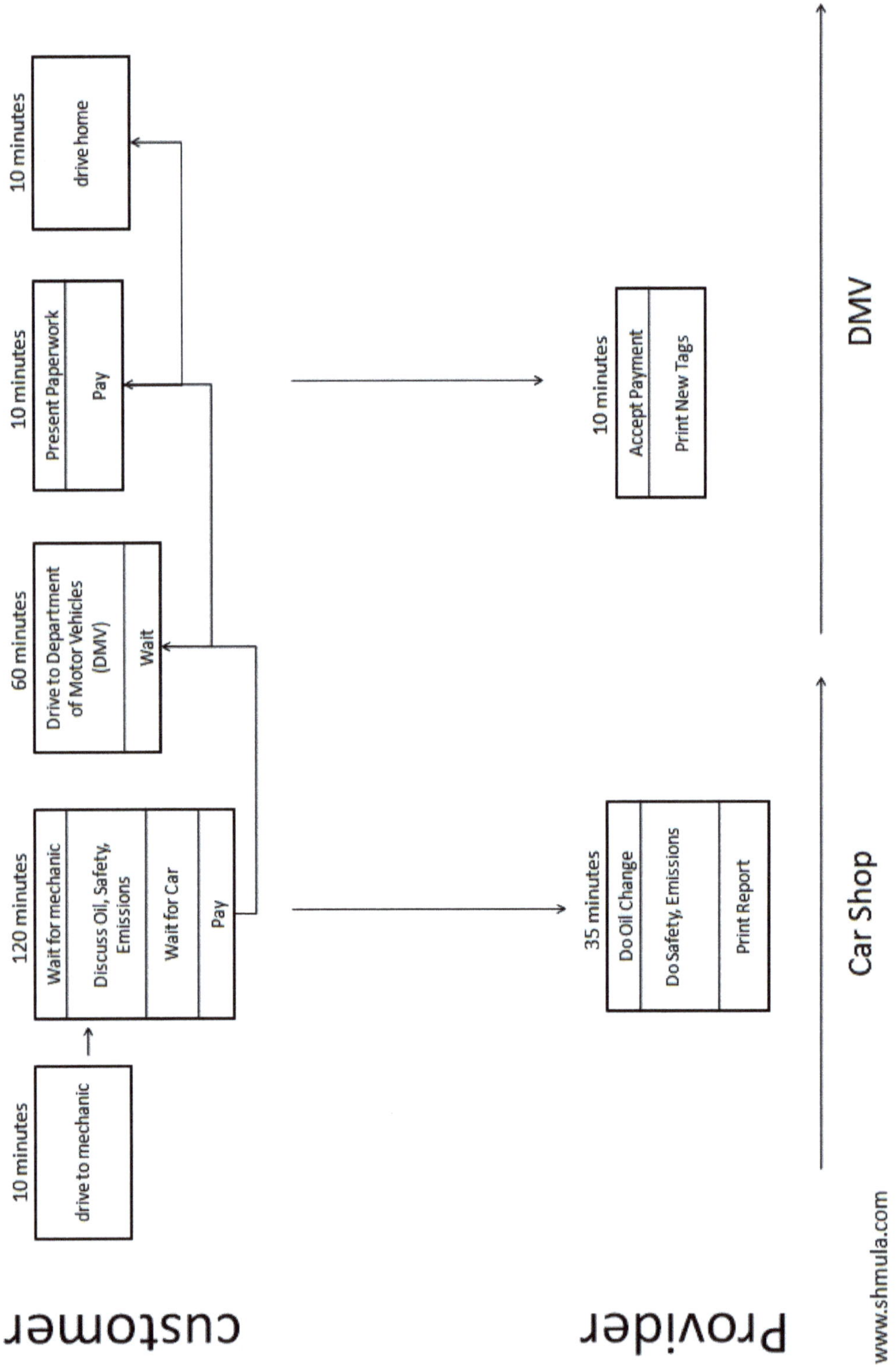

FIGURE 11-7. BEFORE: Inspecting and registering a vehicle takes the customer 210 minutes across two service providers.

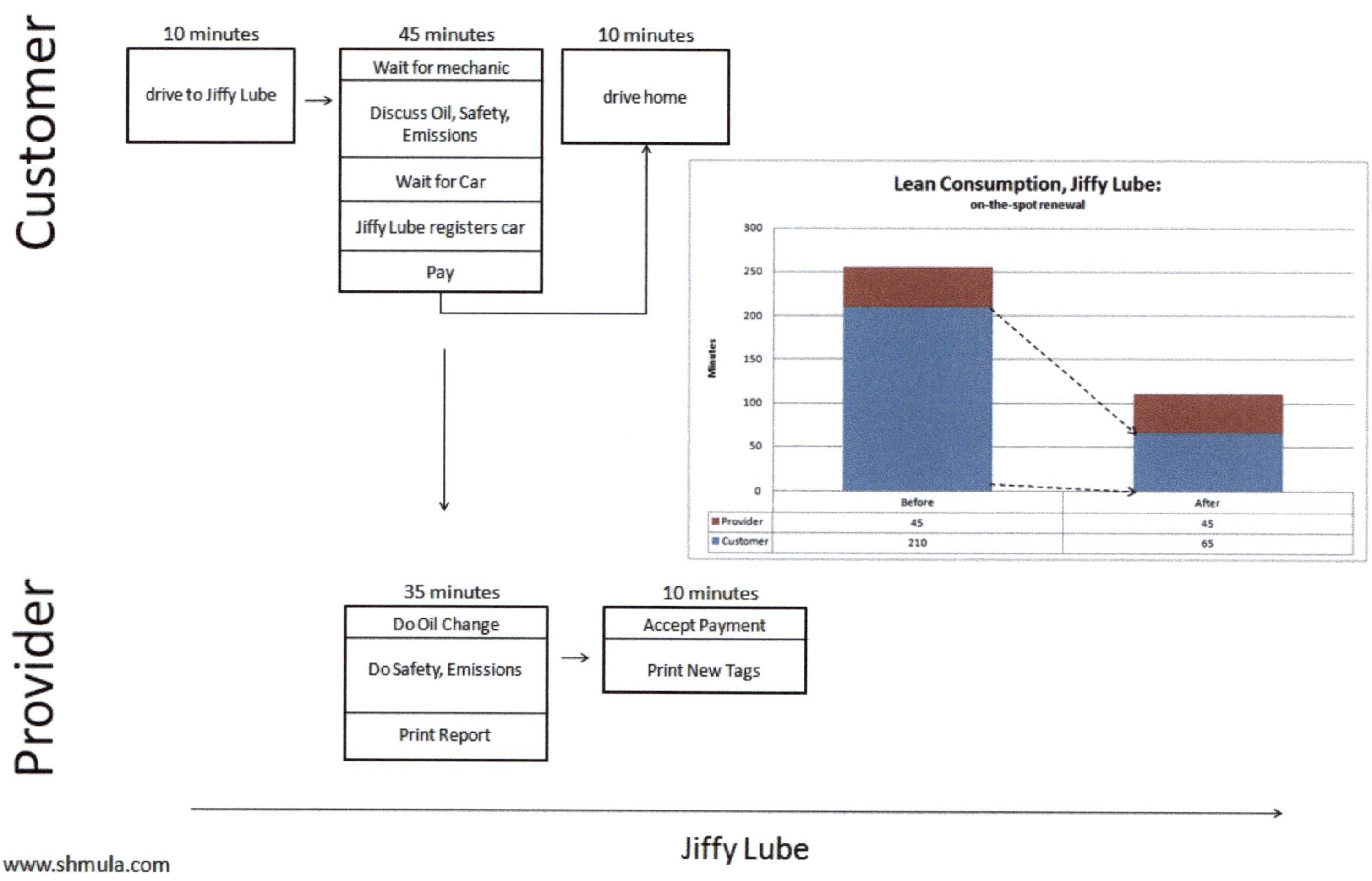

FIGURE 11-8. AFTER: A redesign of the service reduces the time investment for the customer to just 65 minutes.

Build Compassionate Teams

In *Humanocracy: Creating Organizations as Amazing as the People Inside Them*, Gary Hamel and Michele Zanini make a passionate, data-driven argument for excising bureaucracy and empowering everyone in the organization. Drawing on more than a decade of research, they point to companies like Nucor that have built cultures based on freedom and responsibility. The book proposes flipping the traditional hierarchy—making the organization a vehicle for people to achieve their goals, rather than treating people as mere resources.

This connects directly to employee experience work. Empathy for customers is a starting point on the path to achieving customer centricity, but it's not enough. The overall system of value creation must allow for compassion and the ability to take action toward creating an ideal customer experience.

Part of employee experience work must include the development of practices, behaviors, and norms that support customer centricity. Mapping provides a powerful tool for building this culture. By visualizing both the customer and the employee experience, organizations can identify specific moments where employees can internalize customer needs and be empowered to act on them.

Looking at the broad employee journey—from before a person joins a company through their career development—mapping reveals opportunities at each stage:

Recruiting

Journey maps reveal what customer-obsessed behavior looks like in practice. Use these insights to give your prospects a sense of what to expect even before they join your organization. Indicate your commitment to the customer experience up front by signaling what type of employee you are looking for. This helps ensure you get the right people. The very first contact people have with you—as early as coming across a job description—is part of their employee experience and can spark their interest in customer obsession.

Interviewing

Ask prospects about their impression of your company's customer experience during the job interview. For instance, you can ask about their first interaction with your brand or how they might improve the experience. This can give you insight into how they think about customer experience in general and how they may influence it in their role.

Hiring

Put language in your offer letters and other documents that strongly suggests a commitment to providing a world-class customer experience. Reinforce your position on customer experience, clarify your expectations of employees, and indicate their responsibilities with regard to delivering that experience.

Onboarding

Maps are a powerful onboarding tool. As new employees enter the company, show them early on how their experience there will empower them to take action to ensure an ideal customer experience. For example, in his book *The Year Without Pants*, author Scott Berkun discusses his first days working at Automattic, the makers of WordPress. Every new employee at the company answers support tickets from customers. This not only gives them direct contact with customers, but also exposes them to the internal and external systems that affect the customer experience.

Empowering work

Build programs that expose all employees to customer insights. For instance, tax software giant Intuit has established a company-wide "follow me home" program that gets employees out of the office to observe customers in their places of work. In another example, Hyatt Hotels encourages employees to be themselves rather than using scripted texts when speaking to guests, inviting them to engage in more authentic and empathic dialogue with customers.

Career development and growth

Anchor criteria for promotion and advancement in the organization around customer experience. Typically, monetary incentives permeate organizations like invisible girders, driving behaviors and actions from the top down. For instance, executives may have quarterly revenue goals that guide their strategies and actions. Instead, consider how incentives linked to improving the customer experience can be a motivating force. Explicitly reward people for their efforts through bonuses and career opportunities.

Living the brand values

Design ways for employees to experience brand values themselves and to step into the shoes of customers as much as possible. For example, Airbnb directly aligns the employee experience with its core brand identity: "belong anywhere." Its flexible office design enables employees to move freely and work from different desks and areas. The company also supports remote work, so employees

Using Maps to Find Where AI Can Improve the Employee Experience

AI promises to transform work, but where specifically? An MIT study found that 95% of GenAI pilots fail because companies don't understand where AI actually helps versus where it creates friction.*

The 5% that succeed follow a consistent pattern. They build AI systems with learning loops that remember context and improve through corrections. They focus on back-office areas where friction is highest and ROI is most direct. They measure workflows redesigned, not logins or adoption rates. Most importantly, they treat friction as a signal that reveals where systems need to adapt, not as a barrier to eliminate.

Map the employee experience first. Look for repetitive tasks, information bottlenecks, and decision points where employees lack context. These reveal where AI might help.

* Jason Snyder, "MIT Finds 95% of GenAI Pilots Fail Because Companies Avoid Friction," *Forbes* (2025)

But AI doesn't work uniformly. Researchers describe a "jagged technological frontier": AI excels at some tasks while failing at others in ways that aren't intuitive.† A customer service agent might benefit from AI-powered knowledge retrieval but struggle with AI-generated responses that miss emotional nuance.

The strategic questions include: What are the biggest opportunities to improve the employee experience where AI might help? Where does human judgment remain essential? How can AI improve decision quality? Where does AI increase productivity and efficiency without causing rework or negative downstream effects? How might AI improve teamwork and collaboration?

Mapping prevents AI for AI's sake. It grounds decisions in how work actually happens and where employees struggle.

† Fabrizio Dell'Acqua et al., *Navigating the Jagged Technological Frontier* (2023)

Figure 11-9. Make mapping a team activity at regular intervals for an engaging employee experience that puts people in contact with the customer experience.

can collaborate from anywhere in the world. This "belong anywhere" workplace—both physical and virtual—allows employees to live the brand, reinforcing the desired customer experience.

Of course, mapping can also be leveraged to improve the employee experience. Here are some ideas:

Workshop the employee experience as a team internally.
Creating a map is a great first step toward designing a better employee experience. But to activate the insights from the diagram, you'll need to bring management, HR teams, and other stakeholders together in a united effort. Hold a cross-functional workshop to review the employee experience and come to an agreement on action steps. You can use many of the techniques outlined in Chapter 8 to set up and run this workshop.

Use maps of the experience to onboard new employees.
During their initial introduction to the company, review existing experience maps with employees. Consider reserving an entire day or more during onboarding to focus on customers and the customer experience. Use a map not only to describe the customer experience, but also to help new employees consider how they influence it from their position in the company.

Make mapping a regular exercise to get employees into a customer-centric mindset.
As I've said elsewhere in this book, it's not about the map (the noun); it's about the mapping (a verb). Involve employees in creating various maps regularly, perhaps once a quarter. Make sense of the customer experience together, for team building and for a rich employee experience (see **Figure 11-9**).

Organize Around Experience

In his article "Dysfunctional Products Come from Dysfunctional Organizations," design leader Jon Kolko identifies bureaucracy, siloed functions, and a culture of defensiveness as the primary root causes of product failure. He concludes:

> **If the process, culture, and day-to-day experience of the organization is chaotic or broken, we can start to predict that our customers are experiencing an equally broken product or service.... I've observed its validity in many products and companies. Of course, there are exceptions, but on the whole it seems true that bad products point to bad alignment.***

Kolko recommends various activities—all of which can be seen as elements of employee experience—to get teams aligned, such as regular team-building events and alignment workshops. He also highlights the importance of visual models, such as experience maps. More importantly, Kolko points out that building models of the intended experience together aligns the understanding of those creating the customer experience.

But training and workshops aren't enough. They only superficially create an experiential mindset across the organization. Aligning teams for an ideal customer experience is a structural issue as well, and broad change management may be needed.

Every company with more than a few employees has silos. Journey thinking requires cross-silo organization of work. Aligning the functions of your organization to aspects of the customer journey goes a long way toward creating an employee experience that directly supports the customer experience. It's more than just symbolic: org charts that mirror the customer experience reinforce your commitment to a customer-centric company.

This raises the question: who owns the customer experience of an organization? Ultimately, it's the responsibility of the entire company. "Customer experience" and similarly named teams are there to connect the dots, not to assume this responsibility entirely. Their role is to enable and empower everyone in an organization to take care of it.

If we agree that "everyone owns the customer experience," or at least "everyone impacts the customer experience," then how we organize is critical to providing a desired outcome.

For instance, a previous client of mine at an ecommerce provider once introduced himself as a member of the Discovery team. He explained that their role was to help people find the products the company offered, regardless of channel or medium. There were also Purchasing and Success teams. In other words, the company was organized in a way that mirrored the customer journey, not along functional lines or according to technology types (**Figure 11-10**).

Diagrams of the customer journey provide the basis for this type of organization. They reveal a model to follow that mirrors the individual's experience, and thus serve as an organizational blueprint. This can lead to a new way of seeing your offerings, which in turn fosters innovation.

Aligning with the customer experience can also guide goal setting and performance reviews. For instance, a team could use the phases of the customer journey to structure monthly or quarterly objectives and key results (OKRs), or performance reviews could have target outcomes for specific phases, such as increasing awareness or improving the findability of products or services. The organizing principle of a customer journey can appear throughout the organization.

---

* Jon Kolko, "Dysfunctional Products Come from Dysfunctional Organizations," *Harvard Business Review* (2015)

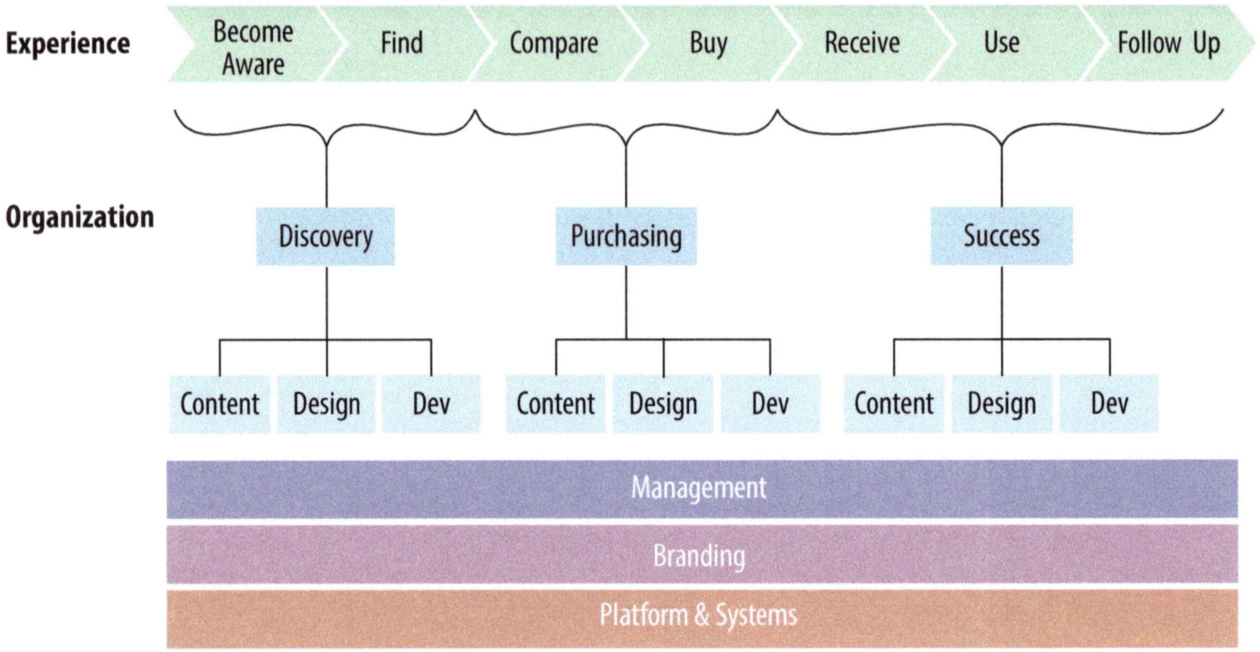

Figure 11-10. Organizing teams around the customer experience keeps it front and center.

If the customer experience matters, you have to organize in a meaningful way to deliver it. Take how USAA, a financial services and insurance provider to military veterans in the US, organized around different "experiences." Rather than maintaining a focus on functional capabilities and services (e.g., checking accounts, credit cards, auto loans, home loans), it shifted to a Life Events model, organizing around milestones such as marriage, having a baby, buying a home, military deployment, and retirement. Instead of siloed product teams, USAA created cross-functional teams that coordinate multiple products and services around these meaningful moments in customers' lives.*

A large publisher I once worked with took a similar approach, first identifying four logical divisions in its offerings that correlated to experiences it wanted to create, then organizing offering teams around those.

Though not embedded in the top-level org chart, the cross-functional teams came together to align around the intended customer experiences. Mapping informed this structure, which resonated with the market and also increased internal collaboration.

Work Across Silos

These examples make it sound straightforward: just reorganize around customer experience, and you're done. What could go wrong?

But there's a deeper problem. Every organization has an invisible skeleton embedded in its financial structure that shapes incentives and drives action.

Ask any chief financial officer how headcount is allocated, and you'll likely get a similar answer: product development or research and development (R&D) on one side, go-to-market (GTM) on the other, with each employee assigned to one of those buckets. The engineer building

* Blake Morgan. "USAA's Proactive Approach to Major Life Events," *Forbes* (2023)

the onboarding flow? R&D. The salesperson doing a discovery call? GTM. The designer trying to bridge that gap? Pick a side.

This division is partly driven by accounting requirements. Companies must follow standard frameworks, such as Generally Accepted Accounting Principles (GAAP) in the US and International Financial Reporting Standards (IFRS) internationally. Investors benchmark against them. Boards track R&D efficiency separately from GTM efficiency, like they're unrelated machines.

This creates perverse incentives. If you're a vice president measured on R&D efficiency, you want engineers working on "real product features," not "helping sales with customer-specific requests." If you're measured on GTM efficiency, you want sellers selling, not "wasting time in product meetings." The financial reporting structure *rewards* isolated behavior.

The result is something that directly affects the employee experience: organizational silos. These divisions prevent horizontal flow of communication, knowledge, and coordination. This directly shapes the employee experience and ultimately is reflected in the customer experience.

Some companies have figured out how to transcend these constraints. For example, Amazon, Intuit, and WL Gore all have silos, but they operate differently:

- Amazon starts every major decision with the customer and works backward.
- Intuit measures success by customer outcomes, not departmental outputs.
- WL Gore has no traditional hierarchy—people organize around what needs to happen, not functional departments.

Here's what makes this possible: companies are networks of collaboration. Work happens across teams, up and down levels, spanning functional boundaries. The real question isn't where someone sits in the org chart or which bucket their salary comes from. It's what they're aligning around.

Look at Pixar's Braintrust, a collaborative process to overcome major challenges or barriers. Directors, writers, animators, and producers across silos gather to answer one question: "Is this making the film better for the audience?" The focus isn't on a timeline, budget, or marketing comfort zone; it's on the customer experience.

These companies prove that the customer is common ground that transcends organizational boundaries. Two practices make this work:

Creating shared models of the experience

Personas and journey maps aren't research deliverables. They're collaboration tools. When the engineer, customer success manager, and product marketer all look at the same journey map, they see the same experience from the customer's perspective. The map becomes shared territory where R&D and GTM meet.

Adopting a common language for creating value

When everyone speaks the language of customer value rather than departmental metrics, collaboration becomes possible even across budgetary boundaries.

Summary

The employee experience is about the overall relationship employees have with an organization—the sum of their actions, thoughts, and feelings over time. It's not enough to satisfy basic requirements of salary and benefits. Organizations also have to create a sense of purpose so people choose to contribute.

As with customer experiences, the employee experience can be mapped for deeper understanding.

Reinventing Organizations

Frederic Laloux's *Reinventing Organizations* maps how organizational structures have evolved throughout history, with each step representing a leap in human collaboration and consciousness. He presents a framework for understanding organizational evolution through different color-coded paradigms (**Figure 11-11**):

- *Red organizations* operate through power and fear. Think street gangs or tribal chiefdoms. Command is immediate and personal.
- *Amber organizations* introduce formal hierarchy and processes. Think the military, the Catholic Church, government bureaucracies. They seek stability through rules and clearly defined roles.
- *Orange organizations* are achievement-oriented machines optimized for efficiency, growth, competition, and innovation. Most modern corporations fall into this category. They rely on hierarchy and functional departments, operating under the assumption that maximizing shareholder value is the ultimate purpose. The R&D-versus-GTM divide reflects classic Orange thinking: separate functions, optimize each independently, measure everything.
- *Green organizations* add stakeholder focus and empowerment. Think Ben & Jerry's or Southwest Airlines. Culture matters. People aren't just resources, though hierarchy remains, even if flattened.
- *Teal organizations* represent a fundamentally different operating model. They self-manage around a common purpose without a traditional hierarchy. People organize around what needs to happen and coordinate without bosses or top-down control. Teal organizations are generally more customer-centric as well. Examples include Buurtzorg (Dutch healthcare), Morning Star (tomato processing), and aspects of Patagonia and Gore.

Laloux doesn't claim Teal is "better." Each model works in its context. But Teal organizations show what's possible when you organize around purpose rather than control.

XLG doesn't require a full Teal transformation, but it moves in that direction, organizing work around customer value rather than functional optimization. Most companies will remain Orange with Green aspects. That's fine. You can still make customer experience matter more within existing structures.

Org type	Metaphor	Description
RED	Wolf Pack	Constant exercise of power by the chief to keep foot soldiers in line. Highly reactive, short-term focus. Thrives in chaotic environments.
AMBER	Army	Highly formal roles within a hierarchical pyramid. Top-down command and control. Future is repetition of the past.
ORANGE	Machine	The goal is to beat the competition; achieve profit and growth. Management by objectives is common (command and control over what, freedom over how).
GREEN	Family	Focus on culture and empowerment to boost member motivation. Stakeholders replace shareholders as the primary purpose.
TEAL	Living organism	Self-management replaces the hierarchical pyramid. Organizations are seen as living entities oriented toward realizing their potential.

Figure 11-11. Frederick Laloux developed a schema showing the evolution of organizational structures.

Visualizing it helps an organization find key opportunities for improvement.

Mapping also helps a company align the customer experience to the employee experience. If you treat employees right, they will treat customers right, and your business will grow. If the customer experience is the brand in action, the employee experience is the company culture in action.

Beyond mapping the employee experience to help encourage passionate employees, organizations can organize around experience by forming teams that align to the customer journey. Companies like Amazon, Intuit, and Gore prove you can transcend silos by making customer experience matter more.

When teams create shared models of the experience and speak a common language about customer value, they can better collaborate across silos. One collaborative mapping session creates shared understanding. Repeated monthly, those sessions shape behaviors and ultimately culture.

The takeaway is that to be customer-obsessed and deliver a great customer experience, you also have to be employee-obsessed and provide a great employee experience.

Further Reading

Denise Lee Yohn, Fusion *(2018)*

Yohn brings together decades of experience advising companies on both brand and culture in this book. She makes a compelling argument for fusing the two, clearly demonstrating how competitive advantage is driven by alignment between customer experience and employee experience. Her website (*deniseleeyohn.com*) includes a range of practical tools for assessment and for building world-class fused companies.

Jacob Morgan, The Employee Experience Advantage *(2017)*

This book stands out in a crowded field of writing on employee experience. It's well organized, easy to read, and, more importantly, thoroughly researched. Morgan presents detailed findings from years of work correlating employee experience with bottom-line business results. He also offers practical tips on how to create an ideal employee experience.

B. Joseph Pine II and James H. Gilmore, The Experience Economy *(1999)*

This landmark book is an expansion of the authors' *Harvard Business Review* article "Welcome to the Experience Economy." At a macro level, they observe the shift from an agrarian economy to an industrial economy, then from a service economy toward an experience-driven economy. Written with rigor and supported by a wealth of evidence, it marks the beginning of an important shift that we are still striving to realize, in part by mapping experiences.

Simon David Clatworthy, The Experience-Centric Organization *(2019)*

Clatworthy distinguishes between being customer-centric and experience-centric, the latter being more holistic and incorporating internal culture. He offers a five-step maturity scale for becoming an experience-centric organization. This book is well researched and rigorous, but also approachable and practical.

Map the Customer Experience to the Employee Experience

Objective	Align a team around the intersection of customer experience and employee experience through visual mapping
Time	2–3 hours
Participants	3–12 people from customer-facing and internal functions
Materials	Whiteboard, sticky notes

Customer journey maps typically show what happens above the surface—customer actions, touchpoints, and emotions. But beneath every customer experience lies a hive of employee activity: the processes, systems, and cross-functional coordination that make that experience possible. Mapping both together reveals the full picture and surfaces opportunities to improve alignment between what customers need and what employees can deliver (FIGURE 11-12).

How it works:

1. Map the customer journey. Based on customer research and data, map step-by-step behavior across the holistic customer journey.
2. Map the employee journey. Below the customer journey, map the employee experience that supports it. Expose the internal workings: the business processes, systems, tools, and cross-functional teams that facilitate the customer experience. Invite representatives from all customer-facing business functions to uncover day-to-day realities.
3. Evaluate the map. Compare customer and employee actions, emotions, moments of truth, and pain points. These present opportunities to either fix an issue or capitalize on a strength to drive loyalty and advocacy. Reframe each moment as a "How might we" (HMW) statement. This creates space for new ideas and encourages collaboration. It also prevents the group from jumping to one solution too quickly.
4. Prioritize. At this point, you'll have several HMW statements that serve as springboards for ideation. Narrow the focus by inviting participants to vote on the most compelling one, reaching democratic consensus on where to start.
5. Ideate. Generate solutions as a group to address each of the pain points you identified. Prioritize the resulting concepts and derive next steps.

Learn more:

Yuri Vedenin, "Employee Experience Journey Map: A Complete Guide + Example + Template," *UXPressia* (2023)

Amanda Wowk, "6 Steps to Mapping the Employee Journey at Your Organization," *Qualtrics* (2020)

Example:

Figure 11-12. You can use this template to align customer experience and employee experience within a team.

Diagram and Image Credits

Figure 11-1: Employee experience map created by UXPressia (uxpressia.com), used with permission

Figure 11-2: Day-in-the-life employee experience diagram created by Chris McGrath, Tangowork: Consultants for Digital Transformation (*tangowork.com*), used with permission

Figure 11-3: Employee experience map based on a template created by Rafa Vivas, creative director at XPLANE (*xplane.com*), used with permission

Figure 11-6: Customer experience/employee experience alignment diagram created by Seema Jain and Emilia Åström in Mural, used with permission

Figures 11-7 and **11-8**: Diagrams from Pete Abilla's blog post "Lean Service: Customer Value and Don't Waste the Customer's Time," used with permission

Figure 11-9: Diagram and photo by design research and visualization expert Nick Bowmast (*bowmast.com*), used with permission.

Figure 11-12: Customer experience/employee experience template by Seema Jain, used with permission

There is only one valid definition of business purpose: to create a customer.

—Peter Drucker, *People and Performance*

IN THIS CHAPTER

- Strategy activation
- Plans versus strategies
- Strategizing around the customer
- Visualizing strategy
- Collaborative methods for mapping strategy

CHAPTER 12

Activating Strategy Through Visual Alignment

Earlier in my career, I encountered a business perspective that shocked me. At a dinner following a multiday strategy workshop I'd facilitated, the director of sales explained his perspective on the workshop's purpose: "We have to figure out how to get customers for all they're worth." He gestured as if wringing out a towel. "If the towel gets dry, you have to squeeze harder. A good leader knows how to do that, and a good strategy makes it easier."

He was serious. I was horrified. "Our markets are not people 'out there' that we shake down for loose change. Customers are our most valuable assets," I thought. Surely we should strive to learn from them so that we can provide better products and services?

The director's perspective seemed shortsighted to me. He believed the sole purpose of our business was to get more sales. That may be fine in the short term, but ultimately, this narrow perspective leads to failure.

Companies frequently don't realize that as a business grows, it must also widen its strategic field of vision. I call this misstep *strategy myopia*. It happens time and time again: organizations focus more on capturing value than creating it. They see growth as a short-term goal, missing more durable, long-lasting ways of generating value.

Successful organizations continually innovate and expand their horizons. Incremental improvements are not enough. Technical R&D is not enough. Instead, they grow by questioning the value they create.

Take Kodak. Many people believe the company failed because it missed out on digital camera technology. In fact, Kodak invented the first digital camera in 1975 and held some of the most important digital camera patents. Its failure came from a myopic view of the business it was in: *film* instead of *storytelling*. It was a nearsighted strategy, not technology, that led to Kodak's downfall.

Diagrams of experiences offer a type of insight that is often overlooked in strategy creation: a view from the customer's perspective.

This chapter shows how mapping serves as a corrective lens for strategy myopia. It focuses on strategy activation, or the broader organizational sensemaking needed to execute strategy, and includes a review of some complementary techniques that extend experience mapping to better visualize strategy.

Close the Gap with Strategy Activation

Creating a new strategic vision is one thing; getting an organization to actually implement it is another.

There's a gap between strategic planning and strategy execution. It's not enough to communicate strategy by flashing a few bullet points on a screen once a quarter. Leaders must consider how strategy involves change for the people executing it. People can't effectively execute a strategy they don't understand or believe in.

Strategy consultant Aric Wood observes in his book *The Strategy Activation Playbook* that most organizations treat strategy as a closed-door activity. Leaders develop plans in isolation, then announce them to the organization, expecting everyone to align and execute. But strategies created this way rarely achieve their intended impact.

Wood advocates for what he calls *strategy activation*—the deliberate practice of bridging strategy and execution by persuading, aligning, and engaging people to move in a new direction. Rather than limiting strategic thinking to a select few executives, organizations benefit when diverse voices contribute to shaping direction. As he says in the book, "The smartest person in the room IS the room."*

Along with human centricity and cocreation, Wood emphasizes the importance of visualization in strategy activation. As he puts it, "If you can't draw a map, you don't know where you're going.... Visual communication accelerates understanding and alignment."

Traditional strategy documents—dense reports, lengthy presentations, abstract mission statements—exclude the people needed to execute the strategy from meaningful participation. They're hard to grasp, harder to discuss, and nearly impossible to act on collectively.

Diagrams, by contrast, invite participation. They make strategy tangible and discussable.

Mapping the company's journey is typically one of the first steps to take in strategy activation. A *vision map* is a simple diagram to compare the company's current state to the desired future state and highlight the gaps between the two. (See **"Strategic Vision Mapping" on page 288** for more on this collaborative method.) Most of the other frameworks in Wood's book include some aspect of visualization as well.

> *People can't effectively execute a strategy they don't understand or believe in.*

Overall, the process of visualizing strategy not only helps correct strategy myopia but also fuels strategy activation. Strategy shifts from something handed down from above to something teams create together. In my experience, the resulting diagrams invariably show a much broader picture of customer needs than a business currently addresses.

Meeting those needs requires the organization as a whole to adopt a new mindset, and this change is made tangible through visualization.

A Plan Is Not a Strategy

Strategy is difficult to define precisely. It is often confused with analysis, which spans everything from market sizing to technical assessments and financial projections, resulting in reports that fill dozens of pages. But you can't analyze your way to strategy—the answers don't magically emerge from data.

* Aric Wood and XPLANE, *The Strategy Activation Playbook* (2022)

Strategy is also frequently conflated with planning. Organizations love to create strategic plans. Leadership teams convene for offsite retreats, emerging with thick documents full of initiatives, budgets, and timelines. These plans get rolled out with fanfare: "Here's our strategy for the next three years."

There's just one problem: neither analysis nor planning is strategy.

Strategy is about determining the optimal way to overcome challenges to reach a desired position (**Figure 12-1**). It is a creative endeavor, not based on analysis and planning alone. Strategy represents the logic that connects those activities. Ultimately, it's how an organization makes sense of its actions and decisions over time.

Roger Martin, former dean of the Rotman School of Management at the University of Toronto, draws a crucial distinction between these concepts. Most so-called strategic planning has nothing to do with actual strategy. Instead, we tend to see a list of activities the company says it will do: improve customer experience,

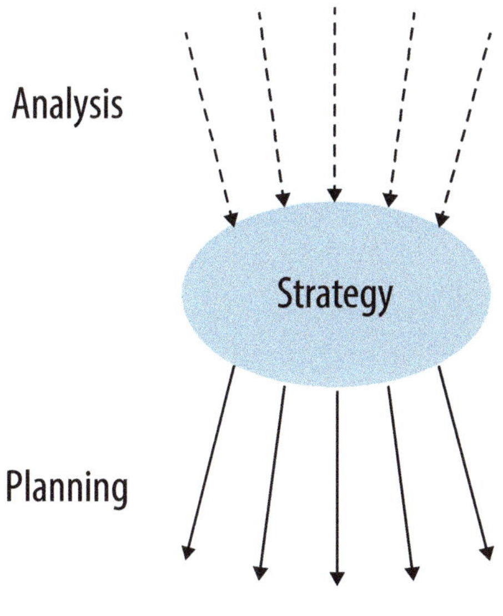

Figure 12-1. Strategy provides the logic connecting analysis and planning.

open a new plant, start a talent development program. These lists typically represent what various departments want, with little coherence about how they collectively accomplish a goal.

Planning feels comfortable because it focuses on resources you control: how many people to hire, which facilities to build, what products to launch. These are on the cost side of the business. You're the customer for these decisions. The plan lists activities. The strategy shows choices and their relationships. The plan focuses on what you'll spend. The strategy focuses on how you'll win.

Consider Southwest Airlines. When it was getting started, Southwest didn't just plan routes—it developed a coherent strategy to offer a substitute for Greyhound buses. Every element of its operating model reinforced this choice: point-to-point flights, a single fleet of 737 aircraft, no in-flight meals, direct customer booking, 15-minute gate turnarounds. These weren't disconnected initiatives but an interlocking system that created a lower cost structure. Other airlines couldn't replicate just one element to compete; they'd need to copy the entire system.

The visualizations discussed in this chapter—strategy maps, canvases, activity system maps—make strategy tangible. They force you to articulate not just what you'll do, but how you'll win. They reveal whether your activities form a coherent system or just a list of departmental wishes.

Techniques like these also open up strategy to input from others. Strategy making doesn't have to be a closed-door activity driven only by an elite few. With visual approaches like the ones described here, it can be inclusive of diverse perspectives. This not only results in higher-quality results but also goes a long way toward getting buy-in.

A New Way of Seeing: Customers First

The context of business has changed dramatically over the last few decades. Consumers have real power: they have access to prices, product information, and alternative providers around the world. Traditional approaches to sales—wringing a market for what it's worth—do not work anymore for sustained growth.

Business is more than a math problem. To succeed, companies must understand customer behavior. It turns out that reaching business goals requires people to act. You need customers to buy your solution, stay loyal, recommend you, and engage with your brand. Human behavior isn't a nuisance; it's central to growth.

In 2019, the Business Roundtable, an association of America's leading CEOs, recognized this broader perspective and updated its definition of corporate purpose to include serving "all stakeholders"—customers, employees, suppliers, and communities—not just shareholders.* This shift demands a fundamental reorientation.

As discussed in Chapter 1, XLG represents this change in action. Rather than competing on product features or sales tactics alone, organizations grow by continually improving the experiences they deliver. Experience becomes the primary differentiator and growth engine.

As a result, organizations need to alter their thinking. Renowned business leader Ram Charan, for one, urges companies to invert the traditional sales perspective. In his book *What the Customer Wants You to Know*, he illustrates a flow of value insight opposite to traditional approaches (**Figure 12-2**). Visualizing the value chain as a team, as outlined in "Value Chain Mapping" on page 105, helps others see the bigger picture.

It turns out that insight about users is not a nice-to-have or, worse, a nuisance; it's a strategic opportunity. The objective is not a *push*, it's a *pull*. You don't sell products; you buy customers.

These ideas run contrary to typical strategic decision making, but it's not an entirely new way of thinking. As early as 1960, renowned Harvard Business School professor Theodore Levitt discussed the importance of focusing on human needs first. In his influential article "Marketing Myopia,"* Levitt writes:

> **An industry begins with the customer and his needs, not with a patent, a raw material, or a selling skill. Given the customer's needs, the industry develops backwards, first concerning**

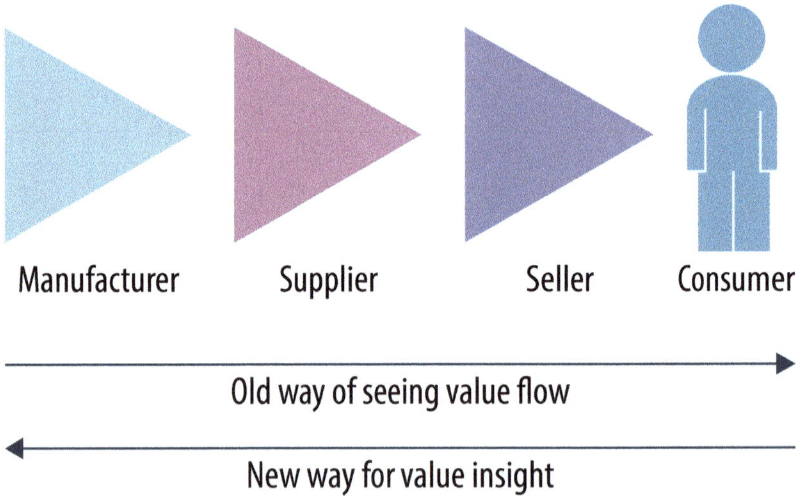

Figure 12-2. Understanding value from the consumer's perspective reverses the flow of insight.

* Business Roundtable, "Purpose of a Corporation" (2019)

> **itself with the physical delivery of customer satisfaction. Then it moves back further to creating the things by which these satisfactions are in part achieved.***

Consider the failure of the railroad industry in the US, a favorite example of Levitt. During their heyday at the beginning of the 20th century, railroads were extremely profitable and attractive to Wall Street investors. No one in that industry could have imagined its sharp decline just a few decades later.

But railroads didn't stop growing in the middle of the century because of competition from emerging technologies such as cars, trucks, planes, and even telephones. They stopped growing because they let rivals take their customers. The railroad companies' intense focus on their own products led to strategy myopia: they saw themselves as in the *railroad* business rather than the *transportation* business.

Though no panacea, mapping experiences provides insight that helps expand the strategic aperture. For example, Tim Brown, CEO of IDEO, describes his company's work with Amtrak in his book *Change by Design*. His firm was brought in to redesign the seats of the Acela trains, with the goal of making the travel experience more pleasurable.

Rather than diving into the seat redesign, however, the team first mapped an end-to-end journey around train travel. They identified about a dozen unique stages in the experience, which led to different conclusions about their focus and how to improve the travel experience.

Brown writes:

> **The insight that proved most striking was that passengers did not take their seats on the train until stage eight—most of the experience of train travel, in other words, did not involve the train at all. The team reasoned that every one of the prior steps was an opportunity to create a positive interaction, opportunities that would have been overlooked if they had focused only on the design of the seats.†**

Alignment diagrams help reveal such new opportunities. They visually align a description of the individual's experience with the offerings of an organization.

Consider the opportunities highlighted at the bottom of the Rail Europe diagram in **Figure 12-3**, created by Chris Risdon. Some suggest tactical solutions, but overall they go beyond that to point to larger, strategic options. Should the company become a provider of travel information? Should it integrate with retailers and ecommerce partners? How can it reinvent support or the ticketing experience? This strategic insight is directly tied to the actual experience of train travel and shown in context in the diagram.

If the railroad companies of the past had followed such customer-centric approaches and had these types of insights, perhaps they would have come to different strategic conclusions.

In this sense, alignment diagrams offer a *new way of seeing* your markets, your organization, and your strategy—from the outside in rather than from the inside out.

---

* Theodore Levitt, "Marketing Myopia," *Harvard Business Review* (1960)

† Tim Brown, *Change by Design* (2009)

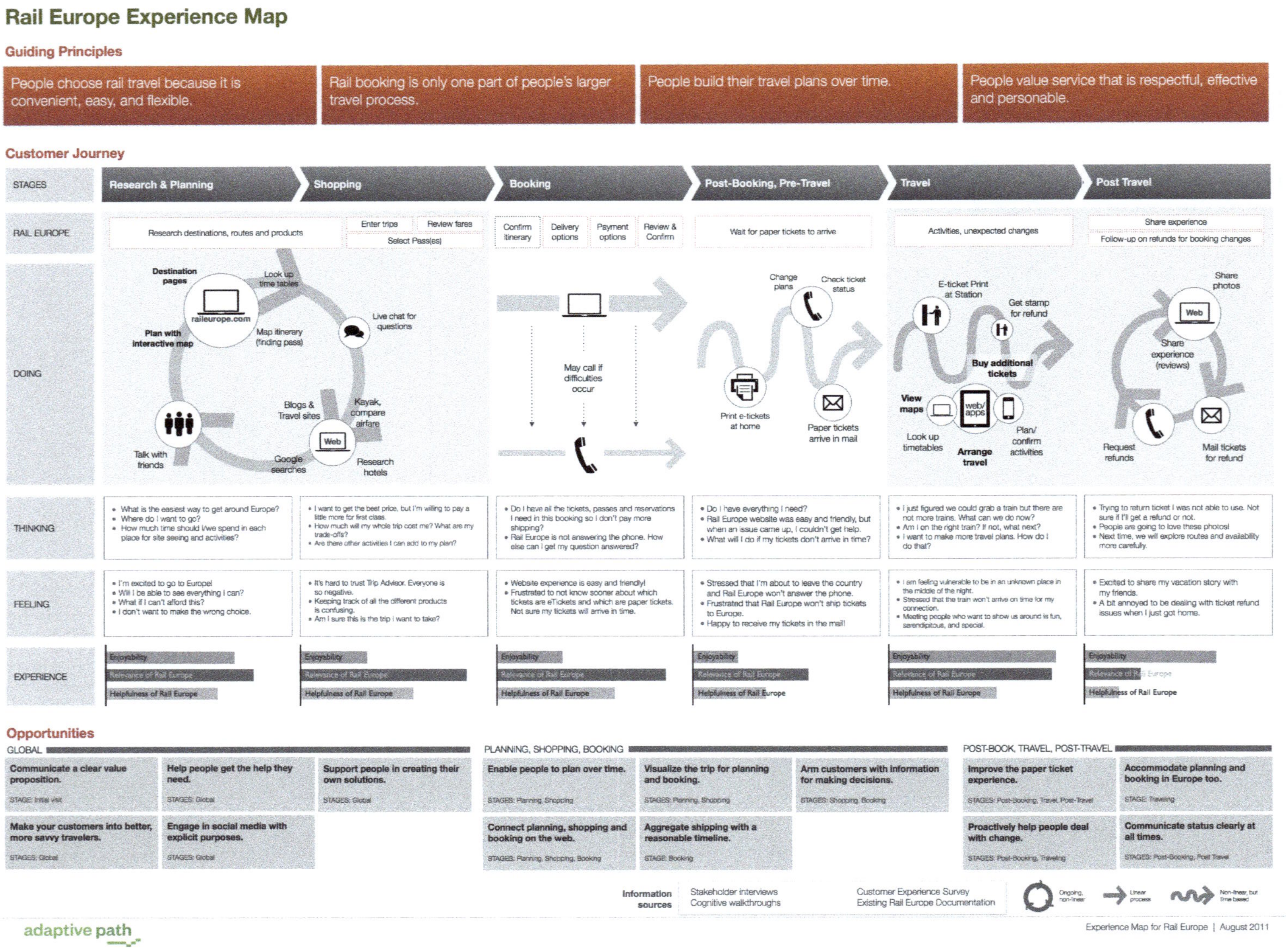

FIGURE 12-3. This experience map of Rail Europe created by Chris Risdon shows the broader context of traveling in Europe.

Mapping Strategy

Strategy is an interlocking set of choices that overcomes obstacles to move an organization to a more favorable position. Making those choices requires collaboration and hard decisions made together. Data alone won't tell you what to choose.

This is where mapping becomes a strategic practice. A journey map, mental model diagram, or ecosystem map reveals patterns and opportunities that spreadsheets obscure. Any visualization of the customer experience can inform strategy. After all, growth depends on customer action. Embedding the customer's perspective in strategy is critical.

What's more, diagrams invite participation. Strategy is no longer something an elite group does behind closed doors. Modern strategy creation is open and inclusive. Mapping provides the forum for those conversations to happen.

Strategy and execution are related: a brilliant strategy that can't be implemented isn't brilliant. Poor communication is only part of the problem. How strategy gets created also matters. The process must overcome gaps in understanding across the entire organization. Otherwise, the realization of strategic intent has no chance.

Business consultant and author Nilofer Merchant has observed a disconnect between the top and bottom layers in many organizations. She describes it as an "Air Sandwich" in her book *The New How*:

> **An Air Sandwich is, in effect, a strategy that has a clear vision and future direction on the top layer, day-to-day action on the bottom, and virtually nothing in the middle—no meaty key decisions that connect the two layers, no rich chewy center filling to align the new direction with the new actions within the company.***

To address the Air Sandwich, companies should view strategy creation as an inclusive endeavor. But the traditional tools only confound the situation. Words are abstract and open to interpretation. Documents bewilder and confuse. Emails and other corporate communications are unintelligible to those who must implement a strategy. This is why visualization becomes essential for strategy activation.

Diagrams are an antidote. They foster broader participation and increased comprehension, leading to stronger buy-in.

The next sections and the collaborative methods at the end of this chapter describe several tools that *complement* alignment diagrams. They all seek to visualize strategy or parts of it. These include the following:

- Activity system maps
- Strategy canvases
- Opportunity-solution trees
- Strategy maps
- Business model canvases
- Vision maps

Diagrams of experiences plug into these techniques, informing customer-related aspects.

Activity System Map

Strategy means choosing what to do and what not to do. But choosing isn't enough. A collection of disconnected initiatives doesn't constitute a strategy. Real strategic advantage comes from how activities fit together and support one another.

---

* Nilofer Merchant, *The New How* (2010)

Michael Porter addresses this in his landmark article "What Is Strategy?"* He argues that competitive advantage emerges from the way a company's activities form a system. Individual activities may be easy to copy, but replicating an entire interconnected system is far more difficult. To visualize these relationships, Porter developed what he calls an *activity system map.*

An activity system map shows the key activities that make up a company's strategy and how they reinforce one another. The diagram reveals not just what a company does, but how those activities connect to create competitive advantage. **Figure 12-4** is Porter's example for Southwest Airlines.

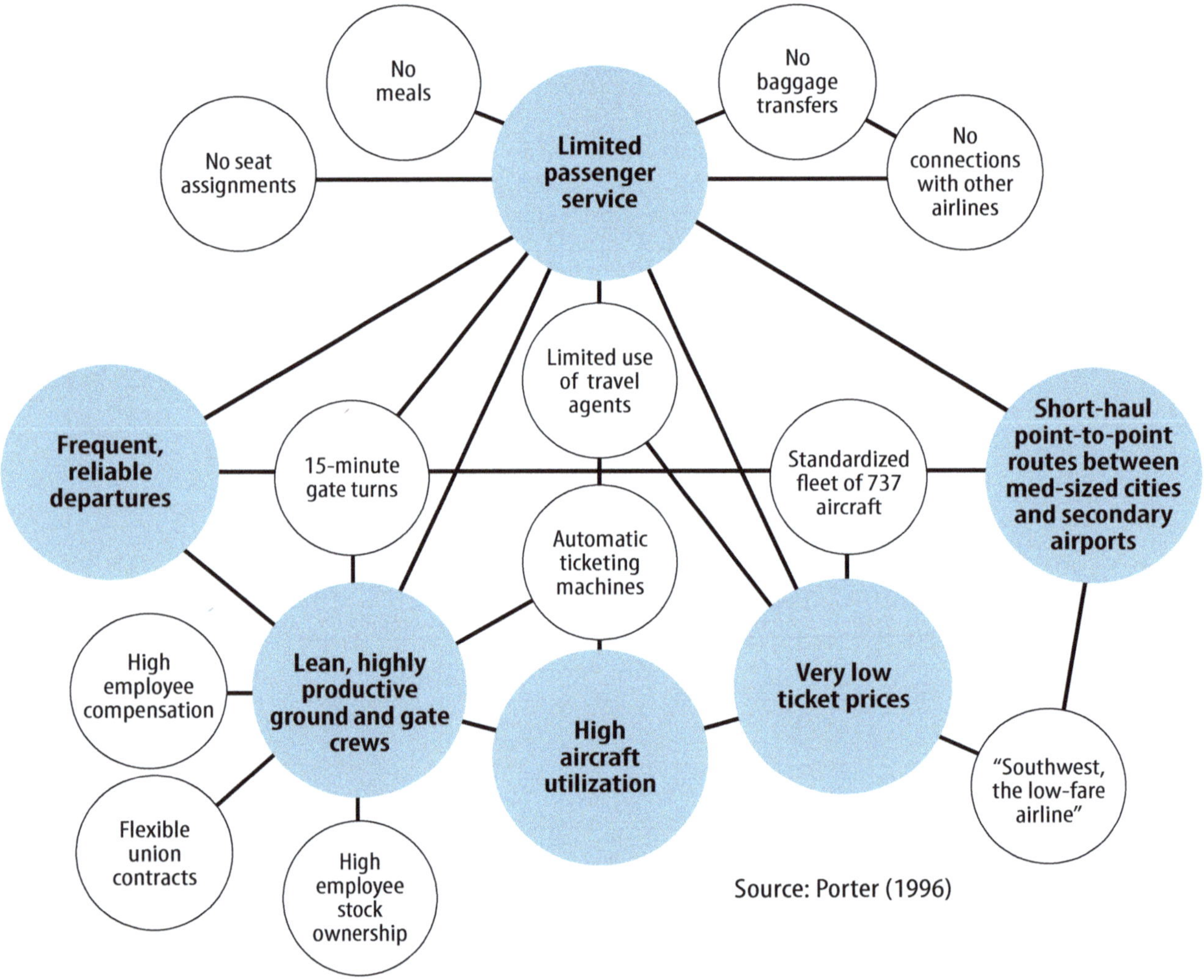

Figure 12-4. This activity system map for Southwest Airlines reveals how the business generates its low cost advantage.

---

* Michael Porter, "What Is Strategy?," *Harvard Business Review* (1996)

The six blue circles represent the foundations of the overall business model at Southwest. All the other activities support those points of the strategy. In a succinct overview, employees get a sense of what's involved in the strategy and the relationship among its parts.

Activity system maps differ from the other visualization tools discussed in this chapter in an important way: they focus on internal activities rather than customer experiences. They show what the organization does and how those activities interlock. This makes them complementary to journey maps and service blueprints, which show the customer's experience and the organization's support for that experience.

Together, these tools provide a complete picture. Journey maps reveal what customers need. Activity system maps show how your organization's strategic choices create value. The connection between them becomes the crucial question: do your strategic activities actually support the experiences customers value?

I've never seen an activity system map focused specifically on design or customer experience activities within an organization, though it would be fascinating to visualize how research, mapping, prototyping, and delivery activities reinforce one another. If you've seen something similar, I'd be curious to know about it.

Strategy Canvas

The *strategy canvas* is a visual tool for both diagnosing existing strategies and building alternative ones. It was developed by W. Chan Kim and Renée Mauborgne around 2000 and featured in their groundbreaking book *Blue Ocean Strategy*.

Figure 12-5 shows an example strategy canvas for Southwest Airlines.* Across the bottom are the primary

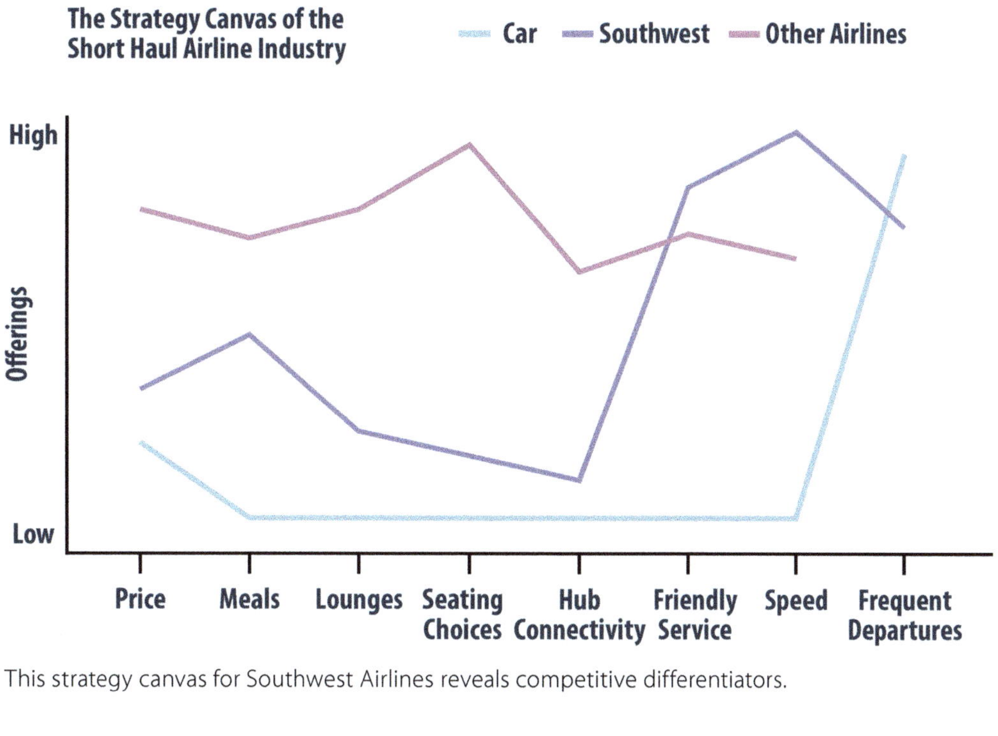

Figure 12-5. This strategy canvas for Southwest Airlines reveals competitive differentiators.

* W. Chan Kim and Renée Mauborgne, *Blue Ocean Strategy* (2005)

factors of competition. These are the aspects that create value for customers and the dimensions along which firms compete. The vertical axis indicates relative performance for each factor, from low to high. This arrangement reveals a picture of how several organizations create value compared to one another.

A strategy canvas reflects the key dynamic in the blue ocean strategy approach. Red oceans, Kim and Mauborgne explain, represent fierce competition among existing industries in a given domain. As the space gets crowded, market share for each organization dwindles, and the waters become bloody.

Blue oceans represent uncontested market space. Demand is *created* rather than fought over. Their advice is clear: don't directly compete with rivals. Instead, make them irrelevant.

To do this you must make difficult trade-offs. Southwest chooses *not* to compete along the traditional factors of airline service. Instead, it focuses on frequent departures from smaller airports. In doing so, it competes with car travel: customers who might otherwise have driven between two cities may now consider flying with Southwest instead.

The process for creating a strategy canvas involves the following steps:

1. ***Determine factors of value creation.*** Coming up with dozens of potential factors may be easy. The key is to focus on the most important ones. This is where alignment diagrams come in: they help identify these factors. They show what problems the organization has and how value is perceived from its perspective.

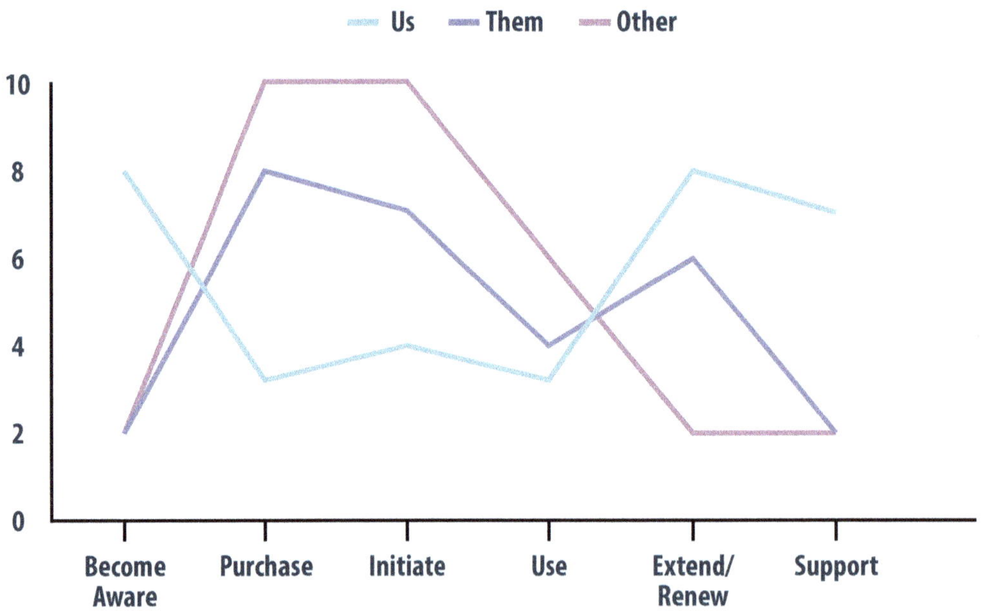

FIGURE 12-6. This experience-based strategy canvas compares experiences provided by the organization, its main competitor, and others.

2. ***Determine competitor types.*** Select a limited set of representative competitors. Three is ideal. Including more than four competitors greatly reduces the impact of the resulting diagram.
3. ***Rate performance for each factor.*** Typically, this is estimated on a relative scale of low to high. It's also possible to get empirical evidence for each rating, such as through a survey.

An alternative approach to determining the factors of value creation is to focus on *types of experiences* individuals have. For instance, from a customer journey map, you may have identified half a dozen or so phases of interaction (e.g., becoming aware, purchasing, initiating the service, using the service, extending and renewing, and getting support). For each of these, you can evaluate your solution's performance relative to those of your main competitor and others (see **FIGURE 12-6**).

This approach may not help you find a blue ocean per se, but it provides valuable insight and an experience-based view of the strategic landscape.

It's also possible to use the strategy canvas to compare the capabilities of specific solutions. For instance, while I was previously working for a content provider, my team wanted to understand why people preferred print resources over digital resources. After interviewing dozens of customers, we found a set of needs that reflected the difference.

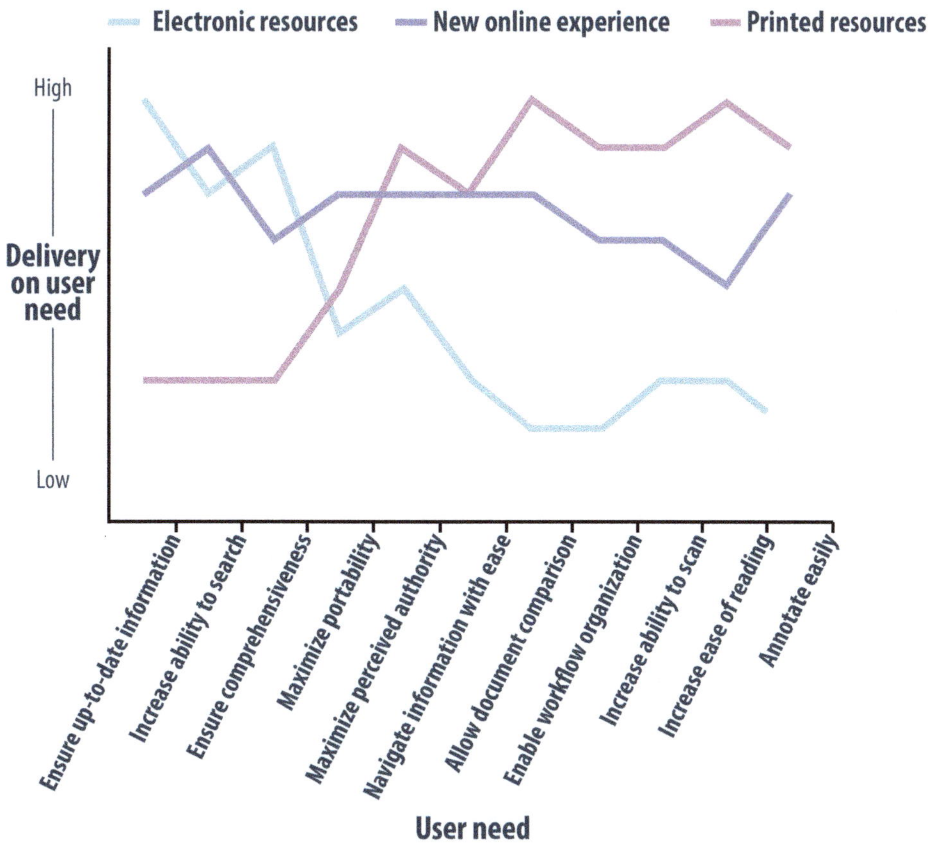

FIGURE 12-7. A graph can help compare advantages based on needs.

We created the graph in **Figure 12-7** to show how the solutions compared in terms of meeting each need. We then hypothesized about what would need to be true for people to more frequently use our online content solutions (labeled "New online experience" in the diagram).

From this visualization, the team could clearly see what to focus on. People in our market needed to annotate documents and compare sources, and they needed help with navigating that was better than what current online content solutions were offering.

Opportunity-Solution Tree

Product teams often struggle to connect their discovery work to strategic outcomes. They conduct customer interviews, gather insights, and brainstorm solutions—but struggle to visualize how all these pieces fit together and ultimately drive business results.

Product discovery coach Teresa Torres created the *opportunity solution tree* (OST) in 2016 to address this challenge. The OST is a visual framework that maps the path from desired business outcomes to validated solutions. It helps teams make implicit assumptions explicit and keeps discovery work organized through what Torres calls the "messy cycles of continuous discovery."*

The structure of an OST includes four key components arranged hierarchically (**Figure 12-8**):

1. ***Outcome.*** At the top of the tree sits a clear, measurable business goal—the metric or result the team aims to improve. This might be revenue growth, customer retention, or satisfaction. The outcome sets the scope for all discovery work below it.
2. ***Opportunities.*** These are customer needs, pain points, and desires that, if addressed, will drive the desired outcome. Torres emphasizes that opportunities should emerge directly from customer conversations, not from sales data or support tickets alone. This ensures that teams work on real, validated customer needs rather than secondhand interpretations.
3. ***Solutions.*** These are the ideas and features the team believes will address the identified opportunities. The OST encourages teams to explore multiple solutions for each opportunity rather than jumping to a single answer. This sets up meaningful compare-and-contrast decisions.
4. ***Experiments.*** At the bottom are tests designed to validate assumptions and evaluate solutions before committing significant resources to building them.

The power of the OST lies in how it connects these elements visually. As Torres writes: "One of the key benefits of using an opportunity solution tree is it helps your team externalize and visualize your thinking, so it's easier to align around what to do when."

Mapping opportunities directly to the outcome and linking solutions to specific opportunities allows teams to see whether their discovery work actually supports their strategic goals. This prevents what Torres calls "feature factory" thinking—shipping outputs without understanding whether they create meaningful outcomes.

The OST also serves as a communication tool. Rather than overwhelming stakeholders with raw interview transcripts or sharing only final conclusions, teams can show their thinking process. Stakeholders can see how customer insights connect to business goals and provide meaningful feedback along the way.

* Teresa Torres, "Opportunity Solution Trees: Visualize Your Discovery to Stay Aligned and Drive Outcomes," *Product Talk* (2023)

For example, a team working on an online coaching platform might have a desired outcome of "improve customer satisfaction with coaching quality." Through customer interviews, they identify opportunities like "customers struggle to find coaches with relevant expertise" and "customers want more flexible scheduling options." For each opportunity, they explore multiple solutions and run experiments to test assumptions before building.

Torres details this approach in her book *Continuous Discovery Habits*, which has become essential reading for product teams. She emphasizes that discovery should be continual, not a quarterly exercise, with teams engaging with customers weekly. The OST keeps this ongoing work organized and prevents teams from losing sight of their strategic goals amid the daily details of product development.

The OST complements journey maps and other alignment diagrams. While journey maps show the current experience, the OST helps teams decide which parts of that experience to improve and validate that their solutions will create meaningful value before investing in development.

To some degree, OSTs resemble strategy maps as pioneered by Robert Kaplan and David Norton in their 2004 book by that name. Even back then, the authors recognized the value of visualizing strategy, noting that "Diagrams open up strategy for broader involvement across an organization and increase general comprehension."*

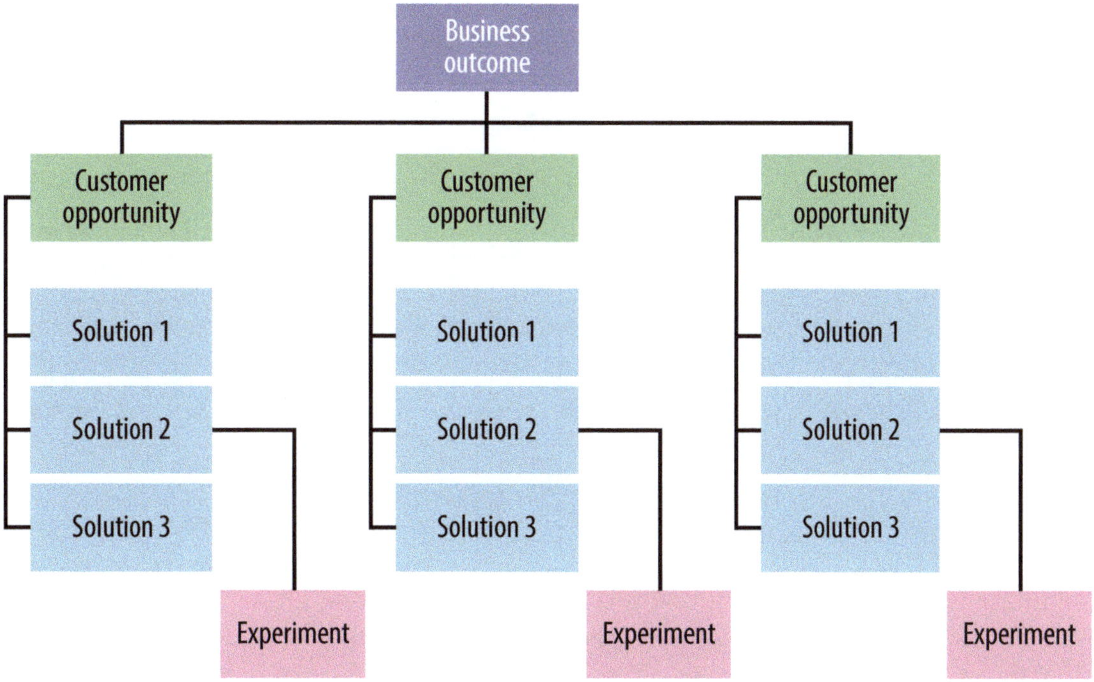

Figure 12-8. This template of an opportunity-solution tree, created by Teresa Torres, shows the basic hierarchy.

* Robert Kaplan and David Norton, *Strategy Maps* (2004)

It's really about *seeing* the cause-and-effect relationships. Consider the simple example strategy map for Patagonia in **Figure 12-9**, created by Michael Ensley, a business consultant with PureStone Partners. Environmental goodwill is a key strategic objective prominent in the diagram. Anchoring it here makes it visible to everyone in the organization.

The center of this example illustrates how Patagonia intends to create customer value. A key internal process is indicated as *solve their [i.e., the customer's] problems*, which is linked to two aspects: *provide extreme gear* and *protect our clients*. Alignment diagrams foster the types of conversations needed to arrive at the problems to solve.

Strategy maps provide a balanced view of the interlocking set of strategic choices an organization makes. They illustrate the relationships in objectives and allow others to see how their activities fit into the strategic whole.

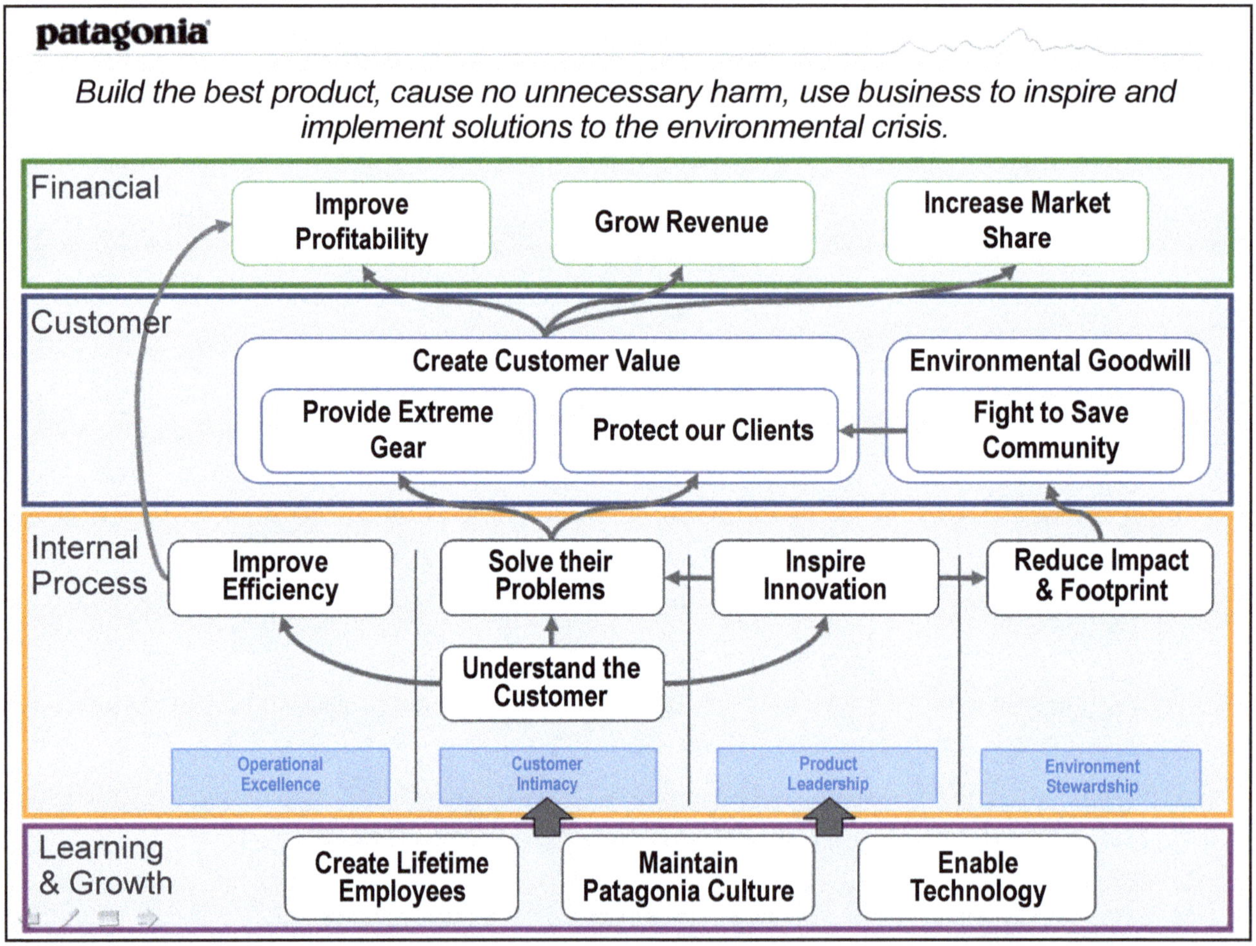

Figure 12-9. This strategy map created for the sportswear company Patagonia shows its focus on environmental goodwill.

Summary

As organizations mature, they often develop strategy myopia unless they actively fight against it—a failure to see the broader landscape of their business and how they can continue to create meaningful value. Successful enterprises start with insights about customer needs and work backward to their strategy. This reverses many existing practices in businesses that seek to push products and services through traditional sales channels.

Strategy is not the same as planning. Plans focus on resources you control and activities you'll undertake. Strategy focuses on how you'll win—the coherent system of choices that creates competitive advantage. Visualizing strategy forces you to articulate not just what you'll do, but how those choices reinforce one another.

To develop an effective strategy, organizations need to reverse their thinking and view value creation from the outside in rather than the inside out. But creating a compelling strategy isn't enough. Making strategy development open and participatory is essential for activation. People can't execute a strategy they don't understand or believe in. Visualization democratizes strategy, allowing diverse voices across the organization to contribute to shaping direction.

Several techniques help illustrate strategy graphically. These include activity system maps, strategy canvases, opportunity-solution trees, and strategy maps, as well as the strategy blueprint and business model canvas. Each offers a different lens for visualizing strategic choices and their relationships. Together, these tools complement and extend alignment diagrams, making strategy not only more understandable but also more inclusive across the organization.

Further Reading

Aric Wood and XPLANE, The Strategy Activation Playbook *(2022)*

Based on years of consulting experience, Wood and the team at XPLANE have gleaned insights from industries around the world and summarized them here. Their practical approach to bringing strategy to life is an essential guide for any strategist. The book includes a range of diagrams and exercises teams can use right away. It's highly recommended for anyone looking to rethink how strategy gets done in any organization.

Roger Martin, "A Plan Is Not a Strategy," Harvard Business Review *[video] (2022)*

Searching for this title will lead you to various resources, including an article with the same name and, more recently, a course on the topic. The best is Martin's 2022 YouTube video, which has gotten millions of views. "Strategy," as Martin says in the video, "is a journey." It's incredibly insightful—as one commenter notes, "I learned more in this 9:31 video than 4 years of business school."

Jonathan Whelan and Stephen Whitla, Visualising Business Transformation *(2020)*

This book details the role of visualizing in general, in strategic conversations and organizational design. The authors do a great job of breaking visual components into workable elements based on their "Visualisation Continuum." Included are discussions of everything from design thinking frameworks and the business model canvas to detailed business process mapping.

A. G. Lafley and Roger Martin, Playing to Win *(2013)*

This book offers a clear framework for understanding strategy, based on five key questions. It is one of the most lucid and useful approaches to strategy development available today, backed up by numerous case studies and examples from the authors' decades of experience.

W. Chan Kim and Renée Mauborgne, Blue Ocean Strategy *(2005)*

This landmark book from the pioneers of blue ocean strategy explains the approach in detail. The key isn't to compete with rivals directly, the authors explain, but rather to make them irrelevant. To do this, organizations need to find new attributes of value creation. Visualizing the landscape in a strategy canvas is an ideal way to identify opportunities of this kind. Many blue ocean strategy tools and resources are available online, for example, at *blueoceanstrategy.com*.

Diagram and Image Credits

Figure 12-2: Diagram re-created and adapted from a figure appearing in Ram Charan's book *What the Customer Wants You to Know*

Figure 12-3: Rail Europe experience map created by Chris Risdon, used with permission

Figure 12-5: Strategy canvas for Southwest Airlines, redrawn and adapted from W. Chan Kim and Renée Mauborgne, *Blue Ocean Strategy*

Figure 12-7: Excerpt of a diagram created by Jim Kalbach for LexisNexis

Figure 12-8: Example opportunity solution tree by Teresa Torres, originally appearing in her article "Engaging Stakeholders with Opportunity Solution Trees: 3 Tactics to Try," used with permission

Figure 12-9: Patagonia strategy map created by Michael Ensley of PureStone Partners, originally appearing in his blog post "Going Green," used with permission

Figure 12-10: Strategy blueprint created by Jim Kalbach

Figure 12-11: Business model canvas by Alexander Osterwalder, downloaded from *https://www.strategyzer.com/library/the-business-model-canvas*, CC BY-SA 3.0

Figure 12-12: Strategy vision map by XPLANE, a TiER 1 studio, used with permission

Cocreate with the Strategy Blueprint

Objective	Explore various aspects of a strategy visually and decide on a direction together
Time	1–2 hours
Participants	3–12
Materials	Strategy blueprint template, whiteboard, sticky notes

The strategy blueprint is a tool I developed. It uses a canvas format to help visualize the relationships among elements of the strategy (**Figure 12-10**). Building strategy is both a creative endeavor and a team sport. The strategy blueprint allows you to explore options with no initial risk. Try alternatives, cross off items, rework ideas, and start over again. Ask "What if?" and "What would need to be true?" to push boundaries.

The blueprint guides the conversations and facilitates collaborative strategy design. There is no prescribed order for completing it. Typically, it's best to start with the challenges and aspirations, but after that, you may find yourself moving freely between the boxes. You can do this individually at first and then aggregate the results in a master version of the blueprint, or you can work on one copy of the blueprint at the same time collectively.

How it works:

1. Identify challenges. Strategy implies the need for change, a desire to move from point A to point B. What are the hurdles to doing so? What opposing forces must you overcome to be able to reach your goals?
2. Define ambitions. What kind of organization do you aspire to be? What do you want for your customers and for society?
3. Determine target areas. Setting a scope for your strategy helps you concentrate effort on the things that matter most. Who will you serve? What regions will you operate in? Which jobs to be done will you target?
4. Set guiding principles. These are the pillars of the strategy that you believe will enable you to overcome the challenges you face. What mantras will unite teams and unify decision making?
5. List key activities. What types of activities are needed to implement the strategy and achieve your aspirations? Note that this is not about making a roadmap or plans, but rather identifying the skills and capabilities you'll ultimately need.
6. Define success measures. How will you know your strategy is on track? How can you show progress and success?

Learn more:

Jim Kalbach, "Strategy Blueprint Revised," *LinkedIn* (2024)

Example:

Strategy Blueprint

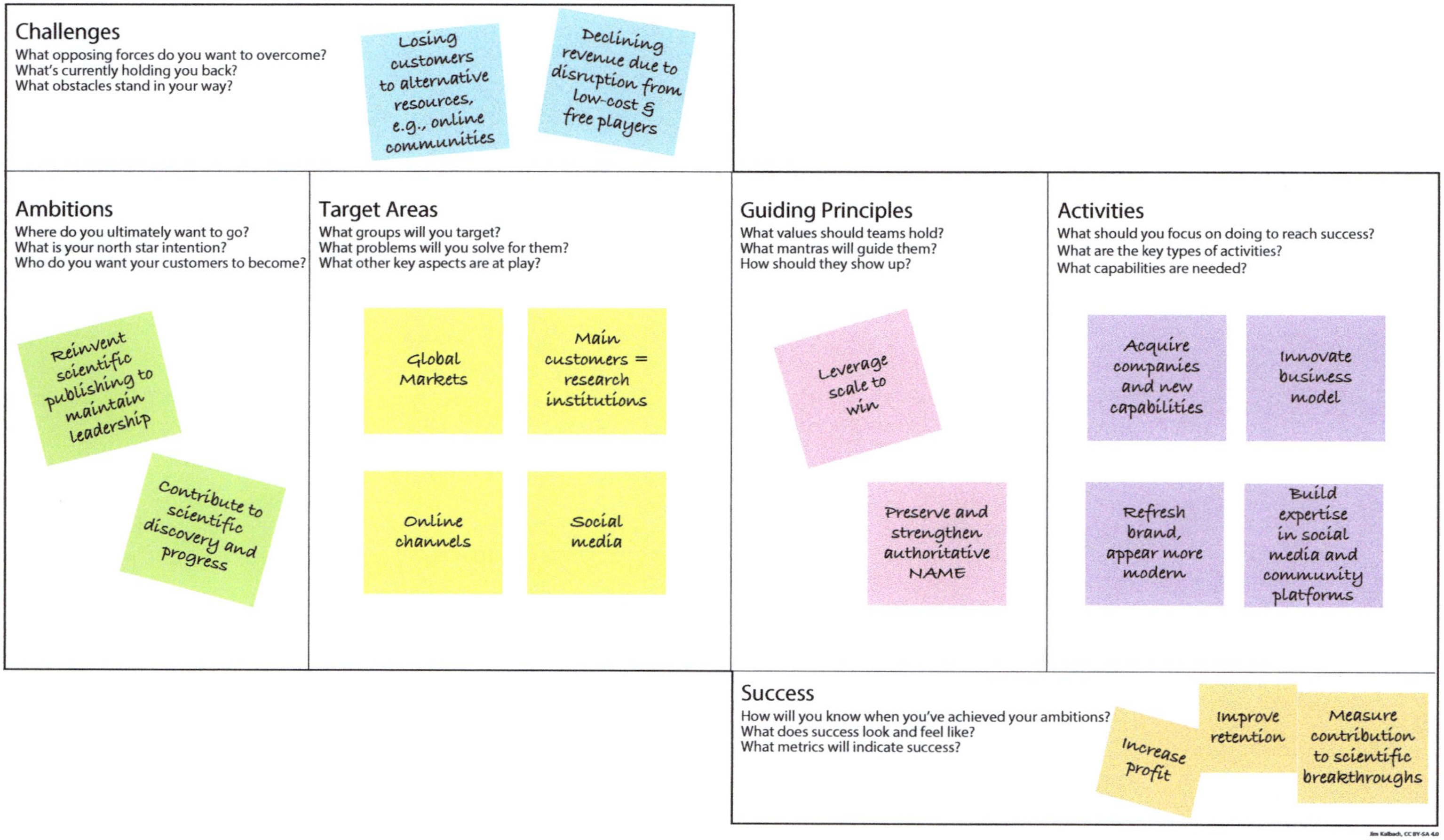

FIGURE 12-10. The strategy blueprint reveals the key logic of strategy, in this case for the fictitious Einstein Media Company.

Business Model Canvas

Objective	Visualize a business model together
Time	1–2 hours
Participants	3–12
Materials	Business model canvas, whiteboard, sticky notes

The business model canvas, developed by Alexander Osterwalder, is a strategic management tool that helps business owners and stakeholders discover different business models. The nine fields of the canvas represent the key components of a business model. The boxes on the right represent market-facing aspects, called the *frontstage*. On the left are the *backstage* elements of a business model—the internal business processes (**Figure 12-11**).

How it works:

1. Start by defining the customer segments and value proposition. On the right side of the canvas, identify who you're serving. Then articulate what unique value you offer them. What problems do you solve? What gains do you create?
2. Explore the customer relationships and channels. Define how you'll interact with customers throughout their journey—self-service, personal assistance, automated services. Then determine how you'll reach them and deliver your value proposition through different channels, partner channels, or a combination.
3. Enumerate revenue streams. Identify how you'll capture value from each customer segment. Will customers pay through one-time purchases, subscriptions, licensing, or other models?
4. Move to the left side and name partners, activities, and resources. Identify the key partnerships needed to deliver your value proposition. Then determine the most important activities your business must perform—production, problem-solving, platform management. Finally, list the critical resources required—physical, intellectual, human, or financial.
5. Complete the cost structure field. At the bottom, outline the major costs involved in operating your business model. What are the most important costs? Which resources and activities are most expensive?
6. Evaluate the model and explore further. Assess the strengths and weaknesses of the model and determine action steps. Explore other models by repeating the activity, and then compare them to one another.

Learn more:

Alexander Osterwalder and Yves Pigneur, *Business Model Generation* (2011)

Example:

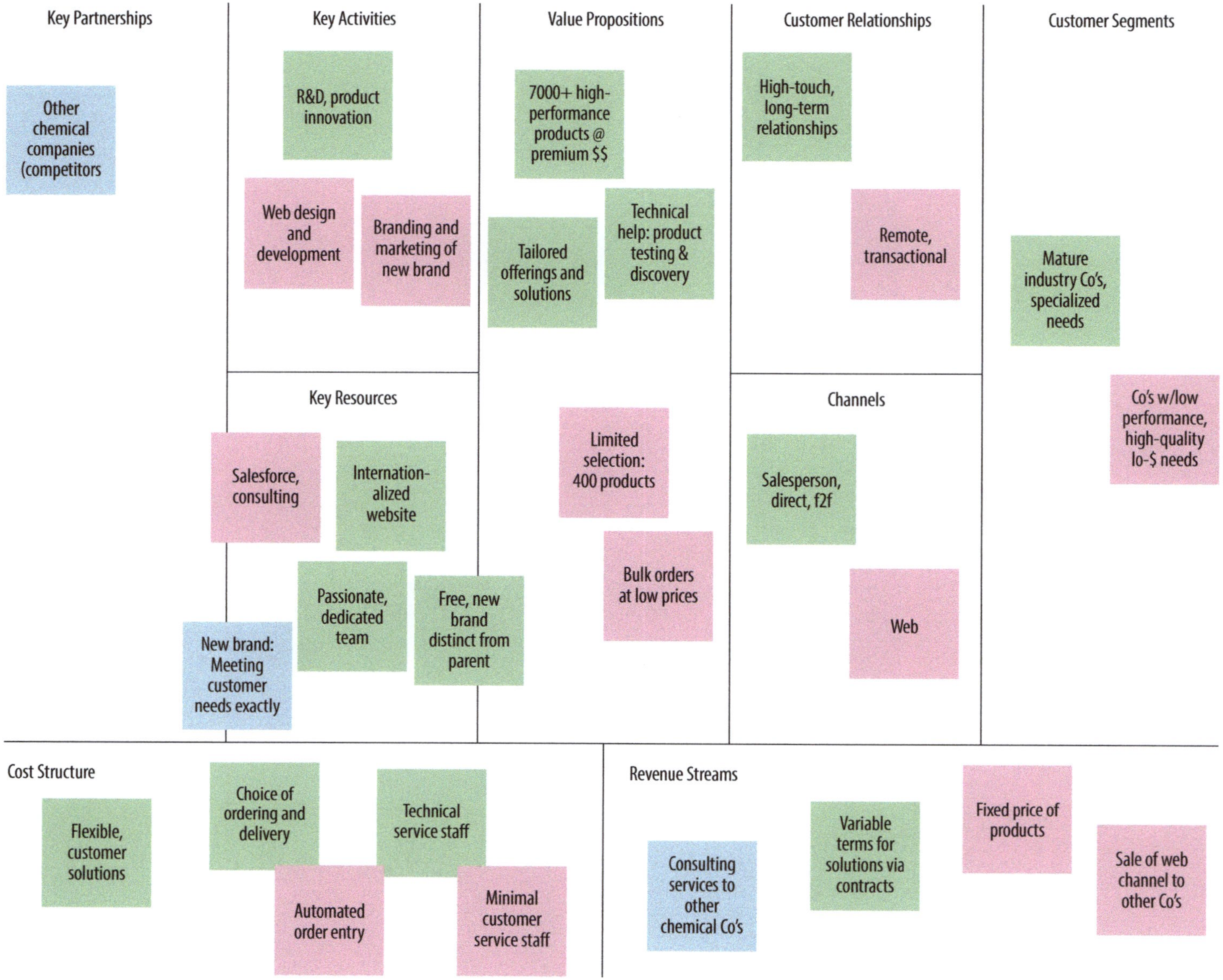

Figure 12-11. This example of a business model canvas compares the business models of Xiameter, a provider of silicon, to its parent, Dow Corning.

Strategic Vision Mapping

Objective	Illustrate your strategic vision together
Time	1–2 hours
Participants	3–8
Materials	Vision map template, whiteboard, sticky notes

A *vision map* is a simple diagram to compare the current state to the future state and highlight the gaps between the two (**Figure 12-12**).

How it works:

1. Give each participant a copy of the template to complete.
2. Describe the current state. Ask the participants to describe or sketch their present situation—what does their world or scenario look like today? What is the case for change?
3. Describe the future state. Invite the participants to describe or sketch their desired to-be state—what do they want their world or scenario to look like in the future? What are the impacts and outcomes?
4. Connect the two states. With both states clearly envisioned, ask the participants to complete the bridge section by identifying specific actions that could be taken or things that would need to change in order for the future state to be realized.
5. Share insights and consolidate. Have each person share their vision with the group, then discuss similarities and differences and identify common themes. These themes become "common ground" for further exploration and alignment on possibilities. Capture the consolidated responses in a separate template to reflect input from across the group.

Learn more:

Aric Wood and XPLANE, *The Strategy Activation Playbook* (2022)

Vision map worksheets: *https://xplane.com/worksheet/vision-map-exercise-worksheet*

Example:

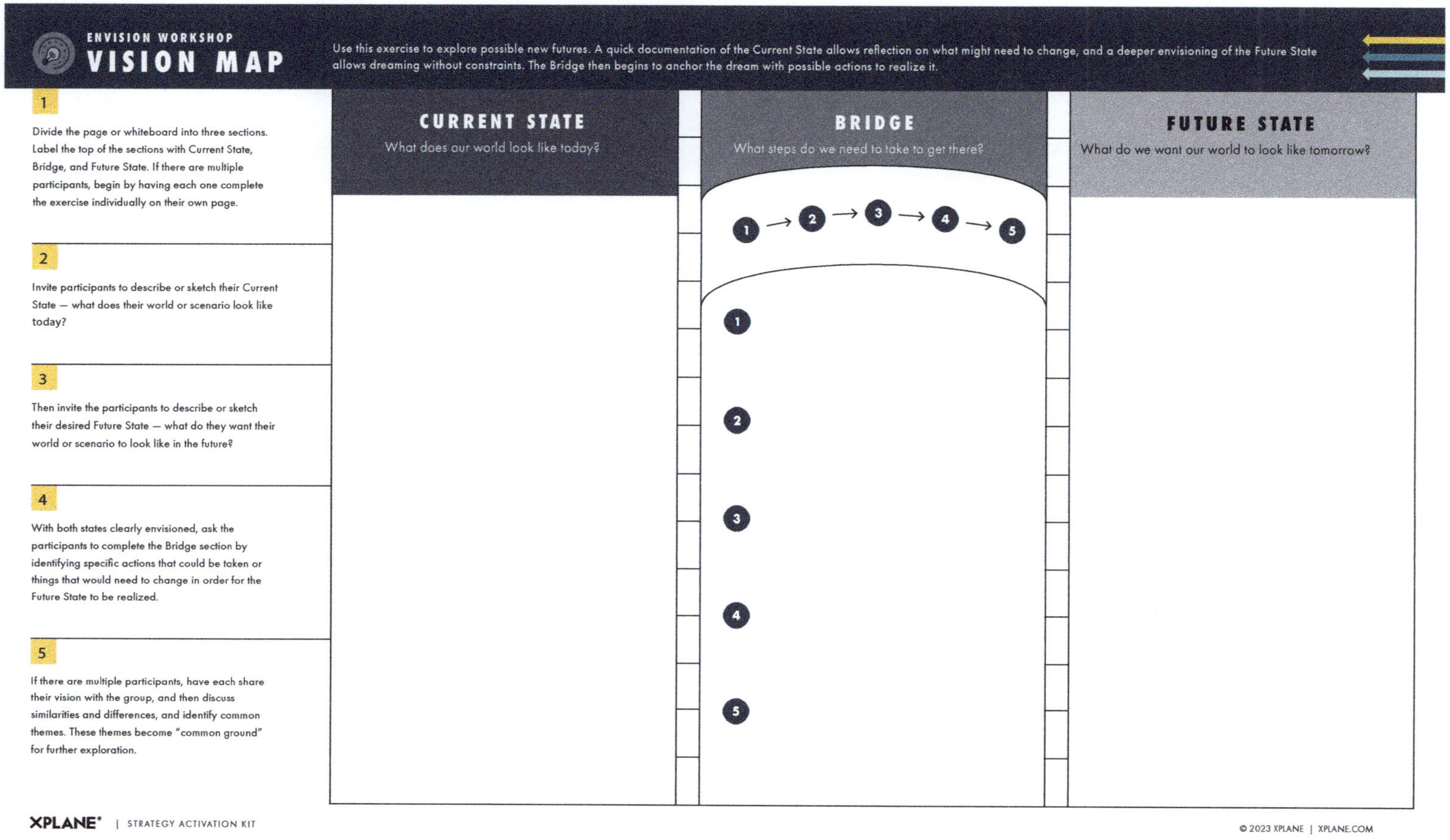

FIGURE 12-12. A vision map is a simple visualization to illustrate your team's strategy journey.

The goal of social innovation is to maximize the satisfaction of all members of the ecosystem with new solutions that will address the needs across the spectrum.

—Sandra Bates, *The Social Innovation Imperative*

IN THIS CHAPTER

- Mapping in noncommercial contexts
- Shared value: profit with social benefit
- System-level mapping for change
- Evaluating social services
- Collaborative method for mapping for social good

CHAPTER 13

Mapping for the Social Good: Prosperity Beyond Profit

Much of the mapping in this book centers on commercial experiences. But mapping isn't limited to businesses. We can map any human experience to help teams understand key challenges and identify viable points of intervention.

Take my experience leading a workshop for Hedayah, a nongovernmental organization (NGO) based in Abu Dhabi, focused on countering violent extremism (CVE). The project centered on understanding the experience of ex-violent extremists—called *formers*—after they disengage from hate groups.

Formers are valuable to CVE efforts. They can hear dog whistles, or encoded messages that appear normal to the general public. They see extremist groups from the inside out. People looking to leave hate groups often confide in formers because they understand what it means to disengage.

My sponsor believed that mapping formers' experiences would provide insight into how to recruit more of them. A search for "mapping experiences" led them to my work. They invited me to lead a two-day workshop. I accepted on a pro bono basis and started planning my trip to Abu Dhabi.

Not knowing much about violent extremism, I did an initial investigation into formers ahead of the event. I wanted to understand enough to keep up with experts in the field and sketch out a hypothesis experience map to validate in the workshop.

The workshop included seven formers from a range of groups: ex-white supremacists, ex-Al Qaeda, and ex-gang members. All had chosen to dedicate their careers and lives to fighting hate. Nine other participants from various CVE organizations, including the US State Department and other NGOs, also attended.

I planned the workshop as I would a typical experience mapping workshop. The focus was a group mapping exercise to foster broad discussion about how the formers got involved in CVE themselves (**Figure 13-1**). They indicated their actions, thoughts, and feelings during their journey to involvement. Together, we identified key moments to concentrate on and moved into ideation before developing concrete solutions.

It was nerve-racking for me—I was way out of my comfort zone. I knew nothing about CVE, yet there I was leading a multiday workshop to explore the topic in a deep and unique way. And I was unsure if any of it would work.

Thankfully, it did. The workshop was a success overall and garnered very positive feedback. One participant representing an NGO said, "This was the best hands-on workshop I've ever attended." A former who participated commented, "Experience mapping changed the way that I look at countering violent extremism. Cultivating empathy by mapping an experience elevates the technique beyond just optimizing business performance and makes it an asset to building a more peaceful world."

My primary output from the multiday session was a map of a former's journey toward involvement, which was included in an in-depth analysis created by Hedayah. **Figure 13-2** shows the path from guilt—a common emotion after leaving an extremist group—toward atonement, a primary motivation for getting involved in CVE.

Overall, the session was an exploration of new ground. No one had ever investigated formers' paths to involvement. The project contributed to a broader, long-term understanding of why some formers get involved in CVE and others don't. The results of the workshop were documented in a detailed report, which was made available to researchers in CVE worldwide to learn from.

From my perspective, the effort reaffirmed that experience mapping techniques have broader application beyond commercial settings. And sharing this story in presentations at conferences and meetups has inspired others to consider social applications of creative techniques like mapping in their own work and lives.

This chapter explores how mapping works across different scales of social impact: helping individuals find purpose after leaving extremist groups, enabling businesses to create value for society alongside profit, and evaluating entire service systems to improve lives. The tools remain the same; what changes is what we're optimizing for.

Figure 13-1. Various techniques from mapping experiences were used in a workshop with former violent extremists.

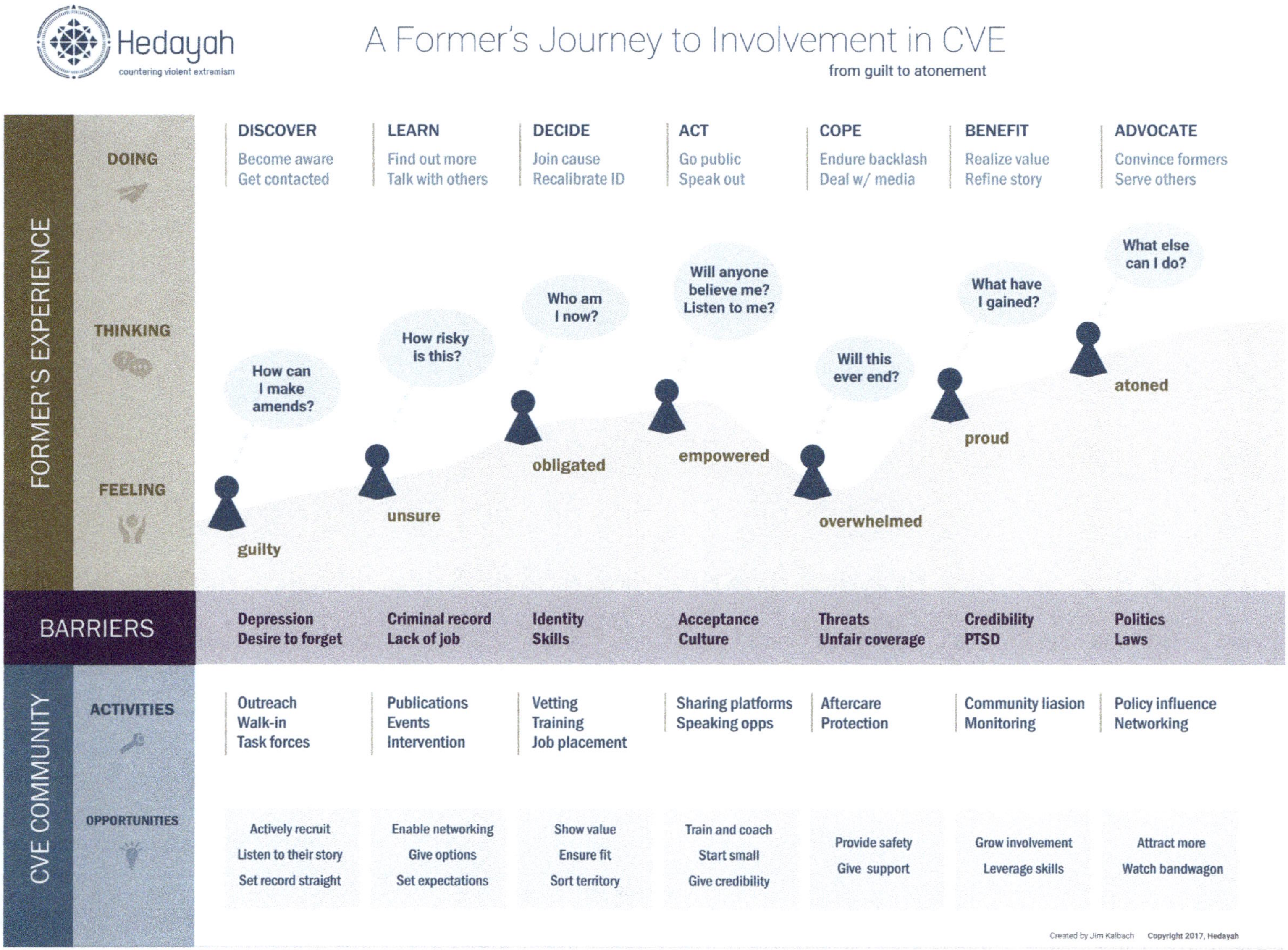

FIGURE 13-2. The final map of a former's journey after denouncing violent extremism shows the process of moving through different stages, from guilt to atonement.

Mapping Human Experiences

The Hedayah project showed me something important: the same collaborative process that works for understanding customer journeys works for any human experience. I wasn't invited to lead the effort because of my knowledge of countering violent extremism—that was almost nonexistent. I was invited because I have expertise in a technique that can help shed light on human experiences via mapping.

In commercial contexts, we optimize for business outcomes: conversion rates, revenue, customer lifetime value, and innovation opportunities. The maps help us make sense of human behaviors and find opportunities to improve the bottom line for customers and users. The same applies to finding opportunities in the employee experience.

In social contexts, we're optimizing for human impact: better lives, transformed systems, and prosperity beyond profit. The techniques are the same, but the goals shift.

In social contexts, we're optimizing for human impact: better lives, transformed systems, and prosperity beyond profit.

Creating Shared Value

After World War II, US corporations assumed a retain-and-reinvest approach to strategy. They put earnings back into the company, benefiting employees and making firms more competitive.

This gave way to a downsize-and-distribute posture in the 1970s. Reducing costs and maximizing financial returns, particularly for shareholders, became the priority. The widely held belief was that profit is good for society: the more companies can earn, the better off we all are.

This policy has not made America more prosperous.* Since the '70s, shareholder value in the form of dividends and CEO wages has experienced a massive upturn. Meanwhile, American workers have been working more and making less. Trust in corporations is at an all-time low. Businesses are increasingly blamed for many social, environmental, and economic problems.

The good news is that the balance is shifting. In their article "Creating Shared Value," strategy experts Michael Porter and Mark Kramer recognize a tipping point in business—companies can no longer operate at the expense of the markets they serve. They write:

> **A big part of the problem lies with companies themselves, which remain trapped in an outdated approach to value creation that has emerged over the past few decades. They continue to view value creation narrowly, optimizing short-term financial performance in a bubble while missing the most important customer needs and ignoring the broader influences that determine their longer-term success.†**

* For a more detailed analysis and supporting data, see William Lazonick, "Profits Without Prosperity," *Harvard Business Review* (2014).

† Michael Porter and Mark Kramer, "Creating Shared Value," *Harvard Business Review* (2011)

Shared value directly links revenue to creating social benefit, which in turn provides a competitive advantage to the organization. It's a win-win approach.

Shared value is not about social responsibility or philanthropy. It goes deeper and touches the heart of an organization's strategy. The aim is to make every customer interaction also create value for society.

There are three ways of thinking about shared value strategically:

Reconceive your offering.

Microsoft built accessibility tools directly into its products—Immersive Reader, live captioning, dictation, and more—that help over 1 billion people with disabilities worldwide. These aren't add-ons or expensive upgrades. They're free, built-in features in Windows, Office 365, and Teams. A 2019 study found these tools improved student learning outcomes while reducing school costs.* Microsoft partners with governments to integrate accessibility into school curricula. The company isn't just selling software—it's democratizing access to education and work.

Innovate how products and services are produced.

In 2009, Intercontinental Hotels Group (IHG) introduced the GreenEngage program to address its environmental footprint. The program led to energy savings of about 25% and helped differentiate IHG in the eyes of customers.† The group is no longer just a provider of hotel rooms; it's helping build more environmentally conscious communities.

* Forrester Consulting, "The Total Economic Impact of Microsoft Accessibility and Assistive Technologies for Education" (2019)

† IHG, "IHG Green Engage System"

Collaborate with partners in new ways.

Nestlé has worked closely with dairy farmers in India for many years, investing in technology to build competitive milk supply systems. Complementary initiatives simultaneously generated social benefits through improvements in education and healthcare.‡ Nestlé doesn't only produce food products; it's in the nutrition business.

The notion of shared value means an organization needs to conceive its value proposition in a way that takes many perspectives into account. Chief among these is a deep understanding of human needs. In a video interview, Porter advises:

> **Figure out what your product is and what your value chain is. Understand where those things touch important social needs and problems. If you're in financial services, let's think about "saving" or "buying a home"—but in a way that actually works for the consumer.**

Consider **Figure 13-3**, a diagram of the home buying experience created by Sofia Hussain, a leading digital strategist in Norway. It shows the services of a fictitious home-listings company in the inner circle, labeled "inside activities." The activities of the user—the "outside activities"—are listed in the bigger circle. Also included are touchpoint types, illustrated with small icons.

Hussain suggests a strategic scenario for the company: it wants to expand its business with services that address more customer needs in this domain. The intent is to move from simply helping people buy homes to helping them settle into those homes. This diagram illustrates how that expansion fits into the overall experience from the customer's perspective.

‡ Meeta Punjabi, "Nestlé India's Dairy Development Initiative in the Punjab Region," FAO (2015)

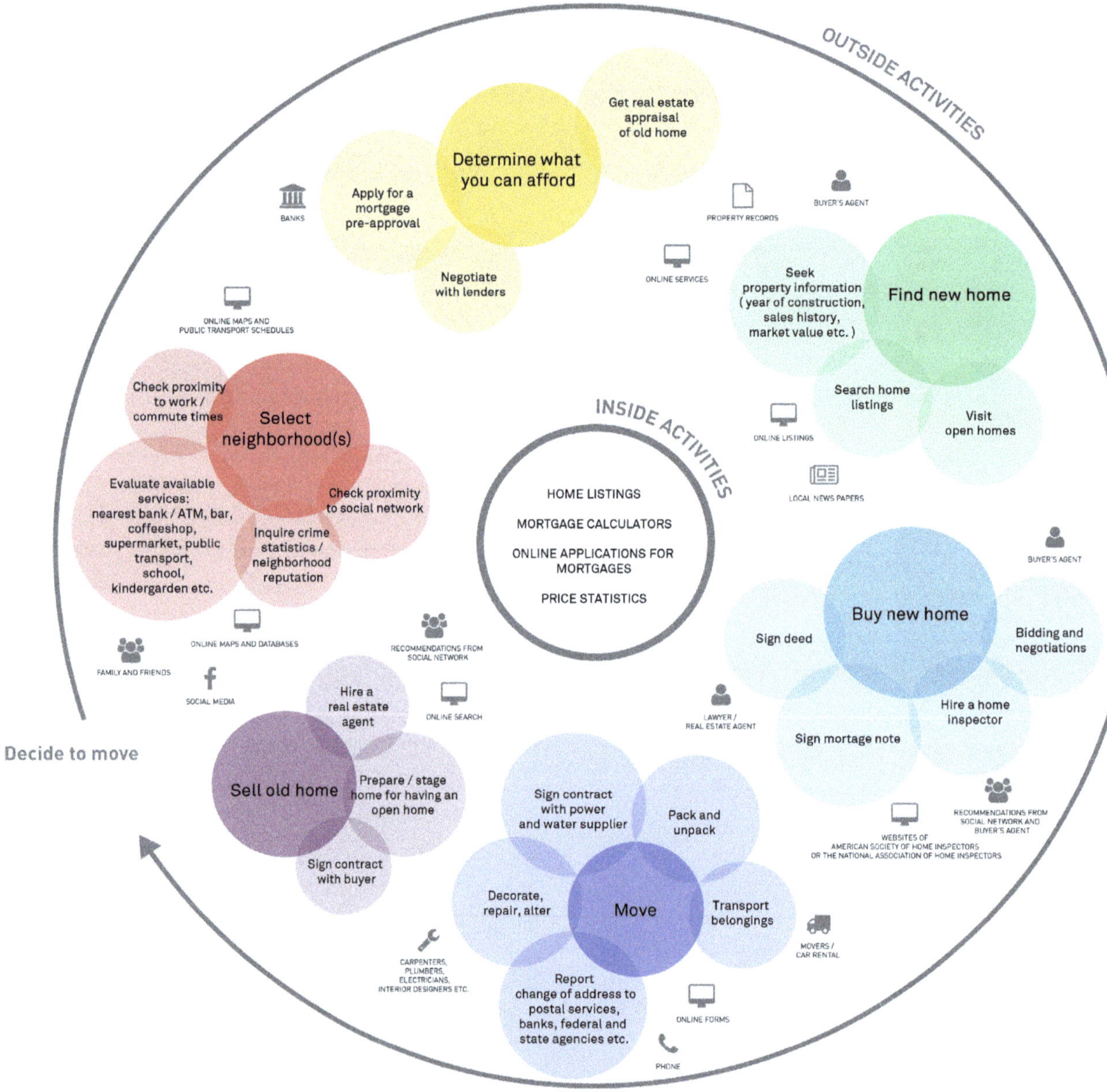

FIGURE 13-3. This map created by Sofia Hussain illustrates the experience of buying a home.

But shared value goes one step further than increasing services or moving into a new playing field. It requires the company to ask how it might also create social benefit.

For example, the company might promote healthier lifestyles by coordinating home listings with information about neighborhood walkability. In the map in **Figure 13-3**, services around selecting a neighborhood and finding a new home are points of interaction where presenting walkability information makes sense. Thanks to potential cost savings, it could also be included in determining what buyers can afford. The system could show how much money could be saved by reducing gas expenses or getting rid of a car altogether.

With shared value in mind, the strategic aspiration becomes even broader. It's not just about buying and settling into a home; it's about creating a healthier, environmentally friendly lifestyle when buying a new home.

Diagrams help us think through interactions and customer needs in a holistic way. Recalling Porter, they enable us to view the offering in a way that actually works for the consumer. Finding shared business value relies on such examinations of the overall human experience. Visualizations help us find opportunities.

With shared value in mind, the strategic aspiration becomes even broader.

Mapping System-Level Change

Shared value at the company level creates important social benefits. But some of the biggest opportunities exist at a systems level. Many social and environmental challenges can't be solved by any single organization. They require understanding the broader ecosystem of actors, relationships, and flows.

Chris Risdon and Patrick Quattlebaum advocate starting with a view of the broader ecosystem in their book *Orchestrating Experiences*. They write:

> **The basic process includes identifying what makes up the ecosystem, identifying the relationships.... An experience ecosystem complements other models, such as personas and customer journeys, which provide insights into your customers and their experiences.***

Figure 13-4 shows an example of an ecosystem map from their book. This particular diagram deals with healthcare in the US, showing various entities and their primary relationships with one another. The concentric circles reflect immediacy and the direct influence of those aspects on the individual, who stands in the center.

The goal is to look at touchpoints and the interactions an individual has while moving along the pathways in the system. Points of integration between various parts of the model emerge, leading to team discussions about opportunities and solutions. This isn't to say you intend to design the ecosystem itself. Rather, the aim is to understand the broader context to be better able to design within it.

* Chris Risdon and Patrick Quattlebaum, *Orchestrating Experiences* (2018)

Visualizations offer an immediacy of comprehension and help us arrive at strategic conclusions. Maps show interrelationships in an ecosystem.

In biology, an ecosystem is a community of living organisms interacting with one another and with nonliving elements in their environment. Think about plants, animals, and insects, and how they move in air, in water, and on land. The sum is greater than its parts: ecosystems are diverse sets of relationships. We can view organizations and the individuals they serve similarly, as a whole rather than a collection of disparate parts.

Ecosystem mapping applies what is called *systems thinking*, or a consideration of multiple entities within a complex environment in a holistic way. Basically, systems thinking is a way of viewing the relationships between multiple components as a whole. This allows teams to identify leverage points—areas they can influence—to find opportunities for change and improvement.

For instance, based on the model in **Figure 13-4**, a team might discuss the role of health standards in the individual's overall health and how there could be a more direct impact. Each aspect in the diagram is intentionally oversimplified to focus on the connections between them, rather than the complexities within each.

Figure 13-4. An ecosystem map provides a high-level view of the relationships among elements in a broader system.

Mapping a Veteran's Life Experience

Consider the diagram in **Figure 13-5**, created by Sarah Brooks, chief design officer at the US Department of Veteran Affairs (VA).

The map has no "awareness" or "purchase" phase because it takes a different point of view from a classic customer journey map. This diagram tells a story of experiences, not a story of transactions. It's quite literally the life story of a military service member.

The VA used this ecosystem view to understand how services needed to connect across an entire lifespan—from enlistment through active duty, transition to civilian life, and ongoing veteran support. No single department could address all of a veteran's needs. The map revealed where services fragmented and where better coordination could improve lives.*

This is systems thinking applied to social good. The map doesn't optimize for a business outcome. It reveals opportunities to design better support for people who have served their country.

Designing for Circular Systems

Ecosystem thinking also applies to environmental challenges. Traditional business models follow a linear path: extract resources, make products, use them, dispose of them. Circular design challenges this. It emphasizes looking beyond single product lifecycles for single users. Products become entities within systems that allow multiple users and usages.

Matt Sinclair and his research team at Loughborough University developed Consumer Intervention Mapping as part of an Engineering and Physical Sciences Research Council project. They were looking at how circular design could integrate with redistributed manufacturing—the type that can occur when production machinery is smaller, cheaper, and more easily localized. 3D printers are the best-known example.

The team realized something important. Most strategic visions of a circular economy see the consumer as fairly disinterested in anything except consuming. But there's this whole other idea of the consumer as someone engaged in designing, making, repairing, and reselling products whose lifecycles don't match those of conventionally conceived consumer goods.

Touchpoint diagrams in commercial settings typically concentrate only on experiences within the value chain that a brand can influence. Consumer interventions such as post-purchase modification, repair, lending, and resale often receive little attention, because brands cannot monetize them. The team realized there's a whole ecosystem of activities carried out by people interested in ideas central to the circular economy that never appear on brands' touchpoint diagrams.

Consumer Intervention Maps were their way of capturing these activities—partly because they found them interesting in their own right, but also because they hoped drawing attention to them might encourage brands to design for them. **Figure 13-6** shows the underlying framework for Consumer Intervention Mapping.

The design follows a conventional brand touchpoint wheel. Touchpoints are defined at the top level as pre-purchase, purchase, or post-purchase experiences. These are subdivided into 6 categories, including new product development—something brands rarely see as an area for consumer involvement—then further divided into 18 subcategories, including maintenance and disposal, which are often left out of touchpoint diagrams.

* For more details, see Kyla Fullenwider, "How Citizen-Centered Design Is Changing the Ways the Government Serves the People," *Fast Company* (2016).

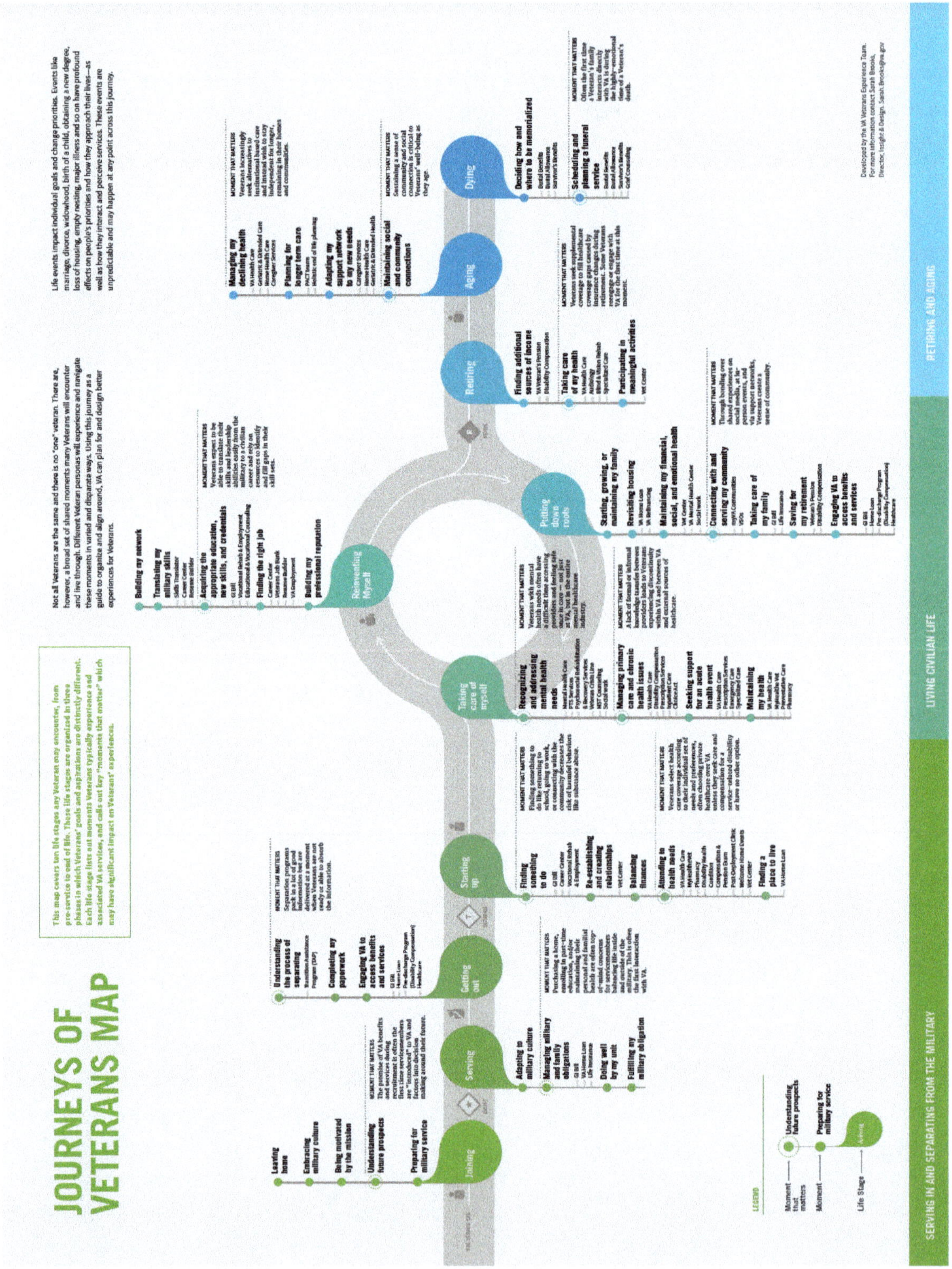

FIGURE 13-5. This map of a military veteran's life experiences reflects a wide range of disparate goals and objectives over time.

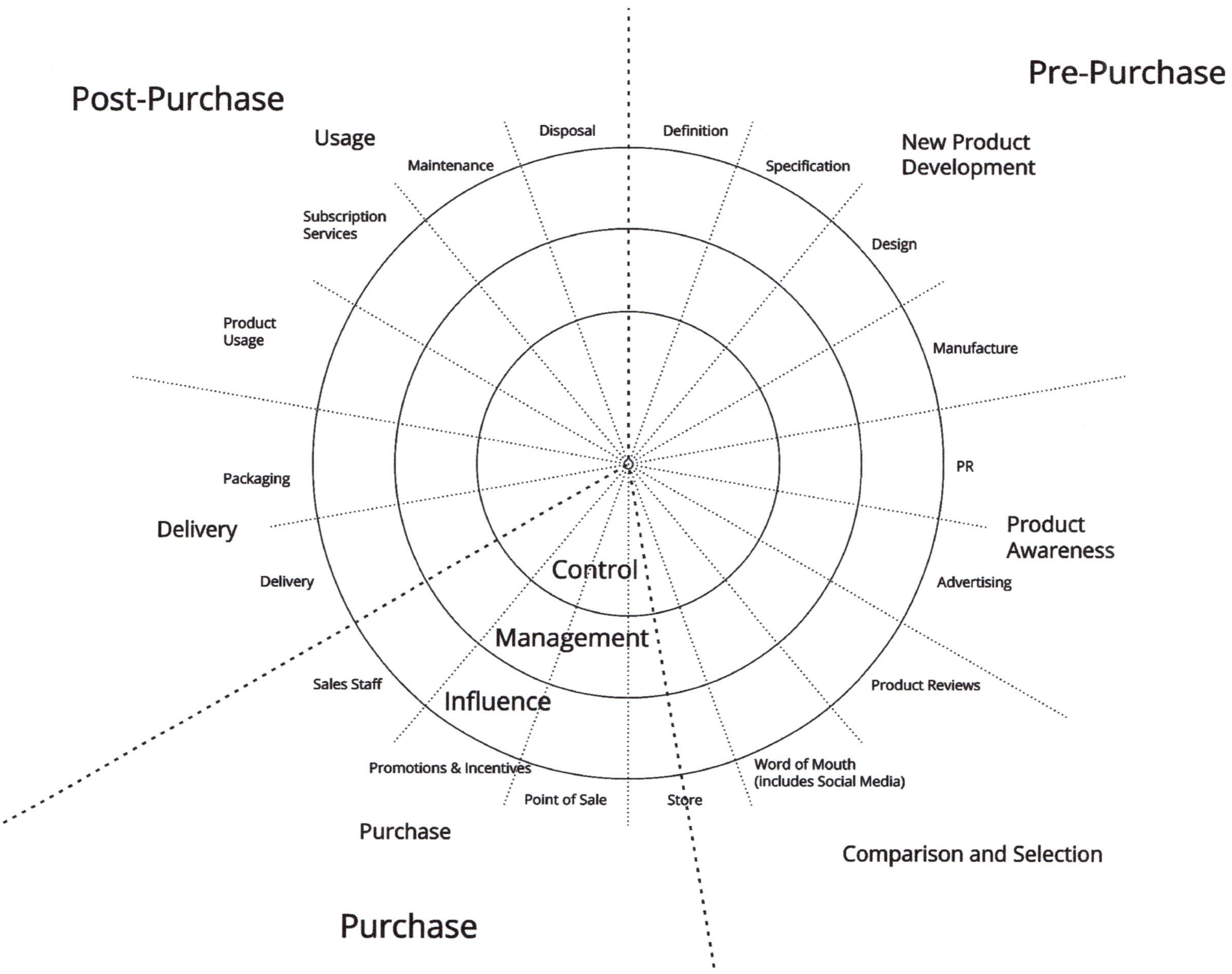

Figure 13-6. The Consumer Intervention space visualizes the broader circular design ecosystem.

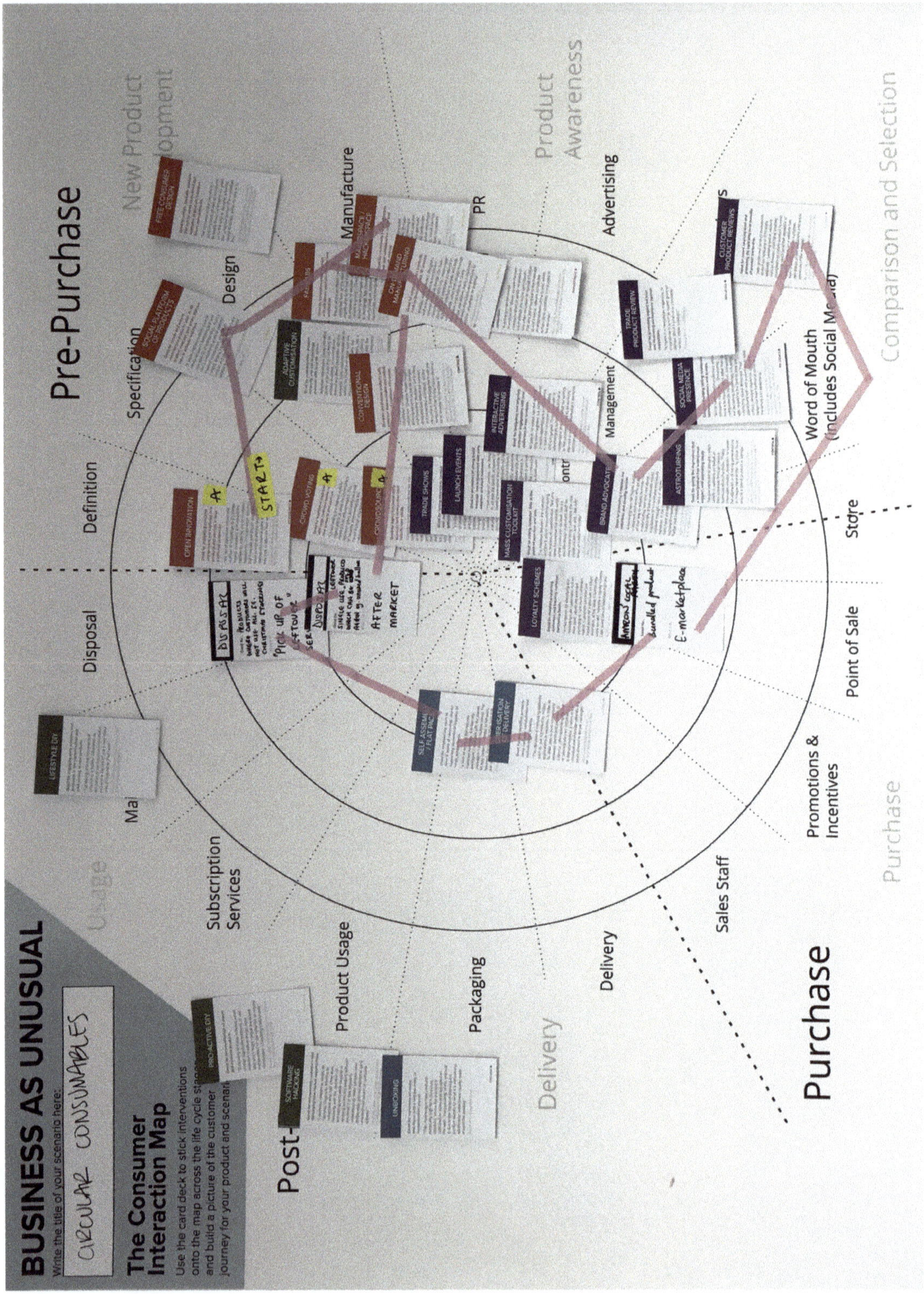

FIGURE 13-7. This Consumer Intervention Map engaged a group of participants in a workshop.

A further refinement adds concentric rings that indicate the degree of control a brand exerts when a consumer intervenes in the product's lifecycle. A brand has much more control when a consumer uses an authorized dealer for a repair rather than purchasing a gray market spare part and repairing a product themselves.

The diagram is populated with touchpoints identified through literature and workshop activities. **Figure 13-7** shows an example.

To a large extent, the value of the tool has been seen in the discussions that have arisen from these exercises. Alternative visions of product strategies and business models have emerged. Workshop participants have commented that it's refreshing to be asked to consider possibilities rather than constraints. The tool's focus on users introduces a perspective that many had not previously considered.

The Consumer Intervention Map is essentially a circular diagram for creating shared value. The mapping reveals opportunities for businesses to design products that last longer and can be repaired or resold. This creates environmental benefits, such as less waste and fewer resources extracted. It also creates social benefits, including the development of local repair economies and accessible secondhand markets. And it can create business value through new service models and deeper customer relationships.

Both the VA map and the Consumer Intervention Map demonstrate the power of ecosystem thinking. When the team members zoom out, they see the full system—all the actors, relationships, and flows. Zooming in, they can spot leverage points that no single organization could identify on its own. This is where mapping creates the conditions for transformation, not just optimization.

Evaluating Social Service Systems

The most challenging social problems don't exist within the boundaries of any single organization. They span multiple agencies, government programs, and nonprofits, each doing important work, but rarely coordinated into a coherent whole.

Traditional evaluation approaches focus on measuring individual programs. Did this shelter serve *X* number of families? Did that counseling program achieve *Y* outcomes? These metrics matter, but they miss something crucial: how does the entire system perform from the perspective of someone trying to navigate it?

Mapping provides a way to evaluate social service ecosystems as complete systems. By visualizing a person's journey across multiple touchpoints, teams can identify where the system works well and where it breaks down—not from an administrative perspective, but from the lived experience of the people it's designed to serve.

For example, Karen Woods, a service design and developmental evaluation consultant in Ottawa, applied mapping to one of society's most challenging problems: domestic violence. Victim support involves a complex web of interconnected services and stakeholders. Mapping helps reveal how these parts interact and where coordination breaks down.

> *The most challenging social problems don't exist within the boundaries of any single organization.*

Woods used the map structure as a data collection mechanism. A journey board was prepared in advance, shown in **Figure 13-8**. Participants used a card sort activity to identify service system touchpoints, then selected up to 10 services with the most impact on their journey.

These services were placed chronologically on the board. The interviewer then walked the participant through data collection, identifying their needs from each service and the stress level they experienced.

One of the biggest surprises was the total number of services the participants interacted with. On average, women experiencing domestic violence reported interacting with 22 different services. The research showed that the system met functional needs fairly well, but some services were less likely to address underlying emotional needs, such as compassion.

Journey mapping allowed the team to identify high- and lower-performing services, information that could be used to guide resource allocation to improve underperforming areas.

To date, over 40 shelter staff and community stakeholders across Ontario have been trained to conduct journey mapping interviews. The process is being used to build capacity to inform and improve services for women living with or escaping domestic violence.

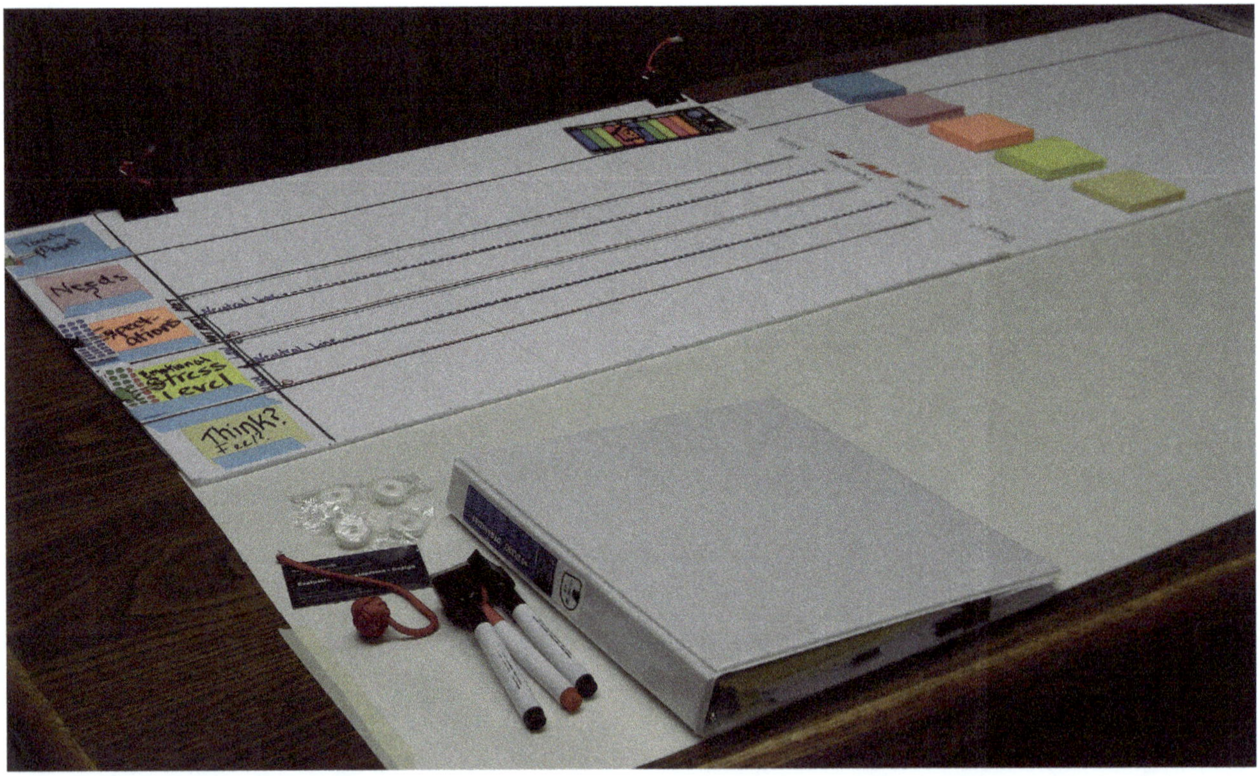

Figure 13-8. The domestic violence journey was mapped with a preformatted grid, colored pens, and sticky notes.

Summary

The collaborative mapping process remains the same whether your aim is to optimize a checkout flow or understand a former extremist's path to atonement. You bring diverse perspectives together, visualize the experience, identify opportunities, and then design interventions.

What changes is what you're optimizing for. In commercial contexts, success might be measured in conversion rates, customer satisfaction scores, or revenue growth. These are all important metrics that help businesses thrive.

In social contexts, success looks different. Metrics might include "fewer women experience violence," "more formers find purpose in fighting hate," and "products are designed for longevity rather than planned obsolescence."

This is the power of mapping for social good. The collaborative techniques that help businesses understand customers also help us design for human prosperity. We can map any human experience to create positive change. The question then becomes: what human experience will you map next?

Further Reading

Attila Bujdosó, ed., Social Design Cookbook *(2019)*

Bujdosó, with contributions from leading designers across Europe, presents 18 international case studies of successful social cooperative formats—from Restaurant Day to OpenStreetMap—that have been replicated across communities and contexts. The book introduces the Social Design Canvas, a framework for analyzing and designing new forms of social collaboration, with stories of social change positioning it as the social and nonprofit equivalent of the business model canvas.

Sandra M. Bates, The Social Innovation Imperative *(2012)*

This book applies corporate innovation best practices to social sector challenges. Bates presents a systematic framework for addressing complex social problems through three phases: Investigate (define challenge, understand needs, examine opportunities), Innovate (devise solution, develop business model), and Implement (ensure diffusion and shared value). She draws on jobs to be done and outcome-driven innovation methodologies to help nonprofits, NGOs, and social enterprises create measurable impact.

Lesley-Ann Noel and Stanford d.school, Design Social Change *(2023)*

This book centers personal identity and lived experience as starting points for design work. Noel presents design strategies grounded in equity and social justice that move from self-reflection outward to community and systemic change. The approach asks designers to examine their own social positions and histories as tools for creating meaningful impact.

Jeanne Liedtka, Randy Salzman, and Daisy Azer, Design Thinking for the Greater Good *(2017)*

This book examines design thinking applications in social sector organizations through a set of case studies. The authors document how government agencies and nonprofits use collaborative creativity to address complex problems in healthcare, education, transportation, and social services. They argue for democratizing innovation beyond specialist designers to include multiple stakeholders in the process.

Social Design Canvas

Objective	Map the essential elements of a social cooperative project to identify opportunities for broader participation and greater impact
Time	60–90 minutes for initial canvas completion
Participants	Project organizers, potential contributors, stakeholders, and beneficiaries—works best with 4–8 people representing diverse perspectives
Materials	Social Design Canvas template, sticky notes

The Social Design Canvas, created by Attila Bujdosó (Head of Research, Innovation Center of Moholy-Nagy University of Art and Design, Budapest), maps the key ingredients of social cooperative processes on a single page (**Figure 13-9**). It helps teams design projects that engage contributors effectively and create lasting social impact.

How it works:

1. Frame the context. Begin by describing the social cooperative project you're designing. What shared goal are you working toward? What problem are you solving? Write this at the top of the canvas.
2. List contributors. Who are the people who will actively contribute to this effort? Group them by their respective contributions and levels of involvement. Remember: typically, a great number of participants contribute little, and a few contribute the most. Use sticky notes to map out different contributor types. Be specific: "local residents," "subject matter experts," "volunteer organizers." Focus on the top three to six most significant contributors.
3. Map contributions. What will contributors provide? This might include physical goods, digital content, money, or voluntarily offered time, skills, knowledge, and expertise. Include help in organizing and communication. For each contributor type, identify their specific contributions, using one sticky note per type. Focus on the substantial contributions to avoid too much detail.
4. Understand motivations. Why would participants get involved and contribute? What do they expect, perceive, or experience as value or benefit from participation? People are more likely to engage in social processes that are directed toward a shared, positive goal or that promise a tangible output. Map the motivations for each contributor group.

5. Define enablers. What makes participation easy and affordable for key participants? What drives down the cost of participation? What removes obstacles and reduces risks? When participation is simple and low-cost, it lowers the time, effort, and experience required, making it accessible to more people.
6. Establish rules. What are the explicit operational rules that define the framework of your cooperative process? Who, where, when, and how can people contribute? What happens to participants' contributions? The best rules are simple, specific, and nonrestrictive, combining freedom with structure. Think of rules as creative constraints: they delimit and guide efforts while offering space for creativity.
7. Select tools. What tools help realize the project? What facilitates communication among involved parties? What supports both participation and organizing efforts? Start with who (contributors) would do what (contribute) and why (motivation) for success. Then figure out how tools can support this. Tools matter only as long as they motivate, enable, or facilitate the involvement of specific contributors.
8. Review and refine. Step back and look at the complete canvas. Are there gaps? Do the motivations align with what you're asking people to contribute? Are the enablers strong enough? Do the rules support or hinder participation? Refine the canvas based on group discussion.

Learn more:

Attila Bujdosó, "Social Design Canvas," *Medium* (2018)

Example:

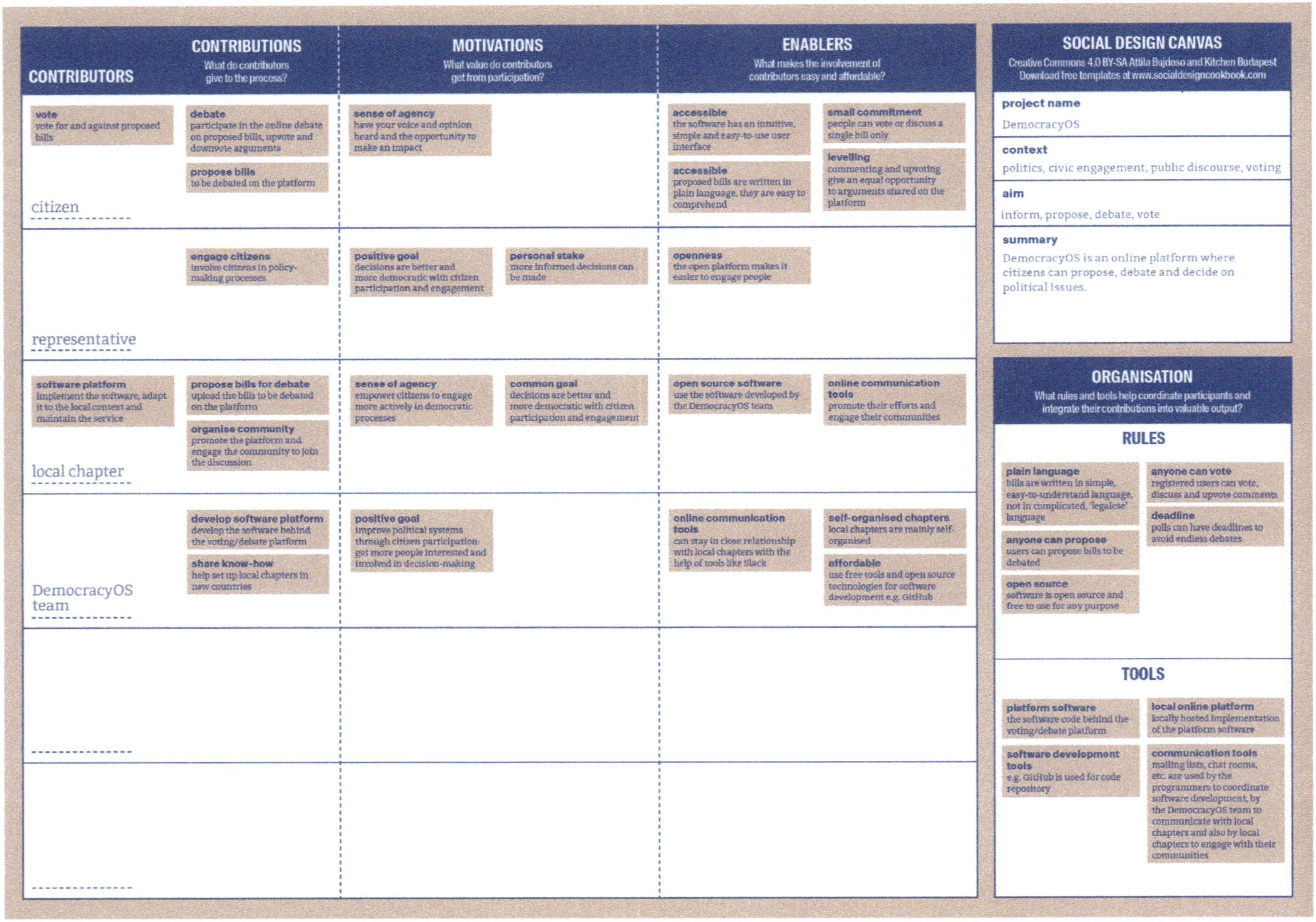

FIGURE 13-9. The Social Design Canvas by Attila Bujdosó helps teams work through the various aspects of social change, in this case for DemocracyOS, an online platform where citizens can meet and debate.

Diagram and Image Credits

Figure 13-1: Photos of a workshop mapping the experience of formers, by Jim Kalbach

Figure 13-2: Experience map of a former's journey from guilt to atonement, by Jim Kalbach

Figure 13-3: Experience diagram for buying a new home by Sofia Hussain, used with permission

Figure 13-4: Ecosystem diagram by Chris Risdon and Patrick Quattlebaum from their book *Orchestrating Experiences*, used with permission

Figure 13-5: Experience map of the veteran experience by Sarah Brooks, used with permission

Figure 13-6: Consumer Intervention Map by Matt Sinclair, used with permission

Figure 13-7: Photo of Consumer Intervention Map from a workshop by Matt Sinclair, used with permission

Figure 13-8: Photo of mapping domestic violence by Karen Woods, used with permission

Figure 13-9: Social Design Canvas by Attila Bujdosó (*bujatt.com*), Head of Research, Innovation Center of Moholy-Nagy University of Art and Design, Budapest, used with permission

Creating the right experiences and then integrating around them to solve a job is critical for competitive advantage.

—Clayton Christensen et al., *Competing Against Luck*

IN THIS CHAPTER

- JTBD fundamentals
- Ecosystem mapping for scoping
- Job mapping techniques
- Upgrading to experience maps
- Collaborative methods for job mapping

CHAPTER 14

Mapping and Jobs to Be Done

Scott Cook, founder of the renowned tax software company Intuit, once made a surprising claim about his company's biggest competitor. It wasn't a rival to the TurboTax software package, or the accountants offering clients tax preparation services.

It was the pencil.

"The pencil is a tough and resilient substitute," Cook noted. "Yet the entire industry had overlooked it."*

Think about it: when you're preparing a tax return, making a calculation on a pad of paper is natural and hard to improve on. Cook realized his software didn't just need to outperform other tax packages. It needed to be more effective than and as simple to use as a pencil.

This insight reframes everything. You don't compete against products in your category as defined by industry analysts. You compete against anything that gets the job done from the user's point of view.

Jobs to be done (JTBD) provides a powerful lens for customer-centered mapping by shifting focus from solutions to the objectives customers aim to accomplish. When you map jobs from their perspective rather than journeys with your product, you can see opportunities others miss.

This chapter briefly outlines the JTBD methodology, without attempting to teach the full framework. JTBD is substantial and requires practice to apply well. For a deeper exploration, please see the references provided throughout.

Our focus here will be on where JTBD and mapping intersect—specifically, ecosystem modeling and job mapping. Ecosystem modeling is about understanding your JTBD landscape to select a strategic focus. Job mapping is about creating a chronological foundation that can be evolved into detailed experience maps. The chapter concludes with methods for turning insights into action.

What Is Jobs to Be Done?

Every day you pursue dozens of objectives: drink coffee to *get energy in the morning*, *commute to work*, *collaborate with colleagues* to *finish a project*, or *plan long-term financial well-being* with an advisor. You might eat chocolate to *reward yourself after a hard day* or *prepare a meal* to enjoy with family.

These are all jobs to be done.

The JTBD approach offers a unique framework for understanding the people you serve. Instead of looking at demographic and psychographic factors, JTBD

* Reported in W. Chan Kim & Renée Mauborgne, "Creating New Market Space," *Harvard Business Review* (1999).

focuses on what people seek to achieve in a given circumstance. People don't hire products because of the demographic they belong to; they employ solutions to get a job done.

In *The Jobs To Be Done Playbook*, I developed a definition of a job that's simple and broad to cover variations in the field: *the process of reaching an objective under given circumstances*. The use of "objective" is deliberate. It reflects the functional nature of a job. I avoid "goals" to prevent associations with broader aspirations like "life goals."

My definition also includes an explicit mention of process, highlighting the dynamic nature of getting a job done. An objective isn't just about an endpoint: it's something that unfolds over time, with a beginning, middle, and end. And there is an experience around that process that we can describe and map.

Three Critical Distinctions

It took me a while to really grasp JTBD, so don't be discouraged if you're still working it out. Broadly speaking, JTBD is a customer discovery approach that makes careful distinctions about the individuals you serve. Understanding the three aspects described here will help you make the mindset shift needed to practice the framework.

Remove all references to technology and solutions

JTBD offers a structured language with rules of grammar and formulation. This language explicitly expunges any references to technology, solutions, methods, companies, or brands—including yours.

This point of view flips the script: rather than seeing people as consumers of your offering, you view them as objective-driven individuals with choices. By foregoing the assumption that people need your product, you open up new opportunities for human-centered growth.

> *Rather than seeing people as consumers of your offering, you view them as objective-driven individuals with choices.*

To achieve this perspective shift, the rules of formulation have a very intentional forcing function. Language matters in JTBD, and how you record insights from the field—typically as discrete statements—is critical to the method.

This may sound easy, but it's harder than you think. I see it all the time in workshops: people forget that common things like sending an email or making a phone call are solutions. In JTBD, we don't mention them. Similarly, Agile and design thinking are methods. It takes practice to remove all these things from your language.

One key advantage of being technology-agnostic is longevity. While solutions and technology trends change rapidly, jobs are stable over time. If a job statement was valid for people decades ago, it will likely remain valid in the future.

Find the right level of altitude

Before you begin with JTBD, answer the question: where do you want to innovate? There is no right or wrong answer. You can innovate your entire corporate strategy or focus on solving a very narrowly defined problem. For instance, a power tool manufacturer might investigate a broad job like *renovate a home* or a narrower one like *mount an object to a wall*. Innovation can happen at any level. It's up to you to determine where you'll investigate.

There is a hierarchy of goals to consider anytime you're dealing with human behavior. I recommend mapping it out before you get started to define your scope. I typically begin with three levels:

- *Aspirations* reflect the ultimate, ideal change of state. It's something the individual desires to become.
- The *focus job* is a broad objective that defines where you'll innovate. Target jobs should be formulated as a process with a beginning, middle, and end—the "done" state.
- *Job steps* break the process into a sequence of discrete actions to get the job done.

You can navigate this hierarchy by asking "Why?" to move up toward aspirations or "How?" to move down toward steps. You may find another level or two depending on the domain you're working in; "Key Elements of the JTBD Framework" on page 314 provides a more complete list.

FIGURE 14-1 shows how the basic levels of the hierarchy work together. A simple triangle can help distinguish the different levels of jobs you may be exploring for a given job performer. The JTBD experts at Vendbridge, a Swiss-based strategy consultancy, detail how to explore the hierarchies inherent in JTBD, writing:

> [The JTBD hierarchy] helps to reframe almost instantly the perspective from an internal, often technology-driven view to an external user view. This change in perspective is especially valuable for companies in a transformation process, where more customer-centricity is a major cultural and organizational goal.*

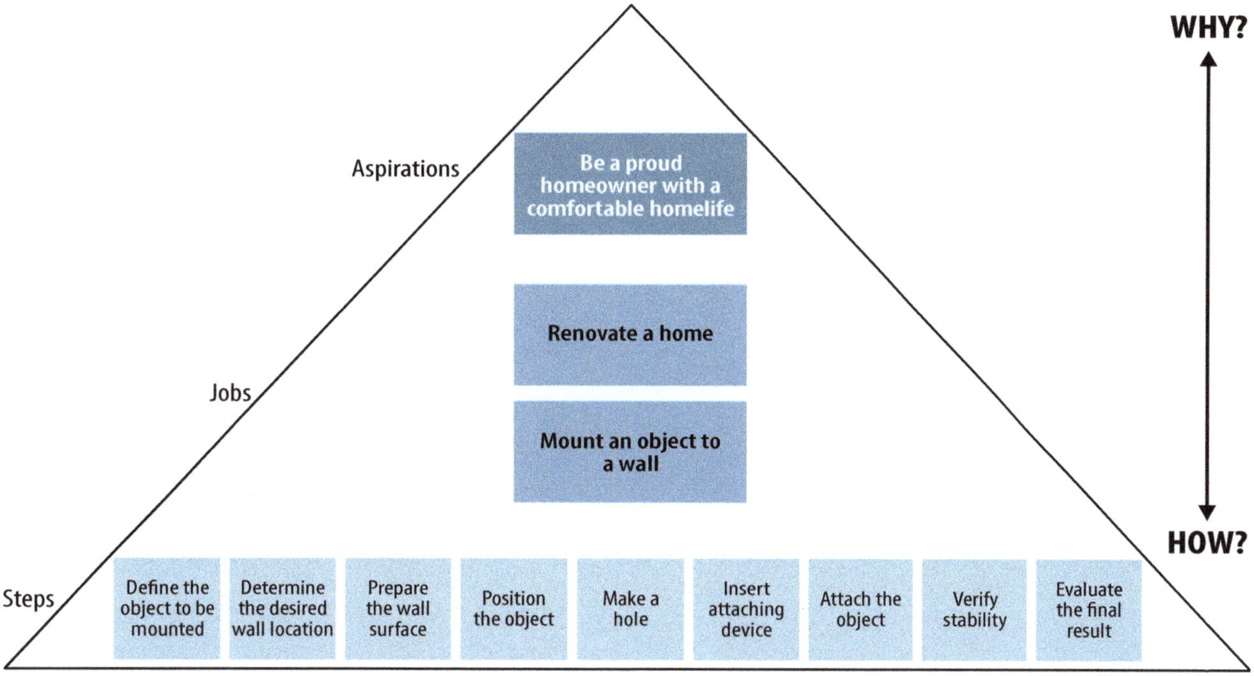

FIGURE 14-1. This example shows a basic hierarchy around home renovations, ranging from broader aspirations to smaller steps.

* Vendbridge, "The Jobs-to-be-Done Hierarchy" (2018)

Be cautious of starting too high in the pyramid; aspirations are often influenced by factors outside your control and can be fulfilled in endless ways. As a rule of thumb, start with a job you can reasonably affect.

Separate job steps from success criteria

Think of JTBD as a filter with different buckets of information that you distill from in-depth research. One of the key aspects of JTBD is the clear separation of the functional steps required to complete a job from the success criteria, the measures performers use to determine how well the job was executed.

Consider a family planning a vacation. During your research, you might hear someone say: "I want to find cheap airfares quickly." That's perfectly natural language you'll find in the field.

But in JTBD terms, we carefully deconstruct key elements—namely, the steps and success criteria. The steps show the sequence of actions that must be taken to complete the job, and the success criteria show how well it got done. So, from that single phrase, we write three separate pieces of information as discrete statements:

1. Job step = Find airfares
2. Success = Minimize the cost of airfares
3. Success = Minimize the time it takes to find airfares

At the end of your investigation, you may have as many as 20 discrete job steps and 50 or more success criteria. Once you've identified all of these, you can compare them to determine which steps and success criteria are most important—or in other words, which present the biggest pain points to the job performer.

Getting this right takes practice, but in the end, JTBD points to hidden opportunities that can ultimately help you outperform the competition.

Key Elements of the JTBD Framework

The JTBD Hypothesis Canvas helps you explore the primary categories of the framework and make the critical distinctions needed for analysis.

Each element has its own rules for formulation. For consistency and clarity, we record each of these elements with a predetermined format, indicated after its definition:

Playing field

What area or domain are you in? Often this corresponds to your industry, but it may differ depending on your area of concern. For instance, in the real estate industry, you might indicate the playing field as "buying and selling homes."

Focus job

Where do you want to create value? The focus job becomes your focus for innovation—the unit of analysis for all subsequent research. It should be a functional job that has a beginning, middle, and end whose description begins with a first-person action verb (e.g., *shop for a new home*).

Job performer

Who are you creating value for? The job performer goes hand in hand with the focus job. For instance, in the field of buying and selling homes there are buyers, sellers, agents, mortgage brokers, and more to consider. The job performer should be indicated as a single group of people. Don't use *and* or *or.*

Related jobs

What else is the job performer striving to get done? Related jobs are at the same level as the focus job, but you're not choosing to investigate them right now. Typically, you'll identify three to six primary related jobs. Like the focus job, related jobs begin with a first-person action verb. For example, apart from *shop for a new home*, a buyer also has to *move homes* and *update address information*, among other things.

Aspirations

Who does the job performer aspire to become by doing the job? Aspirations are what we call "be" goals. These aren't functional tasks; they're identity-level outcomes the job performer is pursuing by doing the job.

Job steps

What is the process of getting the job done? The job steps describe how the job performer gets a job done. They form a chronological sequence reflected in a job map. As sub-jobs to the focus job, job steps are functional jobs that begin with a first-person action verb.

Success criteria

How does the job performer measure success? If the focus job and job steps describe the process, the success criteria describe how well the job is done. Success criteria begin with a verb that shows a change in a downward direction, such as "minimize," "reduce," or "decrease."

Emotions

How does the job performer feel while doing the job? Job performers experience a range of emotions as they try to get a job done. These often drive decision making as much as success criteria. Emotions begin with "feel" or "avoid feeling."

Circumstances

What are the contexts and factors that make a difference? At first, JTBD looks for patterns common to all job performers. But in reality, people get the job done in different ways depending on their context. Circumstances explain those variations. These often include time, place, or manner, but they can be anything that changes how the job is approached. Circumstances begin with the word "whether" to indicate that a condition applies.

Figure 14-2 shows a partially completed canvas for *home buyers* (job performer) who are trying to *shop for a new home* (focus job).

Think of the canvas as a collaboration tool to get clarity and agreement within the team and to explore the JTBD space. It's not designed for collection or detailed analysis. Use a spreadsheet or digital whiteboard for that. The canvas also doesn't replace research—you can't brainstorm your way to the answer.

The JTBD Hypothesis Canvas helps frame your focus, but in complex domains with many potential job performers and jobs, you first need to see the full landscape. The processes outlined in the following sections provide that view.

> *JTBD points to hidden opportunities that can ultimately help you outperform the competition.*

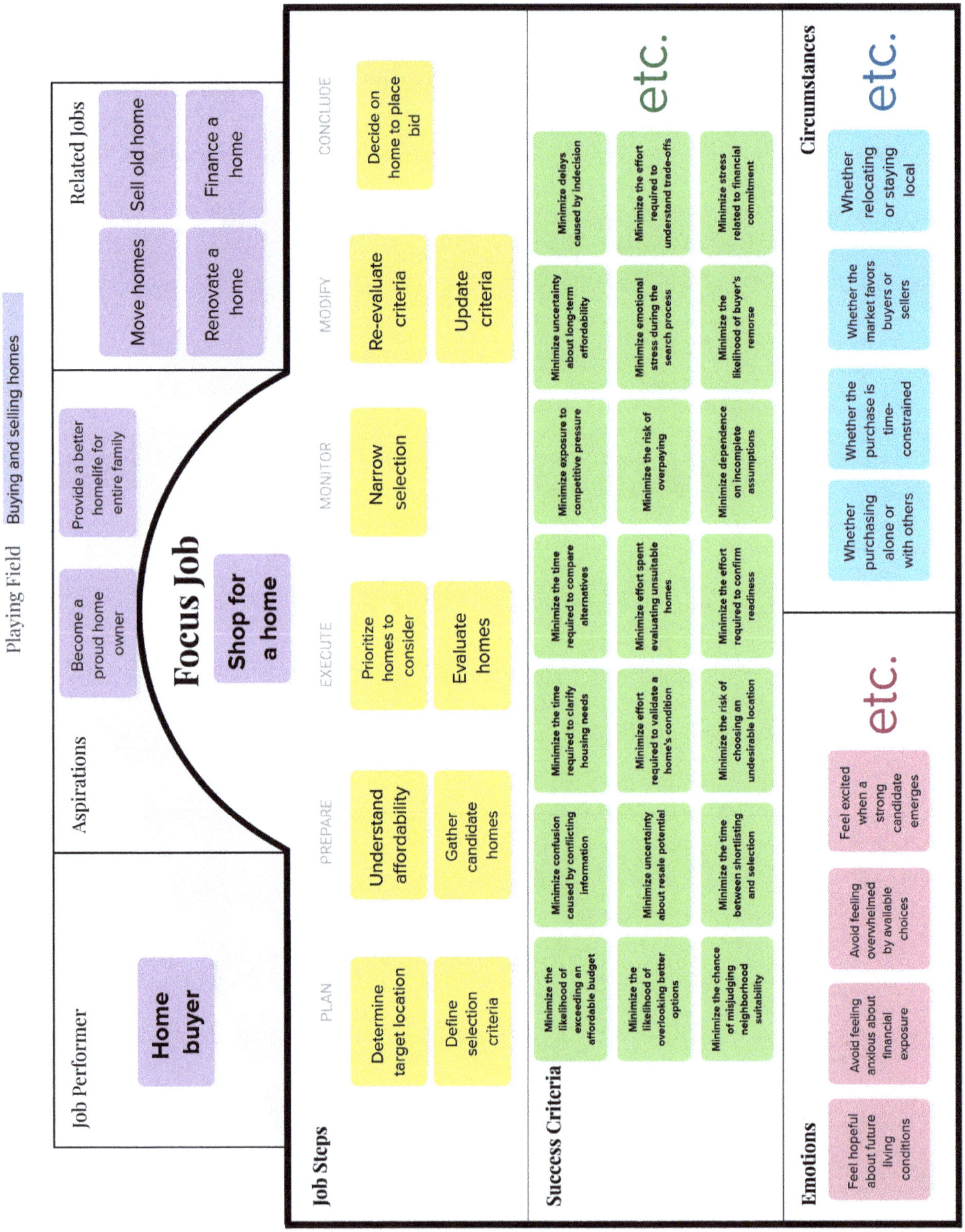

FIGURE 14-2. The JTBD Hypothesis Canvas helps sort insights into the different categories of information within the framework.

A Core Process for JTBD Analysis

A JTBD analysis has three main phases (**Figure 14-3**): Frame (scope your landscape as a hypothesis), Discover (conduct research to uncover jobs and analyze them), and SPIN (activate insights by integrating them into workflows).

Let's examine each of these in more detail.

Frame

The Frame phase determines who you want to create value for (the job performer) and what you want to help them accomplish (the focus job). This shouldn't be done in isolation—you'll need to gather qualitative information from customers via switch interviews or the techniques outlined in Chapter 6.* Also, be sure to consider organizational goals. What's strategically important right now? How do you want to grow? The ideal focus job sits at the intersection of what matters to job performers and what matters to your organization.

In complex domains with multiple potential job performers and focus jobs, use the JTBD Hypothesis Canvas iteratively to explore options. Map out your ecosystem of possibilities, if needed. The choice of focus is strategic—it depends on where you can create the most value while advancing your business goals. The two key activities in the Frame phase are as follows:

- *Scope:* Determine who you want to create value for and what you want to help them accomplish. Identify the job performer and focus job through team discussion and conversations with customers.
- *Hypothesize:* Create initial assumptions about job steps, success criteria, emotions, and circumstances. Use universal frameworks, colleague input, and AI tools to develop a hypothesis job map (discussed in "Create a Hypothesis Job Map" on page 334) before conducting full research.

Discover

The Discover phase is where you investigate how job performers actually get work done. JTBD is a *problem space* methodology that tells you which customer problem to solve, not what solutions to create. Through in-depth interviews and observation, you uncover the real process, pain points, and variations.

AI tools can accelerate this work, but they have limitations: you must validate accuracy and watch for gaps in completeness. AI doesn't replace talking to actual job performers—even a handful of conversations gives you essential context for interpreting results. The two techniques are complementary, with interviews grounding

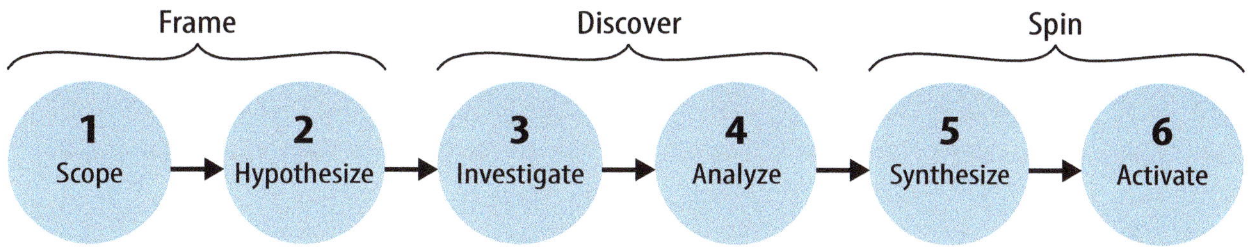

Figure 14-3. The core process for JTBD comprises three phases and six stages.

* Swtich interviews were pioneered by Bob Moesta. See Chris Spiek and Bob Moesta, *Jobs-to-be-Done: The Handbook* (2014).

you in reality and AI helping you scale and synthesize. These are the key activities in the Discover phase:

- ***Investigate:*** Conduct in-depth interviews with job performers about how they get the job done. Use the hypothesis job map as a conversation guide to uncover the process, pain points, and variations.
- ***Analyze:*** Extract and categorize insights from interview data into the framework buckets (job steps, success criteria, emotions, circumstances). Prioritize to identify the biggest opportunities and unmet needs. A powerful technique with the JTBD framework is to quantify the success criteria with a survey.

SPIN

Discovery alone doesn't change organizations. Even well-researched findings fall flat without effective activation. The SPIN phase, developed by Vendbridge as part of Customer Focused Innovation, provides a structured approach to making insights compelling and actionable.* The acronym stands for the following:

- ***Storytell:*** Transform findings into narratives connected to real experiences.
- ***Position:*** Frame insights in terms that resonate with stakeholder priorities.
- ***Integrate:*** Weave insights into existing workflows and decision structures.
- ***Normalize:*** Make insight-driven thinking part of the organizational culture.

SPIN isn't about manipulation, it's about collaboration. Rather than presenting findings as nonnegotiable facts, work with stakeholders to cocreate understanding and buy-in. The key activities in this phase are as follows:

- ***Synthesize:*** Create artifacts like job stories that make insights portable and actionable for downstream teams. Translate research findings into formats that don't require deep JTBD knowledge to understand.
- ***Activate:*** Integrate insights into workflows and decision making through collaborative activities. Use techniques that help teams act on customer needs rather than just read about them.

Ecosystem Mapping and JTBD

Jobs to be done don't come in neat little packages. You have to hunt to uncover them, and explore them. Often, there's an ecosystem of jobs in any given playing field or area of interest. This is particularly true for existing businesses. The first step is to sort out your JTBD landscape. Here, an ecosystem map helps.

The approach presented here draws on the work of Cornelius Rachieru, managing partner at Ampli2de (*ampli2de.com*), a strategic design consultancy in Canada. His process builds an ecosystem map from the bottom up in three layers.

Step 1: Research and Sketching

Start with exploratory research into the problem space. This includes user interviews, competitive research in your industry vertical, and market research.

Begin diagramming with primary and secondary actors in your domain. These might include various entities, but a job performer for JTBD will always be a person.

A low-fidelity sketch is recommended at first. From there, you can iterate as you go. **Figure 14-4** shows a rough sketch of the first layer of actors for an ecosystem map around the topic of "retirement."

* Vendbridge, "Customer-Focused Innovation: Jobs-to-be-Done in Action" (2020)

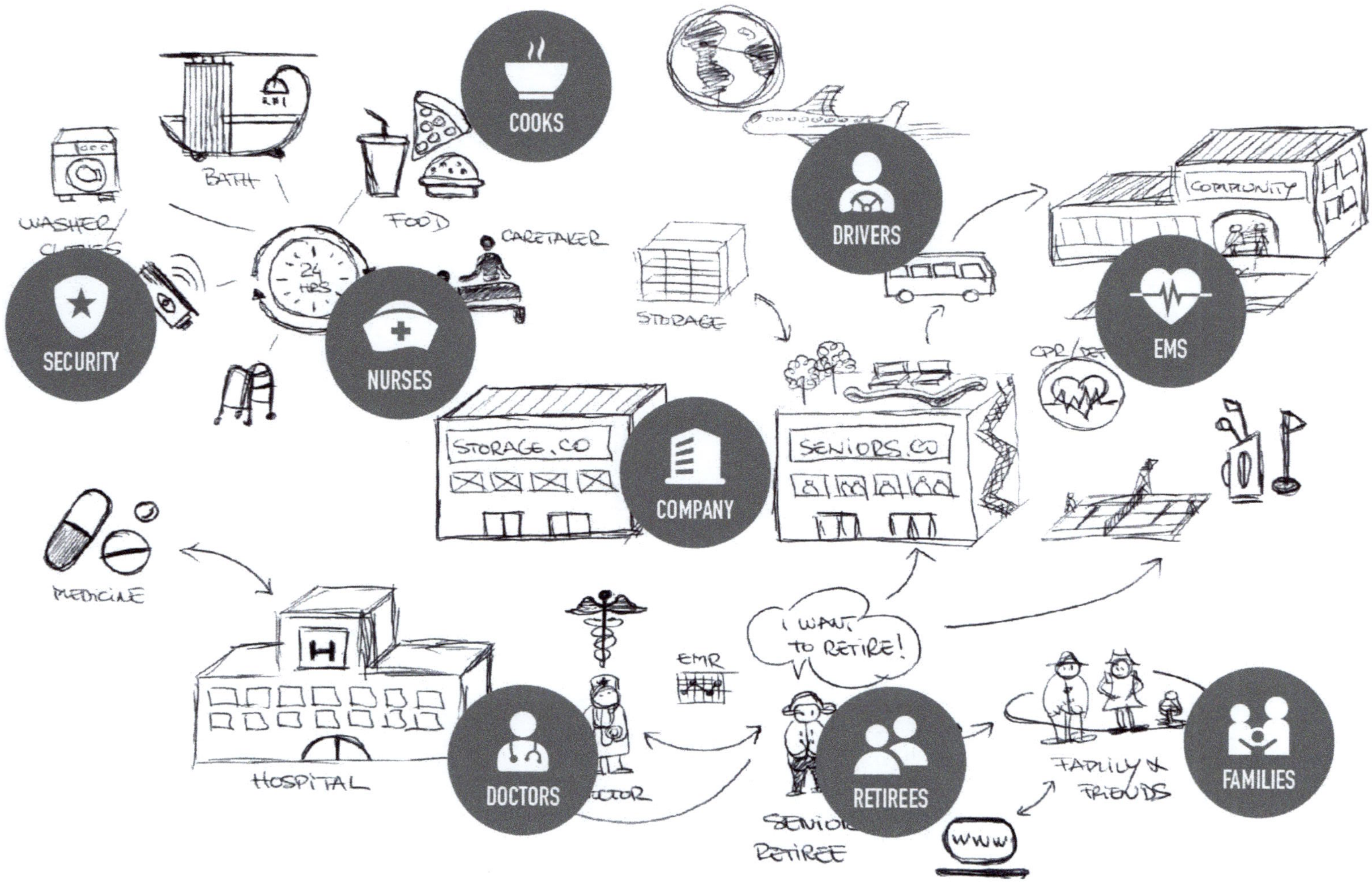

FIGURE 14-4. Ecosystem modeling begins with research and a rough sketch of the entities and actors in the system.

Step 2: Synthesis and Visual Exploration

Next, consider the jobs to be done of each actor type. Map their objectives to service clusters in the model, as shown in **Figure 14-5**.

You can then expand the area of focus by identifying additional clusters. These secondary services are important for understanding the ecosystem as a whole. **Figure 14-6** shows how further clusters of concern were investigated beyond the core model in the example used here. Notice that in this iteration of the model, "retirees" have moved to the center, making that group the primary focus of attention.

Service ecosystems are expansive. At some point, you need to draw a boundary around what to consider for future initiatives, strategically limiting the scope of subsequent efforts.

Step 3: Refinement and Focus

The last step is choosing the data lenses to consider. These should be the factors that are most relevant to the business and the situation. In the retirement example, the focus was on gaps in service provision (shown in red in **Figure 14-7**) and cost to acquire the service (in green). Service providers can then decide which gaps to fill based on the cost of delivery.

The JTBD methodology analyzes the unmet needs of one job performer and one focus job at a time. Your selection is therefore a strategic one. An ecosystem map of people in your domain, along with their key objectives, helps you prioritize as a team.

Scoping the focus job is one of the trickiest—and most important—steps in applying the JTBD framework. There's no absolute right or wrong answer. It's less about finding "the right job" and more about making a smart, informed decision about where to focus next.

The key is to step back and consider a range of areas in the organization: business strategy, enterprise risk management, human resources, diversity, product, and more. Visualizing your playing field in an ecosystem diagram helps your team consider various aspects at once and prioritize collectively.

Determining which job to start with involves two critical lines of inquiry, reflected in **Figure 14-8**:

1. ***What's important to the people you serve?*** You want to identify jobs that truly matter to customers. These should be meaningful, durable, and independent of solutions.
2. ***What's important to the business right now?*** JTBD creates the most value when it's linked to real strategic needs. The focus job should help answer questions your organization is already asking: Where should we invest? What should we build next?

The overlap between these two lines of inquiry is your sweet spot. Bring your ecosystem map into a short working session with your team to prioritize together—it gives you a shared foundation for the strategic conversations ahead. After defining your job performer and focus job, you can follow the steps outlined in "A Core Process for JTBD Analysis" on page 317.

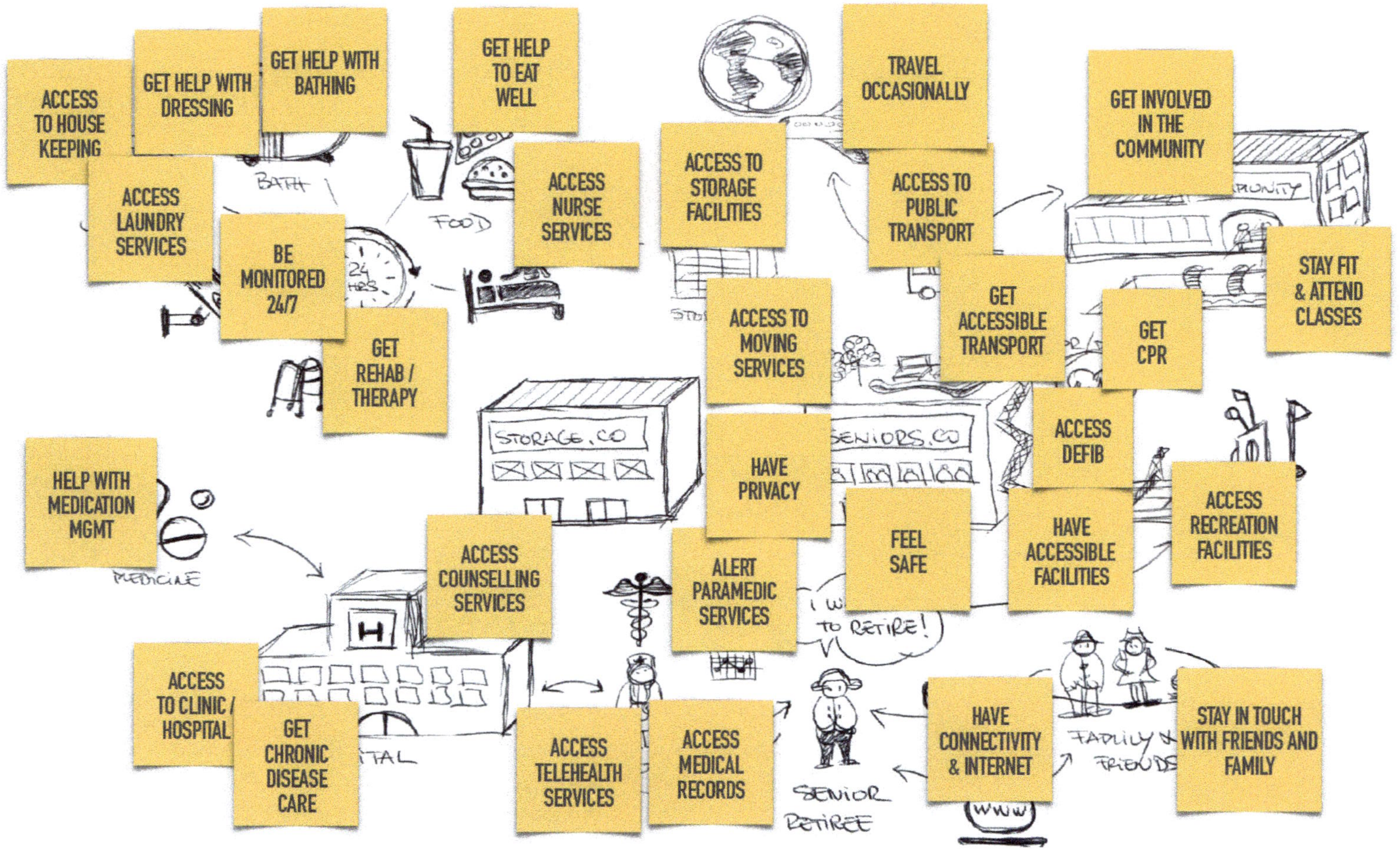

FIGURE 14-5. Overlay the jobs to be done on the model, clustering them into logical groupings.

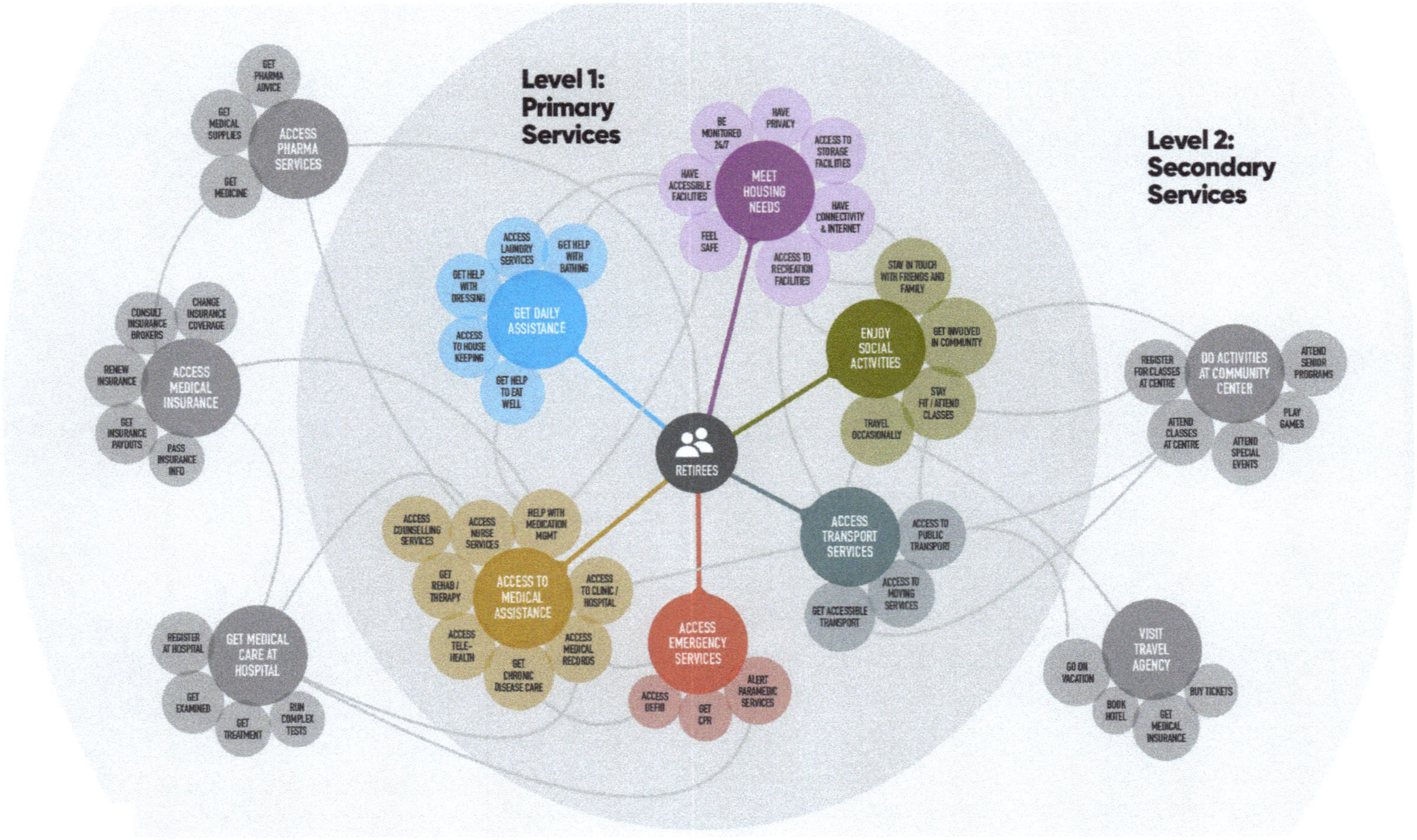

FIGURE 14-6. Extend the ecosystem model to include secondary service clusters.

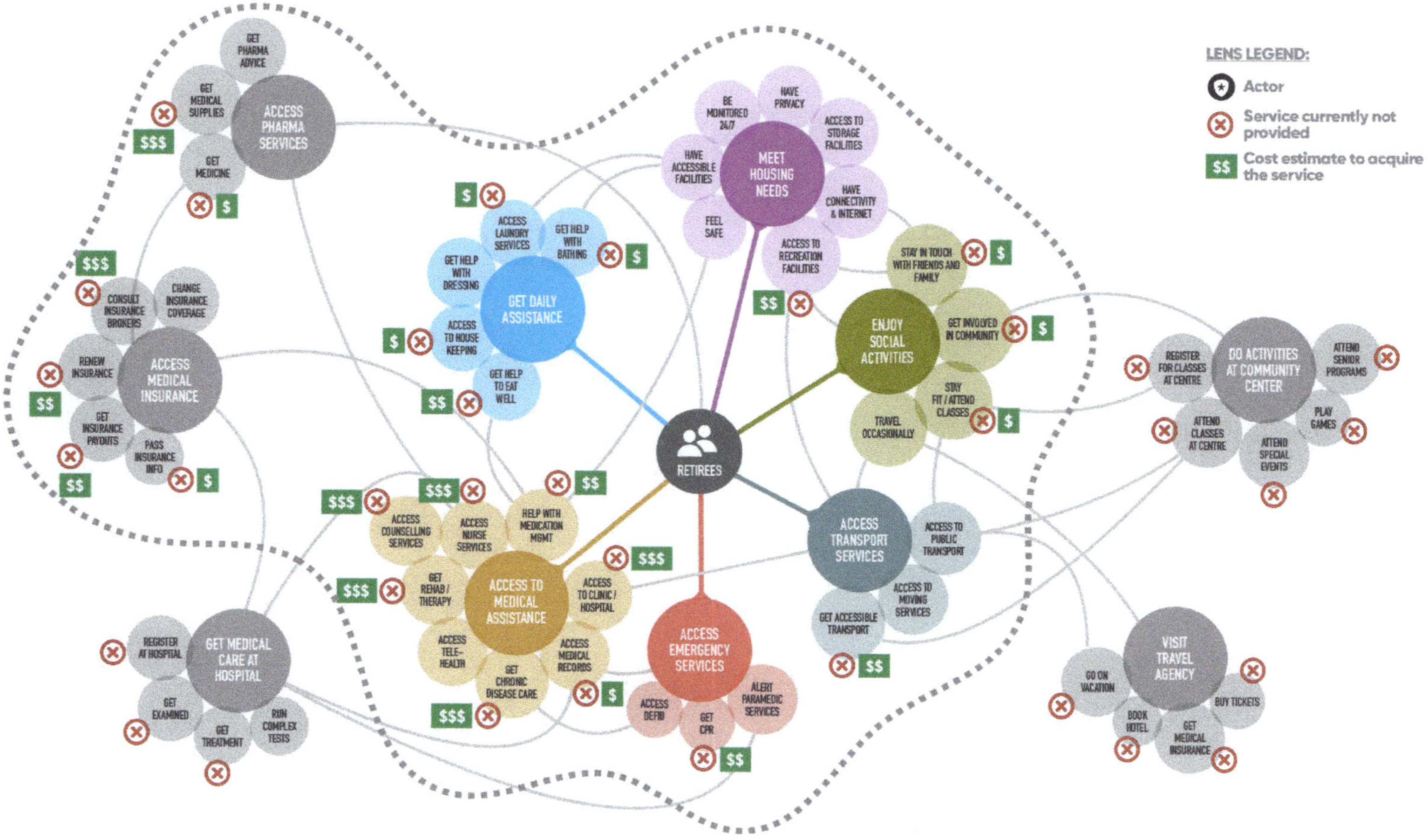

FIGURE 14-7. Overlays of strategic factors to consider provide insight into opportunities and points of intervention.

Figure 14-8. Selecting a focus job involves answering two fundamental questions and finding the overlap between them.

Job Mapping

One of the most powerful things you can do in JTBD practice is map out the customer's job step-by-step. This might seem simple: customers have a job, perform specific actions, and complete it. But when you actually sit down to capture those steps—using their language and stripping away all references to tools or solutions—something remarkable happens. Messy interview notes suddenly become structured. Overlooked details come to the surface. Teams that used to argue about features start aligning around the flow of real customer work.

Think of a job map like a trail guide. If you're hiking, you don't care what brand of boots someone is wearing. You care about the route, the switchbacks, the obstacles, and the summit. A job map works the same way. It shows the path customers follow to get from "not done" to "done." Once you can see the full path, it's much easier to spot where they stumble, where they waste time, or where they need a better way forward.

Job mapping was pioneered by Lance Bettencourt and Tony Ulwick. In their 2008 article "The Customer-Centered Innovation Map," they wrote:

> By deconstructing a job from beginning to end, a company gains a complete view of all the points at which a customer might desire more help from a product or service—namely, at each step in the job. With a job map in hand, a company can analyze the biggest drawbacks of the products and services customers currently use.*

Since then, job mapping has become a core practice within the JTBD methodology.

A job map is not a customer journey map. Though both are chronological, they differ in several important ways:

A job map is solution-free.

Job maps don't include tool actions like "click the button" or "open the app." Instead, you capture what the customer is trying to accomplish, regardless of the solution they use. As a result, a job map does not describe the journey to buy, receive, set up, use, upgrade, clean, or maintain a product.

* Lance Bettencourt and Anthony W. Ulwick, "The Customer-Centered Innovation Map," *Harvard Business Review* (2008)

A job map is timeless and universal.

A good job map works whether someone is using the latest technology, a manual workaround, or no tool at all. Their focus on human intent rather than the tools or processes used to act on it gives job maps longevity far greater than many other types of maps—they often remain valid for years, or even decades.

A job map is a summary, not a workflow.

A job map captures the key steps in a process (commonly around 12–20) that must be completed to get the job done. It doesn't detail every micro-task, nor does it include things like emotions, thoughts, or pain points. You're looking for the essential moments that move the job forward, not documenting every action.

To make this concrete, imagine you're mapping the job of washing clothes. If you ask 10 people to describe it, you'll get 10 different answers: one person starts with "I sort by color," another says "I check for stains," while someone else jumps to "I grab detergent." Without a map, these sound like disconnected anecdotes. But when you put them into a job map, the pattern emerges:

1. Gather dirty clothes
2. Sort and inspect items
3. Load machine and add detergent
4. Run wash cycle
5. Transfer to dryer or hang to dry
6. Fold and put away

Notice what's missing: there's no mention of "pressing the start button" or "selecting cycle type." Those are tool-specific actions. The map stays at the level of work the customer is trying to get done.

Universal Structures

No matter the domain, jobs tend to follow a common rhythm. People start by clarifying what they're trying to accomplish. Then they gather what they need, get set up, do the thing, check on it, fix what goes wrong, and close it out.

Tony Ulwick first identified these common patterns and codified them into a universal job map structure.* I've adapted his approach into six stages here. These labels aren't mandatory—feel free to use language that's more appropriate for your area of interest. You may also skip a stage or break one into two. Think of the universal structure as a mnemonic device to help you think through the beginning, middle, and end of a job:

1. ***Plan:*** Clarify goals, constraints, or resources before beginning. Common job step verbs: plan, select, determine.
2. ***Prepare:*** Set up the environment or organize materials. Common job step verbs: set up, organize, examine.
3. ***Execute:*** Carry out the core transformation from "not done" to "done." Common job step verbs: perform, transact, administer.
4. ***Monitor:*** Assess progress and results as the work happens. Common job step verbs: verify, track, check.
5. ***Modify:*** Adjust, correct, or resolve when something goes wrong. Common job step verbs: update, adjust, maintain, resolve.
6. ***Conclude:*** Wrap up and reset for next time. Common job step verbs: store, finish, close.

* Anthony W. Ulwick, *JTBD: Theory to Practice* (2016). The terms Job Map and Universal Job Map are trademarked by Tony Ulwick and Strategyn; see *https://strategyn.com/jobs-to-be-done/customer-centered-innovation-map*.

These steps form a checklist, not a prescription. They help you remember to cover the entire process from beginning to end. When interviewing customers, the richest opportunities often hide outside the Execute step. Everyone pays attention to the "doing," but key frustrations, delays, and unmet needs often lurk in the "before" (Plan, Prepare) and the "after" (Monitor, Modify, Conclude).

Job Map Formats

Practitioners use different formats for job maps depending on their needs. Each has its place.

The *list format* presents steps as a simple numbered or bulleted sequence (**Figure 14-9**). This works well for quick reference and initial drafts. It's easy to create and share, but it doesn't show structure or enable collaborative analysis.

A *sequence diagram* arranges steps in rows (**Figure 14-10**). This provides more visual structure than a list and can even show decision points or loops, if needed. It also fits neatly onto a slide. This format is more conducive to presentation and discussion, but it doesn't lend itself to hands-on team interaction.

A *column arrangement* organizes steps under stage headers (**Figure 14-11**). This is the format I recommend for most situations: a map with 6–8 stage headers (columns) and 12–20 total steps distributed across those stages. It's scannable. People can quickly see the progression from beginning to end without following arrows or getting lost in boxes.

PLAYING FIELD: Buying and selling homes	**PLAN**	Initiate session engagement
JOB PERFORMER: Home buyer		Define the problem
FOCUS JOB: Shop for a new home		Determine session parameters
	PREPARE	Create a session flow
		Build materials
		Customize session for client
	SET UP	Execute on session logistics
		Set expectations
		Get materials ready for use
	INITIATE	Orient participants
		Warm up
	COLLABORATE	Engage in activities
		Visualize concepts
	SYNTHESIZE	Find patterns
		Make conclusions
		Assess outcomes
	CONCLUDE	Evaluate success of the session
		Set next steps
	FOLLOW UP	Package outcomes
		Share with others

Figure 14-9. It's possible to represent a job map as a simple list of stages and steps, e.g., in a spreadsheet.

The column format creates natural units for team discussion and evaluation. In collaborative sessions, you can assess the map stage by stage, asking, "How well do we support customers here?" The columns become zones of conversation. See "Find the Hotspots with Job Mapping" on page 336 for more details.

Researching Job Maps

A valid job map isn't based on guesswork. It requires listening to how actual job performers get work done, then distilling what you hear into a structured sequence.

Start by conducting interviews where you ask people to walk through the last time they performed the job. Use simple language and frame it in a way they will relate to: "Tell me the last time you *shopped for a new*

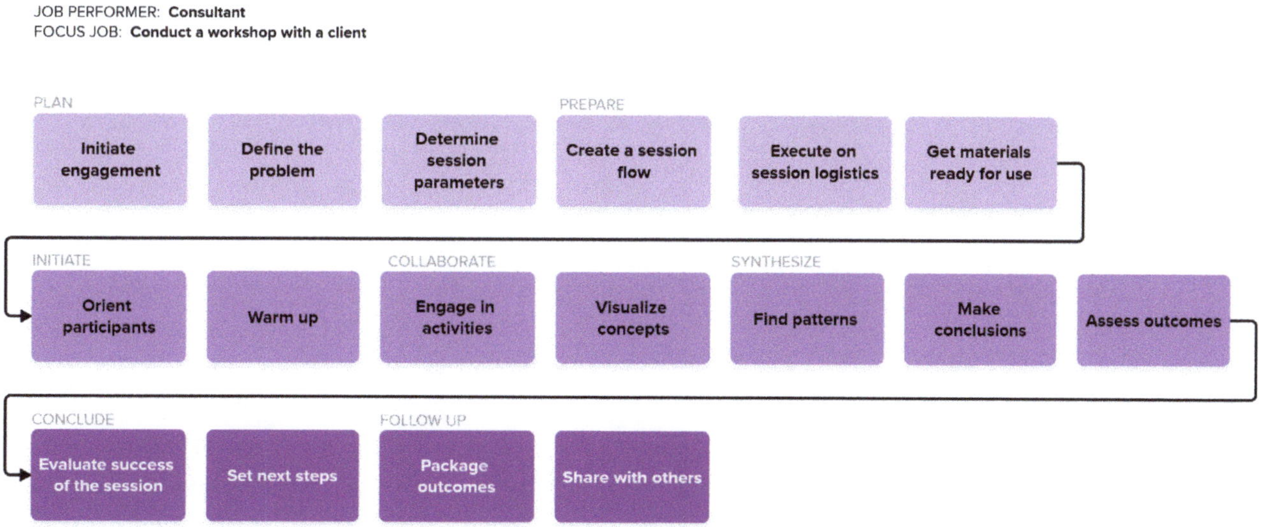

Figure 14-10. Arranging stages and steps as a sequence of boxes adds visual structure.

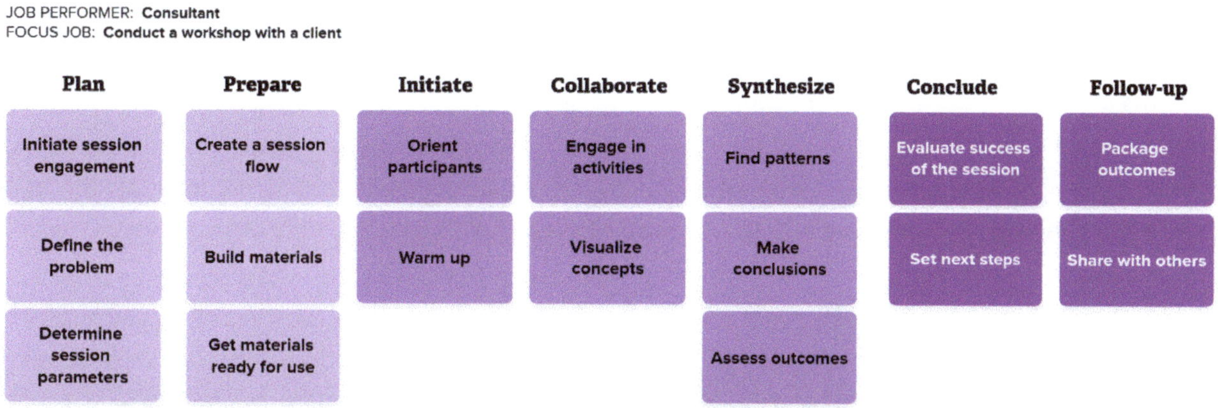

Figure 14-11. A column format with stages and steps is well suited for interactivity—discussions and exercises—during a working session with a team.

home." Listen for action verbs. Note when they say "First I…," "Then I…," and "After that…" These signal the chronological flow.

Don't expect people to describe the job steps in perfect order. They'll jump around. They might start in the middle, backtrack to mention something they forgot, or skip steps they consider obvious. Your aim is to capture everything, then organize it later.

After several interviews, you'll have pages of notes filled with actions, workarounds, checks, and frustrations. Distill these into job steps:

1. ***Look for patterns.*** When multiple people mention the same action or checkpoint, that's a step. When they use different words but describe the same intent, consolidate them into one step.
2. ***Translate to solution-free language.*** If someone says, "I open the app and click Search," translate that to "Identify potential options." If they say, "I check my email for the confirmation," translate it to "Verify completion."
3. ***Keep it at the right altitude.*** You're not documenting every micro-action. You're capturing the essential steps that move the job forward. Aim for 12–20 steps total.
4. ***Test the sequence.*** Put the steps in chronological order and walk through them. Does this flow make sense? Are there gaps? Does it have a clear beginning, middle, and end?
5. ***Validate with job performers.*** Show the draft map to people you interviewed. Ask: "Does this capture how you get the job done? What's missing? What's out of order?" Use their feedback to refine the map.

The result is a job map grounded in real data but expressed in straightforward, universal language that anyone can understand.

Job maps aren't just outputs of research, though—they're tools for conducting it. Once you have a hypothesis job map, you can use it as a conversation guide and validation instrument:

As an interview guide

Walk through the map step-by-step with job performers. Ask them to describe how they accomplish each step. Probe for what's hard, what takes time, what causes anxiety. The map keeps the conversation focused and ensures you cover the full process.

For identifying pain points

Point to each stage and ask, "Where do you struggle most? Which steps cause the most frustration?" The visual representation helps people pinpoint specific moments rather than giving vague answers about "the whole process" being hard.

To explore circumstances

Show job performers the map and ask, "Do any of these steps change depending on your situation?" You'll learn about the contextual factors that create different paths through the job. Maybe solo performers skip certain steps. Maybe tight deadlines force shortcuts. These circumstances become important elements in your full JTBD analysis.

Using the map this way turns research into a dialogue. You're not just extracting information—you're cocreating understanding with job performers. The map gives them something concrete to react to, making the conversation more productive than open-ended "tell me about your process" prompts.

Job maps show the functional process for accomplishing a goal. This focus makes them stable and durable. The steps in a job map don't change much over time or across different solutions. That's why they serve as such a strong foundation for innovation and for upgrading into richer experience maps, as we'll explore next.

From Job Map to Experience Map

A job map gives you the chronological spine of what customers are trying to accomplish. But it leaves out emotional aspects, thoughts, pain points, and contextual details. That's by design: job maps focus on the process.

Once you have a validated job map, you can upgrade it into a full experience map by layering additional dimensions onto that functional flow. This transforms a simple process view into a richer picture of the customer's lived experience.

Most experience maps are solution-centric. They map the journey with your product or service. By starting with a job map, you ensure a human-centric foundation. The job map keeps you honest about what customers are actually trying to accomplish, independent of how you currently serve them.

The process is fairly straightforward.

Step 1: Start with a Validated Job Map

Follow the steps outlined earlier to create and validate your job map. First, define the job performer and focus job to frame your inquiry. Conduct interviews to understand the process. Then, distill well-formed job steps and arrange them chronologically. Finally, validate the resulting job map with job performers to ensure that it accurately reflects how they achieve their objective.

Figure 14-12 shows a job map for a conference organizer (job performer) trying to run a conference (focus job). It's broken into three simple sections: beginning, middle, and end.

The job map alone can guide internal conversations. Use it to identify pain points as a team, or overlay your current projects to see which parts of the job you're addressing and which you're ignoring.

Run a Conference

Beginning			*Middle*			*End*	
DEFINE	**PROMOTE**	**PREPARE**	**OPEN**	**PRESENT**	**ENGAGE**	**CONCLUDE**	**FOLLOW UP**
Determine purpose	Create promotional materials	Track registrations	Open the event	Support speakers	Interact with participants	Conclude the event	Communicate with participants
Define event parameters	Reach audience	Respond to inquiries	Verify attendance	Maintain agenda	Assess satisfaction	Assess results	Update materials
Secure speakers	Monitor promotion performance	Confirm logistics	Initiate proceedings	Oversee sessions	Adjust execution	Determine next steps	Identify improvements

Figure 14-12. This simple job map shows the process of how a conference organizer (job performer) runs a conference (focus job).

Step 2: Create Additional Swim Lanes and Add More Information Types

With the job map as your foundation, add more rows (swim lanes) below it to capture other aspects of the experience. Typically, you'll want to layer three to five additional dimensions onto the job map, such as these:

Thoughts and questions
: What's going through the customer's mind at each step? What uncertainties do they face?

Emotions
: How do they feel as they move through the process? Where are the highs and lows?

Pain points
: Where do they struggle? What causes frustration, anxiety, or delays?

Opportunities
: Based on the struggles and emotions, where can you create value?

Draw from your research to populate these swim lanes. Look for patterns across interviews and highlight those moments.

The job steps (columns) from your job map create natural zones for organizing these experiential elements. Each column becomes a conversation space where you can see the full picture: what customers are trying to do, how they feel about it, and where they need help.

Refer back to Chapter 7 (in particular **Figure 7-11**) for more about aligning swim lanes of information in a rough table format.

Step 3: Refine the Diagram

Once you have the functional flow and experiential layers, refine the diagram for your audience. Clean up the language, adjust the layout for clarity, and add visual elements that make the story clear. The result is a human-centered experience map grounded in jobs, not solutions.

Figure 14-13 shows an example of an experience map based on a simple job map. This diagram was created in collaboration with Hennie Farrow and explored in further detail in Chapter 7.

The top row lists actions based on the job steps. Note that they've been slightly modified in the transition from the job map to the experience map. That's OK—you still get the benefit of starting with a neutral job map.

Below that, additional swim lanes capture thoughts, emotions, pain points, and goals at each stage. This particular example is a graphically refined diagram suitable for presentation, but remember: the power of a diagram lies in the information it shows and the story it tells, not the visual appeal.

Starting to build an experience map from a job map ensures that you're not anchoring it to your solution, or any technology for that matter. This results in something very different from a customer journey map, which shows the interaction of a customer and a provider, or a service blueprint, which details a service encounter with a provider.

This approach also reveals opportunities you might otherwise miss. When you look beyond the parts of the experience where customers interact with you, you can spot where they struggle before they ever reach you, or where they need help after your interaction ends.

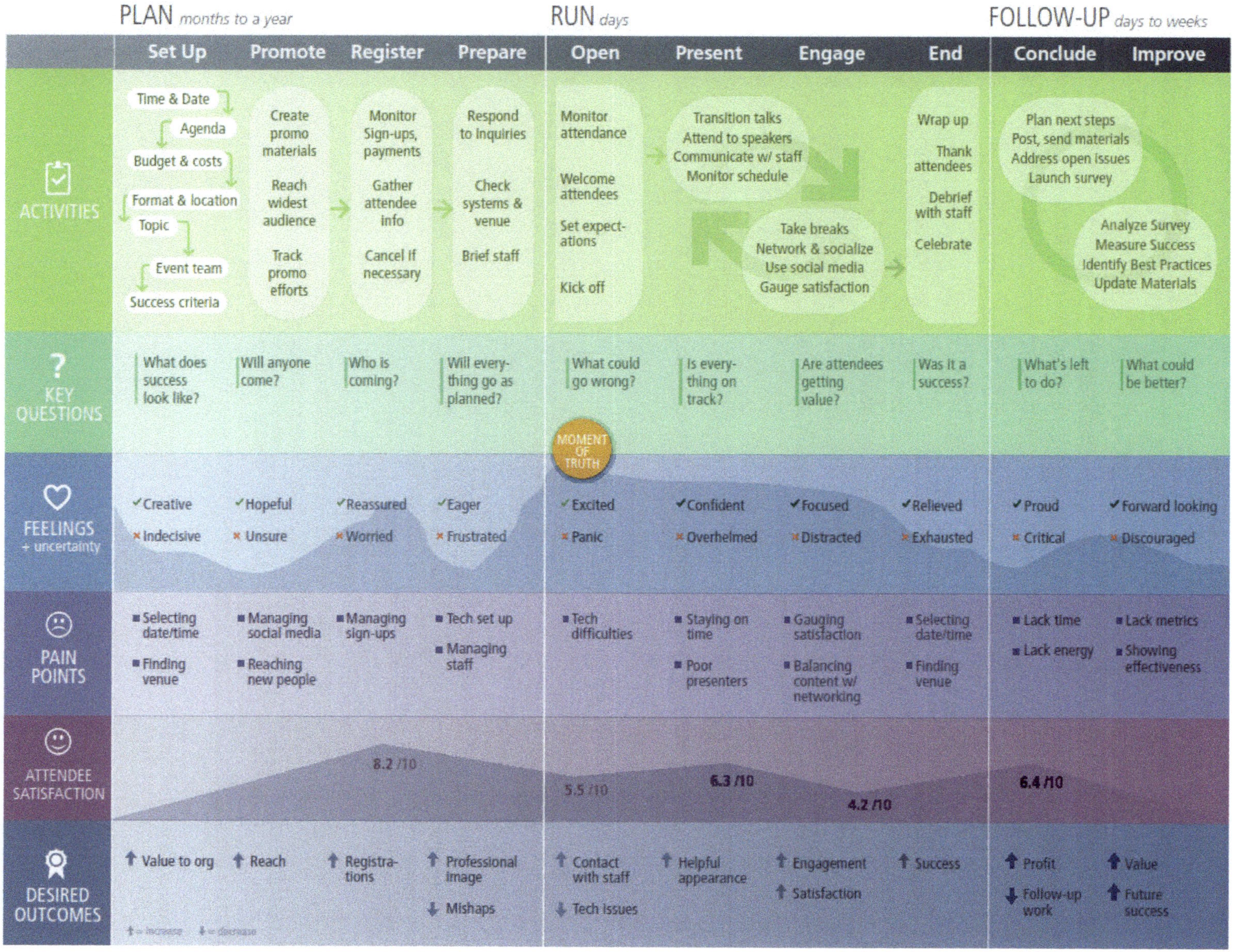

FIGURE 14-13. This experience map shows how to run a conference from the organizer's point of view.

Summary

Jobs to be done theory reframes how you see value creation. Instead of starting with solutions, demographics, or features, you start with the objectives people are trying to accomplish. This shift in perspective reveals opportunities others miss, like Intuit's leader realizing the company was competing against pencils, not just other tax software.

JTBD is a substantial framework. Applying it well requires dedicated practice with its structured language and careful distinctions. This chapter outlined the fundamentals but focused on where mapping strengthens JTBD work.

Ecosystem mapping helps you scope your JTBD landscape when facing multiple potential job performers and focus jobs. It creates a stable reference for strategic decisions about where to innovate.

Job mapping captures the chronological process customers follow to get work done—solution-free, universal, and durable. The column format enables collaborative assessment and upgrades into full experience maps by layering emotions, thoughts, and pain points onto the functional spine.

The methods described at the end of this chapter activate JTBD insights through collaborative mapping. Creating a hypothesis job map together builds shared understanding before research. Finding the hotspots turns a completed map into a conversation about where to focus investment.

Job maps have lasting relevance. Unlike volatile metrics, they represent an investment that pays dividends for years. Use them as foundations for innovation, team alignment, and experience design.

Further Reading

Jim Kalbach, The JTBD Playbook *(2020)*

This book provides practical techniques for applying jobs to be done theory across organizations. It bridges JTBD methodology with user experience practice, offering job mapping, outcome identification, and job stories as tools for turning customer insight into action. Updates to this approach are reflected in this chapter and can be found on the JTBD Toolkit website (*www.jtbdtoolkit.com*).

Anthony W. Ulwick, JTBD: Theory to Practice *(2016)*

This book details Ulwick's Outcome-Driven Innovation process, which applies jobs to be done theory to create predictable innovation with an 86% success rate. Ulwick explains how to define markets around jobs rather than products, identify outcome-based customer needs, and segment customers by unmet needs. The book provides practical frameworks and templates for implementing JTBD methodology, emphasizing that innovation can be managed as a science rather than left to chance.

Lance Bettencourt and Anthony W. Ulwick, "The Customer-Centered Innovation Map," Harvard Business Review *(2008)*

This article introduces job mapping as a foundational methodology in JTBD theory. The authors break customer jobs into eight universal steps. The approach differs from process mapping by focusing on what customers want to accomplish rather than what they currently do. This framework helps identify innovation opportunities at each step of a job.

W. Scott Burleson, The Jobs-to-be-Done Pyramid *(2025)*

This book expands JTBD theory by introducing a five-level framework addressing functional, emotional, and identity-based motivations. Burleson adds Identity Jobs as a distinct category, separating Role Identity from Image Identity. The framework makes social and emotional jobs more actionable by providing structure to understand customer motivations beyond functional tasks.

Diagram and Image Credits

Figure 14-2: JTBD Hypothesis Canvas created by Jim Kalbach and Elaine Matthias via the JTBD Toolkit (*www.jtbdtoolkit.com*), used with permission

Figures 14-4 through **14-7**: Examples of an ecosystem model in different stages created by Cornelius Rachieru, used with permission

Figure 14-13: Experience map created by Jim Kalbach and Hennie Farrow, used with permission

Create a Hypothesis Job Map

Objective	Collaboratively create a hypothesis job map to be updated and validated through research
Time	30–60 minutes
Participants	3–15 (cross-functional team members)
Materials	Whiteboard, sticky notes

In most cases, it's possible to create a hypothesis job map before doing any research (**Figure 14-14**). It's important to remember that this map is based on assumptions and must be validated during the Discover phase of the JTBD analysis process.

How it works:

1. Gather your sources. You can rely on three main sources of information to inform your hypothesis map:
   a. ***The universal job map structure.*** You can place the labels on the whiteboard as guidelines for possible stages to align to. Keep in mind that you can adjust them to suit your particular playing field.
   b. ***Job performers and subject matter experts (SMEs).*** Find a few people on your team or nearby who are job performers or know something about the focus job you're analyzing. Ask them to join the conversation and describe how they might get the job done.
   c. ***Generative AI tools.*** AI can generate decent job maps. You'll have to describe what a job map is and create a prompt for the output you'd like.
2. Identify the steps. Drawing on your sources, generate steps to include. Write each one on a sticky note, and arrange them in chronological order. Write "beginning," "middle," and "end" from left to right on the board to reflect a rough chronology.
3. Arrange the steps into stages. As a team, begin forming the job map. It may be messy at first, but that's OK; you'll have time to refine it after validation with customers. Deduplicate steps and refine their formulation as you go along.
4. Refine the chronology. Continue to work on the map and discuss the sequences and steps.

Learn more:

W. Scott Burleson, "Job Mapping 101," *Product HiveMind* (2025)

Example:

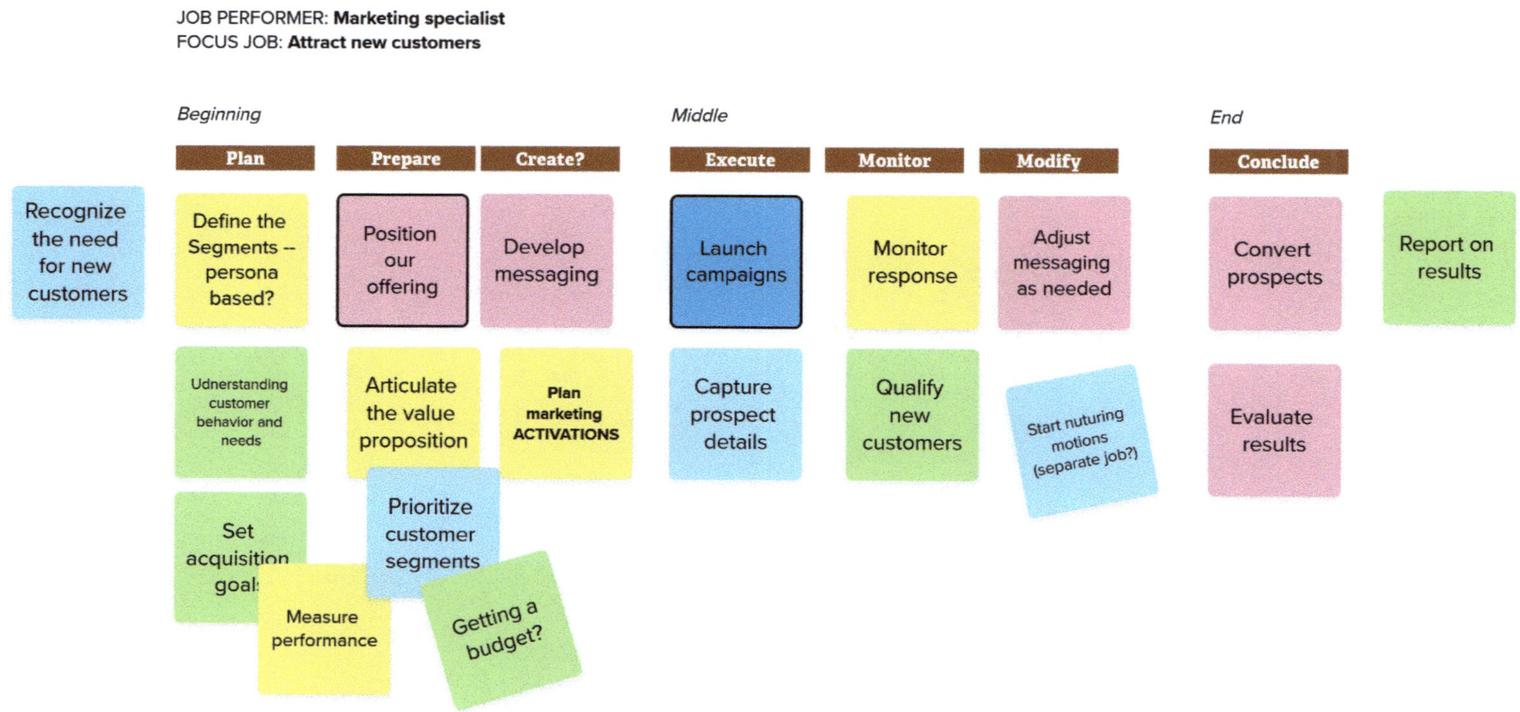

Figure 14-14. Creating a hypothesis job map as a team may feel messy at first, but you'll have time to refine it later. Use the universal job map structure, knowledge you already have access to, and AI to complete the chronology.

Find the Hotspots with Job Mapping

Objective	Collaboratively assess organizational strengths and weaknesses across the customer's job process
Time	90–150 minutes
Participants	3–15 (cross-functional team members)
Materials	Completed job map, sticky notes

A completed job map sitting in a slide deck doesn't change behavior. This activity turns your job map into something more than a research report. By bringing stakeholders together to grade how well you support customers at each stage, you'll build shared understanding of where to focus and create collective ownership of the insights.

How it works:

1. Walk through the job map together. Present the map, and review the stages and steps. Invite clarifying questions and give people an opportunity to fill in major gaps.
2. Grade each stage. For each stage of the job map (the columns), have every participant independently assign a letter grade (A, B, C, D, F) reflecting how well your organization currently supports customers at that stage:
   - A = We excel at supporting customers here.
   - B = We do well, but room for improvement exists.
   - C = We provide adequate support, but with notable gaps.
   - D = We struggle to support customers effectively at this stage.
   - F = We fail to adequately support customers here; major problems exist.
3. Discuss patterns and discrepancies. Display all the grades for each stage and discuss:
   - Where is there strong consensus?
   - Where are there major discrepancies or outliers?
   - What explains these differences in perspective?
4. Prioritize hotspots. Identify three to five *hotspots*—the stages where organizational performance has the biggest opportunity for improvement.
5. Align your roadmap to the hotspots. Review your current roadmap, backlog, or planned initiatives against the identified hotspots. Map each planned item to the job map stage it addresses. Then evaluate:
   - Are we investing in the hotspots we just identified?
   - Do we have initiatives planned for high-performing stages that could be deprioritized?
   - What gaps exist between our hotspots and our current plans?

Example:

A team working on software solutions for consultants (job performer) created a job map for "conducting a workshop with a client" (focus job). **Figure 14-15** shows the seven stages, represented by columns in the diagram.

After presenting the complete job map to a group of four people, we walked through each stage for understanding and clarity. Then, each person independently graded how well our current solution supported consultants at each stage.

When we revealed the grades, we found two stages where we performed particularly poorly. Despite different perspectives across the team, there was a strong consensus that these two stages needed attention. This alignment gave us clear direction for what to prioritize in the upcoming quarter.

Learn more:

Jim Kalbach, "Finding Opportunities with Job Maps," *Medium* (2021)

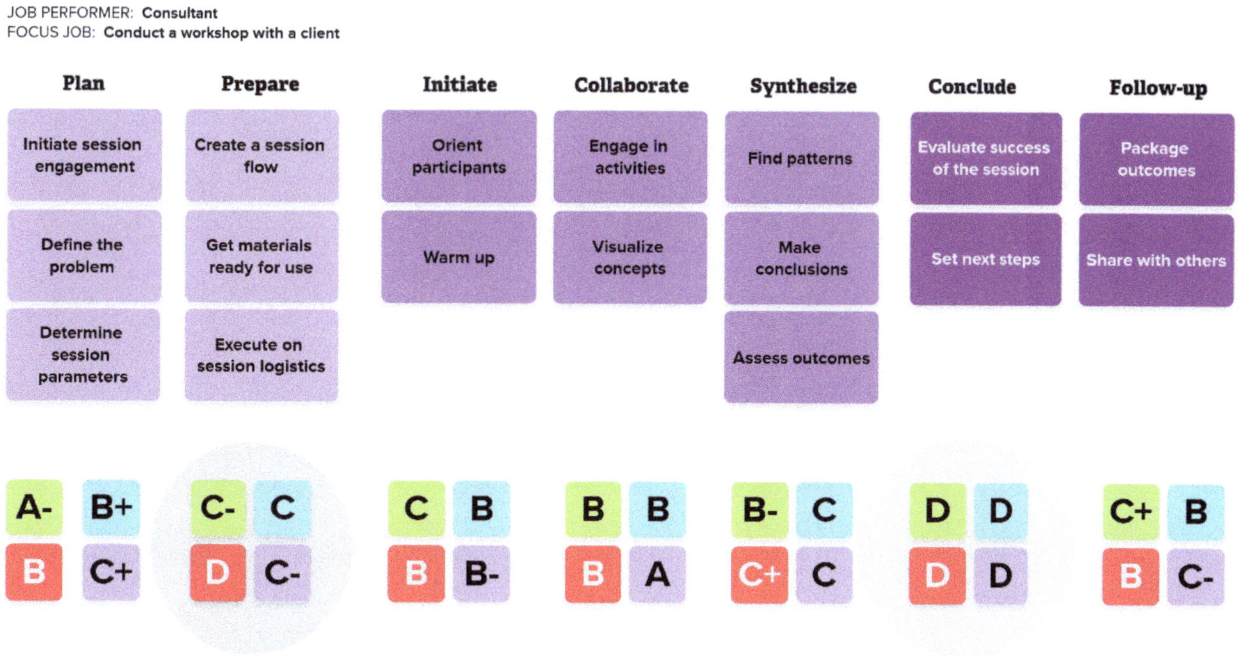

Figure 14-15. Comparing ratings for different stages in this job map enabled identification of hotspots to prioritize for improvement.

References

Aberdeen Group. "Customer Journey Mapping: Lead the Way to Advocacy" (2016)

Abilla, Pete. "Lean Service: Customer Value and Don't Waste the Customer's Time," *Six Sigma* (2010)

Adlin, Tamara, and John Pruitt. *The Essential Persona Lifecycle* (2010)

Alamir, Diego. "What Is a Customer Journey Map?," *HubSpot Service Blog* (2025)

Allen, James, Frederick F. Reichheld, Barney Hamilton, and Rob Markey. "Closing the Delivery Gap," *Bain & Company* (2005)

Angrave, Jerry. *The Journey Mapping Playbook* (2020)

Anthony, Scott, Mark Johnson, Joseph Sinfield, and Elizabeth Altman. *The Innovator's Guide to Growth* (2008)

Arena, Michael. *Adaptive Space* (2018)

Aricò, Marzia. "Organisations Don't Need More Journey Maps," *Design Mavericks* (2025)

Banfield, Richard, C. Todd Lombardo, and Trace Wax. *Design Sprint: A Practical Guidebook for Building Great Digital Products* (2015)

Bates, Sandra M. *The Social Innovation Imperative* (2012)

Battan, Mariano, and Jim Kalbach. *Collaborative Intelligence* (2022)

Berkman, Eric, and Steven Hoober. *Designing Mobile Interfaces* (2011)

Berkun, Scott. *The Myths of Innovation* (2007)

Berkun, Scott. *A Year Without Pants* (2013)

Bettencourt, Lance, and Anthony W. Ulwick. "The Customer-Centered Innovation Map," *Harvard Business Review* (2008)

Beyer, Hugh, and Karen Holtzblatt. *Contextual Design* (1997)

Bitner, Mary Jo, Amy Ostrom, and Felicia Morgan. "Service Blueprinting: A Practical Technique for Service Innovation" [working paper, Center for Leadership Services, Arizona State University] (2007)

Boag, Paul. "Functional Personas with AI: A Lean, Practical Workflow," *Smashing* (2025)

Bough, Victoria, Oliver Ehrlich, Harald Fanderl, and Robert Schiff. "Experience-Led Growth: A New Way to Create Value," *McKinsey* (2023)

Boysen, Mike. "Jobs to Be Done: Imperfection vs. Perfection," *Medium* (2023)

Brown, Dan. "The Delicate Art of Interviewing Stakeholders," *Medium* (2018)

Brown, David. "Supermodeler: Hugh Dubberly," *GAIN: AIGA Journal of Design for the Network Economy* (2001)

Brown, Leonie. "Customer Journey Mapping for Better Experiences," *McKinsey* (2025)

Brown, Maddie. "Personas Are Living Documents: Design Them to Evolve," *NN/g* (2023)

Brown, Tim. *Change by Design* (2009)

Bringhurst, Robert. *The Elements of Typographic Style*, 3rd ed. (2008)

Bujdosó, Attila. "Social Design Canvas," *Medium* (2018)

Bujdosó, Attila, ed. *Social Design Cookbook: Recipes for Social Cooperation* (2019)

Burleson, W. Scott. "Job Mapping 101," *Product HiveMind* (2025)

Burleson, W. Scott. *The Jobs-to-be-Done Pyramid*™ (2025)

Business Roundtable. "Purpose of a Corporation" (2019)

Canvanizer. "Create a New Customer Journey Canvas"

Capital One. "Marking over 10 Years of Experience Design at Capital One," *Capital One Tech* (2025)

Carlzon, Jan. *Moments of Truth* (1987)

Catmull, Ed. *Creativity, Inc.* (2014)

Charan, Ram. *What the Customer Wants You to Know* (2007)

Christensen, Clayton, Karen Dillon, Taddy Hall, and David S. Duncan. *Competing Against Luck* (2016)

Christensen, Clayton, and Michael Raynor. *The Innovator's Solution* (2003)

Clatworthy, Simon David. *The Experience-Centric Organization* (2019)

Colley, Russell. *Defining Advertising Goals for Measured Advertising Results* (1961)

Connor, Adam, and Aaron Irizarry. *Discussing Design: Improving Communication and Collaboration Through Critique* (2015)

Court, David, Dave Elzinga, Susan Mulder, and Ole Jørgen Vetvik. "The Consumer Decision Journey," *McKinsey Quarterly* (2009)

Curedale, Robert. *Mapping Methods 2: Step-by-Step Guide* (2018)

Dam, Rikke Friis, and Teo Yu Siang. "Introduction to the Essential Ideation Techniques," *IxDF* (2020)

Dam, Rikke Friis, and Teo Yu Siang. "Stakeholder Mapping: The Complete Guide to Stakeholder Maps," *IxDF* (2022)

D'Amore, Sebastian. "Boost Empathy Quickly with Proto-Personas," *Mural blog* (2016)

Danielson, David. "Transitional Volatility in Web Navigation," *IT & Society* (2003)

Dell'Acqua, Fabrizio, Edward McFowland III, Ethan Mollick, et al. *Navigating the Jagged Technological Frontier: Field Experimental Evidence of the Effects of AI on Knowledge Worker Productivity & Quality* [Harvard Business School working paper 24-013] (2023)

DiJulius, John. *The Customer Service Revolution* (2015)

Diller, Steve, Nathan Shedroff, and Darrel Rhea. *Making Meaning* (2008)

Downe, Louise. *Good Services: How to Design Services That Work* (2020)

Drucker, Peter. *The Practice of Management* (1954)

Edelman, David C. "Branding in the Digital Age: You're Spending Your Money in All the Wrong Places," *Harvard Business Review* (2010)

Edelman, David C., and Mark Abraham. "Customer Experience in the Age of AI," *Harvard Business Review* (2022)

Emplifi, *11 Key Things Consumers Expect from Their Brand Experiences Today* (2022)

Ensley, Michael. "Going Green," PureStone Partners (2009)

Flowers, Erika. "QuickBooks Billing Experience Overhaul" [case study] (2025)

Flowers, Erika, and Morgan Miller. *Your Guide to Blueprinting the Practical Way* (2023)

Forrester. "Forrester's 2024 US Customer Experience Index: Brands' CX Quality Is at an All-Time Low" [news release] (2024)

Forrester Consulting. "The Total Economic Impact™ of Microsoft Accessibility and Assistive Technologies for Education" [study commissioned by Microsoft] (2019)

Fullenwider, Kyla. "How Citizen-Centered Design Is Changing the Ways the Government Serves the People," *Fast Company* (2016)

Furr, Nathan, and Jeff Dyer. *The Innovator's Method* (2014)

Gallo, Carmine. "The Art of the Elevator Pitch," *Harvard Business Review* (2018)

Gartner. "Using Design Thinking to Improve the Employee Experience: A Conversation with Cox Enterprises" (2019)

Geertz, Clifford. "Thick Description: Toward an Interpretive Theory of Culture," in *The Interpretation of Cultures: Selected Essays* (1973)

Gerber, Ray. "How to Create a Customer Journey Map," *Qualtrics* (2024)

Gibbons, Sarah. "Dot Voting: A Simple Decision-Making & Prioritizing Technique in UX," *NN/g* (2019)

Gibbons, Sarah. "Journey Mapping 101," *NN/g* (2019)

Gibbons, Sarah. "Stakeholder Interviews 101," *NN/g* (2022)

Gibbons, Sarah. "Using Prioritization Matrices to Inform UX Decisions," *NN/g* (2018)

Gilbert, Phil. *Irresistible Change* (2025)

Gothelf, Jeff, and Josh Seiden. *Lean UX*, 2nd ed. (2017)

Gothelf, Jeff, and Josh Seiden. *Sense and Respond* (2017)

Gownder, J. P., and contributors. "Ground Your Workforce AI Strategy in Human Experience: Put Employees at the Center of Your AI Efforts to Drive Business Success," *Forrester* (2025)

Grandin, Temple. *Visual Thinking* (2022)

Gray, Dave, and Sunni Brown. *Gamestorming 2.0* (2025)

Grocki, Megan. "How to Create a Customer Journey Map," *UX Mastery* (2014)

Hall, Erika. *Just Enough Research*, 2nd ed. (2019)

Hamel, Gary, and Michele Zanini. *Humanocracy: Creating Organizations as Amazing as the People Inside Them* (2020)

Hanover Research. *The Power of Customer Journey Mapping* [whitepaper] (2024)

Hansen, Michele. *Deploy Empathy*, 2nd ed. (2025)

Heitner, Ami. "7 User Journey Map Examples to Inspire You in 2025" (2025)

Holtzblatt, Karen, Jessamyn Burns Wendell, and Shelley Wood. *Rapid Contextual Design* (2004)

Horowitz, Ben. *What You Do Is Who You Are* (2019)

Hubert, Lis, and Donna Lichaw. "Storymapping: A MacGyver Approach to Content Strategy, Part 1," *UXmatters* (2014)

Hussain, Sofia. "Designing Digital Strategies, Part 1: Cartography," *UX Booth* (2014)

Hussain, Sofia. "Designing Digital Strategies, Part 2: Connected User Experiences," *UX Booth* (2015)

Hutchens, David. *Story Dash* (2021)

IBM Enterprise Design Thinking. "To-Be Scenario Map" (2018)

IDEO. "Synthesis," in *The Field Guide to Human-Centered Design* (2015)

IHG. "IHG Green Engage System"

Interaction Design Foundation. "Brainwriting"

Interaction Design Foundation. "Customer Experience Mapping"

Interaction Design Foundation. "How to Improve Your UX Designs with Task Analysis" (2023)

InterContinental Hotels Group. "IHG to Reduce Environmental Impact" [press release] (2009)

Jenkins, John. *Marketing and Customer Behaviour* (1972)

Jones, Peter, and Kristel Van Ael. *Design Journeys Through Complex Systems: Practice Tools for Systemic Design* (2022)

Kalbach, Jim. "Alignment Diagrams," *Boxes and Arrows* (2011)

Kalbach, Jim. "Finding Opportunities with Job Maps," *Medium* (2021)

Kalbach, Jim. *The Jobs To Be Done Playbook* (2020)

Kalbach, Jim. "Strategy Blueprint Revised," *LinkedIn* (2024)

Kalbach, Jim, and Paul Kahn. "Locating Value with Alignment Diagrams," *Parsons Journal of Information Mapping* (2011)

Kaner, Sam. *Facilitator's Guide to Participatory Decision-Making*, 3rd ed. (2021)

Kaplan, Kate. "How to Run a Journey-Mapping Workshop: A Step-by-Step Case Study," *NN/g* (2020)

Kaplan, Robert, and David Norton. *Strategy Maps* (2004)

Kendrick, Alita. "Getting Started with Journey Mapping: 27 Tips from Practitioners," *NN/g* (2021)

Khokhra, Shrey. "Why Customer Journey Mapping Matters in 2025," *Userology* (2025)

Kihlström, Greg, Tara DeZao, Raymond Gerber, Eytan Hattem, Mark Smith, and Trent Rossini. *Customer Journey Management & Orchestration: For Marketers & CX Professionals* (2026)

Kim, W. Chan, and Renée Mauborgne. *Blue Ocean Strategy* (2005)

Kim, W. Chan, and Renée Mauborgne. "Creating New Market Space," *Harvard Business Review* (1999)

Knapp, Jake. *Sprint* (2016)

Kolko, Jon. "Dysfunctional Products Come from Dysfunctional Organizations," *Harvard Business Review* (2015)

Krause, Carsten. "Case Study: Starbucks' Success Elevating Customer Experience with Customer Journey Mapping," *CDO Times* (2023)

Lafley, A. G., and Roger Martin. *Playing to Win* (2013)

Laloux, Frederic. *Reinventing Organizations* (2014)

Lavidge, Robert, and Gary Steiner. "A Model for Predictive Measurements of Advertising Effectiveness," *Journal of Marketing* (1961)

Lazonick, William. "Profits Without Prosperity," *Harvard Business Review* (2014)

Leinwand, Paul, and Cesare Mainardi. *The Essential Advantage: How to Win with a Capabilities-Driven Strategy* (2010)

Levin, Michal. *Designing Multi-Device Experiences* (2014)

Levitt, Theodore. "Marketing Myopia," *Harvard Business Review* (1960)

Lichaw, Donna. *The User's Journey: Storymapping Products That People Love* (2016)

Liedtka, Jeanne, Jessica Eldridge, and Karen Hold. *Experiencing Design: The Innovator's Journey* (2021)

Liedtka, Jeanne, Randy Salzman, and Daisy Azer. *Design Thinking for the Greater Good* (2017)

Løvlie, Lavrans, Andy Polaine, and Ben Reason. *Service Design*, 2nd ed. (2025)

Lucier, Chuck. "Herb Kelleher: The Thought Leader Interview," *strategy+business* (2004)

LUMA Institute. "Concept Poster"

LUMA Institute. "Creative Matrix"

LUMA Institute. "Critique"

LUMA Institute. "Importance/Difficulty Matrix"

LUMA Institute. "Round Robin"

LUMA Institute. "Stakeholder Mapping"

LUMA Institute. "Storyboarding"

LUMA Institute. "Visualize the Vote"

Macauley, Arnold. "4 Steps to Experience-Led Growth," *Nansen Insights* (2025)

Manning, Harley, and Kerry Bodine. *Outside In: The Power of Putting Customers at the Center of Your Business* (2012)

Martin, Roger. "A Plan Is Not a Strategy," *Harvard Business Review* [video] (2022)

Maurya, Ash. *Running Lean*, 3rd ed. (2022)

May, Tim. "The Empathy Map: A Human-Centered Tool for Understanding How Your Audience Thinks," *XPLANE blog* (2021)

McKinsey & Company. "Customer Experience: New Capabilities, New Audiences, New Opportunities" (2023)

McMullin, Jess. "Searching for the Center of Design," *Boxes and Arrows* (2003)

Meadows, Donella H. *Thinking in Systems* (2008)

Merchant, Nilofer. *The New How: Creating Business Solutions Through Collaborative Strategy* (2010)

Meyer, Bernard. "What We Can Learn from Omnichannel Statistics for 2022," *Omnisend blog* (2022)

Morgan, Blake. "USAA's Proactive Approach to Major Life Events," *Forbes* (2023)

Morgan, Jacob. *The Employee Experience Advantage* (2017)

Mural. "Maximizing the ROI of Design Thinking" [webinar] (2020)

Nagel, Wolfram. *Multiscreen UX Design* (2015)

Noel, Lesley-Ann, and Stanford d.school. *Design Social Change* (2023)

Nordlund, Cassandra. "How to Create an Effective Customer Journey Map," *Gartner* (2019)

Openprise, *2025 State of RevOps Survey* (2025)

Oppelt, Joran Slane, and Geoffrey T. Nelson. *Facilitation: A Human-Centered Guide to the Art of Collaboration* (2023)

Osterwalder, Alexander, and Yves Pigneur. *Business Model Generation* (2011)

Ozenc, Kursat, and Glenn Fajardo. *Rituals for Virtual Meetings* (2021)

Parker, Priya. *The Art of Gathering* (2018)

Patton, Jeff. *User Story Mapping* (2014)

Pine, B. Joseph II, and James H. Gilmore. *The Experience Economy* (1999)

Polaine, Andy. "Blueprint+: Developing a Tool for Service Design," SDN Conference (2009)

Porter, Michael E. "What Is Strategy?" *Harvard Business Review* (1996)

Porter, Michael E., and Mark R. Kramer. "Creating Shared Value," *Harvard Business Review* (2011)

Portigal, Steve. *Interviewing Users*, 2nd ed. (2023)

Pruitt, John, and Tamara Adlin. *The Persona Lifecycle* (2006)

Pulido, Alfonso, Dorian Stone, and John Strevel. "The Three Cs of Customer Satisfaction: Consistency, Consistency, Consistency," *McKinsey* (2014)

Punjabi, Meeta. "Nestlé India's Dairy Development Initiative in the Punjab Region," FAO (2015)

Puthiyamadam, Tom, and José Reyes. "Experience Is Everything," *PwC* (2018)

PwC. "PwC's 2025 Customer Experience Survey—The Loyalty Illusion: Why Companies Think They're Winning When Customers Are Walking Away" (2025)

PwC. "Future of Customer Experience Survey" (2018)

Qualtrics. "The Complete Guide to Customer Journey Management" (2023)

de Quintanilha, Joana, and contributors. "The Customer Journey Mapping Canvas: A Planning Tool to Help Your Journey Mapping Efforts Succeed," *Forrester* (2025)

de Quintanilha, Joana, and contributors. "The Forrester Wave™: Customer Journey Management Platforms, Q4 2025," *Forrester* (2025)

de Quintanilha, Joana, Melissa Chaudet, and contributors. "The Seven Steps of Highly Effective Journey Mapping: Playbook and Templates," *Forrester* (2026)

de Quintanilha, Joana, Maxie Schmidt, and contributors. "What Journeys Really Are: Customers' Paths and Perceptions as They Pursue a Goal," *Forrester* (2024)

Reichheld, Fred. *The Ultimate Question* (2006)

Ries, Eric. *The Lean Startup* (2011)

Risdon, Chris. "The Anatomy of an Experience Map," *Adaptive Path* (2014)

Risdon, Chris. "Un-Sucking the Touchpoint," *Center Centre* (2014)

Risdon, Chris, and Patrick Quattlebaum. *Orchestrating Experiences* (2018)

Robinson, Simon, and Maria Moraes Robinson. *Designing Customer Experiences with Soul* (2024)

Rosala, Maria. "Task Analysis: Support Users in Achieving Their Goals," *NN/g* (2020)

Salehi, Rani. "The Rise of Experience-Fueled Growth," *Forrester* (2024)

Sauro, Jeff. "Measuring Usability with the System Usability Scale (SUS)," *MeasuringU* (2011)

Schall, Andrew. *The Persona and Journey Map Playbook* (2024)

Schebrova, Anastasia. "Creating a Persona—a Step-By-Step Guide with Tips and Examples," *UXPressia* (2025)

Schmidt, Maxie, and Sam Karpinkski. "Improving CX by 1 Point Can Drive More Than 1 Billion Dollars In Revenue (2022)," *Forrester* (2022)

Schrage, Michael. *Who Do You Want Your Customers to Become?* (2012)

Shaw, Colin, and John Ivens. *Building Great Customer Experiences* (2002)

Shedroff, Nathan. "Bridging Strategy with Design: How Designers Create Value for Businesses" [talk at Interaction South America] (2014)

Sheth, Jagdish, Bruce Newman, and Barbara Gross. *Consumption Values and Market Choices: Theory and Applications* (1991)

Shostack, G. Lynn. "Designing Services That Deliver," *Harvard Business Review* (1984)

Shostack, G. Lynn. "How to Design a Service," *European Journal of Marketing* (1982)

Sinclair, Matt, Leila Sheldrick, Mariale Moreno, and Emma Dewberry. "Consumer Intervention Mapping—A Tool for Designing Future Product Strategies Within Circular Product Service Systems," *Sustainability* (2018)

Snyder, Jason. "MIT Finds 95% of GenAI Pilots Fail Because Companies Avoid Friction," *Forbes* (2025)

Soegaard, Mads. "Top Tips to Create Effective Journey Maps," *IxDF* (2025)

Spengler, Christoph, Werner Wirth, and Renzo Sigrist. "360° Touchpoint Management—How Important Is Twitter for Our Brand?," *Marketing Review St. Gallen* (2010)

Spiek, Chris, and Bob Moesta. *Jobs-to-Be-Done: The Handbook* (2014)

Staikos, Bill. "Journey Management in 2026 Is Finally Becoming What We Pretended It Was," *LinkedIn* (2026)

Star, Susan Leigh, and James R. Griesemer. "Institutional Ecology, 'Translations' & Boundary Objects," *Social Studies of Science* (1989)

Stickdorn, Marc, Markus Edgar Hormess, Adam Lawrence, and Jakob Schneider. *This is Service Design Doing* (2018)

Stickdorn, Marc, and Jakob Schneider. *This is Service Design Thinking* (2012)

Szabo, Peter. *User Experience Mapping* (2017)

Tallec, Christophe, and Paul Kahn. "Customer Journey Mapping Game (Transport)," *Prezi* (2013)

Team Asana. "15 Creative Elevator Pitch Examples for Every Scenario" (2025)

Temkin, Bruce. "It's All About Your Customer's Journey," *Customer Experience Matters* (2010)

Temkin, Bruce. "Mapping the Customer Journey," *Forrester* (2010)

TheyDo. "Lufthansa Group at Forrester CX Summit: From Service Design to System of Record" (2025)

Thompson, Ed, and Esteban Kolsky. "How to Approach Customer Experience Management," *Gartner* (2004)

Tincher, Jim. "Driving Change Through Journey Mapping," *Heart of the Customer* (2017)

Tincher, Jim, and Nicole Newton. *How Hard Is It to Be Your Customer?* (2022)

Torres, Teresa. *Continuous Discovery Habits* (2021)

Torres, Teresa. "Engaging Stakeholders with Opportunity Solution Trees: 3 Tactics to Try," *Product Talk* (2019)

Torres, Teresa. "Opportunity Solution Trees: Visualize Your Discovery to Drive Outcomes," *Product Talk* (2023)

Trusler, Aimee. "Experience-Led Growth: Unleashing the Power of Customer-Centric Strategies," *Forbes Communications Council* (2023)

Tufte, Edward. *Envisioning Information* (1990)

Tufte, Edward. *Visual Explanations* (1997)

Twilio. *State of Personalization Report* (2021)

Ulwick, Anthony W.. *Jobs to Be Done: Theory to Practice* (2016)

Vedenin, Yuri. "Employee Experience Journey Map: A Complete Guide + Example + Template," *UXPressia* (2023)

Vlahovic, Tatiana, and Pedro Rodriguez. "Using Journey Mapping as a Tool for Cross-Functional Research," *Dscout* (2022)

Vendbridge. "The Jobs-to-Be-Done Hierarchy" (2018)

Vendbridge. "Customer-Focused Innovation: Jobs-to-Be-Done in Action" (2020)

Voltage Control. "Journey Mapping in Design Thinking: Best Practices & Tools" (2024)

Walter, Stéphanie. *User Journey Mapping* (2022)

Walters, Jeannie. "Co-Creation with Customers: 5 Ways to Drive Better Results," *Experience Investigators* (2019)

Walters, Jeannie. *Experience Is Everything* (2026)

Walters, Jeannie. "What IS a Customer Touchpoint?," *Customer Think* (2013)

Wang, Tricia. "The Human Insights Missing from Big Data" [TEDxCambridge talk] (2016)

Wang, Tricia. "Why Big Data Needs Thick Data," *Ethnography Matters* (2013)

Whelan, Jonathan, and Stephen Whitla. *Visualising Business Transformation* (2020)

Williams, Luke. *Disrupt: Think the Unthinkable to Spark Transformation in Your Business* (2010)

Womack, James, and Daniel Jones. "Lean Consumption," *Harvard Business Review* (2005)

Womack, James, and Daniel Jones. *Lean Thinking*, 2nd ed. (2010)

Wood, Aric, and XPLANE. *The Strategy Activation Playbook: A Practical Approach to Bringing Your Strategies to Life* (2022)

Wowk, Amanda. "6 Steps to Mapping the Employee Journey at Your Organization," *Qualtrics* (2020)

Yohn, Denise Lee. *Fusion* (2018)

Index

A

F

G

H

I

J

K

L

www.ingramcontent.com/pod-product-compliance
Lightning Source LLC
LaVergne TN
LVHW070521061126
851857LV00023B/2124
9798341672291